SECOND EDITION

JavaScript Cookbook

Shelley Powers

Beijing · Cambridge · Farnham · Köln · Sebastopol · Tokyo

JavaScript Cookbook, Second Edition

by Shelley Powers

Copyright © 2015 Shelley Powers. All rights reserved.

Printed in the United States of America.

Published by O'Reilly Media, Inc., 1005 Gravenstein Highway North, Sebastopol, CA 95472.

O'Reilly books may be purchased for educational, business, or sales promotional use. Online editions are also available for most titles (*http://safaribooksonline.com*). For more information, contact our corporate/institutional sales department: 800-998-9938 or *corporate@oreilly.com*.

Editors: Simon St. Laurent and Brian MacDonald	**Indexer:** Judy McConville
Production Editor: Kara Ebrahim	**Cover Designer:** Ellie Volckhausen
Copyeditor: Jasmine Kwityn	**Interior Designer:** David Futato
Proofreader: Kara Ebrahim	**Illustrator:** Rebecca Demarest

February 2015:   Second Edition

Revision History for the Second Edition:

2015-01-23:   First release

See *http://oreilly.com/catalog/errata.csp?isbn=9781491901885* for release details.

The O'Reilly logo is a registered trademark of O'Reilly Media, Inc. *JavaScript Cookbook, Second Edition*, the cover image of a little egret, and related trade dress are trademarks of O'Reilly Media, Inc.

ISBN: 978-1-491-90188-5

[LSI]

Table of Contents

Part II. JavaScript, All Blown Up

The World of JavaScript

I wrote my first book on JavaScript in 1996. At the time, we had to really dig to fill the book. This was before DHTML, before ECMAScript, before mobile development, and definitely before Node.js. Form validation and popping up alerts were the big things. With this second edition of the *JavaScript Cookbook*, I had the opposite problem: the world of JavaScript is just too immense to stuff into one book. But I gave it my all.

The world of JavaScript is the key to this book. The use of JavaScript has expanded from the browser to the server, to the mobile environment, to the cloud. We've gone beyond simple libraries to complex modular systems; from basic animations to rich data visualizations, with a little audio and video tossed in for fun and giggles. Entire applications are served in one HTML page thanks to sophisticated frameworks, and MEAN is no longer an adjective to apply to nasty folk.

Ajax is still around and still relevant, but now it's joined by direct and immediate bidirectional communication—no more having to fake server-client communication, because we have it, for real. We can connect to Twitter and Dropbox, create apps for Android devices, and open ePub files directly in the browser for reading. The libraries and modules available in both the client and server take care of so much of the complex, tedious bits, that we can focus on creating what's unique to our applications. Ten years ago, we'd be surprised at finding a library that met our needs. Now, we're surprised when we don't.

We have all of this, but we still have JavaScript, the language. We still have String and Number, Array and Function, and the most basic of statements:

```
var someVar = 'Hello, World?';
```

However, today's JavaScript is not the same as the language I first wrote about in 1996. It's growing and expanding, with ECMAScript 5, and now ECMAScript 6, and even the newest additions for ECMAScript 7. It seem as if there's a new addition to the language every month. What am I saying…there *is* a new edition every month.

Just to make it even more interesting and rich is the increasing number of APIs provided by both standards organizations and sevice providers.

There's never been a more *exciting* time to be a JavaScript developer. But it can also be a little overwhelming, and that's the focus of this book: getting a handle on this big wonderful world of JavaScript.

Book Audience

In order to encompass the many subjects and topics reflective of JavaScript in use today, we had to start with one premise: this is not a book for a JavaScript newbie. There are so many good books and tutorials for those new to JavaScript that we felt comfortable setting the bar a little higher than the first edition of the *JavaScript Cookbook*.

If you've been playing around with JavaScript for several months, maybe tried your hand with a little Node or Ajax development, you should be comfortable with the book material. Some of the subjects might be challenging, but in a good way.

Book Architecture or Why Is This Book Organized in This Way?

I originally had this idea of a large graphic diagramming the world of JavaScript, which I would split into fragments, which I would then use to introduce each chapter. It didn't take long for me to realize that no component of JavaScript exists in isolation from the others. If anything, JavaScript is one big Venn diagram, with dozens of intersections— more of a *spirograph* than distinct, connected bubbles. So much for grand visualizations. Instead, I split the book into 18 loosely defined chapters, with overlap handled by cross references.

The book is split into two parts labeled *Classic JavaScript* and *JavaScript, All Blown Up*.

The classic parts of JavaScript are the solid foundations of the language we've had for the last decade, and aren't going away. But they aren't standing still, either. We have our friends String, Number, Boolean, Array, Function, and Object, but thanks to ECMA-Script 5 and 6, there's a lot more we can do with these objects. In addition, before we can get into the more leading-edge, complex uses of JavaScript, we still need to understand how to use Ajax, work with JSON, create and use libraries, as well as incorporate one of the more popular (jQuery) into our applications. We also need to understand how to work within the browser, which is still the working environment for most JavaScript development, as well as test our creations and make sure they're accessible.

Now that video and audio, as well as the Canvas element and SVG, are supported in all modern browsers, a basic understanding of these rich media elements is fundamental.

The *All Blown Up* part of JavaScript is basically everything else. This includes the new objects introduced in ECMAScript 6, JavaScript in the server (Node), complex frameworks (in the server and client), and modular JavaScript. It also includes JavaScript in mobile devices, data visualizatons, graphical tools available in the server, bidirectional client-server communication, and the rich world of available APIs, libraries, and modules.

It seems a bewildering mess at times, but the more examples you try in the different environments, the more you realize that JavaScript is the key that makes it all come together.

A break down of the chapters follows in the next sections.

Part I, Classic JavaScript

Part I focuses on traditional uses of JavaScript as they've been practiced the last several years, but updated to incorporate new ideas, modifications, and improved functionality:

Chapter 1, The JavaScript Not-So-Simple Building Blocks
> Covering use of some familiar old friends: String, Number, Boolean, RegExp, Math, and Date. The coverage goes beyond the basic, and also touches on some of the new extensions that come to us via ECMAScript 5 and 6.

Chapter 2, JavaScript Arrays
> Probably no component of JavaScript, the language, has changed more than the simple, essential Array. This chapter goes beyond basic Array use, and covers some of the newer functionality.

Chapter 3, Functions: The JavaScript Building Blocks
> The ubiquitous Function—what would we do without it? In JavaScript, very little. This chapter covers some of the more advanced function uses, and introduces more modern functional uses. We'll look at the three basic function construction types, as well as the extremely useful IIFE (Immediately Invoked Function Expression).

Chapter 4, The Malleable JavaScript Object
> Following closely on the heels of the Array in undergoing change, both in perception and use, the JavaScript Object is nothing if not malleable, hence the chapter title. Most of the chapter focuses on this malleability, both the good uses and the not as good. I also briefly touch on the increasing popularity of functional programming versus object-oriented.

Chapter 5, JavaScript and Directly Accessing the User Interface
> You can't escape the DOM, the DOM knows all (nless it's Shadow DOM, covered in Chapter 14). It's a whole lot more fun to work with the DOM nowadays, thanks to new querying capabilitiy. And though most folks use jQuery, it's still important

to understand what's happening beneath the surface of this and other popular libraries.

Chapter 6, Preliminary Testing and Accessibility
No matter how new JavaScript is, there are still JavaScript best practices to follow, such as keeping our code clean, testing, and ensuring accessibility. We now have new tools to make these necessary tasks a little easier, and a little more entertaining.

Chapter 7, Creating and Using JavaScript Libraries
Here we'll look at the basics of library creation, including minification, hosting your library in GitHub or CDN, using external libraries (jQuery and Underscore), and converting your library to a jQuery plug-in. We'll take jQuery for a spin, but not all libraries do all things—we'll also take a look at libraries that focus on one single type of task. Once we have the basics of library building under our belt, we can continue with modularizing our code, in Chapter 12.

Chapter 8, Simplified Client-Server Communication and Data
You can't play with the new communication techniques (e.g. WebSockets) without a good understanding of Ajax, as well as how to work with JSON and XML. Yes, XML still does exist. Understanding the technology covered in this chapter is necessary before working with the newer client-server communication covered in Chapter 14.

Chapter 9, Creating Media Rich, Interactive Web Effects
This chapter provides basic usage techniques for the Canvas element and 2D graphics, SVG, and the audio and video elements. It also touches on combining the media types (integrating SVG and Canvas) and altering videos as they run. Data visualizations, more escoteric graphical tools, and server-side graphics are covered in Chapter 16.

Part II, JavaScript, All Blown Up

Part II is labeled *All Blown Up* because a few years ago, JavaScript developers never could have imagined all the things we can do today. Not all of the technology covered is brand new, but most is leading-edge. This part of the book also gets into the more complex uses of JavaScript, such as advanced client-server communication, data visualization, OAuth, and mobile development:

Chapter 10, The New ECMAScript Standard Objects
There are several new objects introduced with ECMAScript 6. I touch on all of them, or at least, all of them known at the time the book was written. (Yes, JavaScript is changing...a bit too fast to keep up with, at times.) What's my favorite new additions? Function generators and iterators.

Chapter 11, Node: JavaScript on the Server

This chapter provides a faster paced introduction to working with Node.js. You don't need past experience with Node to work with the examples in this chapter, but the chapter does move along quickly. It also answers those most commonly asked Node questions: How do you keep a Node server running; how do you run Node on the same server as Apache; how do you automatically restart Node when the application changes, or it goes down for some reason. It also explores how to use Node modules, and how to create a stand alone application based on Node.

Chapter 12, Modularizing and Managing JavaScript

This chapter is all about the new world of JavaScript modularization. It takes the older but still necessary components of code reuse, covered in Chapter 7, and incorporates the many new tools and approaches for creating, distributing, and using modular code. The chapter introduces the different approaches to modularization (AMD and Common JS), creating Node modules, working with RequireJS, Bower, Browserify, and that task master, Grunt. We in JavaScript are nothing if not creative with our application names.

Chapter 13, Fun with APIs

An API is a programmer contract. It's an interface into the inner working of the browser, but it's also a way of accessing services or data from a media server or remote resource. APIs are also used in graphical, data, and mobile applications, covered in Chapters 16 through 18. This chapter introduces three different kinds of APIs: remote APIs built on the principle of REST, new W3C APIs that introduce us to new capabilities in the browser, and remote APIs that act locally.

Chapter 14, JavaScript Frameworks

Some of the more complex JavaScript components are the frameworks, whether they're located on the server (ExpressJS), or in the client (AngularJS, Backbone, or Ember). Frameworks also encompass complex strategies for certain problems or business use, like OAuth for authorization, and the *very* new Web Components.

A few asides about this chapter before moving on: I wanted to include a demonstration of at least one of the popular client-side MV* framework tools in the book, but couldn't decide which one. They do differ enough that covering one results in recipes that aren't helpful for folks not using that specific framework. That's when I decided on deconstructing the ToDoMVC web application, and diving into how it's implemented using three of the more popular framework tools: Angular, Ember.js, and Backbone. Hopefully, the process I used can be used with the other frameworks.

I did go into much more depth with the OAuth framework, because of its increasing use authorizing access for data and services at the many APIs we're interested in using. OAuth is also used with the Twitter API, covered in Chapter 13, as well as the Dropbox Datastores, covered in Chapter 17.

I also covered Web Components, but without reliance on a polyfill (e.g. Google's Polymer), as I'm wary of replying on roprietary technology when learning about something new.

Chapter 15, Advanced Client-Server Communications and Streams
Client-server communications is so much better now that WebSockets and CORS (Cross-Origin Resource Sharing) are standard in all modern browsers. Real-time, bidirectional communication can greatly simplify our lives. And because this type of communication is a stream, this chapter also takes a look at Node's new *transform streams*.

Chapter 16, Data Visualizations and Client/Server Graphics
Some of the graphical applications we had fun with when the Canvas element and SVG first received broader support are giving way to more serious data visualizations, most of which use data provided directly from the server. This chapter takes a closer look at data visualization tools, including one that partners with a Web-Socket server application.

Speaking of the server, we now have access to the same rich visualization and graphics tools in the server that we've had in the client, and we'll explore some of the more interesting possibilities.

Chapter 17, Data and Persistence
Data. The world runs on data. This chapter first checks in with form validation, because a good data system depends on good data. Next, we look at the new data storage mechanisms now available in our browsers, including the more complex IndexedDB. And because JavaScript is now on the server, we take a peek at accessing SQL databases (accessing MongoDB is covered in Chapter 15). Lastly, we'll explore data in the cloud, by working with Dropbox's Datastores.

Chapter 18, JavaScript Hits the (Mobile) Road
The last chapter is about all things mobile. Well, Android and web apps mobile (sorry, no iOS coverage). Thanks to Cordova/PhoneGap, and new mobile APIs, we can now take our mad HTML5, CSS, and JavaScript skills to Android and Kindle Fire tablets and smart phones. How fun is that?

Appendix A, Up and Running in jsBin and jsFiddle
This appendix introduces you to jsBin and jsFiddle, which are useful for trying out the different examples in the book.

Conventions Used in This Book

The following typographical conventions are used in this book:

Italic
Indicates new terms, URLs, email addresses, filenames, and file extensions.

Constant width

Indicates computer code in a broad sense, including commands, arrays, elements, statements, options, switches, variables, attributes, keys, functions, types, classes, namespaces, methods, modules, properties, parameters, values, objects, events, event handlers, XML tags, HTML tags, macros, the contents of files, and the output from commands.

Constant width bold

Shows commands or other text that should be typed literally by the user.

Constant width italic

Shows text that should be replaced with user-supplied values or by values determined by context.

This icon signifies a tip, suggestion, or general note.

This icon indicates a warning or caution.

Websites and pages are mentioned in this book to help you locate online information that might be useful. Normally both the address (URL) and the name (title, heading) of a page are mentioned. Some addresses are relatively complicated, but you can probably locate the pages easier using your favorite search engine to find a page by its name, typically by writing it inside quotation marks. This may also help if the page cannot be found by its address; it may have moved elsewhere, but the name may still work.

Using Code Examples

Supplemental material (code examples, exercises, etc.) is available for download at *https://github.com/shelleyp/javascriptcookbook*.

This book is here to help you get your job done. In general, you may use the code in this book in your programs and documentation. You do not need to contact us for permission unless you're reproducing a significant portion of the code. For example, writing a program that uses several chunks of code from this book does not require permission. Selling or distributing a CD-ROM of examples from O'Reilly books does require permission. Answering a question by citing this book and quoting example code does not require permission. Incorporating a significant amount of example code from this book into your product's documentation does require permission.

We appreciate, but do not require, attribution. An attribution usually includes the title, author, publisher, and ISBN. For example: *JavaScript Cookbook, Second Edition*, by Shelley Powers. Copyright 2015 Shelley Powers, 978-1-491-90188-5.

If you feel your use of code examples falls outside fair use or the permission given here, feel free to contact us at *permissions@oreilly.com*.

Safari® Books Online

 *Safari Books Online* is an on-demand digital library that delivers expert content in both book and video form from the world's leading authors in technology and business.

Technology professionals, software developers, web designers, and business and creative professionals use Safari Books Online as their primary resource for research, problem solving, learning, and certification training.

Safari Books Online offers a range of plans and pricing for enterprise, government, education, and individuals.

Members have access to thousands of books, training videos, and prepublication manuscripts in one fully searchable database from publishers like O'Reilly Media, Prentice Hall Professional, Addison-Wesley Professional, Microsoft Press, Sams, Que, Peachpit Press, Focal Press, Cisco Press, John Wiley & Sons, Syngress, Morgan Kaufmann, IBM Redbooks, Packt, Adobe Press, FT Press, Apress, Manning, New Riders, McGraw-Hill, Jones & Bartlett, Course Technology, and hundreds more. For more information about Safari Books Online, please visit us online.

How to Contact Us

Please address comments and questions concerning this book to the publisher:

O'Reilly Media, Inc.
1005 Gravenstein Highway North
Sebastopol, CA 95472
800-998-9938 (in the United States or Canada)
707-829-0515 (international or local)
707-829-0104 (fax)

We have a web page for this book, where we list errata, examples, and any additional information. You can access this page at *http://bit.ly/js-cookbook-2e*.

To comment or ask technical questions about this book, send email to *bookques tions@oreilly.com.*

For more information about our books, courses, conferences, and news, see our website at *http://www.oreilly.com.*

Find us on Facebook: *http://facebook.com/oreilly*

Follow us on Twitter: *http://twitter.com/oreillymedia*

Watch us on YouTube: *http://www.youtube.com/oreillymedia*

Acknowledgments

My appreciation to my editors, Simon St. Laurent and Brian McDonald, as well as all of the rest of the O'Reilly production staff.

I also want to extend a thank you to my tech reviewers, Dr. Axel Rauschmayer and Semmy Purewal, with the caveat that any errors or gotchas still in the finished work are my responsibility.

I also want to thank the many people in the JavaScript community who generously give their time in extending the language, creating the JavaScript implementations, and the other technologies so many of us have come to depend on and appreciate. I also want to include those who write about the technologies online so the rest of us don't have to stumble around in the dark.

## PART I

Classic JavaScript

Classic JavaScript is the JavaScript that's stable, well used, well known, and still a fundamental component of any and all JavaScript applications. From working with the built-in objects, such as String and Number, to communicating with the server via Ajax and creating media effects with SVG, Canvas, Video, and Audio, the JavaScript in this section has broad support and well defined understanding.

## CHAPTER 1

The JavaScript Not-So-Simple Building Blocks

Most JavaScript functionality comes to us via a very basic set of objects and data types. The functionality associated with strings, numbers, and booleans is provided via the String, Number, and Boolean data types. Other fundamental functionality, including regular expressions, dates, and necessary mathematical operations, are provided via the built-in RegExp, Date, and Math objects, respectively.

The fundamental building blocks of JavaScript have changed over time, but their core functionality remains the same. In this chapter, I'm focusing less on the syntax associated with the objects, and more on understanding their place in JavaScript.

 A good, introductory overview of the JavaScript standard built-in objects can be found in the Mozilla Developer Network JavaScript Reference (*http://mzl.la/1yHWKMr*).

1.1. Differentiating Between a JavaScript Object, Primitive, and Literal

Problem

People toss around terms like *object*, *primitive*, and *literal*. What is the difference between the three, and how can you tell which is which?

Solution

A JavaScript *literal* represents a value of a specific type, such as a quoted string (String), floating-point number (Number), or boolean (Boolean):

```
"this is a string"
1.45
true
```

A JavaScript *primitive* is an instance of a particular *data type*, and there are five such in the language: String, Number, Boolean, null, and undefined. The following are examples of JavaScript primitives:

```
"this is a string"
null
```

Of the primitive data types, three have complementary *constructor objects*: String, Number, and Boolean. These objects provide access to the built-in properties and methods that allow us to do more than simple assignment and subsequent access:

```
var str1 = "this is a string";
console.log(str1.length); // using String object's length property
```

 Many of the examples in this book use the console.log() function to display JavaScript results. "The Console Is Your Friend" on page 589 provides a quick how-to on accessing the JavaScript console in modern browers, and Appendix A also provides directions for setting up your environment and running the code snippets found in the solutions.

Discussion

It may seem as if we're working with simple strings or numbers when we declare a variable:

```
var str1 = "this is a simple string";
```

However, we're actually creating doorways into an extensive set of functionality. Without reliance on JavaScript objects, we can assign a string, number, or boolean value to a variable and then access it at a later time. However, if we want to do more with the variable, we'll need to use the data type's complementary JavaScript object and its properties.

As an example, if we want to see the length of a string, we'll access the String object's length property:

```
var str1 = "this is a simple string";
console.log(str1.length); // prints out 23 to browser console
```

Behind the scenes, when the code accesses a String object's property on the literal, a new String object is created and its value is set to the value of the string contained in the variable. The length property is accessed and printed out, and the newly created String object is discarded.

 JavaScript engines don't have to actually create an object to wrap the primitive when you access object properties; they only have to emulate this type behavior.

There are exactly five *primitive* data types in JavaScript: string, number, boolean, null, and undefined. Only the string, number, and boolean data types have complementary constructor objects. The actual representation of strings, floating-point numbers, integers, and booleans are *literals*:

```
var str1 = "this is a simple string"; // the quoted string is the literal

var num1 = 1.45; // the value of 1.45 is the literal

var answer = true; // the values of true and false are boolean literals
```

We can create primitive boolean, string, and number variables either by using a literal representation or using the object without using the new operator:

```
var str1 = String("this is a simple string"); // primitive string

var num1 = Number(1.45); // primitive number

var bool1 = Boolean(true); // primitive boolean
```

To deliberately instantiate an object, use the new operator:

```
var str2 = new String("this is a simple string"); // String object instance

var num2 = new Number(1.45); // Number object instance

var bool2 = new Boolean(true); // primitive boolean
```

You can quickly tell the difference between a primitive and an object instance when you compare an object instance to a literal value using *strict equality*. For example, running the following code in a browser:

```
var str1 = String("string");
var num1 = Number(1.45);
var bool1 = Boolean(true);

if (str1 === "string") {
  console.log('equal');
}
```

```
if (num1 === 1.45) {
  console.log('equal');
}

if (bool1 === true) {
  console.log('equal');
}

var str2 = new String("string");
var num2 = new Number(1.45);
var bool2 = new Boolean(true);

if (str2 === "string") {
  console.log('equal');
} else {
  console.log('not equal');
}

if (num2 === 1.45) {
  console.log('equal');
} else {
  console.log('not equal');
}

if (bool2 === true) {
  console.log('equal');
} else {
  console.log('not equal');
}
```

Results in the following print outs to the console:

```
equal
equal
equal
not equal
not equal
not equal
```

The primitive variables (those not created with new) are strictly equal to the literals, while the object instances are not. Why are the primitive variables strictly equal to the literals? Because primitives are compared by value, and values *are* literals.

For the most part, JavaScript developers don't directly create object instances for the three primitive data types. Developers just want a number, boolean, or string variable to act like a number, boolean, or string, rather than an object; we don't need the enhanced functionality of the object. More importantly, when developers use *strict equality* or type checking in the code, they want a variable to match their expectations of data type, rather than be defined as "object":

```
var num1 = 1.45;

var num2 = new Number(1.45);

console.log(typeof num1); // prints out number
console.log(typeof num2); // prints out object
```

Code validators, such as JSHint, output a warning if you instantiate a primitive data type object directly for just this reason.

See Also

Recipe 1.3 has a more detailed look at the *strict equality* operators, as compared to the standard equality operators.

1.2. Extracting a List from a String

Problem

You have a string with several sentences, one of which includes a list of items. The list begins with a colon (:) and ends with a period (.), and each item is separated by a comma. You want to extract just the list.

Before:

```
This is a list of items: cherries, limes, oranges, apples.
```

After:

```
['cherries','limes','oranges','apples']
```

Solution

The solution requires two actions: extract out the string containing the list of items, and then convert this string into a list.

Use String's `indexOf()` to locate the colon, and then use it again to find the first period following the colon. With these two locations, extract the string using String's `sub string()`:

```
var sentence = 'This is one sentence. This is a sentence with a list of items:' +
'cherries, oranges, apples, bananas. That was the list of items.';
var start = sentence.indexOf(':');
var end = sentence.indexOf('.', start+1);

var listStr = sentence.substring(start+1, end);
```

Once you have the string consisting of the list items, use the String `split()` to break the string into an array:

```
var fruits = listStr.split(',');
console.log(fruits); // ['cherries', ' oranges', ' apples', ' bananas']
```

Discussion

The indexOf() method takes a search value, as first parameter, and an optional beginning index position, as second.

The list is delimited by a beginning colon character and an ending period. The index
Of() method is used without the second parameter in the first search, to find the colon.
The method is used again but the colon's position (plus *1*) is used to modify the begin-
ning location of the search for the period:

```
var end = sentence.indexOf('.',start+1);
```

If we didn't modify the search for the ending period, we'd end up with the location of
the first sentence's period rather than the period for the sentence containing the list.

Once we have the beginning and ending location for the list, we'll use the sub
string() method, passing in the two index values representing the beginning and ending positions of the string:

```
var listStr = sentence.substring(start+1, end);
```

The extracted string is:

```
cherries, oranges, apples, bananas
```

We'll finish by using split() to split the list into its individual values:

```
var fruits = listStr.split(',') ; // ['cherries', ' oranges',
              ' apples', ' bananas']
```

There is another string extraction method, substr(), that begins extraction at an index
position marking the start of the substring and passing in the length of the substring as
the second parameter. We can easily find the length just by subtracting the beginning
position of the string from the end position:

```
var listStr = sentence.substr(start+1, end-start);

var fruits = listStr.split(',');
```

See Also

Another way to extract the string is to use regular expressions and the RegExp object,
covered beginning in Recipe 1.5.

Advanced

The result of splitting the extracted string is an array of list items. However, the items come with artifacts (leading spaces) from sentence white space. In most applications, we'll want to clean up the resulting array elements.

We'll discuss the Array object in more detail in Chapter 2, but for now, we'll use the Array `forEach()` method in addition to the String object's `trim()` method to clean up the array:

```
fruits = listStr.split(',');

console.log(fruits); // [' cherries', ' oranges', ' apples', ' bananas']

fruits.forEach(function(elmnt,indx,arry) {
            arry[indx] = elmnt.trim();
});

console.log(fruits); // ['cherries', 'oranges', 'apples", "bananas"]
```

The `forEach()` method applies the function passed as parameter (the *callback*) to each array element. The callback function supports three arguments: the array element value, and optionally, the array element index and the array itself.

Another simpler approach is to pass a regular expression to the `split()` that trims the result before it's returned:

```
var fruits = listStr.split(/\s*,\s*/);
```

Now the matching returned value is just the string without the surrounding white space.

 The `forEach()` method is also covered in Recipe 2.5. The code in this section *mutates the array in place*, which means it actually modifies the array as it's traversed. Another nondestructive approach is to use the newer `map()` Array method, covered in Recipe 2.7.

Extra: Simplifying the Code Using Chaining

The example code in this recipe is correct, but a little verbose. We can compress the code by using JavaScript's *method chaining*, allowing us to attach one method call to the end of a previous method call if the object and methods allow it. In this case, we can *chain* the `split()` method directly to the `substring()` method:

```
var start = sentence.indexOf(":");
var end = sentence.indexOf(".", start+1);

var fruits = sentence.substring(start+1, end).split(",");
```

The code isn't more accurate, but it uses less space and can be easier to read. I'll cover method chaining in more detail in Recipe 4.9.

1.3. Checking for an Existing, Nonempty String

Problem

You want to verify that a variable is defined, is a string, and is not empty.

Solution

The simplest solution when testing for a nonempty string is the following:

```
if (typeof unknownVariable === 'string' && unknownVariable.length > 0)
```

If the variable isn't a string, the test will fail, and if the string's length isn't longer than zero (0), it will fail.

However, if you're interested in testing for a string, regardless of whether it's a String object or a string literal, you'll need a different typeof test, as well as test to ensure the variable isn't null:

```
if (((typeof unknownVariable != 'undefined' && unknownVariable) &&
    unknownVariable.length() > 0) &&
    typeof unknownVariable.valueOf() == 'string') ...
```

Discussion

You can use length to find out how long the string is and test whether the string variable is an *empty string* (zero length):

```
if (strFromFormElement.length == 0) // testing for empty string
```

However, when you're working with strings and aren't sure whether they're set or not, you can't just check their length, as you'll get an *undefined* JavaScript error if the variable has never been set (or even declared). You have to combine the length test with another test for existence and this brings us to the typeof operator.

The JavaScript typeof operator returns the type of a variable. The list of possible returned values are:

- number if the variable is a number
- string if the variable is a string
- boolean if the variable is a Boolean
- function if the variable is a function
- object if the variable is null, an array, or another JavaScript object

- `undefined` if the variable is undefined

Combining the test for a string and a test on the string length ensures our app knows if the variable is a non-zero length string or not:

```
if (typeof unknownVariable == 'string' && unknownVariable.length > 0) ...
```

However, if you're looking for a nonempty string regardless of whether the string is a literal or an object, than things get a little more interesting. A string that's created using the String constructor:

```
var str = new String('test');
```

has a `typeof` value equal to `object` not `string`. We need a more sophisticated test.

First, we need a way to test whether a variable has been defined *and* isn't null. The `typeof` can be used to ensure the variable isn't undefined:

```
if (typeof unknownVariable != 'undefined')...
```

But it's not sufficient, because `null` variables have a `typeof` value equal to `object`.

So the defined and not null test is changed to check to see if the variable is defined and isn't `null`:

```
if (typeof unknownVariable != 'undefined' && unknownVariable) ...
```

Just listing the variable is sufficient to test whether it's `null` or not.

We still don't know, though, if the variable is a nonempty string. We'll return the `length` test, which should allow us to test whether the variable is a string, and is not empty:

```
if ((typeof unknownVariable != 'undefined' && unknownVariable) &&
    unknownVariable.length > 0) ...
```

If the variable is a number, the test fails because a number doesn't have a `length`. The String object and string literal variables succeed, because both support `length`. However, an array also succeeds, because the Array object also supports `length`.

To finish the test, turn to a little used method, `valueOf()`. The `valueOf()` method is available on all JavaScript objects, and returns the primitive (unwrapped) value of the object. For Number, String, and Boolean, `valueOf()` returns the primitive value. So if the variable is a String object, `valueOf()` returns a string literal. If the variable is already a string literal, applying the `valueOf()` method temporarily wraps it in a String object, which means the `valueOf()` method will still return a string literal.

Our finished test then becomes:

```
if(((typeof unknownVariable != "undefined" && unknownVariable) &&
    (typeof unknownVariable.valueOf() == "string")) &&
```

Now, the test functions without throwing an error regardless of the value and type of the unknown variable, and only succeeds with a nonempty string, regardless of whether the string is a string object or literal.

 Our use of `valueOf()` is limited. The method is primarily used by the JavaScript engine, itself, to handle conversions in instances when a primitive is expected and the engine is given an object.

The process is complex, and normally your application usually won't have to be this extensive when testing a value. You'll typically only need to test whether a variable has been set (`typeof` returns the correct data type), or find the length of a string in order to ensure it's not an empty string.

Extra: Loose and Strict Equality Operators

I used *loose equality* (== and !=) in this section, but I use *strict equality* (=== and !==) elsewhere in the book. My use of both types of operators is not a typo.

Some folks (Douglas Crockford being the most outspoken) consider the loose equality operators (== and !=) to be evil, and discourage their use. The main reason many developers eschew loose equality operators is that they test primitive values rather than the variable object, in totality, and the results of the test can be unexpected.

For instance, the following code succeeds:

```
var str1 = new String('test');
if (str1 == 'test') { ...}
```

whereas this code fails:

```
var str1 = new String('test');
if (str1 === 'test') { ...}
```

The first code snippet succeeds because the string literal (`test`) and the primitive value the `str1` variable contains are identical. The second code snippet fails the conditional test because the objects being compared are not equivalent, though they both share the same primitive value (`test`): the `str1` variable is a String object, while the compared value is a string literal.

While results of this comparison are relatively intuitive, others are less so. In the following code snippet, a string is compared to a number, and the results may be unexpected:

```
var num = 0;
var str = '0';
```

```
console.log(num == str); // true
console.log(num === str); // false
```

In the Abstract Equality Comparison Algorithm (*http://es5.github.io/#x11.9.3*), when a string is compared to a number, the *loose equality* comparison is treated as if the following occurs:

```
console.log(num === toNumber(str));
```

And therein lies the risk of loose equality: not understanding the implicit type conversion.

Sometimes, though, the very nature of the loose equality operator can be useful. For instance, the following code snippet demonstrates how the loose equality operator saves us time and code. The test to see if the variable is "bad" succeeds with standard equality regardless of whether the variable is undefined or null, where it wouldn't succeed if strict equality had been used:

```
var str1;

if (str1 == null) {
  console.log('bad variable');
}
```

Rather than using the first typeof in the solution, I could shorten the test to the following and get the same result:

```
if ((unknownVariable != null && unknownVariable.length > 0) &&
    typeof unknownVariable.valueOf() == 'string') ...
```

Should you always use strict equality except in these rare instances? Just to ensure you don't get unexpected results?

I'm going to buck the industry trend and say "No." As long as you're cognizant of how the equality operators work, and your code is such that you're either only interested in primitive values or you want the object type coercion I just demonstrated, you can use loose equality operators in addition to strict equality.

Consider the following scenario: in a function, you're testing to see if a counter is a certain value (100, for example). You're expecting the counter, passed into the function, to be a number, but the developer who sent the value to your function passed it as a string.

When you perform the test, you *are* only interested in the value of the variable, not whether it's a string or number. In this case, strict equality would fail, but not because the value isn't what you're testing for, but because the tested value and the function argument are different types. And the failure may be such that the developer using your function thinks that the application generating the value is in error, not that a type conversion hasn't been made.

You don't care in your function that the variable is a string and not a number. In this case, what you're implicitly doing is converting the variable to what you expect and then doing the comparison. The following are equivalent:

```
if (counter == 100) ...
```

```
if (parseInt(counter) === 100) ...
```

 If the type is critically important, then a first test should be on the type and a relevant error generated. But this is what I mean by being cognizant of your code.

In a more realistic scenario, you may be working with a string, and you don't care if the person who passed the string value to your function used a String constructor to create the string, or used a string literal—all you care about is the primitive value:

```
var str = 'test';
var str2 = new String('test');

doSomething(str);
doSomething(str2);
...

function doSomething (passedString) {

  if (passedString == 'test')
    ...
}
```

See Also

For more on the equality operators and their differences, as well as a view from the other side on the issue, I recommend JS101: Equality (*http://dailyjs.com/2012/08/27/equality/*). The Mozilla Developer Network has a lovely, in-depth overview of the comparison operators and how they work in their documentation on comparison operators (*http://mzl.la/1z2y92i*). And do check out the Abstract Equality Comparison Algorithm (*http://es5.github.io/#x11.9.3*), directly.

1.4. Inserting Special Characters

Problem

You want to insert a special character, such as a line feed, into a string.

Solution

Use one of the *escape sequences* in the string. For instance, to include the copyright symbol in a block of text to be added to the page (shown in Figure 1-1), use the escape sequence \u00A9:

```
var resultString = "<p>This page \u00A9 Shelley Powers </p>";

// print out to page
 var blk = document.getElementById("result");
 blk.innerHTML = resultString;
```

This page © Shelley Powers

Figure 1-1. Using an escape sequence to create the copyright symbol

Discussion

The escape sequences in JavaScript all begin with the *backslash character*, (\). This character signals the application processing the string that what follows is a sequence of characters that need special handling. Table 1-1 lists the other escape sequences.

Table 1-1. Escape sequences

Sequence	Character
\'	Single quote
\"	Double quote
\\	Backslash
\b	Backspace
\f	Form feed
\n	Newline
\r	Carriage return
\t	Horizontal tab
\ddd	Octal sequence (3 digits: *ddd*)
\xdd	Hexadecimal sequence (2 digits: *dd*)
\udddd	Unicode sequence (4 hex digits: *dddd*)

The last three escape sequences in Table 1-1 are patterns, where providing different numeric values will result in differing escape sequences. The copyright symbol in the solution is an example of the Unicode sequence pattern.

The escape sequences listed in Table 1-1 can also be represented as a *Unicode sequence*. Unicode is a computing standard for consistent encoding, and a Unicode sequence is a specific pattern for a given character. For instance, the horizontal tab (\t), can also be represented as the Unicode escape sequence, \u0009. Of course, if the user agent disregards the special character, as browsers do with the horizontal tab, the use is moot.

One of the most common uses of escape sequences is to include double or single quotes within strings delimited by the same character:

```
var newString = 'You can\'t use single quotes ' +
                'in a string surrounded by single quotes.' +
                'Oh, wait a sec...yes you can.';
```

1.5. Replacing Patterns with New Strings

Problem

You want to replace all matched substrings with a new substring.

Solution

Use the String's `replace()` method, with a regular expression:

```
var searchString = "Now is the time, this is the tame";
var re = /t\w{2}e/g;
var replacement = searchString.replace(re, "place");
console.log(replacement); // Now is the place, this is the place
```

Discussion

The solution also makes use of a global search. Using the global flag (g) with the regular expression in combination with the String `replace()` method will replace all instances of the matched text with the replacement string. If we didn't use the global flag, only the first match would trigger a replacement.

The literal regular expression begins and ends with a slash (/). As an alternative, I could have used the built-in RegExp object:

```
var re = new RegExp('t\\w{2}e',"g");
var replacement = searchString.replace(re,"place");
console.log(p);
```

The difference is the surrounding slashes aren't necessary when using RegExp, but the use of the backslash in the pattern has to be escaped. In addition, the global indicator is a second, optional argument to the RegExp constructor.

You can use a regular expression literal or a RegExp object instance interchangeably. The primary difference is that the RegExp constructor allows you to create the regular expression dynamically.

Extra: Regular Expression Quick Primer

Regular expressions are made up of characters that are used alone or in combination with special characters. For instance, the following is a regular expression for a pattern that matches against a string that contains the word *technology* and the word *book*, in that order, and separated by one or more whitespace characters:

```
var re = /technology\s+book/;
```

The backslash character (\) serves two purposes: either it's used with a regular character, to designate that it's a special character, or it's used with a special character, such as the plus sign (+), to designate that the character should be treated literally. In this case, the backslash is used with *s*, which transforms the letter *s* to a special character designating a whitespace character (space, tab, line feed, or form feed). The \s special character is followed by the plus sign, \s+, which is a signal to match the preceding character (in this example, a whitespace character) one or more times. This regular expression would work with the following:

```
technology book
```

It would also work with the following:

```
technology     book
```

It would not work with the following, because there is no white space between the words:

```
technologybook
```

It doesn't matter how much whitespace is between *technology* and *book*, because of the use of \s+. However, using the plus sign does require at least one whitespace character.

Table 1-2 shows the most commonly used special characters in JavaScript applications.

Table 1-2. Regular expression special characters

Character	Matches	Example
^	Matches beginning of input	/^This/ matches *This is…*
$	Matches end of input	/end$/ matches *This is the end*
*	Matches zero or more times	/se*/ matches *seeee* as well as *se*
?	Matches zero or one time	/ap?/ matches *apple* and *and*
+	Matches one or more times	/ap+/ matches *apple* but not *and*

Character	Matches	Example
{n}	Matches exactly *n* times	/ap{2}/ matches *apple* but not *apie*
{n,}	Matches *n* or more times	/ap{2,}/ matches all p's in *apple* and *appple* but not *apie*
{n,m}	Matches at least *n*, at most *m* times	/ap{2,4}/ matches four p's in *apppppple*
.	Any character except newline	/a.e/ matches *ape* and *axe*
[...]	Any character within brackets	/a[px]e/ matches *ape* and *axe* but not *ale*
[^...]	Any character but those within brackets	/a[^px]/ matches *ale* but not *axe* or *ape*
\b	Matches on word boundary	/\bno/ matches the first *no* in *nono*
\B	Matches on nonword boundary	/\Bno/ matches the second *no* in *nono*
\d	Digits from 0 to 9	/\d{3}/ matches 123 in *Now in 123*
\D	Any nondigit character	/\D{2,4}/ matches *Now '* in *'Now in 123;*
\w	Matches word character (letters, digits, underscores)	/\w/ matches *j* in javascript
\W	Matches any nonword character (not letters, digits, or underscores)	/\W/ matches *%* in *100%*
\n	Matches a line feed	
\s	A single whitespace character	
\S	A single character that is not whitespace	
\t	A tab	
(x)	Capturing parentheses	Remembers the matched characters

 Regular expressions are powerful but can be tricky. I'm only covering them lightly in this book. If you want more in-depth coverage of regular expressions, I recommend the excellent *Regular Expressions Cookbook* by Jan Goyvaerts and Steven Levithan (O'Reilly).

See Also

Recipe 1.7 shows variations of using regular expressions with the String `replace` method, including the use of *capturing parenthesis*.

1.6. Finding and Highlighting All Instances of a Pattern

Problem

You want to find all instances of a pattern within a string.

Solution

Use the `RegExp` `exec` method and the global flag (g) in a loop to locate all instances of a pattern, such as any word that begins with *t* and ends with *e*, with any number of characters in between:

```
var searchString = "Now is the time and this is the time and that is the time";
var pattern = /t\w*e/g;
var matchArray;

var str = "";

// check for pattern with regexp exec, if not null, process
while((matchArray = pattern.exec(searchString)) != null) {
  str+="at " + matchArray.index + " we found " + matchArray[0] + "\n";
}
console.log(str);
```

The results are:

```
at 7 we found the
at 11 we found time
at 28 we found the
at 32 we found time
at 49 we found the
at 53 we found time
```

Discussion

The RegExp `exec()` method executes the regular expression, returning `null` if a match is not found, or an object with information about the match, if found. Included in the returned array is the actual matched value, the index in the string where the match is found, any parenthetical substring matches, and the original string:

- `index`: The index of the located match
- `input`: The original input string
- [0]: The matched value
- [1],…,[n]+: Parenthesized substring matches, if any

The parentheses *capture* the matched values. Given a regular expression like that in the following code snippet:

```
var re = /a(p+).*(pie)/ig;
var result = re.exec("The apples in the apple pie are tart");
console.log(result);
console.log(result.index);
console.log(result.input);
```

the resulting output is:

```
["apples in the apple pie", "pp", "pie"]
4
"The apples in the apple pie are tart"
```

The array results contain the complete matched value at index zero (0), and the rest of the array entries are the parenthetical matches. The `index` is the index of the match, and the `input` is just a repeat of the string being matched. In the solution, the index where the match was found is printed out in addition to the matched value.

The solution also uses the global flag (g). This triggers the RegExp object to preserve the location of each match, and to begin the search after the previously discovered match. When used in a loop, we can find all instances where the pattern matches the string. In the solution, the following are printed out:

```
at 7 we found the
at 11 we found time
at 28 we found the
at 32 we found time
at 49 we found the
at 53 we found time
```

Both *time* and *the* match the pattern.

Let's look at the nature of global searching in action. In Example 1-1, a web page is created with a `textarea` and an input text box for accessing both a search string and a pattern. The pattern is used to create a RegExp object, which is then applied against the string. A result string is built, consisting of both the unmatched text and the matched text, except the matched text is surrounded by a `span` element (with a CSS class used to highlight the text). The resulting string is then inserted into the page, using the `innerHTML` for a `div` element.

Example 1-1. Using exec and global flag to search and highlight all matches in a text string

```html
<!DOCTYPE html>
<html>
<head>
<title>Searching for strings</title>
<style>
.found
{
  background-color: #ff0;
}
</style>

</head>
<body>
  <form id="textsearch">
    <textarea id="incoming" cols="150" rows="10">
    </textarea>
    <p>
```

```
        Search pattern: <input id="pattern" type="text" />
      </p>
    </form>
    <button id="searchSubmit">Search for pattern</button>
    <div id="searchResult"></div>

<script>

    document.getElementById("searchSubmit").onclick=function() {

      // get pattern
      var pattern = document.getElementById("pattern").value;
      var re = new RegExp(pattern,"g");

      // get string
      var searchString = document.getElementById("incoming").value;

      var matchArray;
      var resultString = "<pre>";
      var first=0;
      var last=0;

      // find each match
      while((matchArray = re.exec(searchString)) != null) {
        last = matchArray.index;

        // get all of string up to match, concatenate
        resultString += searchString.substring(first, last);

        // add matched, with class
        resultString += "<span class='found'>" + matchArray[0] + "</span>";
        first = re.lastIndex;
      }

      // finish off string
      resultString += searchString.substring(first,searchString.length);
      resultString += "</pre>";

      // insert into page
      document.getElementById("searchResult").innerHTML = resultString;
  }

</script>
</body>
</html>
```

Figure 1-2 shows the application in action on William Wordsworth's poem, "The Kitten and the Falling Leaves" after a search for the following pattern:

```
lea(f|ves)
```

The bar (|) is a conditional test, and will match a word based on the value on either side of the bar. So *leaf* matches, as well as *leaves*, but not *leap*.

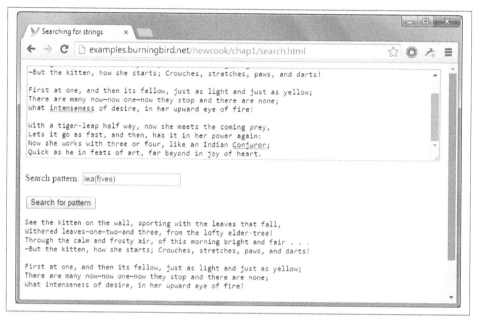

Figure 1-2. Application finding and highlighting all matched strings

You can access the last index found through the RegExp's `lastIndex` property. The `lastIndex` property is handy if you want to track both the first and last matches.

See Also

Recipe 1.5 describes another way to do a standard find-and-replace behavior, and Recipe 1.7 provides a simpler approach to finding and highlighting text in a string.

1.7. Swapping Words in a String Using Capturing Parentheses

Problem

You want to accept an input string with first and last name, and swap the names so the last name is first.

Solution

Use *capturing parentheses* and a regular expression to find and remember the two names in the string, and reverse them:

```
var name = "Abe Lincoln";
var re = /^(\w+)\s(\w+)$/;
var newname = name.replace(re,"$2, $1");
```

Discussion

Capturing parentheses allow us to not only match specific patterns in a string, but to reference the matched substrings at a later time. The matched substrings are referenced numerically, from left to right, as represented by $1 and $2 in the `replace()` method.

In the solution, the regular expression matches two words separated by a space. Capturing parentheses were used with both words, so the first name is accessible using $1, the last name with $2.

The capturing parentheses aren't the only special characters available with `replace()`. Table 1-3 shows the other special characters that can be used with regular expressions and String `replace()`.

Table 1-3. String.replace special patterns

Pattern	Purpose
$$	Allows a literal dollar sign ($) in replacement
$&	Inserts matched substring
$`	Inserts portion of string before match
$'	Inserts portion of string after match
$*n*	Inserts *n* th captured parenthetical value when using RegExp

The second pattern, which reinserts the matched substring, can be used to provide a simplified version of the Example 1-1 application shown in Recipe 1.6. That example found and provided markup and CSS to highlight the matched substring. It used a loop to find and replace all entries, but in Example 1-2 we'll use `replace()` with the matched substring special pattern ($&).

Example 1-2. Using String.replace and special pattern to find and highlight text in a string

```
<!DOCTYPE html>
<html>
<head>
<title>Searching for strings</title>
<style>
.found
{
```

```
    background-color: #ff0;
}
</style>
</head>
<body>
  <form id="textsearch">
    <textarea id="incoming" cols="100" rows="10">
    </textarea>
    <p>
      Search pattern: <input id="pattern" type="text" />
    </p>
  </form>
  <button id="searchSubmit">Search for pattern</button>
  <div id="searchResult"></div>

<script>

  document.getElementById("searchSubmit").onclick=function() {

    // get pattern
    var pattern = document.getElementById("pattern").value;
    var re = new RegExp(pattern,"g");

    // get string
    var searchString = document.getElementById("incoming").value;

    // replace
    var resultString = searchString.replace(re,"<span class='found'>$&</span>");

    // insert into page
    document.getElementById("searchResult").innerHTML = resultString;
 }

</script>
</body>
</html>
```

This is a simpler alternative, but the result isn't quite the same: the line feeds aren't preserved with Example 1-2, but they are with Example 1-1.

The captured text can also be accessed via the RegExp object using the exec() method. Let's return to the Recipe 1.7 solution code, this time using exec():

```
    var name = "Abe Lincoln";
    var re = /^(\w+)\s(\w+)$/;
    var result = re.exec(name);
    var newname = result[2] + ", " + result[1];
```

This approach is handy if you want to access the capturing parentheses values, but without having to use them within a string replacement.

1.8. Replacing HTML Tags with Named Entities

Problem

You want to paste example markup into a web page, and escape the markup (i.e., have the angle brackets print out rather than have the contents parsed).

Solution

Use regular expressions to convert angle brackets (<>) into the named entities < and >:

```
var pieceOfHtml = "<p>This is a <span>paragraph</span></p>";
pieceOfHtml = pieceOfHtml.replace(/</g,"&lt;");
pieceOfHtml = pieceOfHtml.replace(/>/g,"&gt;");
console.log(pieceOfHtml);
```

Discussion

It's not unusual to want to paste samples of markup into another web page. The only way to have the text printed out, as is, without having the browser parse it, is to convert all angle brackets into their equivalent *named entities*.

The process is simple with the use of regular expressions and the `String replace` method, as demonstrated in the solution. The key is to remember to use the global flag with the regular expression, to match all instances of the angle brackets.

 Of course, if the regular expression finds the use of > or < in a mathematical or conditional expression, it will replace these, too.

1.9. Converting an ISO 8601 Formatted Date to a Date Object Acceptable Format

Problem

You need to convert an ISO 8601 formatted date string into values that can be used to create a new Date object instance.

Solution

Parse the ISO 8601 string into the individual date values, and use it to create a new JavaScript Date object instance:

```
var dtstr= "2014-3-04T19:35:32Z";

dtstr = dtstr.replace(/\D/g," ");
var dtcomps = dtstr.split(" ");

// modify month between 1 based ISO 8601 and zero based Date
dtcomps[1]--;

var convdt = new Date(Date.UTC.apply(null,dtcomps));

console.log(convdt.toString()); // Tue, 04 Mar 2014 19:35:32 GMT
```

Discussion

The ISO 8601 is an international standard that defines a representation for both dates and times. It's not unusual for applications that provide APIs to require ISO 8601 formatting. It's also not unusual for most dates to and from APIs to be in UTC, rather than local time.

The solution shows one variation of ISO 8601 formatting. The following demonstrate some others:

- 2009
- 2009-10
- 2009-10-15
- 2009-10-15T19:20
- 2009-10-15T19:20:20
- 2009-10-15T19:20:20.50

The values are year, month, date, then T to represent time, and hours, minutes, seconds, and fractions of sections. The time zone also needs to be indicated. If the date is in UTC, the time zone is represented by the letter Z, as shown in the solution:

```
2014-3-04T19:35:32Z
```

Otherwise, the time zone is represented as +hh:mm to represent a time zone ahead of UTC, and -hh:mm to represent a time zone behind UTC.

If you attempt to create a JavaScript Date with an ISO 8601 formatted string, you'll get an invalid date error. Instead, you have to convert the string into values that can be used with the JavaScript Date.

The simplest way to parse an ISO 8601 formatted string is to use the String split() method. To facilitate using split(), all non-numeric characters are converted to one specific character. In the solution, the non-numeric characters are converted to a space:

```
dtstr = dtstr.replace(/\D/g, " ");
```

The ISO-formatted string would be converted to:

```
2014 03 04 19 35 32
```

ISO months are one-based values of 1 through 12. To use the month value in JavaScript `Dates`, the month needs to be adjusted by subtracting 1:

```
dtcomps[1]--;
```

Finally, the new `Date` is created. To maintain the UTC setting, the Date's `UTC()` method is used to create the date in universal time, which is then passed to the `Date` constructor. Rather than listing out each and every single date value, the `apply()` method is used, with `null` as the first value, and all of the arguments as an array as the second:

```
var convdt = new Date(Date.UTC.apply(null,dtcomps));
```

The task gets more challenging when you have to account for the different ISO 8601 formats. Example 1-3 shows a JavaScript application that contains a more complex JavaScript function that converts from ISO 8601 to allowable `Date` values. The first test in the function ensures that the ISO 8601 format can be converted to a JavaScript Date. This means that, at a minimum, the formatted string must have a month, day, and year.

Example 1-3. Converting ISO 8601 formatted dates to JavaScript Dates

```
<!DOCTYPE html>
<html>
<head>
   <title>Converting ISO 8601 date</title>
</head>
<body>
  <form>
    <p>Datestring in ISO 8601 format: <input type="text" id="datestring" />
    </p>
  </form>
  <button id="dateSubmit">Convert Date</button>
  <div id="result"></div>

<script type="text/javascript">
  document.getElementById("dateSubmit").onclick=function() {

    var dtstr = document.getElementById("datestring").value;
    var convdate = convertISO8601toDate(dtstr);
    document.getElementById("result").innerHTML=convdate;
  }

  function convertISO8601toDate(dtstr) {

    // replace anything but numbers by spaces
    dtstr = dtstr.replace(/\D/g," ");

    // trim any hanging white space
    dtstr = dtstr.replace(/\s+$/,"");
```

```
    // split on space
    var dtcomps = dtstr.split(" ");

    // not all ISO 8601 dates can convert, as is
    // unless month and date specified, invalid
    if (dtcomps.length < 3) return "invalid date";

    // if time not provided, set to zero
    if (dtcomps.length < 4) {
        dtcomps[3] = 0;
        dtcomps[4] = 0;
        dtcomps[5] = 0;
    }

    // modify month between 1 based ISO 8601 and zero based Date
    dtcomps[1]--;

    var convdt = new Date(Date.UTC.apply(null,dtcomps));

    return convdt.toUTCString();
  }
 </script>

</body>
</html>
```

Another test incorporated into Example 1-3 is whether a time is given. If there aren't enough array elements to cover a time, then the hours, minutes, and seconds are set to zero when the UTC date is created.

There are other issues related to dates not covered in the application. For instance, if the ISO 8601 formatted string isn't in UTC time, converting it to UTC can require additional code, both to parse the time zone and to adjust the date to incorporate the time zone.

 Eventually, you won't need this special processing, because ECMA-Script 5 includes support for ISO 8601 dates in methods such as Date parse(). However, implementation is still inconsistent across all major browsers—nonexistent in older browsers—so you'll need these workarounds, or a *shim*, for now. See Recipe 1.17 for more on using a shim.

1.10. Using Function Closures with Timers

Problem

You want to provide a function with a timer, but you want to add the function directly into the timer method call.

Solution

Use an *anonymous function* as first parameter to the `setInterval()` or `setTimeout()` method call:

```
intervalId=setInterval(
           function() {
              x+=5;
              var left = x + "px";
              document.getElementById("redbox").style.left=left;
           },100);
```

Discussion

Unlike the other material covered in this chapter, JavaScript timers don't belong to any of the basic built-in objects. Instead, they're part of the basic Web API (previously known as the Browser Object Model, or BOM). In the browser, they're properties of the Window object, the browser's global object, though we don't need to specify `window` when accessing them. In Node.js, the two timer functions are part of the global object.

When you're creating timers using `setTimeout()` and `setInterval()`, you can pass in a function variable as the first parameter:

```
function bing() {
   alert('Bing!');
}

setTimeout(bing, 3000);
```

However, you can also use an anonymous function, as demonstrated in the solution. This approach is more useful, because rather than have to clutter up the global space with a function just to use with the timer, you can embed the function directly. In addition, you can use a variable local to the scope of the enclosing function when you use an anonymous function.

Example 1-4 demonstrates an anonymous function within a `setInterval()` method call. The approach also demonstrates how the use of this *function closure* allows access to the parent function's local variables within the timer method. In the example, clicking the red box starts the timer, and the box moves. Clicking the box again clears the timer, and the box stops. The position of the box is tracked in the x variable, which is within scope for the timer function, as it operates within the scope of the parent function.

Example 1-4. Using an anonymous function within a setInterval timer parameter

```
<!DOCTYPE html>
<head>
<title>interval and anonymous function</title>
<style>
#redbox
{
  position: absolute;
  left: 100px;
  top: 100px;
  width: 200px; height: 200px;
  background-color: red;
}
</style>
</head>
<body>
<div id="redbox"></div>

<script>
  var intervalId=null;

  document.getElementById('redbox').addEventListener('click',startBox,false);

  function startBox() {
    if (intervalId == null) {
      var x = 100;
      intervalId=setInterval(
          function() {
            x+=5;
            var left = x + "px";
            document.getElementById("redbox").style.left=left;
          },100);
    } else {
      clearInterval(intervalId);
      intervalId=null;
    }
  }
</script>

</body>
```

There's no guarantee that the timer event fires when it is supposed to fire. Timers run on the same execution thread as all other user interface (UI) events, such as mouse-clicks. All events are queued and blocked, including the timer event, until its turn. So, if you have several events in the queue ahead of the timer, the actual time could differ —probably not enough to be noticeable to your application users, but a delay can happen.

See Also

John Resig offers an excellent discussion on how timers work (*http://ejohn.org/blog/how-javascript-timers-work/*), and especially the issues associated with event queues and single threads of execution.

Function closures are covered in more detail in Recipe 3.5. See function closures in timers in action in Recipe 1.11.

1.11. Tracking Elapsed Time

Problem

You want to track the elapsed time between events.

Solution

Create a Date object when the first event occurs, a new Date object when the second event occurs, and subtract the first from the second. The difference is in milliseconds; to convert to seconds, divide by 1,000:

```
var firstDate = new Date();

setTimeout(function() {
  doEvent(firstDate);
}, 25000);

function doEvent() {
  var secondDate = new Date();
  var diff = secondDate - firstDate;
  console.log(diff); // approx. 25000
}
```

Discussion

Some arithmetic operators can be used with Date, but with interesting results. In the example, one Date instance can be subtracted from another, and the difference between the two is returned as milliseconds. However, if you add two dates together, the result is a string with the second Date instance concatenated to the first:

```
Thu Oct 08 2009 20:20:34 GMT-0500 (CST)Thu Oct 08 2009 20:20:31 GMT-0500 (CST)
```

If you divide the Date instances, the dates are converted to their millisecond value, and the result of dividing one by the other is returned. Multiplying two dates will return a very large millisecond result.

Only the Date instance subtraction operator really makes sense, but it's interesting to see what happens with arithmetic operators and the Date object.

1.12. Converting a Decimal to a Hexadecimal Value

Problem

You have a decimal value, and need to find its hexadecimal equivalent.

Solution

Use the Number `toString()` method:

```
var num = 255;

// displays ff, which is hexadecimal equivalent for 255
console.log(num.toString(16));
```

Discussion

By default, numbers in JavaScript are base 10, or decimal. However, they can also be converted to a different *radix*, including hexadecimal (16) and octal (8). Hexadecimal numbers begin with 0x (a zero followed by lowercase x), and octal numbers always begin with zero:

```
var octoNumber = 0255; // equivalent to 173 decimal
var hexaNumber = 0xad; // equivalent to 173 decimal
```

A decimal number can be converted to another radix, in a range from 2 to 36:

```
var decNum = 55;
var octNum = decNum.toString(8); // value of 67 octal
var hexNum = decNum.toString(16); // value of 37 hexadecimal
var binNum = decNum.toString(2); // value of 110111 binary
```

To complete the octal and hexadecimal presentation, you'll need to concatenate the zero to the octal, and the 0x to the hexadecimal value.

Although decimals can be converted to any base number (between a range of 2 to 36), only the octal, hexadecimal, and decimal numbers can be manipulated, directly as numbers. In addition, when using JavaScript *strict mode*, only decimal and hexadecimal literals are supported, as octal integers are no longer supported in JavaScript.

Extra: Speaking of Strict Mode

Strict mode is an ECMAScript 5 addition that signals the use of a more restricted version of the JavaScript language. Strict mode can be implemented for an entire script or only for a function. Triggering is simple:

```
'use strict';
```

or:

```
"use strict";
```

This code should be the first line in your script block or function.

When strict mode is engaged, a mistake that would normally be ignored now generates an error. What kind of mistake?

- Typos in variable names in assignment throw an error.
- Assignments that would normally fail quietly now throw an error.
- Attempting to delete an undeletable property fails.
- Using nonunique property names.
- Using nonunique function parameter names.

Strict mode also triggers other requirements:

- Octals aren't supported in strict mode.
- The eval() statement is limited, and with is not supported.
- When constructing a new object, new is required for this to function correctly.

Bottom line: strict mode helps eliminate unexpected and unexplainable results.

1.13. Summing All Numbers in a Table Column

Problem

You want to sum all numbers in a table column.

Solution

Traverse the table column containing numeric string values, convert to numbers, and sum the numbers:

```
var sum = 0;

// use querySelector to find all second table cells
var cells = document.querySelectorAll("td:nth-of-type(2)");
```

```
    for (var i = 0; i < cells.length; i++) {
      sum+=parseFloat(cells[i].firstChild.data);
    }
```

Discussion

The global functions `parseInt()` and `parseFloat()` convert strings to numbers, but `parseFloat()` is more adaptable when it comes to handling numbers in an HTML table. Unless you're absolutely certain all of the numbers will be integers, `parseFloat()` can work with both integers and floating-point numbers.

As you traverse the HTML table and convert the table entries to numbers, sum the results. Once you have the sum, you can use it in a database update, print it to the page, or pop up a message box, as the solution demonstrates.

You can also add a sum row to the HTML table. Example 1-5 demonstrates how to convert and sum up numeric values in an HTML table, and then how to insert a table row with this sum, at the end. The code uses `document.querySelectorAll()`, which uses a different variation on the CSS selector, `td + td`, to access the data this time. This selector finds all table cells that are preceded by another table cell.

Example 1-5. Converting table values to numbers and summing the results

```
<!DOCTYPE html>
<html>
<head>
<title>Accessing numbers in table</title>
</head>
<body>
<table id="table1">
   <tr>
      <td>Washington</td><td>145</td>
   </tr>
   <tr>
      <td>Oregon</td><td>233</td>
   </tr>
   <tr>
      <td>Missouri</td><td>833</td>
   </tr>
</table>
<script type="text/javascript">

   var sum = 0;

   // use querySelector to find all second table cells
   var cells = document.querySelectorAll("td + td");

   for (var i = 0; i < cells.length; i++)
      sum+=parseFloat(cells[i].firstChild.data);
```

```
// now add sum to end of table
var newRow = document.createElement("tr");

// first cell
var firstCell = document.createElement("td");
var firstCellText = document.createTextNode("Sum:");
firstCell.appendChild(firstCellText);
newRow.appendChild(firstCell);

// second cell with sum
var secondCell = document.createElement("td");
var secondCellText = document.createTextNode(sum);
secondCell.appendChild(secondCellText);
newRow.appendChild(secondCell);

// add row to table
document.getElementById("table1").appendChild(newRow);

</script>
</body>
</html>
```

Being able to provide a sum or other operation on table data is helpful if you're working with dynamic updates via an Ajax operation, such as accessing rows of data from a database. The Ajax operation may not be able to provide summary data, or you may not want to provide summary data until a web page reader chooses to do so. The users may want to manipulate the table results, and then push a button to perform the summing operation.

Adding rows to a table is simple, as long as you remember the steps:

1. Create a new table row using `document.createElement("tr")`.

2. Create each table row cell using `document.createElement("td")`.

3. Create each table row cell's data using `document.createTextNode()`, passing in the text of the node (including numbers, which are automatically converted to a string).

4. Append the text node to the table cell.

5. Append the table cell to the table row.

6. Append the table row to the table. Rinse, repeat.

If you perform this operation frequently, you can create functions for these operations, and package them into JavaScript libraries that you can reuse. Also, many of the available JavaScript libraries can do much of this work for you.

See Also

Wonder why I'm not using `forEach()` with the results of the query? That's because the `querySelectorAll()` returns a NodeList, not an array, and `forEach()` is an Array method. But there is a workaround, covered in Recipe 2.6.

Extra: Modularization of Globals

The `parseFloat()` and `parseInt()` methods are global methods. As part of a growing effort to *modularize* JavaScript, both methods are now attached to the Number object, as new *static* methods, in ECMAScript 6:

```
var num = Number.parseInt('123');
```

The motive is good, but at the time this book was written, only Firefox supported the Number methods.

1.14. Converting Between Degrees and Radians

Problem

You have an angle in degrees. To use the value in the Math object's trigonometric functions, you need to convert the degrees to radians.

Solution

To convert degrees to radians, multiply the value by (`Math.PI / 180`):

```
var radians = degrees * (Math.PI / 180);
```

To convert radians to degrees, multiply the value by (180 / `Math.PI`):

```
var degrees = radians * (180 / Math.PI);
```

Discussion

All Math trigonometric methods (`sin()`, `cos()`, `tin()`, `asin()`, `acos()`, `atan()`, and `atan2()`), take values in radians, and return radians as a result. Yet it's not unusual for people to provide values in degrees rather than radians, as degrees are the more familiar unit of measure. The functionality covered in the solution provides the conversion between the two units.

1.15. Find the Radius and Center of a Circle to Fit Within a Page Element

Problem

Given the width and height of a page element, you need to find the center and radius of the largest circle that fits within that page element.

Solution

Find the smaller of the width and height; divide this by 2 to find the radius:

```
var circleRadius = Math.min(elementWidth, elementHeight) / 2;
```

Given the page element's width and height, find the center by dividing both by 2:

```
var x = elementWidth / 2;
var y = elementHeight / 2;
```

Discussion

Working with graphics requires us to do things such as finding the center of an element, or finding the radius of the largest circle that will fit into a rectangle (or largest rectangle that can fit in a circle).

Example 1-6 demonstrates both of the solution calculations, modifying an SVG circle contained within an HTML document so that the circle fits within the div element that surrounds it.

Example 1-6. Fitting a SVG circle into a div element

```
<!DOCTYPE html>
<html>
<head>
<title>Using Math method to fit a circle</title>
<style type="text/css">

#elem
{
   width: 600px;
   height: 400px;
   border: 1px solid black;
}
</style>
<script type="text/javascript">

window.onload = window.onresize = function() {
  var box = document.getElementById("elem");
  var style = window.getComputedStyle(box,null);
```

```javascript
    var height = parseInt(style.getPropertyValue("height"));
    var width = parseInt(style.getPropertyValue("width"));

    var x = width / 2;
    var y = height / 2;

    var circleRadius = Math.min(width,height) / 2;

    var circ = document.getElementById("circ");
    circ.setAttribute("r",circleRadius);
    circ.setAttribute("cx",x);
    circ.setAttribute("cy",y);
}

</script>

</head>
<body>
<div id="elem">
   <svg width="100%" height="100%">
      <circle id="circ" width="10" height="10" r="10" fill="red" />
   </svg>

</div>
</body>
```

Figure 1-3 shows the page once it's loaded. There are techniques in SVG that can accomplish the same procedure using the SVG element's viewPort setting, but even with these, at some point in time you'll need to dust off your basic geometry skills if you want to work with graphics. However, as the example demonstrates, most of the math you'll need is basic.

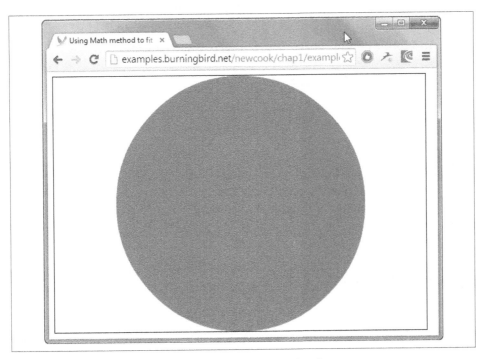

Figure 1-3. Page with SVG circle fit into rectangular div element

1.16. Calculating the Length of a Circular Arc

Problem

Given the radius of a circle, and the angle of an arc in degrees, find the length of the arc.

Solution

Use `Math.PI` to convert degrees to radians, and use the result in a formula to find the length of the arc:

```
// angle of arc is 120 degrees, radius of circle is 2
var radians = degrees * (Math.PI / 180);
var arclength = radians * radius; // value is 4.18879020478...
```

Discussion

The length of a circular arc is found by multiplying the circle's radius times the angle of the arc, in radians.

If the angle is given in degrees, you'll need to convert the degree to radians first, before multiplying the angle by the radius.

See Also

Recipe 1.14 covers how to convert between degrees and radians.

1.17. Using ES6 String Extras Without Leaving Users in the Dirt

Problem

You want to use new ECMAScript 6 features, such as the *string extras* like `starts With()` and `endsWith()`, but you don't want your applications to break for people using browsers that don't support this newer functionality.

Solution

Use an ECMAScript 6 (or ES 6) *shim* to provide support for the functionality in browsers not currently implementing it. Example 1-7 demonstrates how a shim enables support for the new ES 6 String functionality.

Example 1-7. Using a shim to enable ES 6 functionality

```
<!DOCTYPE html>
<html>
<head>
<meta charset="utf-8">
<title>ES 6 String</title>
<script type="text/javascript" src="es6-shim.js"></script>
</head>
<body>

<script type="text/javascript">

  // quote from "To Kill a Mockingbird"
  var str = "Mockingbirds don't do one thing except make music " +
  "for us to enjoy. They don't eat up people's gardens, " +
  "don't nest in corn cribs, " +
  "they don't do one thing but sing their hearts out for us. " +
  "That's why it's a sin to kill a mockingbird."

  console.log(str.startsWith("Mockingbirds")); // true
  console.log(str.startsWith("autos", 20)); // false

  console.log(str.endsWith("mockingbird.")); // true
  console.log(str.endsWith("kill", str.length-15)); // true

  var cp = str.codePointAt(50); // 102 for 'f'
  var cp2 = str.codePointAt(51); // 111 for 'o'
  var cp3 = str.codePointAt(52); // 114 for 'r'
```

```
    var str2 = String.fromCodePoint(cp,cp2,cp3);

    console.log(str2); // for
</script>
</body>
</html>
```

Discussion

JavaScript (or ECMAScript, the more proper name) is advancing much more rapidly now than in the past, but uneven implementation is still an issue. We do live in better times, as the major browser companies are more ready to embrace new features more quickly, and automated browser upgrades help eliminate some of the bogging down we had with a browser such as IE 6. In addition, until we see complete cross-browser support for a new feature, we can still make use of enhancements in Node.js applications on the server, and via the use of *shims* in the client. I'll cover Node.js in a later chapter, but for now, let's look at shims, JavaScript compatibility, and what they mean for something like the new String object enhancements.

 The shim (*https://github.com/paulmillr/es6-shim/*) used in the example is the ES6-shim created by Paul Miller. There are other shims and libraries known as *polyfills*, which you'll see used elsewhere in this book.

The latest formal release of ECMAScript (ES) is ECMAScript 5, and I make use of several ES 5 features throughout the book. Work is underway, though, on the next generation of ES, appropriately named ES.Next (ECMA-262 Edition 6), but commonly referred to as ES 6.

As consensus is reached on new ES features, they're added to the existing draft specification. They're also listed in ES compatibility tables, such as the ones Mozilla incorporates in much of its documentation, and the exceedingly helpful ECMAScript 6 Compatibility Table (*http://kangax.github.io/es5-compat-table/es6/*).

Among the ES 6 additions are the following new `String.prototype` methods:

- `startsWith`: Returns `true` if string begins with characters from another string
- `endsWith`: Returns `true` if string ends with characters from another string
- `contains`: Returns `true` if string contains another string
- `repeat`: Repeats the string a given number of times and returns the result
- `codePointAt`: Returns the Unicode code point (unicode number) that starts at the given index

Both `startsWith()` and `endsWith()` require a string to examine as first parameter, and an optional integer as second parameter. For `startsWith()`, the integer marks the position in the string to begin the search; for `endsWith()`, the integer represents the position in the string where the search should terminate.

The `contains()` method also takes two parameters—search string and optional starting position for search—but it returns `true` or `false` depending on whether it found the search string *anywhere* in the string:

```
console.log(str.contains("gardens")); // true
```

The `repeat()` method takes a given string and repeats it however many times is given in the only parameter, returning the result:

```
var str2 = 'abc';
console.log(str2.repeat(2)); // abcabc
```

The `codePointAt()` method returns the UTF-16 encoded code point value for the character found at the position in the string. In addition, there's also a new *static* method, `fromCodePoint`, which returns a string created by a sequence of code points:

```
var cp = str.codePointAt(50); // 102 for 'f'
var cp2 = str.codePointAt(51); // 111 for 'o'
var cp3 = str.codePointAt(52); // 114 for 'r'

var str2 = String.fromCodePoint(cp,cp2,cp3);

console.log(str2); // for
```

At the time of this writing, if I were to access the web page in Example 1-7 without the use of the ES 6 shim, the JavaScript would fail for all but a developer release of Firefox. With the use of the shim, the JavaScript works for all modern browsers.

See Also

Another alternative to a shim is a *transpiler* that compiles tomorrow's code into today's environment. Google's version, Traceur, is introduced in Recipe 2.11, and demonstrated more fully in Recipe 10.8.

JavaScript Arrays

There is no array data type in JavaScript. Instead, support for arrays is managed through the JavaScript Array object.

Array object support has changed considerably over the years—going from simple array access and assignment to sophisticated functionality allowing us to search and sort arrays, as well as manipulate the array elements using more efficient techniques. This chapter focuses on how to best utilize these more modern Array additions.

Most modern browsers support the solutions presented in this chapter. To support folks not using modern browsers, there are several *shims* you can use to ensure applications work for most. Recipe 1.17 described some of the shims, and demonstrated how you can use them.

2.1. Searching Through an Array

Problem

You want to search an array for a specific value and get the array element index if found.

Solution

Use the Array methods `indexOf()` and `lastIndexOf()`:

```
var animals = new Array("dog","cat","seal","elephant","walrus","lion");
console.log(animals.indexOf("elephant")); // prints 3
```

Discussion

Though support for both `indexOf()` and `lastIndexOf()` has existed in browsers for some time, their use wasn't standardized until the release of ECMAScript 5. Both methods take a search value that is then compared to every element in the array. If the value is found, both return an index representing the array element. If the value is not found, −1 is returned. The `indexOf()` method returns the first one found, the `lastIndex Of()` returns the last one found:

```
var animals = new Array("dog","cat","seal","walrus","lion", "cat");

console.log(animals.indexOf("cat")); // prints 1
console.log(animals.lastIndexOf("cat")); // prints 5
```

Both methods can take a starting index, setting where the search is going to start:

```
var animals = ["dog","cat","seal","walrus","lion", "cat"];

console.log(animals.indexOf("cat",2)); // prints 5
console.log(animals.lastIndexOf("cat",4)); // prints 1
```

If your interest goes beyond just finding an exact match, you can use the ECMAScript 6 (ES 6) Array method `findIndex()`, providing a function that tests each array value, returning the index of the array element when the test is successful.

An example use of `findIndex()` is the following, using the new method to find an array element whose value equals or exceeds 100:

```
var nums = [2, 4, 19, 15, 183, 6, 7, 1, 1];

var over = nums.findIndex(function(element) {
  return (element >= 100);
});

console.log(nums[over]);
```

A comparable ES 6 Array method is `find()`, which does the same process but returns the value of the element that successfully passes the given test. Both methods take a *callback function*, and an optional second argument to act as this in the function. The callback function has three arguments, the array element, index, and array, itself, but only the first is required. Neither method mutates the original array.

See Also

See Recipe 3.5 for more on callback functions.

Extra: Array Literal or Array Object Instance?

The solutions demonstrated in this recipe show two different ways of creating an array: creating an instance of an Array object, or assigning an array literal. So, which is better? As with most of JavaScript, the answer is, it depends.

An array literal is simpler to create and takes less space in the file. Some JavaScript developers would say it looks more elegant, too. When you use the Array object constructor, the JavaScript engine has to spend more time understanding exactly what it is that you want to do: you're creating an object, OK, what kind of object, and so on. However, if you *use* an array literal in a function, JavaScript instantiates the array each time the function is called. And, if you need to create a specifically sized array, you should use the Array contructor.

Tools such as JSLint will complain if you use the Array constructor, as will as most JavaScript developers. Based on this, I use array literals, but its use isn't inherently wrong.

 jsPerf (*http://jsperf.com*) is a site that allows you to quickly create JavaScript test cases and run the tests. You can then share your test case and results with the world. I cover it in more detail in Recipe 6.4.

2.2. Flattening a Two-Dimensional Array with concat() and apply()

Problem

You want to flatten a two-dimensional array.

Solution

Use the Array object concat() method to merge the multidimensional array into a single-dimensional array:

```
var fruitarray = [];
fruitarray[0] = ['strawberry','orange'];
fruitarray[1] = ['lime','peach','banana'];
fruitarray[2] = ['tangerine','apricot'];
fruitarray[3] = ['raspberry','kiwi'];

// flatten array
var newArray = fruitarray.concat.apply([],fruitarray);
console.log(newArray[5]); // tangerine
```

Discussion

The Array object `concat()` method takes one or more arrays and appends the array elements on to the end of the contents of the parent array on which the method was called. The merged array is then returned as a new array. One use for this type of functionality is to return a single-dimensional array made up of elements from a multidimensional array, as shown in the solution.

I could have flattened the array using the following:

```
var newArray = fruitarray[0].concat(fruitarray[1],fruitarray[2],fruitarray[3]);
```

But if the array has several members, this approach is tedious and error prone. I could also have used a loop or recursion, but these approaches can be equally tedious. Instead, I used the `apply()` method. This method allows us to apply the function being called (`concat`) given an array of arguments. In this case, the array of arguments is the original multidimensional array.

In order for this to work, an empty array is passed as the first parameter to `apply()`, because `concat()` works by concatenating the arrays onto an existing array. I can't use the first element of the array, because its values will be repeated in the final result.

2.3. Removing or Replacing Array Elements

Problem

You want to find occurrences of a given value in an array, and either remove the element or replace with another value.

Solution

Use the Array `indexOf()` and `splice()` to find and remove/replace array elements:

```
var animals = new Array("dog","cat","seal","walrus","lion", "cat");

// remove the element from array
animals.splice(animals.indexOf("walrus"),1); // dog,cat,seal,lion,cat

// splice in new element
animals.splice(animals.lastIndexOf("cat"),1,"monkey");

// dog,cat,seal,lion,monkey
console.log(animals.toString());
```

Discussion

The `splice()` method takes three parameters: the first parameter is required, as it's the index where the splicing is to take place; the second, optional parameter is the number of elements to remove; the third parameter, also optional, is a set of the replacement elements (if any). If the index is negative, the elements will be spliced from the end rather than the beginning of the array:

```
var animals = ["cat","walrus","lion", "cat"];

// splice in new element
animals.splice(-1,1,"monkey"); // cat,walrus,lion,monkey
```

If the number of elements to splice is not provided, all elements from the index to the end will be removed:

```
var animals = ["cat","walrus","lion", "cat"];

// remove all elements after second
animals.splice(2); // cat,walrus
```

The last parameter, the replaced value, can be a set of replacement elements, separated by commas:

```
var animals = ["cat","walrus","lion", "cat"];

// replace second element with two
animals.splice(2,1,"zebra","elephant"); // cat,walrus,zebra,elephant,cat
```

Removing or replacing one element is handy, but being able to remove or replace all instances of a particular element is even handier. In Example 2-1, an array is created with several elements, including multiple instances of a specific value. The `splice()` method is used in a loop to replace all of the elements with a given value. The `splice()` method is used again, in a separate loop, to remove the newly spliced elements.

Example 2-1. Using looping and splice to replace and remove elements

```
var charSets = ["ab","bb","cd","ab","cc","ab","dd","ab"];

// replace element
while (charSets.indexOf("ab") != -1) {
  charSets.splice(charSets.indexOf("ab"),1,"**");
}

// ["**", "bb", "cd", "**", "cc", "**", "dd", "**"]
console.log(charSets);

// delete new element
while(charSets.indexOf("**") != -1) {
  charSets.splice(charSets.indexOf("**"),1);
}
console.log(charSets); // ["bb", "cd", "cc", "dd"]
```

2.4. Extracting a Portion of an Array

Problem

You want to extract out a portion of an array but keep the original array intact.

Solution

The Array slice() method extracts a *shallow copy* of a portion of an existing array:

```
var animals = ['elephant','tiger','lion','zebra','cat','dog','rabbit','goose'];

var domestic = animals.slice(4,7);

console.log(domestic); // ['cat','dog','rabbit'];
```

Discussion

The slice() makes a copy of a portion of an existing array, returning a new array. It makes a *shallow copy*, which means that if the array elements are objects, both arrays point to the same object—modifications to the object in the new array is reflected in the same object in the old array. In the following, slice() is used on an array of array elements to extract out of the arrays. The contents are modified and both arrays are printed out. The changes to the new array are reflected in the old:

```
var mArray = [];
mArray[0] = ['apple','pear'];
mArray[1] = ['strawberry','lemon'];
mArray[2] = ['lime','peach','berry'];

var nArray = mArray.slice(1,2);
console.log(mArray[1]); // ['strawberry','lemon']

nArray[0][0] = 'raspberry';
console.log(nArray[0]); // ['raspberry','lemon']
console.log(mArray[1]); // ['raspberry','lemon']
```

The values are copied *by reference*. If the array element is a primitive data type, such as a string or number, the elements are copied *by value*—changes to the new array won't be reflected in the old.

2.5. Applying a Function Against Each Array Element

Problem

You want to use a function to check an array value, and replace it if it matches a given criterion.

Solution

Use the Array method `forEach()` to apply a callback function to each array element:

```
var charSets = ["ab","bb","cd","ab","cc","ab","dd","ab"];

function replaceElement(element,index,array) {
  if (element == "ab") array[index] = "**";
}

// apply function to each array element
charSets.forEach(replaceElement);
console.log(charSets); // ["**", "bb", "cd", "**", "cc", "**", "dd", "**"]
```

Discussion

In Example 2-1, we used a `while` loop to traverse an array and replace a value. Most of the tedious bits are eliminated by using the `forEach()` method.

The `forEach()` method takes one argument, the callback function. The function itself has three parameters: the array element, an index of the element, and the array. All three were used in the function, `replaceElement`, though only the first argument is required.

In the function, the value is tested to see if it matches a given string, *ab*. If matched, the array element's index is used to modify the array element's value with the replacement string, **.

> Don't return a value from the function passed to the `forEach()` method, as the value will be discarded.

See Also

The solution *mutates the array in place*. If you wish to make a copy of the modified array rather than replacing the original, use `map()`, which is covered in Recipe 2.7.

Extra: About That Conditional Statement

The solution used a single line for the conditional statement, sans braces:

```
if (element == "ab") array[index] = "**";
```

Using this single line syntax without braces can be frowned upon because it doesn't account for the possibility of future additions to the conditional block:

```
if (element == "ab") {
  array[index] = "**";
```

```
        //some other line of code
    }
```

However, we should be aware of what we're doing with our code, enough so that we'll know if there's a strong possibility of additional code within the conditional block. I don't see any harm in using a single line when warranted, such as when the conditional stands alone and isn't part of an if-then-else construct.

Of course, we can be even more cryptic and use the following:

```
(element == "ab") && (array[index] = "**");
```

If the element has a value of *ab*, the assignment in the second set of parenthesis is performed. This syntax not only works, it can be faster than the original approach. However, those not familiar with this cryptic conditional could have problems understanding what's happening, as the approach is less readable than using the traditional if statement.

2.6. Traversing the Results from querySelectorAll() with forEach() and call()

Problem

You want to use forEach() on the nodeList returned from a call to querySelector All().

Solution

You can coerce forEach() into working with a NodeList (the collection returned by querySelectorAll()) using the following:

```
// use querySelector to find all second table cells
var cells = document.querySelectorAll("td + td");

[].forEach.call(cells,function(cell) {
    sum+=parseFloat(cell.firstChild.data);
  });
```

Discussion

The forEach() is an Array method, and the results of querySelectorAll() is a NodeList, which is a different type of object than an Array.

In the solution, to get forEach() to work with the NodeList, we're calling the method on an empty array, and then using call() on the object to emulate the effect of an Array method on the NodeList, as if it were an actual array.

Simple, but there are drawbacks. Unless you convert the NodeList into an Array, the coercion is a one-shot that has to be repeated if you need to use the same functionality again. In addition, later in the code you may automatically try another Array method on the NodeList, only to have it fail because you didn't use coercion.

See Also

This approach is also used to convert both NodeLists and function arguments into an array, as detailed in Recipe 3.6.

2.7. Applying a Function to Every Element in an Array and Returning a New Array

Problem

You want to convert an array of decimal numbers into a new array with their hexadecimal equivalents.

Solution

Use the Array map() method to create a new array consisting of elements from the old array that have been modified via a callback function passed to the method:

```
var decArray = [23, 255, 122, 5, 16, 99];

var hexArray = decArray.map(function(element) {
  return element.toString(16);
});

console.log(hexArray); // ["17", "ff", "7a", "5", "10", "63"]
```

Discussion

Like the forEach() method in Recipe 2.5, the map() method applies a *callback* function to each array element. Unlike forEach(), though, the map() method results in a new array rather than modifying the original array. You don't return a value when using forEach(), but you must return a value when using map().

The function that's passed to the map() method has three parameters: the current array element, and, optionally, the array index and array. Only the first is required.

2.8. Creating a Filtered Array

Problem

You want to filter element values in an array and assign the results to a new array.

Solution

Use the Array `filter()` method:

```
var charSet = ["**","bb","cd","**","cc","**","dd","**"];

var newArray = charSet.filter(function(element) {
  return (element !== "**");
});

console.log(newArray); // ["bb", "cd", "cc", "dd"]
```

Discussion

The `filter()` method is another ECMAScript 5 addition, like `forEach()` and `map()` (covered in Recipe 2.5 and Recipe 2.7, respectively). Like them, the method is a way of applying a callback function to every array element.

The function passed as a parameter to the `filter()` method returns either `true` or `false` based on some test against the array elements. This returned value determines if the array element is added to a new array: it's added if the function returns `true`; otherwise, it's not added. In the solution, the character string (**) is filtered from the original array when the new array is created.

The function has three parameters: the array element, and, optionally, the index for the element and the original array.

2.9. Validating Array Contents

Problem

You want to ensure that array contents meet certain criteria.

Solution

Use the Array `every()` method to check that every element passes a given criterion. For instance, the following code checks to ensure that every element in the array consists of alphabetical characters:

```
// testing function
function testValue (element,index,array) {
```

```
    var textExp = /^[a-zA-Z]+$/;
    return textExp.test(element);
}

var elemSet = ["**",123,"aaa","abc","-",46,"AAA"];


// run test
var result = elemSet.every(testValue);

console.log(result); // false

var elemSet2 = ["elephant","lion","cat","dog"];

result = elemSet2.every(testValue);

console.log(result); // true
```

Or use the Array some() method to ensure that one or more of the elements pass the criteria. As an example, the following code checks to ensure that at least some of the array elements are alphabetical strings:

```
var elemSet = new Array("**",123,"aaa","abc","-",46,"AAA");

// testing function
function testValue (element) {
    var textExp = /^[a-zA-Z]+$/;
    return textExp.test(element);
}

// run test
var result = elemSet.some(testValue);

console.log(result); // true
```

Discussion

Unlike the Array methods I covered earlier in the chapter, every() and some() functions do not work against all array elements: they only process as many array elements as necessary to fulfill their functionality.

The solution demonstrates that the same callback function can be used for both the every() and some() methods. The difference is that when using every(), as soon as the function returns a false value, the processing is finished, and the method returns false. The some() method continues to test against every array element until the callback function returns true. At that time, no other elements are validated, and the method returns true. However, if the callback function tests against all elements, and doesn't return true at any point, some() returns false.

Which method to use depends on your needs. If all array elements must meet certain criteria, then use every(); otherwise, use some().

The callback function takes three parameters: the element, and an optional element index and array.

Extra: Using Anonymous Functions in Array Methods

In Recipe 2.8, I used an *anonymous function*, but in this solution, I use a named function. When to use which depends on the context and your own preferences.

The advantage to a named function is it shows up in a stack trace when you're debugging your code, while an anonymous function doesn't. This isn't an issue when you're dealing with simple, targeted functionality, as demonstrated in all of these solutions. However, it can very much be an issue in functionality that's deeply nested, or is asynchronous.

Another advantage to the named function is you can use it in multiple places. Again, though, it doesn't make sense to reuse a function targeted to a specific Array method callback for any reason other than that specific callback. And the disadvantage is that you are cluttering up the global space when you use a named function.

A final possible advantage is that named functions perform better in all browsers than anonymous functions in the context of an Array method callback. Now, this might be the best reason for using a named function.

2.10. Using an Associative Array to Store Form Element Names and Values

Problem

You want to store form element names and values for later validation purposes.

Solution

Use an associative array to store the elements, using the element identifiers as array index:

```
var elemArray = new Object(); // notice Object, not Array
var elem = document.forms[0].elements[0];
elemArray[elem.id] = elem.value;
```

Iterate over the array using a combination of keys() and forEach():

```
Object.keys(elemArray).forEach(function (key) {
        var value = elemArray[key];
        console.log(value);
    });
```

Discussion

Typically, JavaScript arrays use a numeric index:

```
arr[0] = value;
```

However, you can create an *associative array* in JavaScript, where the array index can be a string representing a keyword, mapping that string to a given value. In the solution, the array index is the identifier given the array element, and the actual array value is the form element value.

You *can* create an associative array, but you're not using the Array object to do so. Using the Array object is risky and actively discouraged—especially if you're using one of the built-in libraries that use the `prototype` attribute for extending objects, as people discovered when the popular Prototype.js library was first released several years ago.

When we use an Array to create an associative array, what we're really doing is adding new properties to the Array, rather than adding new array elements. You could actually create an associative array with a RegExp or String, as well as an Array. All are JavaScript objects, which *are* associative arrays. When you're adding a new array, `element`:

```
obj[propName] = "somevalue";
```

what you're really doing is adding a new object property:

```
obj.propName = "somevalue";
```

Additionally, when you use an Array to create an associative array, you can no longer access the array elements by numeric index, and the length property returns zero.

Instead of using an Array to create the associative array, use the JavaScript Object directly. You get the exact same functionality, but avoid the clashes with libraries that extend the base Array object using `prototype`.

Example 2-2 shows a web page with a form. When the form is submitted, all of the form elements of type text are accessed and stored in an associative array. The element IDs are used as the array keyword, and the values assigned to the array elements. Once collected, the associative array is passed to another function that could be used to validate the values, but in this case just creates a string of keyword/value pairs that are displayed.

Example 2-2. Demonstrating associative array with form elements

```
<!DOCTYPE html>
<html>
<head>
<title>Associative Array</title>
</head>
<body>
<form id="picker">
  <label>Value 1:</label> <input type="text" id="first" /><br />
```

```
   <label>Value 2:</label> <input type="text" id="second" /><br />
   <label>Value 3:</label> <input type="text" id="third"  /><br />
   <label>Value 4:</label> <input type="text" id="four"   /><br />
   <button id="validate">Validate</button>
</form>
<div id="result"></div>
<script>

   // get the form element names and values and validate
   document.getElementById('validate').addEventListener('click',function (evnt) {
      evnt.preventDefault();

      // create array of element key/values
      var elems = document.getElementById("picker").elements;
      var elemArray = new Object();
      for (var i = 0; i < elems.length; i++) {
         if (elems[i].type == "text") elemArray[elems[i].id] = elems[i].value;
      }

      var str = '';
      Object.keys(elemArray).forEach(function (key) {
           var value = elemArray[key];
           str+=key + '->' + value + '<br />';
        });

      document.getElementById("result").innerHTML = str;
   }, false);

</script>

</body>
</html>
```

In the example, notice that the array index is formed by the form element's id. The Object keys() returns an array of the object's enumerable properties, and forEach() traverses the array.

Figure 2-1 shows the example after values are typed into the form fields and the form is submitted.

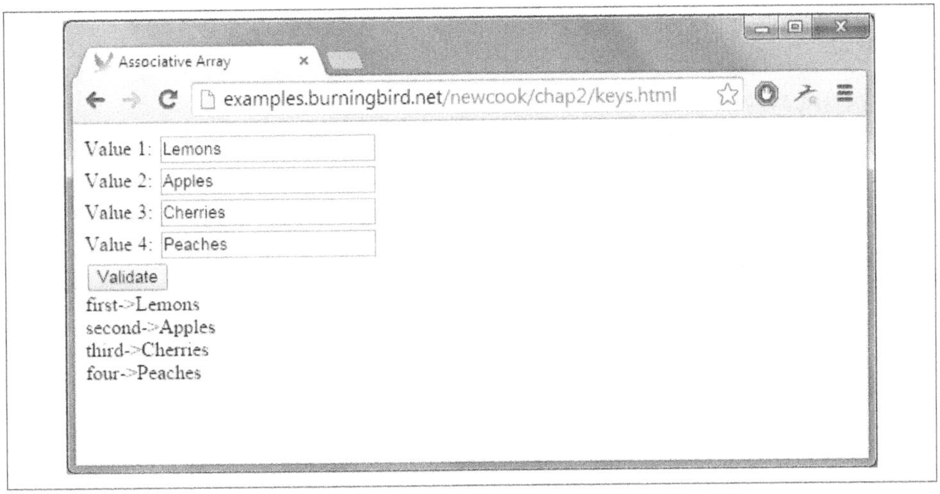

Figure 2-1. Demonstration of associative array and traversing form elements

See Also

For additional information on the risks associated with associative arrays in JavaScript, read JavaScript "Associative Arrays" Considered Harmful (*http://bit.ly/1J9vRon*).

Extra: The dict Pattern

Dr. Axel Rauschmayer discusses a pattern called the *dict pattern* (*http://www.2ality.com/ 2013/10/dict-pattern.html*). Rather than creating a standard object, create one that has a null prototype to avoid inheriting existing properties that can muck up the applications.

The difference between using a standard object and using one with a null prototype is demonstrated in the following code snippet:

```
var newMap = {};

var key = 'toString';

console.log(key in newMap);
console.log(newMap[key]);

var secondMap = Object.create(null);
console.log(key in secondMap);

secondMap[key] = 'something diff';
console.log(key in secondMap);
console.log(secondMap[key]);
```

Here's the result of the code (run in jsBin):

```
true
function toString() { [native code] }
false
true
"something diff"
```

The toString() method is, of course, a standard Object method. So when we test to see if it exists in a regularly created object, it does. However, if we create the null prototype object, toString() doesn't exist. Not until we add it as a key.

2.11. Using a Destructuring Assignment to Simplify Code

Problem

You want to assign array element values to several variables, but you really don't want to have assign each, individually.

Solution

Use ECMAScript 6's *destructuring assignment* to simplify array assignment:

```
var stateValues = [459, 144, 96, 34, 0, 14];

var [Arizona, Missouri, Idaho, Nebraska, Texas, Minnesota] = stateValues;

console.log(Missouri); // 144
```

Discussion

In the solution, variables are declared and instantiated with values in an Array, starting with the Array index at position zero. If the number of variables is less than the array elements, they're assigned the element values up until all variables have been assigned. If there are more variables than array elements, the unmatched variables are created, but they're set to undefined.

The *destructuring assignment* is less a new feature in ECMAScript 6, and more an enhancement of existing functionality. It's not *necessary* functionality, as it's not providing access to functionality we've not had and can't emulate. It's an improvement in the language that will, according to the specification, "Allow for destructuring of arrays and objects using syntax that mirrors array and object initialisers."

Unfortunately, implementation of the functionality is extremely limited, and there is no shim that I know of that can emulate it. However, things change quickly in the world of JavaScript, and it's good to be aware of what's coming down the road.

Extra: Harmony Flags and Using Traceur

V8 JavaScript Engine developers have signaled future implementation of destructuring assignment, which means the capability will also be available in Node.js, as well as browsers like Chrome and Opera (in addition to existing support in Firefox).

Enabling the newest, latest ECMAScript features is typically off by default in most browsers and environments. However, you can signal that you want to enable support for newer features in some of the environments.

In Chrome and Opera, you can enable ES 6 feature support by accessing the URL *chrome://flags*. This opens up the flags page, where you can search for a flag labeled *Experimental JavaScript* and enable it. Note that this can add to the instability of your JavaScript applications.

In addition to enabling ES 6 support in browsers and Node, Google created Traceur, an application that takes ECMAScript.next code and *transpiles* (translates and compiles) it into ECMAScript.current code, which should be executable in all modern environments. An example of using Traceur is the following, the results of using the application on the solution code:

```
$traceurRuntime.ModuleStore.getAnonymousModule(function() {
  "use strict";
  var stateValues = [459, 144, 96, 34, 0, 14];
  var $__3 = stateValues,
      Arizona = $__3[0],
      Missouri = $__3[1],
      Idaho = $__3[2],
      Nebraska = $__3[3],
      Texas = $__3[4],
      Minnesota = $__3[5];
  console.log(Missouri);
  return {};
});
```

 The Traceur results were derived using Google's Traceur REPL (Read-Eval-Print) application (*http://bit.ly/1yHX8dy*). Just copy the code into the given space on the left side of the application, and it produces the translated and compiled results on the right.

Traceur can be accessed via the Traceur GitHub page (*https://github.com/google/traceur-compiler*). It's also an option in jsBin (see Appendix A for more on working with jsBin).

There are also *polyfills* and *shims* to enable ES 6 support. Addy Osmani's page Tracking ECMAScript 6 Support (*http://bit.ly/1J9yiaG*) tracks ES 6 support tools and technology.

See Also

Recipe 10.8 contains a detailed description on how to use Traceur with your browser-based applications. A more detailed discussion on support for ECMAScript 6 (Harmony) features in different browsers can be found in Recipe 10.1.

## CHAPTER 3

Functions: The JavaScript Building Blocks

JavaScript functions provide a way to encapsulate a block of code in order to reuse the code several times. They are *first-class objects* in JavaScript, which means they can be treated as an object, as well as an expression or statement.

There are three basic ways to create a function:

Declarative function
> A declarative function is a statement triggered by the `function` keyword; declarative functions are parsed when the JavaScript application is first loaded.

Anonymous function or function constructor
> An anonymous function is constructed using the `new` operator and referencing the `Function` object. It's anonymous because it isn't given a name, and access to the function occurs through a variable or another object property. Unlike the declarative function, an anonymous function is parsed each time it's accessed.

Function literal or function expression
> A literal function is a function expression, including parameter and body, which is used in place—such as a callback function in an argument to another function. Similar to the declarative function, function literals are also parsed only once, when the JavaScript application is loaded. The function literal can also be anonymous.

3.1. Placing Your Function and Hoisting

Problem

You're not sure where to place your function to ensure it's accessible when needed.

Solution

If you're using a declarative function, you can place the function anywhere in the code. However, if you're using a function expression, you must do so before the function is used. The reasons are given in the discussion.

Discussion

An important concept to remember when considering the different ways you can create a function is *hoisting*. In JavaScript, all variable declarations are moved, or *hoisted* to the top of their current scope. That's *declaration*, though, not instantiation. The difference is critical. If you access a variable that's not declared, you'll get a reference error. However, if you access a variable before it's declared, but it is declared within the scope at a later time, you'll get an undefined:

```
console.log(a); // undefined
var a;
```

If you don't assign a value to the variable when you declare it, you'll still get an undefined when you access the variable:

```
console.log(a); // undefined
var a = 1;
```

This is because the variable *declaration* is hoisted, not the assignment, which happens in place.

What does this have to do with functions? Quite a bit. If you create a declarative function, hoisting will ensure the function definition is moved to the top of the current scope before it's accessed:

```
console.log(test()); // 'hello'
function test() {
  return 'hello';
}
```

However, if you use a functional expression, you're basically toast:

```
console.log(test());
var test = function() {
  return 'hello';
  };
```

A reference error results because the variable test may be declared, but it's not instantiated, and your code is trying to treat this noninstantiated variable as a function.

3.2. Passing a Function As an Argument to Another Function

Problem

You want to pass a function as an argument to another function.

Solution

For the following function:

```
function otherFunction(x,y,z) {
   x(y,z);
}
```

Use a function expression (literal function) as argument:

```
var param = function(arg1, arg2) { alert(arg1 + " " + arg2); };
otherFunction(param, "Hello", "World");
```

or:

```
otherFunction(function(arg1,arg2) {
              alert(arg1 + ' ' + arg2); }, "Hello","World");
```

Discussion

The `function` keyword is an operator as well as a statement, and can be used to create a function as an expression. Functions created this way are called *function expressions*, *function literals*, and *anonymous functions*.

A function name can be provided with literal functions, but it's only accessible within the function:

```
var param = function inner() { return typeof inner; }
console.log(param()); // "function"
```

> The main benefit with naming the function expression is when you're debugging your JavaScript, the named function appears by its name in a stack trace, rather than just an anonymous function.

You can pass a function as an argument to another function as a named variable, or even directly within the argument list, as shown in the solution. Function literals are parsed when the page is loaded, rather than each time they're accessed.

Extra: Functional Programming and JavaScript

A function that accepts another function as a parameter, or returns a function, or both, is known as a *higher order function*. The concept is from a programming paradigm known as *functional programming*. Functional programming is a way of abstracting out the complexity of an application, replacing complicated loops and conditional statements with nice, clean function calls.

 Our more traditional JavaScript development approach using conditionals, loops, and associated procedures is called *imperative programming*.

As an example of functional programming, consider something simple: sum all the numbers in an array. One way of doing so is to create a variable to hold the sum, iterate through the array using a for loop, and adding the value of each array element to the sum variable:

```
var nums = [1, 45, 2, 16, 9, 12];
var sum = 0;
for (var i = 0; i < nums.length; i++) {
  sum+=nums[i];
}
console.log(sum); // 85
```

Now examine how the function `Array.reduce()`, one of the ECMAScript 5 additions to JavaScript, performs the same functionality:

```
var nums = [1, 45, 2, 16, 9, 12];
var sum = nums.reduce(function(n1,n2) { return n1 + n2; });
console.log(sum); // 85
```

The results are the same, but the difference is less verbose code, and a clearer understanding of what's happening to drive the result: the array elements are traversed, some operation is performed until the end result is *reduced* to a single value—in this case, a sum of all array element values.

The real benefit to functional programming, however, is more reliable code. When you break your application down into functional bits, and each function performs a single task, and the *only data* available to that function comes in via function arguments, the *only* output from the operation is that returned by the function, you reduce unintended *side effects* in the code.

A function that always delivers the same result given the same argument values, and that never modifies any external data or triggers any side effects is known as a *pure function*.

In other words, no matter what happens elsewhere in the application—in any library, with any global variable—the effects of applying a function such as `Array.reduce()` will always be consistent.

See Also

See Recipe 3.3 for a demonstration of using a named function literal in recursion. See Recipe 3.4 for a demonstration of using a callback function to prevent blocking.

3.3. Implementing a Recursive Algorithm

Problem

You want to implement a function that will recursively traverse an array and return a string of the array element values, in reverse order.

Solution

Use a function literal recursively until the end goal is met:

```
var reverseArray = function(x,indx,str) {
   return indx == 0 ? str :
                reverseArray(x,--indx,(str+= " " + x[indx]));
}

var arr = ['apple','orange','peach','lime'];
var str = reverseArray(arr,arr.length,"");
console.log(str);

var arr2 = ['car','boat','sun','computer'];
str = reverseArray(arr2,arr2.length,"");
console.log(str);
```

Discussion

Before looking at the solution, I want to cover the concept of recursion first, and then look at functional recursion.

Recursion is a well-known concept in the field of mathematics, as well as computer science. An example of recursion in mathematics is the *Fibonacci Sequence*:

```
f(n)= f(n-1) + f(n-2),
   for n= 2,3,4,...,n and
   f(0) = 0 and f(1) = 1
```

A Fibonacci number is the sum of the two previous Fibonacci numbers.

Another example of mathematical recursion is a *factorial*, usually denoted with an exclamation point (4!). A factorial is the product of all integers from 1 to a given number *n*. If *n* is 4, then the factorial (4!) would be:

```
4! = 4 x 3 x 2 x 1 = 24
```

These recursions can be coded in JavaScript using a series of loops and conditions, but they can also be coded using functional recursion. A common example of JavaScript recursion is the solution for a Fibonacci:

```
var fibonacci = function (n) {
   return n < 2 ? n : fibonacci(n - 1) + fibonacci(n - 2);
}
```

or a factorial:

```
function factorial(n) {
   return n == 1 ? 1 : n * Factorial(n -1);
}
```

In the Fibonacci example, *n* is tested to see if it is less than 2. If it is, it's returned; otherwise the Fibonacci function is called again with (*n* – 1) and with (*n* – 2), and the sum of both is returned.

 Neither function works with negative values. Negative numbers are not extensible to factorial, and the function given for the Fibonacci is not adjusted for negative values.

A little convoluted? The second example with the `factorial` might be clearer. In this example, when the function is first called, the value passed as argument is compared to the number 1. If *n* is less than or equal to 1, the function terminates, returning 1.

However, if *n* is greater than 1, what's returned is the value of *n* times a call to the `factorial` function again, this time passing in a value of *n* – 1. The value of *n*, then, decreases with each iteration of the function, until the terminating condition (or base) is reached.

What happens is that the interim values of the function call are pushed onto a stack in memory and kept until the termination condition is met. Then the values are popped from memory and returned, in a state similar to the following:

```
return 1;
return 1;
return 1 * 2;
return 1 * 2 * 3;
return 1 * 2 * 3 * 4;
```

In the solution, we reverse the array elements by using a recursive function literal. Instead of beginning at index zero, we begin the array from the end length, and decrement this value with each iteration. When the value is zero, we return the string.

If we want the reverse—to concatenate the array elements, in order, to a string—modify the function:

```
var orderArray = function(x,indx,str) {
  return indx == x.length-1 ? str : orderArray(x,++indx,(str+=x[indx] + " "));
}

var arr = ['apple','orange','peach','lime'];
var str = orderArray(arr,-1,"");

// apple orange peach lime
console.log(str);
```

Rather than the length of the array, we start with an index value of –1, and continue the loop until one less than the length of the array. We increment the index value rather than decrement it with each loop.

Most recursive functions can be replaced with code that performs the same function linearly, via some kind of loop. The advantage of recursion is that recursive functions can be fast and efficient. In addition, it adheres to the functional programming paradigm, which means the code is going to be more reliable and consistent.

The downside, though, is that recursive functions can be very memory-intensive. However, the next section explains why this is likely to change in future implementations of JavaScript.

Advanced: Tail Call Optimization

Promised in ECMAScript 6 is a new JavaScript feature called *tail call optimization*, or more properly, *proper tail calls*.

In the following recursive factorial function (less cryptically displayed than the one I provided previously):

```
function factorial(num)
{
  if (num == 0) {
    return 1;
  }
  // Otherwise, call this recursive procedure again.
  else {
    return (num * factorial(num - 1));
  }
}
```

The call to the function at the end of the function is the *tail call*. Currently, each time the recursive function is called, another frame is added to the *call stack*. Basically what's happening is the JavaScript engine is keeping track of the function call and the data passed to it. Enough calls, and the memory is exhausted and you get a `RangeError`.

What the *proper tail call* (optimization) does is reuse the same frame rather than add a new one. Once this feature is incorporated, the possibility of a `RangeError` error happening is eliminated.

 At the time this was written, no browser or other JavaScript engine has implemented *proper tail call* functionality. There is a way of working around the lack of this optimization by using what is known as a *trampoline*. However, the approach is not for the faint of heart. For more on using a trampoline, I recommend reading Reginald Braithwaite's Functional JavaScript—Tail Call Optimization and Trampolines (*http://bit.ly/1J9BoeR*).

See Also

Some of the negative consequences of recursive functions can be mitigated via *memoization*, covered in Recipe 3.8. Accessing the outer variable internally with the recursive function is covered in Recipe 3.5, which goes into function scope.

3.4. Preventing Code Blocking with a Timer and a Callback

Problem

You have a piece of code that can be time consuming, and you don't want to block the rest of the code from processing while waiting for it to finish. But you do need to perform some functionality when the time-consuming function is finished.

Solution

Use a *callback* function in conjunction with `setTimeout()` with timer set to zero (0).

In Example 3-1, `factorial()` is called twice: once with a value of 3 and once with a value of 4. In `factorial()`, the value of the parameter is printed out to the console in each iteration. In `noBlock()`, a `setTimeout()` is used to call `factorial()`, passing to it its first parameter. In addition, an optional second parameter is called if the second parameter is a function. `noBlock()` is called twice with other JavaScript statements printing nonessential text to the `console` inserted preceding, between, and after the two calls. It's also called a third time, in the callback for the very first call to `noBlock()`.

Example 3-1. Using a timer and callback function to prevent code blocking

```
function factorial(n) {
  console.log(n);
  return n == 1 ? 1 : n * factorial(n -1);
}

function noBlock(n, callback) {
  setTimeout(function() {
    var val = factorial(n);
    if (callback && typeof callback == 'function') {
      callback(val);
    }
  },0);
}

console.log("Top of the morning to you");

noBlock(3, function(n) {
  console.log('first call ends with ' + n);
  noBlock(n, function(m) {
    console.log("final result is " + m);
  });
});

var tst = 0;
for (i = 0; i < 10; i++) {
  tst+=i;
}

console.log("value of tst is " + tst);

noBlock(4, function(n) {
  console.log("end result is " + n);
});

console.log("not doing too much");
```

The result of this application run in jsBin is the following output:

```
"Top of the morning to you"
"value of tst is 45"
"not doing too much"
```

```
3
2
1
"first call ends with 6"
4
3
2
1
"end result is 24"
6
5
4
3
2
1
"final result is 720"
```

Even though the calls to noBlock() occur before a couple of the extraneous con
sole.log() calls, the function's process doesn't block the other JavaScript from processing. In addition, the calls to callBack() are processed in the proper order: the two
outer calls complete, before the second one invoked in the callback for the first call to
callBack() is processed.

Discussion

Regardless of the underlying system or application, JavaScript is not multithreaded: all
processes are run on a single thread of execution. Normally this isn't an issue except for
those times when you're running an extremely lengthy bit of code and you don't want
to block the rest of the application from finishing its work. In addition, you may want
to hold off on running another piece of code until *after* the lengthy code is finished.

One solution for both programming challenges is to use a JavaScript timer in conjunction with a *callback* function—a function passed as parameter to another function, and
called within that function in certain circumstances and/or at the end of a process.

When a JavaScript timer event occurs, like any other asynchronous event in JavaScript,
it's added to the end of the event queue rather than getting pushed into the queue immediately. Exactly how and where it enters the queue varies by browser and application
environment, but generally, any functionality associated with the timer event is processed after any other functionality within the same queue.

This can be a bit of an annoyance if you want a process to run *exactly* after so many
seconds, but the functionality can also be a handy way of not blocking an application
while waiting for a time-intensive event. By setting the setTimeout() timer to zero (0),
all we've done in the solution is to create an event that's pushed to the end of the execution
queue. By putting the time-intensive event into the timer's process, we're now no longer
blocking, while waiting for the process to complete.

And because we usually want to perform a final operation when a time-consuming process finishes, we pass a callback function to the timer process that's called only when the process is ended.

In the program output, the three outer console.log() calls are processed immediately, as is the outer loop within the program execution queue:

```
"Top of the morning to you"
"value of tst is 45"
"not doing too much"
```

The next event in the queue is the first noBlock() function call, where the code called factorial() logged its activity as it ran, followed by a call to the callback function logging the function's result:

```
3
2
1
"first call ends with 6"
```

The second call to callBack() operated the same way and again factorial() logged its activity, and the callback logged the result:

```
4
3
2
1
"end result is 24"
```

Only then is the third call to callBack(), invoked in the callback function for the first callBack(), and using the end result of the first function call:

```
6
5
4
3
2
1
"final result is 720"
```

 The concept of a callback and not blocking while waiting on long processes or events is essential for event handling for mouse clicks and Ajax calls, as well as underlying the processing architecture for Node.js, which we'll explore in more detail later in the book.

3.5. Creating a Function That Remembers Its State

Problem

You want to create a function that can remember data, but without having to use global variables and without resending the same data with each function call.

Solution

Create an outer function that takes one or more parameters, and then an inner function that also takes one or more parameters but uses both its and its parent function's parameters. Return the inner function from the outer function, and assign it to a variable. From that point, use the variable as a function:

```
function greetingMaker(greeting) {
   function addName(name) {
      return greeting + " " + name;
   }
   return addName;
}

// Now, create new partial functions
var daytimeGreeting = greetingMaker("Good Day to you");
var nightGreeting = greetingMaker("Good Evening");

...

// if daytime
console.log(daytimeGreeting(name));

// if night
console.log(nightGreeting(name));
```

Discussion

We want to avoid cluttering up the global space with variables, as much as possible. However, there are times when you need to store data to be used across several function calls, and you don't want to have to repeatedly send this information to the function each time.

A way to persist this data from one function to another is to create one of the functions within the other, so both have access to the data, and then return the inner function from the outer. Returning one function from another, when the returned function is using the outer function's *scope*, is known as a *function closure*. Before I get into the specifics of function closure, I want to spend a few minutes on functions and scope.

In the solution, the *inner function* addName() is defined in the *outer function* greeting Maker(). Both of the functions have one argument. The inner function has access to both its argument and the outer function's argument, but the outer function cannot access the argument passed to the inner function. The inner function can operate on the outer function's parameters because it is operating within the same context, or *scope*, of the outer function.

In JavaScript, there is one scope that is created for the outermost application environment. All global variables, functions, and objects are contained within this outer scope.

When you create a function, you create a new scope that exists as long as the function exists. The function has access to all variables in its scope, as well as all of the variables from the outer scope, but the outer scope does not have access to the variables in the function. Because of these scoping rules, we can access window and document objects in all of our browser applications, and the inner function in the solution can also access the data passed to, or originating in, the outer function that wraps it.

 This also explains how the recursive functions in Recipe 3.3 can internally access the variables they're assigned to in the outer application scope.

However, the outer function cannot access the inner function's arguments or local data because they exist in a different scope.

When a function returns a function that refers to the outer function's local scope:

```
function outer (x) {
  return function(y) { return x * y; };
}

var multiThree = outer(3);
alert(multiThree(2)); // 6 is printed
alert(multiThree(3)); // 9 is printed
```

The returned function forms a *closure*. A JavaScript closure is both a function and an environment that existed at the time it was created. In addition, the example also demonstrates *partial application*, where a function's arguments are partially filled (our *bound*) before it's executed.

When the inner function is returned from the outer function, its application scope at the time, including all references to the outer function's variables, persist with the function. So even though the outer function's application scope no longer exists, the inner function's scope exists *at the time the function was returned* including a snapshot of the outer function's data. It will continue to exist until the application is finished.

Another way a closure can be made is if an inner function is assigned to a global variable.

So what happens to these variables when an application scope is released? JavaScript supports automatic garbage collection, which means that you and I don't have to manually allocate or deallocate memory for our variables. Instead, the memory for variables is created automatically when we create variables and objects, and deallocated automatically when the variable scope is released.

In the solution, the outer function greetingMaker() takes one argument, which is a specific greeting. It also returns an inner function, addName(), which itself takes the person's name. In the code, greetingMaker is called twice, once with a daytime greeting, assigned to a variable called daytimeGreeting, and once with a nighttime greeting, assigned to a variable called nightGreeting.

Now, whenever we want to greet someone in daytime, we can use the daytime greeting function, daytimeGreeting, passing in the name of the person. The same applies to the nighttime greeting function, nightGreeting. No matter how many times each is used, the greeting string doesn't need to be re-specified: we just pass in a different name. The specialized variations of the greeting remain in scope until the application terminates.

Closures are interesting and useful, especially when working with JavaScript objects, as we'll see later in the book. But there is a downside to closures that turn up when we create accidental closures.

An accidental closure occurs when we code JavaScript that creates closures, but aren't aware that we've done so. Each closure takes up memory, and the more closures we create, the more memory is used. The problem is compounded if the memory isn't released when the application scope is released. When this happens, the result is a persistent memory leak.

Here's an example of an accidental closure:

```
function outerFunction() {
    var doc = document.getElementById("doc");
    var newObj = { 'doc' : doc};
    doc.newObj = newObj;
}
```

The newObj contains one property, doc, which contains a reference to the page element identified by doc. But then this element is given a new property, newObj, which contains a reference to the new object you just created, which in turn contains a reference to the page element. This is a circular reference from object to page element, and page element to object.

The problem with this circular reference is exacerbated in earlier versions of IE, because these older IE versions did not release memory associated with DOM objects (such as the doc element) if the application scope was released. Even leaving the page does not reclaim the memory: you have to close the browser.

Other browsers and newer versions of IE detect this type of situation and perform a cleanup when the user leaves the application (the web page where the JavaScript resided). However, function closures should be deliberate, rather than accidental.

See Also

Mozilla provides a nice, clean description of closures at *http://mzl.la/1z2yXUY*.

John Resig's Partial Application in JavaScript (*http://ejohn.org/blog/partial-functions-in-javascript/*) has a good write up and demonstration on the concept of *partial application*. Another example can be found in Recipe 3.7.

3.6. Converting Function Arguments into an Array

Problem

You want to use Array functionality on a function's arguments, but the `arguments` object isn't an array.

Solution

Use `Array.prototype.slice()` and then the function `call()` method to convert the `arguments` collection into an array:

```
function someFunc() {
    var args = Array.prototype.slice.call(arguments);
    ...
}
```

Or, here's a simpler approach:

```
function someFunc() {
    var args = [].slice.call(arguments);
}
```

Discussion

The `arguments` object is available within a function (and only available within a function) and is an array-like object consisting of all arguments passed to the function. I say "array like" because the only Array property available to the object is `length`.

There could be any number of times when our function may get an unknown number of arguments and we're going to want to do something with them, such as iterate over the batch and perform some process. It would be nice to be able to use a handy Array method like reduce() with the arguments:

```
function sumRounds() {
  var args = [].slice.call(arguments);

  return args.reduce(function(val1,val2) {
    return parseInt(val1,10) + parseInt(val2,10);
  });
}

var sum = sumRounds("2.3", 4, 5, "16", 18.1);

console.log(sum); // 45
```

The slice() method returns a shallow copy of a portion of an array, or all of an array if a begin or ending value is not given. The slice() method is also a function, which means functional methods like call() can be used with it. In the code snippet, call() is passed the function arguments, which performs the necessary conversion on the argument list, passing in the resulting array to slice().

The call() method's first argument is a this value—typically the calling object itself, followed by any number of arguments. In the solution, this is the slice() method, and the outer function's arguments are passed as arguments for slice(). What this technique has effectively done is coerce the outer function's arguments into an acceptable format to serve as argument for slice().

See Also

The Advanced section in Recipe 3.7 has a twist on the argument conversion process.

Extra

The approach described for converting arguments into an array can also be used to convert a NodeList into an array. Given HTML with the following:

```
<div>test</div>
<div>test2</div>
<div>test3</div>
```

A query for all div elements results in a NodeList. You can process each node using forEach() if you first convert the NodeList to an array:

```
var nlElems = document.querySelectorAll('div');
var aElems = [].slice.call(nlElems);

aElems.forEach(function(elem) {
```

```
      console.log(elem.textContent);
   });
```

This code prints out:

```
test
test2
test3
```

You can also use `forEach()` on the NodeList directly, as covered in Recipe 2.6.

3.7. Reducing Redundancy by Using a Partial Application

Problem

You have a function with three arguments (has an *arity* of three (3)) but the first two arguments are typically repeated based on specific use. You want to eliminate the repetition of arguments whenever possible.

Solution

Create one function that manipulates three values and returns a result:

```
function makeString(ldelim, str, rdelim) {
   return ldelim + str + rdelim;
}
```

Now create another function that accepts two arguments, and returns the previously created function, but this time, encoding two of the arguments:

```
function quoteString(str) {
   return makeString("'",str,"'");
}

function barString(str) {
   return makeString("-", str, "-");
}

function namedEntity(str) {
   return makeString("&#", str, ";");
}
```

Only one argument is needed for the new functions:

```
console.log(quoteString("apple")); // "'apple'"
console.log(barString("apple")); // "-apple-"

console.log(namedEntity(169)); // "&#169; - copyright symbol
```

Discussion

Reducing the arity of a function is a classic example of *partial application* as demonstrated earlier in Recipe 3.5 and in this solution.

One function performs a process on a given number of arguments and returns a result, while a second function acts as a *function factory*: churning out functions that return the first function, but with arguments already encoded. As the solution demonstrates, the encoded arguments can be the same, or different.

Advanced: A Partial Function Factory

We can reduce the redundancy of our function factory even further by creating a generic function, named `partial()`, capable of reducing any number of arguments for any number of functions:

```
function partial( fn /*, args...*/) {
  var args = [].slice.call( arguments, 1 );

  return function() {
    return fn.apply( this, args.concat( [].slice.call( arguments ) ) );
  };
}
```

We'll need a copy of the arguments passed to `partial()` but we don't want the first, which is the actual function. Typically, to convert a function's arguments into an array, we'd use syntax like the following:

```
var args = [].slice.call(arguments);
```

In `partial()`, we specify the beginning value for `slice()`, in this case *1*, skipping over the first argument. Next, an anonymous function is returned that consists of returning the results of the `apply()` method on the function passed as an argument to `partial()`, passing in the anonymous function as `this`, and concatenating the arguments passed to `partial()` to whatever arguments are also passed to the newly generated function. The `apply()` method is similar to `call()` in that it calls the function (represented by `this`), but accepts an array-like list of arguments, rather than an actual array of arguments.

Now we can create functions to generate strings, or add a constant to numbers, or any other type of functionality:

```
function add(a,b) {
  return a + b;
}

var add100 = partial(add, 100);
console.log(add100(14)); // 114
```

However, we have to be aware, of the order of arguments. In the case of the delimited string function, we need to remember that `partial()` concatenates whatever is passed to the generated function to the end of the argument list passed to `partial()`:

```
function makeString(ldelim, rdelim, str) {
  return ldelim + str + rdelim;
}

var namedEntity = partial(makeString, "&#", ";");

console.log(namedEntity(169));
```

I had to modify `makeString()` to expect the inserted string to be at the end of the argument list, rather than in the middle, as was demonstrated in the solution.

Extra: Using bind() to Partially Provide Arguments

ECMAScript 5 simplifies the creation of partial applications via the `Function.proto type.bind()` method. The `bind()` method returns a new function, setting `this` to whatever is provided as first argument. All the other arguments are prepended to the argument list for the new function.

Rather than having to use `partial()` to create the named entity function, we can now use `bind()` to provide the same functionality, passing in `undefined` as the first argument:

```
function makeString(ldelim, rdelim, str) {
  return ldelim + str + rdelim;
}

var named = makeString.bind(undefined, "&#", ";");

console.log(named(169)); // "&#169;"
```

Now you have two good ways to simplify your functions.

See Also

Many of us conflated *partial application* with *currying* when we first started exploring this capability in JavaScript (guilty as charged). But there is a difference. Partial application is a way of fixing however many arguments to a returned function, which is then invoked with whatever new arguments are necessary to finish the task. Currying, on the other hand, keeps returning functions for however many arguments are passed.

For an excellent look at partial applications compared to currying, I recommend Ben Alman's blog post "Partial Application in JavaScript" (*http://bit.ly/1J9Qfpt*).

3.8. Improving Application Performance with Memoization (Caching Calculations)

Problem

You want to optimize your JavaScript applications and libraries by reducing the need to repeat complex and CPU-intensive computations.

Solution

Use function *memoization* in order to cache the results of a complex calculation. Here, I'm borrowing an example from Douglas Crockford's book, *JavaScript: The Good Parts* (O'Reilly), as applied to the code to generate a Fibonacci number:

```
var fibonacci = function () {
  var memo = [0,1];
  var fib = function (n) {
    var result = memo[n];
    if (typeof result != "number") {
      result = fib(n -1) + fib(n - 2);
      memo[n] = result;
    }
    return result;
  };
  return fib;
}();
```

Discussion

Memoization is the process where interim values are cached rather than recreated, cutting down on the number of iterations and computation time. It works especially well with something like the Fibonacci numbers or factorials, both of which operate against previously calculated values. For instance, we can look at a factorial, 4!, as follows:

return 1;

return 1;

return 1 * 2;

return 1 * 2 * 3;

return 1 * 2 * 3 * 4;

But we can also view it as: 3! * 4 // 4!

In other words, if we cache the value for 2! when creating 3!, we don't need to recalculate *1 * 2* and if we cache 3! when calculating 4!, we don't need *1 * 2 * 3*, and so on.

Memoization is built into some languages, such as Java, Perl, Lisp, and others, but not into JavaScript. If we want to memoize a function, we have to build the functionality

---

ourselves. The key to the effective use of memoization is being aware that the technique doesn't result in performance improvements until the number of operations is significant enough to compensate for the extra effort.

Example 3-2 shows the memoized and nonmemoized versions of the Fibonacci function that Crockford provided in his book. Note that the calculations are intense and can take a considerable time. Save any work you have in other tabs. You may have to override a message given by the browser, too, about killing a script that's running a long time.

Example 3-2. A demonstration of memoization

```
// Memoized Function
var fibonacci = function () {
  var memo = [0,1];
  var fib = function (n) {
    var result = memo[n];
    if (typeof result != "number") {
      result = fib(n -1) + fib(n - 2);
      memo[n] = result;
    }
    return result;
  };
  return fib;
}();

// nonmemoized function
var fib = function (n) {
  return n < 2 ? n : fib(n - 1) + fib(n - 2);
};
// run nonmemo function, with timer
console.time("non-memo");
for (var i = 0; i <= 10; i++) {
  console.log(i + " " + fib(i));
}
console.timeEnd("non-memo");

// now, memo function with timer
console.time("memo");
for (var i = 0; i <= 10; i++) {
  console.log(i + " " + fibonacci(i));
}
console.timeEnd("memo");
```

First, the code is run in 10 times in a loop, in jsFiddle via Firefox:

```
non-memo: 14ms
memo: 8ms
```

The result generates one big "meh." In the second run, though, the code is edited to run the code in a for loop of 30. The result is as follows:

```
non-memo: 4724ms
memo: 19ms
```

A major change. When I tried to run the example in a loop of 50 iterations, my browser crashed.

See Also

There's little information on JavaScript memoization online. Crockford provides a generic "memoize" function in his book, as does Addy Osmani in "Faster JavaScript Memoization for Improved Application Performance" (*http://bit.ly/1J9Ru8h*). In addition, the Underscore.js library also provides a `memoize()` function.

3.9. Using an Anonymous Function to Wrap Global Variables

Problem

You need to create a variable that maintains state between function calls, but you want to avoid global variables.

Solution

Use an *Immediately-Invoked Function Expression* (IIFE) to wrap variables and functions both:

```
<!DOCTYPE html>
<head>
<title>faux Global</title>
<script>

  (function() {
    var i = 0;

    function increment() {
      i++;
      alert("value is " + i);
    }

    function runIncrement() {
      while (i < 5) {
        increment();
      }
    }

    window.onload=function() {
      runIncrement();
    }
```

```
    })();

</script>
</head>
<body>
</body>
</html>
```

Discussion

An anonymous function surrounds the global values, is immediately evaluated, and then never evaluated again. Ben Allam gave the pattern the name of *Immediately-Invoked Function Expression* (IIFE or "iffy"), though functionality demonstrated in the solution has existed for some time. IIFEs are used in many major libraries and frameworks, including the popular jQuery, as a way of wrapping plug-in functions so that the code can use the jQuery dollar sign function ($) when the jQuery plug-in is used with another framework library.

The approach consists of surrounding the code block with parentheses, beginning with the anonymous function syntax, and following up with the code block and then the final function closure. It could be the following, if there's no parameter passed into the code block:

```
    })();
```

or the following, if you are passing a parameter into the function:

```
    })(jQuery);
```

Now you can create as many variables as you need without polluting the global space or colliding with global variables used in other libraries.

See Also

Ben Alman coined the IIFE phrase in Immediately-Invoked Function Expression (*http://bit.ly/i-ife*). In addition to the writing on IIFE, take time to read the articles Ben links in the "Further Reading" section.

3.10. Providing a Default Parameter

Problem

You want to specify a default value for a parameter if no argument value is given when a function is called.

Solution

Use the new ECMAScript 6 (ES 6) default parameter functionality:

```
function makeString(str, ldelim = "'", rdelim = "'") {

  return ldelim + str + rdelim;

}

console.log(makeString(169)); // "'169'"
```

Discussion

One of the biggest gaps in JavaScript is the lack of a default parameter. Yes, we can emulate the same functionality, but nothing is simpler and more elegant than having support for a default parameter built in.

The use is simple: if one or more arguments can be optional, you can provide a default parameter using syntax like the following:

```
ldelim = "'"
```

Just assign the default value (in whatever data type format) to the parameter.

The default parameter functionality can be used with any parameter. To maintain the proper argument position, you can pass a value of undefined in the argument:

```
console.log(makeString(169,undefined,"-")); // "'str-"
```

At the time I wrote this, only Firefox had implemented default parameter functionality. To ensure future compatibility, test the parameter for the undefined value and adjust accordingly:

```
function makeString(str, ldelim="'", rdelim="'") {
   ldelim = typeof ldelim !== 'undefined' ? ldelim : "'";
   rdelim = typeof rdelim !== 'undefined' ? rdelim : "'";

  return ldelim + str + rdelim;

}
```

## CHAPTER 4

The Malleable JavaScript Object

With the increased interest in functional programming, you might think there's less interest in JavaScript's object-based capability. However, JavaScript is a flexible, adaptable language, and is just as happy to embrace both functional programming and object-oriented development.

There is a caveat related to JavaScript's object-oriented capabilities: unlike languages such as Java or C++, which are based on classes and class instances, JavaScript is based on *prototypical inheritance*. What prototypical inheritance means is that reuse occurs through creating new instances of existing objects, rather than instances of a class. Instead of extensibility occurring through class inheritance, prototypical extensibility happens by enhancing an existing object with new properties and methods.

Prototype-based languages have an advantage in that you don't have to worry about creating the classes first, and then the applications. You can focus on creating applications, and then deriving the object framework via the effort.

It sounds like a mishmash concept, but hopefully as you walk through the recipes you'll get a better feel for JavaScript's prototype-based, object-oriented capabilities.

A Brief Note About Functional Programming and Object-Oriented Development

In the last few years, especially after the explosive growth of jQuery and Node.js, the trend is to use *functional programming* (discussed in Chapter 2) as a development approach over the more traditional `prototype` object-oriented techniques.

Functional programming does have benefits. There is less chance of unwanted side effects, the coding can be simpler to read and maintain, and at times, it seems we're spending less time on the fussy "get everything together" parts.

But object-oriented development is a long-established and understood development paradigm, with well-understood design principles. In addition, there is strong support for object-oriented development in JavaScript, and much of the history of the language has been focused on this approach.

The thing is, JavaScript supports both, and is completely neutral as to which approach is best. That is its benefit, and its bane:

> As far as JavaScript development is concerned, what are the pros and cons of each paradigm? The biggest drawback is that the language supports both paradigms but leaves it up to you. It supports both but doesn't mandate (or make particularly suitable) any. Frameworks exist to simplify object-oriented JavaScript as well as function-oriented JavaScript.
>
> — Dino Esposito

Read more of Dino Esposito's comparison of functional programming and object-oriented development in "Functional vs. Object-Oriented JavaScript Development" (*http://msdn.microsoft.com/en-us/magazine/gg476048.aspx*).

4.1. Keeping Object Members Private

Problem

You want to keep one or more object properties private, so they can't be accessed outside the object instance.

Solution

When creating the private data members, do *not* use the this keyword with the member:

```
function Tune(song,artist) {
  var title = song;
  this.concat = function() {
    return title + " " + artist;
  }
}

var happySongs = [];
happySongs[0] = new Tune("Putting on the Ritz", "Ella Fitzgerald");

console.log(happySongs[0].title); // undefined

// prints out correct title and artist
console.log(happySongs[0].concat());
```

Discussion

Variables in the object constructor (the function body), are not accessible outside the object unless they're attached to that object using this. If they're redefined using the var keyword or passed in as parameters only, the Tune's *inner function*, the concat() method, can access these now-private data members.

This type of method—one that can access the private data members, but is, itself, exposed to public access via this—has been termed a *privileged method* by Douglas Crockford, the father of JSON (JavaScript Object Notation). As he himself explains (*http://www.crockford.com/javascript/private.html*):

> This pattern of public, private, and privileged members is possible because JavaScript has closures. What this means is that an inner function always has access to the vars and parameters of its outer function, even after the outer function has returned. This is an extremely powerful property of the language [. . . .] Private and privileged members can only be made when an object is constructed. Public members can be added at any time.

Be aware, though, that the privacy of the variable is somewhat illusory. One can easily assign a value to that property outside the constructor function, and overwrite the private data:

```
happySongs[0].title = 'testing';
```

```
console.log(happySongs[0].title); // testing
```

However, the "privacy" of the data isn't meant to ensure security of the object. It's a contract with the developer, a way of saying, "This data isn't meant to be accessed directly, and doing so will probably mess up your application." As such, developers also typically use a naming convention where private data members begin with an underscore, to highlight that they aren't meant to be accessed or set directly:

```
function Tune(song,artist) {
  var _title = song;
  this.concat = function() {
    return _title + " " + artist;
  }
}
```

See Also

See Recipe 3.5 for more on function closures. See Recipe 4.2 for more on adding public members after the object has been defined.

4.2. Using Prototype to Create Objects

You want to create a new object, but you don't want to add all the properties and methods into the constructor function.

Solution

Use the object's `prototype` to add the new properties:

```
Tune.prototype.addCategory = function(categoryName) {
   this.category = categoryName;
}
```

Discussion

Object is the ancestor for every object in JavaScript; objects inherit methods and properties from the Object via the Object `prototype`. It's through the `prototype` that we can add new methods to existing objects:

```
var str = 'one';

String.prototype.exclaim = function() {
  if (this.length == 0) return this;
  return this + '!';
}

var str2 = 'two';

console.log(str.exclaim()); // one!
console.log(str2.exclaim()); // two!
```

Before ECMAScript 5 added `trim()` to the `String` object, applications used to extend the `String` object by adding a `trim` method through the `prototype` object:

```
String.prototype.trim = function() {
   return (this.replace(/^[\s\xA0]+/, "").replace(/[\s\xA0]+$/, ""));
}
```

Needless to say, you'd want to use extreme caution when using this functionality. Applications that have extended the `String` object with a homegrown `trim` method may end up behaving differently than applications using the new standard `trim` method. To avoid this, libraries test to see if the method already exists before adding their own.

We can also use `prototype` to add properties to our own objects. In Example 4-1, the new object, `Tune`, is defined using function syntax. It has two private data members, a `title` and an `artist`. A publicly accessible method, `concatTitleArtist()`, takes these two private data members, concatenates them, and returns the result.

After a new instance of the object is created, and the object is extended with a new method (`addCategory()`) and data member (`category`) the new method is used to update the existing object instance.

Example 4-1. Instantiating a new object, adding values, and extending the object

```
function Tune(title,artist) {
  this.concatTitleArtist = function() {
```

```
      return title + " " + artist;
  }
}


// create instance, print out values
var happySong = new Tune("Putting on the Ritz", "Ella Fitzgerald");

// extend the object
Tune.prototype.addCategory = function(categoryName) {
  this.category = categoryName;
}

// add category
happySong.addCategory("Swing");

// print song out to new paragraph
var song = "Title and artist: " + happySong.concatTitleArtist() +
     " Category: " + happySong.category;

console.log(song);
```

The result of running the code is the following line printed out to the console:

```
"Title and artist: Putting on the Ritz Ella Fitzgerald Category: Swing"
```

One major advantage to extending an object using prototype is increased efficiency. When you add a method directly to a function constructor, such as the concat TitleArtist() method in Tune, every single instance of the object then has a copy of this function. Unlike the data members, the function isn't unique to each object instance. When you extend the object using prototype, as the code did with addCategory(), the method is created on the object itself, and then shared equally between all instances of the objects.

Of course, using prototype also has disadvantages. Consider again the concat TitleArtist() method. It's dependent on access to data members that are not accessible outside the object. If the concatTitleArtist() method was defined using prototype and then tried to access these data members, an error occurs.

If you define the method using prototype directly in the constructor function, it is created in the scope of the function and does have access to the private data, but the data is overridden each time a new object instance is created:

```
    function Tune(title,artist) {
      var title = title;
      var artist = artist;
      Tune.prototype.concatTitleArtist = function() {
        return title + " " + artist;
      }
    }
```

```
var sad = new Tune('Sad Song', 'Sad Singer')
var happy = new Tune('Happy', 'Happy Singer');

console.log(sad.concatTitleArtist()); // Happy Happy Singer
```

The only data unique to the prototype function is what's available via this. There are twisty ways around this, but they not only add to the complexity of the application, they tend to undermine whatever efficiency we get using prototype.

Generally, if your function must deal with private data, it should be defined within the function constructor, and without using prototype. Otherwise, the data should be available via this, or static and never changing once the object is created.

4.3. Inheriting an Object's Functionality

Problem

When creating a new object type, you want to inherit the functionality of an existing JavaScript object.

Solution

Use Object.create() to implement the inheritance:

```
function origObject() {
  this.val1 = 'a';
  this.val2 = 'b';
}

origObject.prototype.returnVal1 = function() {
  return this.val1;
};

origObject.prototype.returnVal2 = function() {
  return this.val2;
};

function newObject() {
  this.val3 = 'c';
  origObject.call(this);
}

newObject.prototype = Object.create(origObject.prototype);
newObject.prototype.constructor=newObject;

newObject.prototype.getValues = function() {
  return this.val1 + " " + this.val2 + " "+ this.val3;
};
```

```
var obj = new newObject();

console.log(obj instanceof newObject); // true
console.log(obj instanceof origObject); // true

console.log(obj.getValues()); "a b c"
```

Discussion

The Object.create() method introduced with ECMAScript 5 provides classical inheritance in JavaScript. The first parameter is the object that serves as prototype for the newly created object, and the second optional parameter is a set of properties defined for the object, and equivalent to the second argument in Object.defineProperties().

In the solution for this recipe, the prototype for the original object is passed in the Object.create() call, assigned to the new object's own prototype. The new object's constructor property is set to the new object's constructor function. The new object's prototype is then extended with a new method, getValues(), which returns a string consisting of concatenated properties from both objects. Note the use of instanceof demonstrating how both the old and new object prototypes are in the new object's prototype chain.

In the constructor function for the new object, you need to use call() to chain the constructors for both objects. If you want to pass the argument list between the two objects, use apply() instead, as demonstrated in Example 4-2.

Example 4-2. Demonstrating classical inheritance in JavaScript with Object.create

```
function Book (title, author) {
   this.getTitle=function() {
      return "Title: " + title;
   };
   this.getAuthor=function() {
      return "Author: " + author;
   };
}

function TechBook (title, author, category) {

   this.getCategory = function() {
      return "Technical Category: " + category;
   };

   this.getBook=function() {
      return this.getTitle() + " " + author + " " + this.getCategory();
   };

   Book.apply(this, arguments);
}
```

```
TechBook.prototype = Object.create(Book.prototype);
TechBook.prototype.constructor = TechBook;

// get all values
var newBook = new TechBook("The JavaScript Cookbook",
  "Shelley Powers", "Programming");

console.log(newBook.getBook());

// now, individually
console.log(newBook.getTitle());
console.log(newBook.getAuthor());
console.log(newBook.getCategory());
```

In jsBin, the output for the application is:

```
"Title: The JavaScript Cookbook Shelley Powers Technical Category: Programming"
"Title: The JavaScript Cookbook"
"Author: Shelley Powers"
"Technical Category: Programming"
```

4.4. Extending an Object by Defining a New Property

Problem

You can easily slap a new property onto an object, but you want to do so in such a way that you have more control of how it's used.

Solution

Use the `defineProperty()` method to add the property.

Given the following object:

```
var data = {}
```

If you want to add the following two properties with the given characteristics:

- type: Initial value set and can't be changed, can't be deleted or modified, but can be enumerated

- id: Initial value set, but can be changed, can't be deleted or modified, and can't be enumerated

Use the following JavaScript:

```
var data = {};

Object.defineProperty(data, 'type', {
```

```
  value: 'primary',
  enumerable: true
});

console.log(data.type); // primary
data.type = 'secondary';
console.log(data.type); // nope, still primary

Object.defineProperty(data, 'id', {
  value: 1,
  writable: true
});

console.log(data.id); // 1
data.id=300;
console.log(data.id); // 300

for (prop in data) {
  console.log(prop); // only type displays
}
```

Discussion

The defineProperty() is a way of adding a property to an object other than direct assignment that gives us some control over its behavior and state. There are two variations of property you can create with defineProperty(): a data descriptor, as demonstrated in the solution, and an accessor descriptor, defined with a getter-setter function pair.

 The defineProperty() Object method for accessor descriptors replaces the now deprecated __defineGetter and __defineSetter.

An example of an accessor descriptor is the following:

```
var data = {};

var group = 'history';

Object.defineProperty(data, "category", {
  get: function () { return group; },
  set: function (value) { group = value; },
  enumerable: true,
  configurable: true
});

console.log(data.category); // history
```

```
group = 'math';
console.log(data.category); // math

data.category = 'spanish';
console.log(data.category); // spanish
console.log(group); // spanish
```

Changes to the value for `data.category` and `group` are now interconnected.

The `Object.defineProperty()` supports three parameters: the object, the property, and a descriptor object. The latter consists of the following options:

- configurable: `false` by default; controls whether the property descriptor can be changed
- enumerable: `false` by default; controls whether the property can be enumerated
- writable: `false` by default; controls whether the property value can be changed through assignment
- value: The initial value for the property
- get: `undefined` by default; property getter
- set: `undefined` by default; property setter

The `defineProperty()` method has wide support in all modern browsers, but with caveats. Safari does not allow its use on a DOM object, while IE8 only supports it on a DOM object (IE9 and later support it on all objects).

See Also

Recipe 4.5 details how to prevent the addition of new properties to an object, and Recipe 4.6 covers freezing an object against any further change.

4.5. Preventing Object Extensibility

Problem

You want to prevent others from extending an object.

Solution

Use the ECMAScript 5 `Object.preventExtensions()` method to lock an object against future property additions:

```
'use strict';

var Test = {
  value1 : "one",
```

```
    value2 : function() {
      return this.value1;
    }
  };

  try {
    Object.preventExtensions(Test);

    // the following fails, and throws a TypeError in Strict mode
    Test.value3 = "test";

  } catch(e) {
    console.log(e);
  }
```

Discussion

The `Object.preventExtensions()` method prevents developers from extending the object with new properties, though property values themselves are still writable. It sets an internal property, `Extensible`, to `false`. You can check to see if an object is extensible using `Object.isExtensible`:

```
if (Object.isExtensible(obj)) {
  // extend the object
}
```

If you attempt to add a property to an object that can't be extended, the effort will either fail silently, or, if `strict mode` is in effect, will throw a `TypeError` exception:

```
TypeError: Can't add property value3, object is not extensible
```

Though you can't extend the object, you can edit existing property values, as well as modify the object's property descriptor.

See Also

Recipe 4.4 covers property descriptors. `strict mode` was covered in "Extra: Speaking of Strict Mode" on page 33.

4.6. Preventing Any Changes to an Object

Problem

You've defined your object, and now you want to make sure that its properties aren't redefined or edited by other applications using the object.

Solution

Use `Object.freeze()` to freeze the object against any and all changes:

```
'use strict';

var test = {
  value1 : 'one',
  value2 : function() {
    return this.value1;
  }
}

try {
  // freeze the object
  Object.freeze(test);

  // the following throws an error in Strict Mode
  test.value2 = 'two';

  // so does the following
  test.newProperty = 'value';

  var val = 'test';

  // and the following
  Object.defineProperty(test, 'category', {
    get: function () { return test; },
    set: function (value) { test = value; },
    enumerable: true,
    configurable: true
  });
} catch(e) {
  console.log(e);
}
```

Discussion

ECMAScript 5 brought us several Object methods for better object management. The least restrictive is `Object.preventExtensions(obj)`, covered in Recipe 4.5, which disallows adding new properties to an object, but you can still change the object's property descriptor or modify an existing property value.

The next, more restrictive method is `Object.seal()`, which prevents any modifications or new properties from being added to the property descriptor, but you can modify an existing property value.

The most restrictive method is `Object.freeze()`. This method disallows extensions to the object and restricts changes to the property descriptor. In addition,

`Object.freeze()` also prevents any and all edits to existing object properties. Literally, once the object is frozen, that's it—no additions, no changes to existing properties.

The first property modification in the solution code:

```
test.value2 = "two";
```

results in the following error (in Chrome):

```
TypeError: Cannot assign to read only property 'value2' of #<Object>
```

If we comment out the line, the next object adjustment:

```
test.newProperty = "value";
```

throws the following error:

```
TypeError: Can't add property newProperty, object is not extensible
```

Commenting out this line leaves the use of `defineProperty()`:

```
var val = 'test';

// and the following
Object.defineProperty(test, "category", {
  get: function () { return test; },
  set: function (value) { test = value; },
  enumerable: true,
  configurable: true
});
```

We get the final exception, for the use of `defineProperty()` on the object:

```
TypeError: Cannot define property:category, object is not extensible.
```

If we're not using strict mode, the first two assignments fail silently, but the use of `defineProperty()` still triggers an exception (this mixed result is another good reason for using strict mode).

Check if an object is frozen using the companion method, `Object.isFrozen()`:

```
if (Object.isFrozen(obj)) ...
```

4.7. Namespacing Your JavaScript Objects

Problem

You want to encapsulate your data and functions in such a way as to prevent clashes with other libraries.

Solution

Use an object *literal*, what I call a *one-off object*, to implement the JavaScript version of namespacing. An example is the following:

```
var jscbObject = {

  // return element
  getElem : function (identifier) {
    return document.getElementById(identifier);
  },

  stripslashes : function(str) {
    return str.replace(/\\/g, '');
  },

  removeAngleBrackets: function(str) {
    return str.replace(/</g,'&lt;').replace(/>/g,'&gt;');
  }
};

var sample = "<div>testing\changes</div>";

var result = jscbObject.stripslashes(sample);
result = jscbObject.removeAngleBrackets(result);

console.log(result); //&lt;div&gt;testingchanges&lt;/div&gt;
```

Discussion

As mentioned elsewhere in this book, all built-in objects in JavaScript have a literal representation in addition to their more formal object representation. For instance, an `Array` can be created as follows:

```
var newArray = new Array('one','two','three');
```

or using the array literal notation:

```
var newArray = ['one','two','three'];
```

The same is true for objects. The notation for object literals is pairs of property names and associated values, separated by commas, and wrapped in curly brackets:

```
var newObj = {
  prop1 : "value",
  prop2 : function() { ... },
    ...
};
```

The property/value pairs are separated by colons. The properties can be scalar data values or they can be functions. The object members can then be accessed using the object dot-notation:

```
    var tmp = newObj.prop2();
```

or:

```
    var val = newObj.prop1 * 20;
```

or:

```
    getElem("result").innerHTML=result;
```

Using an object literal, we can wrap all of our library's functionality in such a way that the functions and variables we need aren't individually in the global space. The only global object is the actual object literal, and if we use a name that incorporates functionality, group, purpose, author, and so on, in a unique manner, we effectively namespace the functionality, preventing name clashes with other libraries.

Advanced

I use the term *one-off* with the object literal rather than the more commonly known *singleton* because, technically, the object literal doesn't fit the singleton pattern.

A singleton pattern is one where only one instance of an object can be created. We can say this is true of our object literal, but there's one big difference: a singleton can be instantiated at a specific time rather than exist as a static construct, which is what the solution defines.

I went to Addy Osmani's *JavaScript Design Patterns* (O'Reilly) to get an example of a good implementation of a singleton:

```
var mySingleton = (function () {

  // Instance stores a reference to the Singleton
  var instance;

  function init() {

    // Singleton

    // Private methods and variables
    function privateMethod(){
        console.log( "I am private" );
    }

    var privateVariable = "Im also private";

    var privateRandomNumber = Math.random();

    return {

      // Public methods and variables
      publicMethod: function () {
        console.log( "The public can see me!" );
```

```
          },

          publicProperty: "I am also public",

          getRandomNumber: function() {
            return privateRandomNumber;
          }

        };

      };

      return {

        // Get the Singleton instance if one exists
        // or create one if it doesn't
        getInstance: function () {

          if ( !instance ) {
            instance = init();
          }

          return instance;
        }

      };

    })();

    singleA = mySingleton.getInstance();
    var singleB = mySingleton.getInstance();
    console.log( singleA.getRandomNumber() === singleB.getRandomNumber() );
```

The singleton uses an Immediately-Invoked Function Expression (IIFE) to wrap the object, which immediately returns an instance of the object. But not just any instance —if an instance already exists, it's returned rather than a new instance. The latter is demonstrated by the object's `getRandomNumber()` function, which returns a random number that is generated when the object is created, and returns the same random number regardless of which "instance" is accessed.

 Access Addy Osmani's *Learning JavaScript Design Patterns* online (*http://bit.ly/ZQNe8L*), or you can purchase a digital and/or paper copy directly at O'Reilly, or from your favorite book seller.

See Also

Chapter 7 covers external libraries and packaging your code into a library for external distribution. Chapter 12 covers another important pattern, the *module pattern*, and how modularization works with JavaScript.

4.8. Rediscovering this with Prototype.bind

Problem

You want to control the scope assigned a given function.

Solution

Use the bind() method:

```
window.onload=function() {

  window.name = "window";

  var newObject = {
    name: "object",

    sayGreeting: function() {
      alert("Now this is easy, " + this.name);
      nestedGreeting = function(greeting) {
        alert(greeting + " " + this.name);
        }.bind(this);

        nestedGreeting("hello");
    }
  };

  newObject.sayGreeting("hello");
};
```

Discussion

this represents the owner or scope of the function. The challenge associated with this in JavaScript libraries is that we can't guarantee which scope applies to a function.

In the solution, the object has a method, sayGreeting(), which outputs a message and maps another nested function to its property, nestedGreeting.

Without the Function's bind() method, the first message printed out would say, "Now this is easy, object", but the second would say, "hello window". The reason the second printout references a different name is that the nesting of the function disassociates the inner function from the surrounding object, and all *unscoped* functions automatically become the property of the window object.

What the bind() method does is use the apply() method to bind the function to the object passed to the object. In the example, the bind() method is invoked on the nested function, binding it with the parent object using the apply() method.

bind() is particularly useful for timers, such as setInterval(). Example 4-3 is a web page with a script that uses setTimeout() to perform a countdown operation, from 10 to 0. As the numbers are counted down, they're inserted into the web page using the element's innerHTML property.

Example 4-3. Demonstrating the utility of bind

```
<!DOCTYPE html>
<head>
<html>
<title>Using bind with timers</title>
<meta charset=utf-8" />
<style type="text/css">
  #item {
    font-size: 72pt;
    margin: 70px auto;
    width: 100px;
  }
</style>
</head>
<body>
  <div id="item">
    10
  </div>
  <script>

    var theCounter = new Counter('item',10,0);
    theCounter.countDown();

    function Counter(id,start,finish) {
      this.count = this.start = start;
      this.finish = finish;
      this.id = id;
      this.countDown = function() {
        if (this.count == this.finish) {
          this.countDown=null;
            return;
        }
        document.getElementById(this.id).innerHTML=this.count--;
        setTimeout(this.countDown.bind(this),1000);
      };
    }
  </script>
```

```
</body>
</html>
```

If the `setTimeout()` function in the code sample had been the following:

```
setTimeout(this.countDown, 1000);
```

the application wouldn't have worked, because the object scope and counter would have been lost when the method was invoked in the timer.

Extra: self = this

An alternative to using `bind()`, and one that is still in popular use, is to assign `this` to a variable in the outer function, which is then accessible to the inner. Typically `this` is assigned to a variable named `that` or `self`:

```
window.onload=function() {

  window.name = "window";

  var newObject = {
    name: "object",

    sayGreeting: function() {
      var self = this;
      alert("Now this is easy, " + this.name);
      nestedGreeting = function(greeting) {
        alert(greeting + " " + self.name);
      };

      nestedGreeting("hello");
    }
  };

  newObject.sayGreeting("hello");
};
```

Without the assignment, the second message would reference "window", not "object".

4.9. Chaining Your Object's Methods

Problem

You wish to define your object's methods in such a way that more than one can be used at the same time, similar to the following, which retrieves a reference to a page element *and* sets the element's `style` property:

```
document.getElementById("elem").setAttribute("class","buttondiv");
```

Solution

The ability to directly call one function on the result of another in the same line of code is known as *method chaining*. It requires specialized code in whatever method you want to chain.

For instance, if you want to be able to chain the `TechBook.changeAuthor()` method in the following code snippet, you must also return the object after you perform whatever other functionality you need:

```
function Book (title, author) {
  this.getTitle=function() {
    return "Title: " + title;
  };

  this.getAuthor=function() {
    return "Author: " + author;
  };

  this.replaceTitle = function (newTitle) {
    var oldTitle = title;
    title = newTitle;
  };

  this.replaceAuthor = function(newAuthor) {
    var oldAuthor = author;
    author = newAuthor;
  };
}

function TechBook (title, author, category) {
  this.getCategory = function() {
    return "Technical Category: " + category;
  };

  Book.apply(this,arguments);

  this.changeAuthor = function(newAuthor) {
    this.replaceAuthor(newAuthor);

    return this;  // necessary to enable method chaining
  };
}

var newBook = new TechBook("I Know Things", "Smart Author", "tech");
console.log(newBook.changeAuthor("Book K. Reader").getAuthor());
```

Discussion

The key to making method chaining work is to return a reference to the object at the end of the method, as shown in the `changeAuthor()` method in the solution:

```
this.changeAuthor = function(newAuthor) {
  this.replaceAuthor(newAuthor);

  return this;  // necessary to enable method chaining
};
```

Chaining is used extensively in JavaScript objects, and demonstrated throughout this book when we see functionality such as:

```
var result = str.replace(/</g,'&lt;').replace(/>/g,'&gt;');
```

Libraries such as jQuery also make extensive use of method chaining, as we'll see later in the book.

## CHAPTER 5

JavaScript and Directly Accessing the User Interface

The user interface in JavaScript applications is typically the web page in which the script is embedded. The page may open in an Android tablet or a traditional computer browser, but the concepts are the same.

Nowadays, most people use libraries and frameworks in order to manipulate the web page. However, no matter how helpful and sophisticated the library, you still need to have a good idea of what you can, and cannot, do to the web page before making effective use of a library. More importantly, you need to have a good idea of the best practices to use when modifying the web page.

5.1. Accessing a Given Element and Finding Its Parent and Child Elements

Problem

You want to access a specific web page element, and then find its parent and child elements.

Solution

Give the element a unique identifier:

```
<div id="demodiv">
  <p>
    This is text.
  </p>
</div>
```

Use `document.getElementById()` to get a reference to the specific element:

```
var demodiv = document.getElementById("demodiv");
```

Find its parent via the `parentNode` property:

```
var parent = demodiv.parentNode;
```

Find its children via the `childNodes` property:

```
var children = demodiv.childNodes;
```

Discussion

A web document is organized like an upside-down tree, with the topmost element at the root and all other elements branching out beneath. Except for the root element (HTML), each element has a parent node, and all of the elements are accessible via the document.

There are several different techniques available for accessing these document elements, or *nodes* as they're called in the Document Object Model (DOM). Today, we access these nodes through standardized versions of the DOM, such as the DOM Levels 2 and 3. Originally, though, a de facto technique was to access the elements through the browser object model, sometimes referred to as DOM Level 0. The DOM Level 0 was invented by the leading browser company of the time, Netscape, and its use has been supported (more or less) in most browsers since. The key object for accessing web page elements in the DOM Level 0 is the document object.

The most commonly used DOM method is `document.getElementById()`. It takes one parameter: a case-sensitive string with the element's identifier. It returns an `element` object, which is referenced to the element if it exists; otherwise, it returns null.

 There are numerous ways to get one specific web page element, including the use of selectors, covered later in the chapter. But you'll always want to use the most restrictive method possible, and you can't get more restrictive than `document.getElementById()`.

The returned `element` object has a set of methods and properties, including several inherited from the node object. The node methods are primarily associated with traversing the document tree. For instance, to find the parent node for the element, use the following:

```
var parent = document.getElementById("demodiv").parentNode; // parent node
```

You can find out the type of element for each node through the `nodeName` property:

```
var type = parent.nodeName; // BODY
```

If you want to find out what children an element has, you can traverse a collection of them via a NodeList, obtained using the `childNodes` property:

```
var demodiv = document.getElementById("demodiv");
var outputString = "";

if (demodiv.hasChildNodes()) {
  var children = demodiv.childNodes;
  for (var i = 0; i < children.length; i++) {
    outputString+="has child " + children[i].nodeName + " ";
  }
}
console.log(outputString);
```

Given the element in the solution, the output would be:

```
"has child #text has child P has child #text "
```

You might be surprised by what appeared as a child node. In this example, whitespace before and after the paragraph element is itself a child node with a nodeName of #text. For the following `div` element:

```
<div id="demodiv" class="demo">
  <p>Some text</p>
  <p>Some more text</p>
</div>
```

the `demodiv` element (node) has five children, not two:

```
has child #text
has child P
has child #text
has child P
has child #text
```

 In the last code snippet, IE8 only picks up the two paragraph elements, which demonstrates why it's important to be specific with the queries and check nodeName to ensure you're accessing the correct elements.

The best way to see how messy the DOM can be is to use a debugger such as Firebug or the Chrome developer tools, access a web page, and then utilize whatever DOM inspection tool the debugger provides. I opened a simple page in Chrome and used the developer tools to display the element tree, as shown in Figure 5-1.

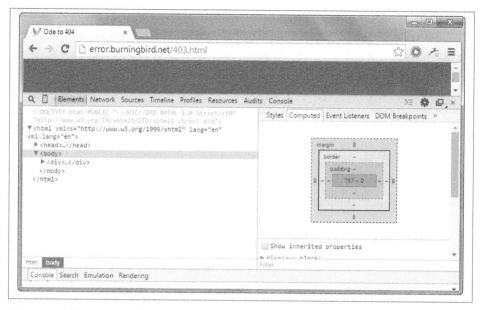

Figure 5-1. Examining the element tree of a web page using Chrome's developer tools

5.2. Accessing All Images in the Web Page

Problem

You want to access all img elements in a given document.

Solution

Use the document.getElementsByTagName() method, passing in *img* as the parameter:

```
var imgElements = document.getElementsByTagName('img');
```

Discussion

The document.getElementsByTagName() method returns a collection of nodes (a NodeList) of a given element type, such as the img tag in the solution. The collection can be traversed like an array, and the order of nodes is based on the order of the elements within the document (the first img element in the page is accessible at index 0, etc.):

```
var imgElements = document.getElementsByTagName('img');
for (let i = 0; i < imgElements.length; i++) {
    var img = imgElements[i];
    ...
}
```

The NodeList collection can be traversed like an array, but it isn't an Array object—you can't use Array object methods, such as push() and reverse(), with a NodeList. Its only property is length, and its only method is item(), returning the element at the position given by an index passed in as parameter:

```
var img = imgElements.item(1); // second image
```

NodeList is an intriguing object because it's a live collection, which means changes made to the document after the NodeList is retrieved are reflected in the collection. Example 5-1 demonstrates the NodeList live collection functionality, as well as getEle mentsByTagName.

In the example, three images in the web page are accessed as a NodeList collection using the getElementsByTagName method. The length property, with a value of 3, is output to the console. Immediately after, a new paragraph and img elements are created, and the img is appended to the paragraph. To append the paragraph following the others in the page, getElementsByTagName is used again, this time with the paragraph tags (p). We're not really interested in the paragraphs, but in the paragraphs' parent elements, found via the parentNode property on each paragraph.

The new paragraph element is appended to the paragraph's parent element, and the previously accessed NodeList collection's length property is again printed out. Now, the value is 4, reflecting the addition of the new img element.

Example 5-1. Demonstrating getElementsByTagName and the NodeList live collection property

```
<!DOCTYPE html>
<html>
<head>
<title>NodeList</title>
</head>
<body>
  <p><img src="firstimage.jpg" alt="image description" /></p>
  <p><img src="secondimage.jpg" alt="image description" /></p>
  <p><img src="thirdimage.jpg" alt="image description" /></p>

<script>
   var imgs = document.getElementsByTagName('img');
   console.log(imgs.length);
   var p = document.createElement("p");
   var img = document.createElement("img");
   img.src="someimg.jpg";
   p.appendChild(img);

   var paras = document.getElementsByTagName('p');
   paras[0].parentNode.appendChild(p);

   console.log(imgs.length);
```

```
        </script>

</body>
</html>
```

In addition to using `getElementsByTagName()` with a specific element type, you can also pass the universal selector (*) as a parameter to the method to get all elements:

```
var allelems = document.getElementsByTagName('*');
```

 IE7, or IE8 running in IE7 mode, will return an empty NodeList if you use the universal selector with `getElementsByTagName()`.

See Also

In the code demonstrated in the discussion, the children nodes are traversed using a traditional for loop. Array functionality, such as `forEach()`, can't be used directly with a NodeList because it's not an Array. You can coerce the NodeList, as is demonstrated in Recipe 2.6, but this type of coercion has its own drawbacks.

Extra: Namespace Variation

Like most of the DOM API access methods, there is a variation of `getElementsByTag Name()`, `getElementsByTagNameNS`, which can be used in documents that support multiple namespaces, such as an XHTML web page with embedded MathML or SVG.

In Example 5-2, an SVG document is embedded in XHTML. Both the XHTML document and the embedded SVG make use of the `title` element. The `title` element in the XHTML document is part of the default XHTML namespace, but the `title` in the SVG is part of the Dublin Core namespace.

When the `title` element is accessed, information about the `title`, including its namespace, the prefix, the `localName`, and the `textContent`, are printed out. The prefix is the dc component of `dc:title`, and the `localName` is the title part of `dc:title`. The `textContent` is a new property, added with the DOM Level 2, and is the text of the element. In the case of `title` (either the XHTML or the Dublin Core element), it would be the `title` text.

Example 5-2. The differences between the namespace and nonnamespace variation of getElementsByTagName

```
<!DOCTYPE html>
<html xmlns="http://www.w3.org/1999/xhtml" xml:lang="en">
<head>
```

```
<title>Namespace</title>
<script type="text/javascript">
//<![CDATA[

window.onload=function () {

    var str = "";
    var title = document.getElementsByTagName("title");
    for (var i = 0; i < title.length; i++) {
        str += title.item(i).namespaceURI + " " +
                title.item(i).prefix + " " +
                title.item(i).localName + " " +
                title.item(i).text + " ";
    }
    alert(str);

    str = "";
    if (!document.getElementsByTagNameNS) return;
    var  titlens =
document.getElementsByTagNameNS("http://purl.org/dc/elements/1.1/",
"title");
    for (var i = 0; i < titlens.length; i++) {
        str += titlens.item(i).namespaceURI + " " +
                titlens.item(i).prefix + " " +
                titlens.item(i).localName + " " +
                titlens.item(i).textContent + " ";
    }
    alert(str);}
//]]>

</script>
</head>
<body>
<h1>SVG</h1>
<svg id="svgelem" height="800" width="800" xmlns="http://www.w3.org/2000/svg">
        <circle id="redcircle" cx="300" cy="300" r="300"
          fill="red" />
  <metadata>
    <rdf:RDF xmlns:cc="http://web.resource.org/cc/"
xmlns:dc="http://purl.org/dc/elements/1.1/"
xmlns:rdf="http://www.w3.org/1999/02/22-rdf-syntax-ns#">
      <cc:Work rdf:about="">
        <dc:title>Sizing Red Circle</dc:title>
        <dc:description></dc:description>
        <dc:subject>
          <rdf:Bag>
            <rdf:li>circle</rdf:li>
            <rdf:li>red</rdf:li>
            <rdf:li>graphic</rdf:li>
          </rdf:Bag>
        </dc:subject>
        <dc:publisher>
```

```
      <cc:Agent rdf:about="http://www.openclipart.org">
        <dc:title>Testing RDF in SVG</dc:title>
      </cc:Agent>
    </dc:publisher>
    <dc:creator>
      <cc:Agent>
        <dc:title id="title">Testing</dc:title>
      </cc:Agent>
      </dc:creator>
    <dc:rights>
      <cc:Agent>
        <dc:title>testing</dc:title>
      </cc:Agent>
      </dc:rights>
    <dc:date></dc:date>
    <dc:format>image/svg+xml</dc:format>
    <dc:type
        rdf:resource="http://purl.org/dc/dcmitype/StillImage"/>
    <cc:license
        rdf:resource="http://web.resource.org/cc/PublicDomain"/>
    <dc:language>en</dc:language>
  </cc:Work>
  <cc:License
        rdf:about="http://web.resource.org/cc/PublicDomain">
    <cc:permits
        rdf:resource="http://web.resource.org/cc/Reproduction"/>
    <cc:permits
        rdf:resource="http://web.resource.org/cc/Distribution"/>
    <cc:permits
      rdf:resource="http://web.resource.org/cc/DerivativeWorks"/>
    </cc:License>
  </rdf:RDF>
</metadata>
</svg>
</body>
</html>
```

The result of the application can vary between browsers. When using Firefox and later versions of IE, and accessing title using getElementsByTagName(), the only title returned is the XHTML document title. However, when using the namespace variation (getElementsByTagNameNS()), and specifying the Dublin Core namespace (*http://purl.org/dc/elements/1.1/*), all of the Dublin Core titles in the RDF within the SVG are returned.

When using getElementsByTagName with title in Chrome and Opera, both the XHTML title and the Dublin Core titles are returned, as shown in Figure 5-2.

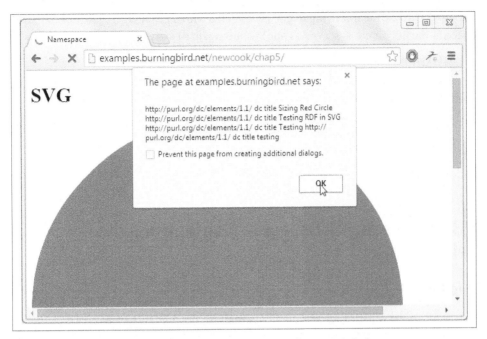

Figure 5-2. Using getElementsByTagNameNS to get namespaced elements

Though IE8 doesn't directly support the XHTML MIME type, if the page is served as text/html using some form of content negotiation, IE will process the page as HTML. However, though the getElementsByTagName() works with IE, the *namespaced* version of the method, getElementsByTagNameNS(), does not. All of the values are returned as undefined. IE8 doesn't return the dc:title entries in the SVG, either.

If the Dublin Core namespace is declared in the html element, instead of in the svg element, IE8 *does* return all of the dc:title entries, as well as the XHTML title:

```
<html xmlns="http://www.w3.org/1999/xhtml"
                    xmlns:dc="http://xml:lang="en">
```

An alternative approach uses a tag name string that concatenates the prefix and localName. All of the browsers will find the dc:title using the following:

```
var titles = document.getElementsByTagName("dc:title");
```

However, you can't access the namespace-specific properties using the pseudonamespace method. Your applications can't access the namespace properties using the IE approach of embedding all of the namespace declarations in the html tag, but you can find out the namespace URI via Microsoft's tagURN property:

```
console.log(title[i].tagURN); // for dc:title
```

Browsers can use the following to get all elements with a given tag, regardless of namespace, if the document is served as `application/xhtml+xml` or other XML type:

```
var titles = document.getElementsByTagNameNS("*","title");
```

This JavaScript returns both the default XHTML namespace title and the titles in the Dublin Core namespace.

 As mentioned earlier, IE8 doesn't properly support namespaces, but later versions do, thanks to support for XHTML.

5.3. Discovering All Images in Articles Using the Selectors API

Problem

You want to get a list of all `img` elements that are descendants of `article` elements, without having to traverse an entire collection of elements.

Solution

Use the Selectors API and access the `img` elements contained within `article` elements using CSS-style selector strings:

```
var imgs = document.querySelectorAll("article img");
```

Discussion

The Selectors API has achieved support in all modern browser versions, though there are quirks in support among the browsers.

There are two selector query API methods. The first, `querySelectorAll()`, is demonstrated in the solution; the second is `querySelector()`. The difference between the two is `querySelectorAll()`, which returns all elements that match the selector criteria, while `querySelector()` only returns the first found result.

The selectors syntax is derived from CSS selector syntax, except that rather than style the selected elements, they're returned to the application. In the example, all `img` elements that are descendants of `article` elements are returned. To access all `img` elements regardless of parent element, use:

```
var imgs = document.querySelectorAll("img");
```

In the solution, you'll get all `img` elements that are direct or indirect descendants of an `article` element. This means that if the `img` element is contained within a `div` that's within an `article`, the `img` element will be among those returned:

```
<article>
  <div>
      <img src="..." />
  </div>
</article>
```

If you want only those `img` elements that are direct children of an `article` element, use the following:

```
var imgs = document.querySelectorAll("article> img");
```

If you're interested in accessing all `img` elements that are immediately followed by a paragraph, use:

```
var imgs = document.querySelectorAll("img + p");
```

If you're interested in an `img` element that has an empty `alt` attribute, use the following:

```
var imgs = document.querySelectorAll('img[alt=""]');
```

If you're only interested in `img` elements that don't have an empty `alt` attribute, use:

```
var imgs = document.querySelectorAll('img:not([alt=""])');
```

The negation pseudoselector (`:not`) is used to find all `img` elements with `alt` attributes that are not empty.

All of the queries demonstrated in this section should get the same result in all modern browsers. Unfortunately, IE8 has only limited support for selectors—the code in the solution does not work.

Unlike the collection returned with `getElementsByTagName()` covered earlier, the collection of elements returned from `querySelectorAll()` is *not* a "live" collection. Updates to the page are not reflected in the collection if the updates occur after the collection is retrieved.

Though the Selectors API is a wonderful creation, it shouldn't be used for every document query. You should always use the most restrictive query when accessing elements. For instance, it's more efficient to use `getElementById()` to get one specific element given an identifier.

Extra: Namespace Variation and CSS Selectors

The following is how to define a namespace in CSS3, via the Namespace module:

```
@namespace svg "http://www.w3.org/2000/svg";
```

If an element is given with a namespace prefix, such as the following:

```
<q:elem>...</q:elem>
```

to style the element, use:

```
@namespace q "http://example.com/q-markup";
q|elem { ... }
```

and to style an attribute, you could use:

```
@namespace foo "http://www.example.com";
[foo|att=val] { color: blue }
```

Recipe 5.2 covered the concept of namespaces when querying against the document, and introduced the namespace-specific method `getElementsByTagNameNS()`. Because the CSS selectors allow for resolving namespaces, we might assume we could use namespaces with `querySelector()` and `querySelectorAll()`. In fact, we could with earlier iterations of the API Selectors draft, but there is no way to do so today.

Now, a namespace error will be thrown if the namespace is not resolved before using the Selectors API methods. Unfortunately, the Selectors API doesn't provide an approach to resolve the namespace before using one of the methods. Instead, the Selectors API specification recommends using JavaScript processing to handle namespaces. For instance, to find all of the `dc:title` elements within an SVG element in a document, use the following:

```
var list = document.querySelectorAll("svg title");
var result = new Array();
var svgns = "http://www.w3.org/2000/svg"

for(var i = 0; i < list.length; i++) {
  if(list[i].namespaceURI == svgns) {
    result.push(list[i]);
}
```

In the example code, querying for all of the titles that are descendants of the `svg` element will return both SVG titles and any Dublin Core or other titles used in the SVG block. In the loop, if the title is in the Dublin Core namespace, it's pushed on to the new array; otherwise, if the title is in some other namespace, including the SVG namespace, it's disregarded.

The workaround is not an elegant approach, but it is serviceable, and also the only option available for namespaces and the Selectors API at this time. Luckily, having to deal with namespaces in web development happens rarely.

See Also

There are three different CSS selector specifications, labeled as Selectors Level 1, Level 2, and Level 3. CSS Selectors Level 3 (*http://www.w3.org/TR/css3-selectors/*) contains links to the documents defining the other levels. These documents provide the definitions of, and examples for, the different types of selectors. The CSS3 Namespace module (*http://www.w3.org/TR/css3-namespace/*) is also located at the W3C. The Selectors API Level 1 (*http://www.w3.org/TR/selectors-api/*) is a W3C Recommendation.

John Resig, the creator of the popular jQuery library, has provided a comprehensive test suite for selectors (*http://ejohn.org/apps/selectortest/*) (GitHub source (*http://github.com/jeresig/selectortest/*)). The CSS3.info site also has a nice selectors test (*http://tools.css3.info/selectors-test/test.html*). This one is a little easier to view, and provides links with each test to the example code.

5.4. Setting an Element's Style Attribute

Problem

You want to add or replace a style setting on a specific web page element.

Solution

To change one CSS property, modify the property value via the element's `style` property:

```
elem.style.backgroundColor="red";
```

To modify one or more CSS properties for a single element, you can use `setAttribute()` and create an entire CSS style rule:

```
elem.setAttribute("style",
  "background-color: red; color: white; border: 1px solid black");
```

Or you can predefine the style rule, assign it a class name, and set the `class` property for the element:

```
.stripe{
  background-color: red;
  color: white;
  border: 1px solid black;
}

...

elem.setAttribute("class", "stripe");
```

Discussion

An element's CSS properties can be modified in JavaScript using one of three approaches. As the solution demonstrates, the simplest approach is to set the property's value directly using the element's `style` property:

```
elem.style.width = "500px";
```

If the CSS property contains a hyphen, such as `font-family` or `background-color`, use the *CamelCase notation* for the property:

```
elem.style.fontFamily = "Courier";
elem.style.backgroundColor = "rgb(255,0,0)";
```

The CamelCase notation removes the dash, and capitalizes the first letter following the dash.

You can also use `setAttribute()` to set the `style` property:

```
elem.setAttribute("style","font-family: Courier; background-color: yellow");
```

The `setAttribute()` method is a way of adding an attribute or replacing the value of an existing attribute for a web page element. The first argument to the method is the attribute name (automatically lowercased if the element is an HTML element), and the new attribute value.

When setting the `style` attribute, all CSS properties that are changed settings must be specified at the same time, as setting the attribute erases any previously set values. However, setting the `style` attribute using `setAttribute()` does not erase any settings made in a stylesheet, or set by default by the browser.

A third approach to changing the style setting for the element is to modify the `class` attribute:

```
elem.setAttribute("class", "classname");
```

Advanced

Rather than using `setAttribute()` to add or modify the attribute, you can create an attribute and attach it to the element using `createAttribute()` to create an `Attr` node, set its value using the `nodeValue` property, and then use `setAttribute()` to add the attribute to the element:

```
var styleAttr = document.createAttribute("style");
styleAttr.nodeValue = "background-color: red";
someElement.setAttribute(styleAttr);
```

You can add any number of attributes to an element using either `createAttribute()` and `setAttribute()`, or `setAttribute()` directly. Both approaches are equally efficient, so unless there's a real need, you'll most likely want to use the simpler approach of setting the attribute name and value directly using setAttribute().

When would you use createAttribute()? If the attribute value is going to be another entity reference, as is allowed with XML, you'll need to use createAttribute() to create an Attr node, as setAttribute() only supports simple strings.

Extra: Accessing an Existing Style Setting

For the most part, accessing existing attribute values is as easy as setting them. Instead of using setAttribute(), use getAttribute():

```
var className = document.getElementById("elem1").getAttribute("class");
```

Getting access to a style setting, though, is much trickier, because a specific element's style settings at any one time is a composite of all settings merged into a whole. This *computed style* for an element is what you're most likely interested in when you want to see specific style settings for the element at any point in time. Happily, there is a method for that: getComputedStyle(). Unhappily, older versions of IE (IE8 and older) don't support the method. Instead, you have to use Microsoft's currentStyle to access the computed style.

In addition to having to having to use a different technique with older versions of IE, you also have to change the property name. When accessing a CSS property using getComputedStyle(), you'll use the CSS property name. However, with current Style, you have to use CamelCase. Example 5-3 demonstrates one cross-browser approach to getting an element's background-color.

Example 5-3. Getting a computed CSS property that works cross-browser

```
<!DOCTYPE html>
<html>
<head>
  <meta charset="utf-8">
  <title>CSS Computed Style</title>
  <style>
    #test {
      background-color: red;
      width: 100px;
      height: 100px;
    }
  </style>
</head>
<body>
  <div id="test"><p>Hi</p></div>
  <script>
    var elem = document.getElementById("test");

    var bkcolor = elem.currentStyle ? elem.currentStyle['backgroundColor'] :
```

```
        window.getComputedStyle(elem).getPropertyValue("background-color");

    console.log(bkcolor);
  </script>
</body>
</html>
```

In all versions of IE (old and new), the alert message reads red, while Firefox and Chrome return rgb(255,0,0), and Opera returns #ff0000.

As I said, getting CSS style information is tricky.

5.5. Applying a Striped Theme to an Unordered List

Problem

You want to modify the appearance of unordered list items so that the list appears striped.

Solution

Use the Selectors API to query for every other item in the list, and then change the background color by changing the class for the element or setting the style attribute on the element using setAttribute():

```
var lis = document.querySelectorAll('li:nth-child(2n+1)');
for (var i = 0; i < lis.length; i++) {
   lis[i].setAttribute("style","background-color: #ffeeee");
}
```

or:

```
var lis = document.querySelectorAll('li:nth-child(odd)');
for (var i = 0; i < lis.length; i++) {
   lis[i].setAttribute("style","background-color: #eeeeff");
}
```

or access the list parent element and then traverse its child nodes, changing the background color of every other element, using the arithmetic modulo operator:

```
var parentElement = document.getElementById("thelist");
var lis = parentElement.getElementsByTagName("li");
for (var i = 0; i < lis.length; i++) {
   if (i % 2 == 0) {
      lis[i].setAttribute("style","background-color: #eeffee");
   }
}
```

Discussion

The `:nth-child()` pseudoclass allows us to specify an algorithm pattern, which can be used to find elements that match a certain pattern, such as 2n+1, to find every other element. You can also use the odd and even arguments to access the odd or even elements of the type:

```
var lis = document.querySelectorAll('li:nth-child(odd)');
```

Not all browsers support this selector type. Firefox, Opera, Safari, and Chrome do, but IE8 doesn't support the first two approaches given in the solution, and older versions of most other browsers don't. If you need to support older browsers, you'll want to use the third approach in the solutions: get access to all of the elements using whatever method, and then use the `modulo` arithmetic operator to filter the elements. `modulo` returns the remainder of dividing the first operand by the second. Dividing the numbers 0, 2, 4, 6, and so on by 2 returns 0, satisfying the conditional test, and the element's style is altered.

In the solution, the even elements are the ones altered. To alter the odd elements, use the following:

```
if ((i + 1) % 2) {
  ...
}
```

See Also

See Recipe 5.3 for more details on the Selectors API and the `querySelector()` and `querySelectorAll()` methods. See Recipe 5.4 for more on using `setAttribute()`.

5.6. Finding All Elements That Share an Attribute

Problem

You want to find all elements in a web document that share the same attribute.

Solution

Use the *universal selector* (*) in combination with the attribute selector to find all elements that have an attribute, regardless of its value:

```
var elems = document.querySelectorAll('*[class]');
```

The universal selector can also be used to find all elements with an attribute that's assigned the same value:

```
elems = document.querySelectorAll('*[class="red"]');
```

Discussion

The solution demonstrates a rather elegant query selector, the *universal selector* (*). The universal selector evaluates all elements, so it's the one you want to use when you need to verify *something* about each element. In the solution, we want to find all of the elements with a given attribute.

To test whether an attribute exists, all you need to do is list the attribute name within square brackets (*[attrname]*). In the solution, we're first testing whether the element contains the class attribute. If it does, it's returned with the element collection:

```
var elems = document.querySelectorAll('*[class]');
```

Next, we're getting all elements with a class attribute value of *red*. If you're not sure of the class name, you can use the substring-matching query selector:

```
var elements = document.querySelectorAll('*[class*="red"]');
```

Now any class name that contains the substring "red" matches.

You could also modify the syntax to find all elements that don't have a certain value. For instance, to find all div elements that don't have the target class name, use the :not negation operator:

```
var elems = document.querySelectorAll('div:not(.red)');
```

 The examples all work with all modern browsers. Both of the selector syntax examples in the solution work with IE8, but the use of the negation operator, :not, does not.

See Also

See Recipe 5.3 for more details on the Selectors API and the querySelector() and querySelectorAll() methods.

5.7. Inserting a New Paragraph

Problem

You want to insert a new paragraph just before the third paragraph within a div element.

Solution

Use some method to access the third paragraph, such as getElementsByTagName(), to get all of the paragraphs for a div element. Then use the createElement() and insert

`Before()` DOM methods to add the new paragraph just before the existing third paragraph:

```
// get the target div
var div = document.getElementById("target");

// retrieve a collection of  paragraphs
var paras = div.getElementsByTagName("p");

// if a third para exists, insert the new element before
// otherwise, append the paragraph to the end of the div
var newPara = document.createElement("p");
if (paras[3]) {
   div.insertBefore(newPara, paras[3]);
} else {
   div.appendChild(newPara);
}
```

Discussion

The `document.createElement()` method creates any HTML element, which then can be inserted or appended into the page. In the solution, the new paragraph element is inserted before an existing paragraph using `insertBefore()`.

Because we're interested in inserting the new paragraph before the existing third paragraph, we need to retrieve a collection of the `div` element's paragraphs, check to make sure a third paragraph exists, and then use `insertBefore()` to insert the new paragraph before the existing one. If the third paragraph doesn't exist, we can append the element to the end of the `div` element using `appendChild()`.

See Also

Recipe 5.8 contains a complete example demonstrating how to access the `div` element and the paragraphs, and add a paragraph with text just before the second paragraph.

5.8. Adding Text to a New Paragraph

Problem

You want to create a new paragraph with text and insert it just before the second paragraph within a `div` element:

```
// use getElementById to access the div element
var div = document.getElementById("target");

// use getElementsByTagName and the collection index
// to access the second paragraph
var oldPara = div.getElementsByTagName("p")[1]; // zero based index
```

```
// create a text node
var txt =
 document.createTextNode("The new paragraph will contain this text");

// create a new paragraph
var para = document.createElement("p");

// append the text to the paragraph, and insert the new para
para.appendChild(txt);
div.insertBefore(para, oldPara);
```

Discussion

The text within an element is, itself, an object within the DOM. Its type is a Text node, and it is created using a specialized method, createTextNode(). The method takes one parameter: the string containing the text.

Example 5-4 shows a web page with a div element containing four paragraphs. The JavaScript creates a new paragraph from text provided by the user via a prompt. The text could just as easily have come from a server communication or other process.

The provided text is used to create a text node, which is then appended as a child node to the new paragraph. The paragraph element is inserted in the web page before the first paragraph.

Example 5-4. Demonstrating various methods for adding content to a web page

```
<!DOCTYPE html>
<html>
<head>
<title>Adding Paragraphs</title>
</head>
<body>
<div id="target">
  <p>
    There is a language 'little known,'<br />
    Lovers claim it as their own.
  </p>
  <p>
    Its symbols smile upon the land, <br />
    Wrought by nature's wondrous hand;
  </p>
  <p>
    And in their silent beauty speak,<br />
    Of life and joy, to those who seek.
  </p>
  <p>
    For Love Divine and sunny hours <br />
    In the language of the flowers.
  </p>
```

```
</div>
<script>

  // use getElementById to access the div element
  var div = document.getElementById("target");

  // get paragraph text
  var txt = prompt("Enter new paragraph text","");

  // use getElementsByTagName and the collection index
  // to access the first paragraph
  var oldPara = div.getElementsByTagName("p")[0]; //zero based index

  // create a text node
  var txtNode = document.createTextNode(txt);

  // create a new paragraph
  var para = document.createElement("p");

  // append the text to the paragraph, and insert the new para
  para.appendChild(txtNode);

  div.insertBefore(para, oldPara);
</script>
</body>
</html>
```

 Inserting user-supplied text directly into a web page without scrubbing the text first is not a good idea. When you leave a door open, all sorts of nasty things can crawl in. Example 5-4 is for demonstration purposes only.

5.9. Deleting Rows from an HTML Table

Problem

You want to remove one or more rows from an HTML table.

Solution

Use the removeChild() method on an HTML table row, and all of the child elements, including the row cells, are also removed:

```
var parent = row.parentNode;
var oldrow = parent.removeChild(parent);
```

Discussion

When you remove an element from the web document, you're not only removing the element, you're removing all of its child elements. In this *DOM pruning* you get a reference to the removed element if you want to process its contents before it's completely discarded. The latter is helpful if you want to provide some kind of *undo* method in case the person accidentally selects the wrong table row.

To demonstrate the nature of DOM pruning, in Example 5-5, DOM methods `crea teElement()` and `createTextNode()` are used to create table rows and cells, as well as the text inserted into the cells. As each table row is created, an event handler is attached to the row's *click* event. If any of the new table rows is clicked, a function is called that removes the row from the table. The removed table row element is then traversed and the data in its cells is extracted and concatenated to a string, which is printed out.

Example 5-5. Adding and removing table rows and associated table cells and data

```
<!DOCTYPE html>
<head>
<title>Adding and Removing Elements</title>
<style>
table {
   border-collapse: collapse;
}
td, th {
   padding: 5px;
   border: 1px solid #ccc;
}
tr:nth-child(2n+1)
{
   background-color: #eeffee;
}
</style>

</head>
<body>
<table id="mixed">
  <tr><th>Value One</th><th>Value two</th><th>Value three</th></tr>
</table>
<div id="result"></div>

<script>

  var values = new Array(3);
  values[0] = [123.45, "apple", true];
  values[1] = [65, "banana", false];
  values[2] = [1034.99, "cherry", false];

  var mixed = document.getElementById("mixed");

  var tbody = document.createElement("tbody");
```

```
    // for each outer array row
    for (var i = 0 ; i < values.length; i++) {
        var tr = document.createElement("tr");

        // for each inner array cell
        // create td then text, append
        for (var j = 0; j < values[i].length; j++) {
            var td = document.createElement("td");
            var txt = document.createTextNode(values[i][j]);
            td.appendChild(txt);
            tr.appendChild(td);
        }

        // attache event handler
        tr.onclick=prunerow;

        // append row to table
        tbody.appendChild(tr);
        mixed.appendChild(tbody);
    }

    function prunerow() {

        // remove row
        var parent = this.parentNode;
        var oldrow = parent.removeChild(this);

        // datastring from removed row data
        var datastring = "";
        for (var i = 0; i < oldrow.childNodes.length; i++) {
            var cell = oldrow.childNodes[i];
            datastring+=cell.firstChild.data + " ";
        }

        // output message
        var msg = document.createTextNode("removed " + datastring);
        var p = document.createElement("p");
        p.appendChild(msg);
        document.getElementById("result").appendChild(p);

    }
</script>

</body>
```

5.10. Adding a Page Overlay

Problem

You want to overlay the web page in order to display a message, photo, or form.

Solution

Provide a stylesheet setting for a `div` element that is sized and positioned to cover the entire web page. It could be completely opaque, but most overlays are transparent enough to see the underlying page material:

```css
.overlay
{
   background-color: #000;
   opacity: .7;
   filter: alpha(opacity=70);
   position: absolute; top: 0; left: 0;
   width: 100%; height: 100%;
   z-index: 10;
}
```

Create a `div` element (or other element) on demand, adding whatever other content is to be displayed to the element:

```javascript
function expandOverlay() {

   var overlay = document.createElement("div");
   overlay.setAttribute("id","overlay");
   overlay.setAttribute("class", "overlay");
   document.body.appendChild(overlay);
}
```

When the overlay is no longer needed, remove it from the page:

```javascript
function restore() {
   document.body.removeChild(document.getElementById("overlay"));
}
```

Discussion

Creating an overlay in a web page consists of creating an element set to a `z-index` higher than anything else in the page, absolutely positioned at the upper left of the page, and sized 100%.

In the solution to this recipe, this is achieved more easily by creating a CSS style setting for the `overlay` class that manages the appearance of the element, and then using `document.createElement()` and `appendChild()` to add it to the page. To restore the page, the `overlay` element is removed.

Page overlays are popular for displaying photos, videos, ads, logins, or providing important site messages. Example 5-6 contains a web page with a message. Clicking on the message block removes the overlay and message.

Example 5-6. Creating an overlay for displaying a message

```
<!DOCTYPE html>
<head>
<title>Overlay</title>
<style>

.overlay
{
   background-color: #000;
   opacity: .5;
   filter: alpha(opacity=50);
   position: fixed; top: 0; left: 0;
   width: 100%; height: 100%;
   z-index: 10;
}
.overlaymsg
{
  position: absolute;
  background-color: yellow;
  padding: 10px;
  width: 200px;
  height: 200px;
  font-size: 2em;
  z-index: 11;
  top: 50%;
  left: 50%;
  margin-left: -100px;
  margin-top: -100px;
}
</style>
<script>

function displayPopup() {

    // create overlay and append to page
    var overlay = document.createElement("div");
    overlay.setAttribute("id","overlay");
    overlay.setAttribute("class", "overlay");
    document.body.appendChild(overlay);

    // create message and append to overlay
    var msg = document.createElement("div");
    var txt =
       document.createTextNode("Please join our mailing list! (Click to close.)");
    msg.appendChild(txt);
    msg.setAttribute("id", "msg")
    msg.setAttribute("class","overlaymsg");

    // click to restore page
    msg.onclick=restore;

    // append message to overlay
```

```
    document.body.appendChild(msg);

}

// restore page to normal
function restore() {

    document.body.removeChild(document.getElementById("overlay"));
    document.body.removeChild(document.getElementById("msg"))
}


window.onload=function() {
    displayPopup();
}

</script>

</head>
<body>
<p>Existing material.</p>
</body>
```

Example 5-6 creates an overlay that fits the size of the page as it's currently opened. Note the CSS setting for the overlay, in particular the `fixed` positioning. This ensures that the overlay fits the window even if the contents require you to scroll to the right, or down, to see all of the contents.

The message is positioned in the center using a CSS trick: set the left and top position to 50% of the page's width and height, and then set the block's margins to a negative value equal to half the block's height and width.

We could append the message directly to the overlay, and when the overlay is removed, the message is also removed with `removeChild()`. However, the overlay's `opacity` setting would impact on its child elements. To ensure the message is bright and easy to read, it's appended to the web page document, but its `z-index` setting is set higher than the overlay, placing it on top of the overlay.

 Most publications that use overlays to display messages when the page is first accessed, use graphics with a "close this" or "X" to indicate where to click to close the message.

We could also statically create a section to display and hide it when not in use, but this just clutters up the page contents and can, depending on how it's formatted, have adverse impact on screen readers. In addition, if you want the same overlay on all pages, it's simpler to create it as part of the site's JavaScript library and automatically include it in each page that uses the library.

See Also

See Recipe 5.9 for more information on `removeChild()`, Recipe 5.8 about adding text to a web page element, and Recipe 5.7, which covers how to create new page elements.

5.11. Creating Collapsible Form Sections

Problem

You have a large form that takes up a lot of space. You only want to display sections of the form as they are needed.

Solution

Split the form into display blocks using `div` elements, and then change the block's styling to control the display of the form section. When the page is loaded, hide all of the form blocks by changing the display value to `none` using JavaScript:

```
theformblock.setAttribute("style","display: none");
```

or:

```
theformblock.style.display="none";
```

To expand the section, change the display setting to `block` using `setAttribute`:

```
theformblock.setAttribute("style","block");
```

or set the value directly:

```
theformblock.style.display="block";
```

Discussion

There are multiple ways you can prevent `form` elements from taking up page space. For one, you can clip the element by setting the clipping area. Another approach is to resize the element to zero height. The best approach, though, and the one most applications use, is to employ a *collapsible section*.

A collapsible section is a form of widget—a set of elements, CSS, and JavaScript packaged together and generally considered one object. The typical implementation consists of one element that acts as a label that is always displayed, another element that holds the content, and all contained within a third, parent element.

The collapsible section may or may not be used with other collapsible sections to form a higher level widget, the *accordion*. The accordion widget is a grouping of collapsible sections with an additional behavior: depending on preference, any number of collapsible sections can be expanded, or only one section can be expanded at a time.

To demonstrate how collapsible sections can be used with forms, Example 5-7 shows a form that's split into two sections. Notice that each form block has an associated label that expands the collapsed form section when clicked. When the label is clicked again, the form section is collapsed again.

Example 5-7. Collapsed form element

```
<!DOCTYPE html>
<head>
<title>Collapsed Form Elements</title>
<style>
.label
{
  width: 400px;
  margin: 10px 0 0 0;
  padding: 10px;
  background-color: #ccccff;
  text-align: center;
  border: 1px solid #ccccff;
}
.elements
{
  border: 1px solid #ccccff;
  padding: 10px;
  border: 1px solid #ccccff;
  width: 400px;
}
button
{
    margin: 20px;
}
</style>
</head>
<body>
<form>
  <div>
    <div id="section1" class="label">
      <p>Checkboxes</p>
    </div>
    <div id="section1b" class="elements">
      <input type="checkbox" name="box1" /> - box one<br />
      <input type="checkbox" name="box1" /> - box one<br />
      <input type="checkbox" name="box1" /> - box one<br />
      <input type="checkbox" name="box1" /> - box one<br />
      <input type="checkbox" name="box1" /> - box one<br />
    </div>
```

```
    </div>
  <div>

  <div id="section2" class="label">
    <p>Buttons</p>
  </div>
  <div class="elements">
    <input type="radio" name="button1" /> - button one<br />
    <input type="radio" name="button1" /> - button one<br />
    <input type="radio" name="button1" /> - button one<br />
    <input type="radio" name="button1" /> - button one<br />
    <input type="radio" name="button1" /> - button one<br />
    <button>Submit</button>
  </div>
</div>
</form>
<script>

  var elements = document.getElementsByTagName("div");

  // collapse all sections
  for (var i = 0; i < elements.length; i++) {
    if (elements[i].className == "elements") {
      elements[i].style.display="none";
    } else if (elements[i].className == "label") {
      elements[i].onclick=switchDisplay;
    }
  }

  //collapse or expand depending on state
  function switchDisplay() {

    var parent = this.parentNode;
    var target = parent.getElementsByTagName("div")[1];

    if (target.style.display == "none") {
      target.style.display="block";
    } else {
      target.style.display="none";
    }
    return false;
  }
</script>
</body>
```

There are numerous ways you can map the click activity in one element by changing the display in another. In Example 5-7, I wrapped both the label and the content elements in a parent element. When you click on a label, the parent to the label element is accessed in JavaScript and its children returned as an HTML collection. The second element's display toggles—if the element's display is none, it's changed to block; if the display is block, it's changed to none.

In the example, notice that the `form` elements are displayed when the page loads, and only collapsed after the elements are loaded. This is because the `form` elements are displayed by default if JavaScript is disabled.

Extra: JavaScript or HTML5?

The example in this recipe uses JavaScript to collapse and display portions of a form. HTML5 provides two elements, `details` and `summary`, that implement this effect without any need for scripting.

When should you use one over the other? If you want to add sections into the page that are displayed or hidden based on the user action, it's just as simple to use the HTML5 elements. However, if you need special effects, or want to attach other behavior when the page section is displayed or hidden, you need to stick with JavaScript.

5.12. Hiding Page Sections

Problem

You want to hide an existing page element and its children until needed.

Solution

You can set the CSS `visibility` property to hide and show the message:

```
msg.style.hidden="visible"; // to display
msg.style.hidden="hidden"; // to hide
```

or you can use the CSS `display` property:

```
msg.style.display="block"; // to display
msg.style.display="none"; // to remove from display
```

Discussion

Both the CSS `visibility` and `display` properties can be used to hide and show elements. There is one major difference between the two that impacts which one you'll use.

The `visibility` property controls the element's visual rendering, but its physical presence still affects other elements. When an element is hidden, it still takes up page space. The `display` property, on the other hand, removes the element completely from the page layout.

The `display` property can be set to several different values, but four are of particular interest to us:

- none: When display is set to none, the element is removed completely from display.
- block: When display is set to block, the element is treated like a block element, with a line break before and after.
- inline-block: When display is set to inline-block, the contents are formatted like a block element, which is then flowed like inline content.
- inherit: This is the default display, and specifies that the display property is inherited from the element's parent.

There are other values, but these are the ones we're most likely to use within JavaScript applications.

Unless you're using absolute positioning with the hidden element, you'll want to use the CSS display property. Otherwise, the element will affect the page layout, pushing any elements that follow down and to the right, depending on the type of hidden element.

There is another approach to removing an element out of page view, and that is to move it totally offscreen using a negative left value. This could work, especially if you're creating a slider element that will slide in from the left. It's also an approach that the accessibility community has suggested using when you have content that you want rendered by assistive technology (AT) devices, but not visually rendered.

See Also

Speaking of accessibility, Recipe 6.5 demonstrates how to incorporate accessibility into forms feedback, and Recipe 6.6 touches on creating an updatable, accessible page region.

5.13. Creating Hover-Based Pop-Up Info Windows

Problem

You like the Netflix website's pop-up window that displays when the mouse cursor is over a movie thumbnail, and you want to incorporate this functionality into your own application.

Solution

The Netflix-style of pop-up info window is based on four different functionalities.

First, you need to capture the mouseover and mouseout events for each image thumbnail, in order to display or remove the pop-up window, respectively. In the following code, the cross-browser event handlers are attached to all images in the page:

```
window.onload=function() {
    var imgs = document.getElementsByTagName("img");
```

```
    for (var i = 0; i < imgs.length; i++) {
      imgs[i].addEventListener("mouseover",getInfo, false);
      imgs[i].addEventListener("mouseout",removeWindow, false);
    }
  }
```

Second, you need to access something about the item you're hovering over in order to know what to use to populate the pop-up bubble. The information can be in the page, or you can use web server communication to get the information:

```
function getInfo() {

  // prepare request
  if (!xmlhttp) {
    xmlhttp = new XMLHttpRequest();
  }
  var value = this.getAttribute("id");
  var url = "photos.php?photo=" + value;
  xmlhttp.open('GET', url, true);
  xmlhttp.onreadystatechange = showWindow;
  xmlhttp.send(null);

  return false;
}
```

Third, you need to either show the pop-up window, if it already exists and is not displayed, or create the window. In the following code, the pop-up window is created just below the object, and just to the right when the web server call returns with the information about the item. The getBoundingClientRect() method is used to determine the location where the pop up should be placed, and createElement() and create TextNode() are used to create the pop up:

```
  // compute position for pop up
  function compPos(obj) {
      var rect = obj.getBoundingClientRect();
      var height;
      if (rect.height) {
        height = rect.height;
      } else {
        height = rect.bottom - rect.top;
      }
      var top = rect.top + height + 10;
      return [rect.left, top];
  }

  // process return
  function showWindow() {
    if(xmlhttp.readyState == 4 && xmlhttp.status == 200) {
      var response = xmlhttp.responseText.split("#");
      var img = document.getElementById(response[0]);

      if (!img) return;
```

```
        // derive location for pop up
        var loc = compPos(img);
        var left = loc[0] + "px";
        var top = loc[1] + "px";

        // create pop up
        var div = document.createElement("popup");
        div.id = "popup";
        var txt = document.createTextNode(response[1]);
        div.appendChild(txt);

        // style pop up
        div.setAttribute("class","popup");
        div.setAttribute("style","left: " + left + "; top: " + top);
        document.body.appendChild(div);
    }
}
```

Lastly, when the mouseover event fires, you need to either hide the pop-up window or remove it—whichever makes sense in your setup. Since the application created a new pop-up window in the mouseover event, it removes the pop-up in the mouseout event handler:

```
function removeWindow() {
    var popup = document.getElementById("popup");
    if (popup)
        popup.parentNode.removeChild(popup);

    return false;
}
```

Discussion

Creating a pop-up information or help window doesn't have to be complicated if you keep the action simple and follow the four steps outlined in the solution. If the pop up provides help for form elements, then you might want to cache the information within the page, and just show and hide pop-up elements as needed. However, if you have pages like the ones at Netflix, which can have hundreds of items, you'll have better performance if you get the pop-up window information on demand via a web service call (i.e., Ajax or WebSockets). The solution demonstrates that using web calls doesn't add significant additional complexity to the application.

When I positioned the pop up in the example, I didn't place it directly over the object. The reason is that I'm not capturing the mouse position to have the pop up follow the cursor around, ensuring that I don't move the cursor directly over the pop up. But if I statically position the pop up partially over the object, the web page readers could move their mouse over the pop up, which triggers the event to hide the pop up...which then triggers the event to show the pop up, and so on. This creates a flicker effect, not to mention a lot of network activity.

If, instead, I allowed the mouse events to continue by returning true from either event handler function, when the web page readers move their mouse over the pop up, the pop up won't go away. However, if they move the mouse from the image to the pop up, and then to the rest of the page, the event to trigger the pop-up event removal won't fire, and the pop up is left on the page.

The best approach is to place the pop up directly under (or to the side, or a specific location in the page) rather than directly over the object. This is the approach Netflix uses on its site.

5.14. Displaying a Flash of Color to Signal an Action

Problem

Based on some action, you want to display a visual cue to signify the success of the action.

Solution

Use a flash to signal the success or failure of an action. While a red flash is standard for signaling either a successful deletion or an error, a yellow flash is typically used to signal a successful update or action:

```
var fadingObject = {
  yellowColor : function (val) {
    var r="ff";   var g="ff";
    var b=val.toString(16);
    var newval = "#"+r+g+b;
    return newval;
  },

  fade : function (id,start,finish) {
   this.count = this.start = start;
   this.finish = finish;
   this.id = id;
   this.countDown = function() {
     this.count+=30;
     if (this.count >= this.finish) {
       document.getElementById(this.id).style.background=
                                          "transparent";
       this.countDown=null;
       return;
     }
     document.getElementById(this.id).style.backgroundColor=
       this.yellowColor(this.count);
```

```
      setTimeout(this.countDown.bind(this),100);
    }
  }
};
...
// fade page element identified as "one"
fadingObject.fade("one", 0, 300);
fadingObject.countDown();
```

Discussion

A flash, or *fade* as it is frequently called, is a quick flash of color. It's created using a recurring timer that gradually changes the background color of the object being flashed. The color is varied by successively changing the values of the nondominant RGB colors, or colors from a variation of 0 to 255, while holding the dominant color or colors at *FF*. If, for some reason, the color can't be perceived (because of color blindness or other factor), the color shows as successions of gray. As you progress down the figure, the color gets progressively paler, as the nondominant red and blue values are increased, from initial hexadecimal values of *00* (0) to *FF* (255).

The color yellow used in the solution kept the red and green values static, while changing the blue. A red flash would keep the red color static, while adjusting both the green and blue.

In the solution, I'm setting the beginning and ending colors for the flash when the application calls the `fade` method on the object, `fadingObject`. Thus, if I don't want to start at pure yellow or end at white, I can begin or end with a paler color.

A color flash is used to highlight an action. As an example, a red flash can signal the deletion of a table row just before the row is removed from the table. The flash is an additional visual cue, as the table row being deleted helps set the context for the flash. A yellow flash can do the same when a table row is updated.

A flash can also be used with an alert message. In the following code snippet, I created an alert that displayed a solid color until removed from the page. I could also have used a red flash to highlight the message, and left the background a pale pink at the end:

```
function generateAlert(txt) {

    // create new text and div elements and set
    // Aria and class values and id
    var txtNd = document.createTextNode(txt);
    msg = document.createElement("div");
    msg.setAttribute("role","alert");
    msg.setAttribute("id","msg");

    // fade
    obj.fade("msg", 0, 127);
    obj.redFlash();
```

```
    msg.setAttribute("class","alert");

    // append text to div, div to document
    msg.appendChild(txtNd);
    document.body.appendChild(msg);
}
```

The only requirement for the solution would be to either make the color-fade effect more generic, for any color, or add a new, specialized `redFlash` method that does the same as the yellow.

Also note the use of the ARIA `alert role` in the code snippet. Including an accessible effect ensures all your users will benefit, and as the code demonstrates, it doesn't add any extra effort.

See Also

Recipe 6.5 demonstrates how to incorporate accessibility into forms feedback, and Recipe 6.6 touches on creating an updatable, accessible page region.

## CHAPTER 6

Preliminary Testing and Accessibility

Best developer practices run the gamut from keeping the cruft out of your code to ensuring your code is accessible to *all* your application or site's users. In this chapter, I'm focusing on two specific components: preliminary testing and accessibility.

There are various forms of testing, including running tools that highlight bad practices, unit testing, performance testing, as well as testing your applications in a variety of environments.

Regardless of how well the code tests out, if it isn't accessible to all your audience, then it fails. At the end of the chapter, we'll look at a couple of approaches you can take to ensure your code is accessible as well as accurate and efficient.

6.1. Cleaning Up Your Code with JSHint

Problem

You want to check your code for any gotchas that may not trigger a failure, but also aren't the best coding practices.

Solution

Use a *lint* tool such as JSHint to highlight potential problems or less than optimal code.

Discussion

The simplest approach to ensuring your code meets a minimum standard of acceptable coding standards is to use the *strict* setting at the beginning of your code or function:

```
'use strict';
```

This setting ensures certain programming standards are met, such as always defining variables, and never using `eval()`. And of course, the most reliable way of ensuring your code meets standards is whatever error mechanism is built into the tools you're using to run the code, typically explored in depth using your favorite debugging tool.

There are a set of coding practices, though, that don't typically trigger an error or warning, but should be avoided because they may introduce unwanted application behaviors or results that are hard to discover. That's where a *linting* tool comes in. And the most popular of the JavaScript lint tools is JSHint.

JSHint is a *fork* of a previously popular lint tool named JSLint. JSHint is now more popular because it is more configurable and less rigid—as well as being actively maintained.

 Documentation and installation source and instruction for JSHint can be found at the JSHint home page (*http://www.jshint.com/install/*), which includes links and references to various JSHint plug-ins available in a variety of environments.

JSHint can be installed using npm, part of the world of Node.js that is covered in Chapter 11:

```
npm install jshint -g
```

When JSHint is installed using npm, you can run it against any JavaScript using command-line syntax such as the following:

```
jshint scriptfile.js
```

Though workable, running JSHint at the command line is a bit tedious. A preferred option is to use a plug-in or browser tool. Both of the JavaScript online playgrounds— JS Bin and jsFiddle—I used to test most of the examples for this book either use JSHint by default or provide an option to run the tool.

When running JSHint, you're running with a default group of settings. Among some of the default settings are those that prevent *bitwise operators* from being used, requiring curly brackets ({}) for every block, and the use of *strict equality* ("==="). You can see all of the options in the *.jshintrc* file (*http://bit.ly/1GVO2Ku*).

If you want to change a default setting, use one of four techniques:

- From the command line you can use the `--config` flag and specify the name of the file containing the configuration settings.
- Create a local version of the *.jshintrc* file.
- Add settings to your project's *package.json* file (more on this in Chapter 11).

- Embed JSHint settings directly in your code.

When you're using an integrated tool that may not provide a way to add an override file for changing JSHint options, you can embed JSHint comments to change default settings directly in the JavaScript. For instance, one of my chronic code foibles is mixing quotes (single and double) in the same code. To prevent this, I can add the following to my JavaScript:

```
/*jshint quotmark:true */
```

And I'll get a warning that I used both types of quotes in the code. If I want to use standard equality operators without warnings, I can use the following:

```
/*jshint quotmark:true, eqeqeq:false */
var test1 = "today";
var test2 = 'tomorrow';

if (test == tomorrow)
    console.log("nope");
```

Using a linting tool such as JSHint doesn't mean you have to create perfect code based on some arbitrary standard. However, it does help ensure that when you decide to write code that bucks the standards, you do so deliberately, rather than accidentally.

See Also

See "Extra: Speaking of Strict Mode" on page 33 for more on *use strict*, and the concept of strict equality. See Chapter 11 for more on Node, and Recipe 12.14 about using JSHint with a task runner.

6.2. Unit Testing Your Code with QUnit

Problem

You want to ensure the robustness of your application or library. A part of this is performing unit testing, but you don't want to create the tests manually.

Solution

Use a tool such as QUnit to incorporate unit testing into your application at the earliest possible stage. For instance, we're interested in testing a new function, addAndRound():

```
function addAndRound(value1,value2) {
    return Math.round(value1 + value2);
}
```

A QUnit test case could look like the following, which performs two *assertion* tests: equal, to test whether the function returns a value given as the first parameter, and ok which just checks the truthfulness (the *truthy* value) of the function's return:

```
test( "testing addAndRound", function() {
  equal(6, addAndRound(3.55, 2.33), "checking valid");
  ok(addAndRound("three", "4.12"), "checking NaN");
});
```

The first test succeeds because both parameters are numbers, or can be coerced into being numbers, and the function result is 6. The second fails when the function call returns NaN because the first parameter can't be coerced into a number, as shown in Figure 6-1.

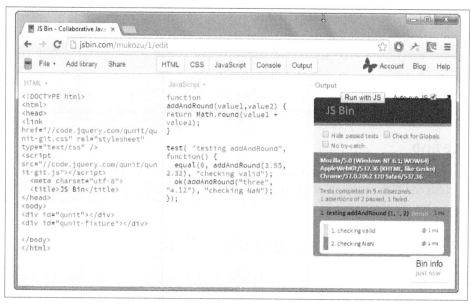

Figure 6-1. Result of running QUnit assertion tests in JS Bin

Discussion

There are multiple types of tests, such as tests for security, usability, and performance, but the most basic form of testing is *unit testing*. Unit testing consists of performing tests of discrete source code units, verifying that the unit behaves as expected, and that operations on data provided to or returned from the unit also meet expectations. In JavaScript, a unit is typically a function.

A good rule of thumb when it comes to unit testing is that every requirement or use case for a function should have an associated test case (or cases). The unit test checks that the requirement is met, and the function performs as expected. You can develop your own tests, but using something like QUnit simplifies the test writing.

 You can download QUnit at the QUnit website (*https://qunitjs.com/*), as well as the jQuery CDN (Content Delivery Network) (*https://code.jquery.com/*). You can also install it using npm, and it's available as a library in JS Bin.

Depending on how you're using QUnit, you'll need to add links to the library to your test page. If you're using something like JS Bin, selecting the QUnit option adds all relevant script source files. At a minimum, you'll need to add a link to the QUnit CSS file, as well as the script. You'll also need to add two div elements for the QUnit output. QUnit gives the following as a minimum QUnit test page:

```
<!DOCTYPE html>
<html>
<head>
  <meta charset="utf-8">
  <title>QUnit Example</title>
  <link rel="stylesheet" href="qunit.css">
</head>
<body>
  <div id="qunit"></div>
  <div id="qunit-fixture"></div>
  <script src="qunit.js"></script>
  <script src="tests.js"></script>
</body>
</html>
```

The unit tests will be in the *tests.js* file.

The QUnit website provides very good documentation on using the product, so I'm only going to touch on some of the more common components, demonstrated in the solution.

The tests are included within an outer function named test(). This is the most commonly used way to trigger the QUnit testing, and is used to perform a synchronous test. The first parameter is a label for the test results, the second a callback function that includes the tests.

QUnit supports several assertion tests, including the two demonstrated in the solution:

- deepEqual: Tests for deep, strict equality
- equal: Tests for standard equality
- notDeepEqual: The inversion of deepEqual testing for deep, strict nonequality
- notEqual: The inversion of equal testing for standard nonequality

- `notPropEqual`: Tests an object's properties for inequality
- `notStrictEqual`: Tests for strict inequality
- `ok`: Tests whether first argument equates to true
- `propEqual`: Tests an object's properties for equality
- `strictEqual`: Tests for strict equality
- `throws`: Tests if callback throws an exception, and can optionally compare thrown error

When the QUnit test is run, a display is output to the page specifying which tests failed and succeeded, each associated with the test label passed to the assertions.

Extra: Writing Tests First

(((programming, TDD vs. BDD approach))Modern development practices have embraced the idea of writing the tests before much of the functionality for the application (and libraries) is written. This Test-Driven Development (TDD) is a component of the Agile development paradigm.

TDD takes some getting used to. Rather than a more formal *structured programming* or *waterfall* project design, with TDD you define the tests, do some coding, run the tests, do some refacturing to remove duplicate code, and then repeat the process until the entire functionality is finished. Previous approaches incorporated testing only at the very end of the process, when much of the code has already been created.

The Microsoft Developer Network has a page (*http://bit.ly/1GVPBYK*) describing a typical scenario. In addition, there are several books and publications online describing both TDD and Agile software development.

In addition, another well-known Agile component is behavior-driven development (BDD), developed by Dan North. If you're interested in utilizing BDD with your JavaScript applications, there is a tool, Cucumber.js (*https://github.com/cucumber/cucumber-js*), specifically designed for BDD in JS.

6.3. Testing Your Application in Various Environments

Problem

You have a set of environments (operating system and browser) you need to support, but you don't have enough machines to test your application or library in each environment.

Solution

Use an emulating tool or browser testing service that can test your application in all of your environments. These aids help you not only test the integrity of the code, but the appearance and behavior of your user interface.

Discussion

In-house testing works if your customer uses a finite set of machines and you can easily re-create the environments, or you work for a large enough corporation that can afford to set up *one of everything*. For most other situations, you either need to use some form of emulation tool or a service.

This is especially critical when you're testing client-side JavaScript. Web or mobile development environments are undergoing rapid change, and a technology you think is safe to use may end up blowing up in your face when you test the functionality in environments other than the ones you use for development.

Emulators are a favorite for mobile developers. Some are specific to a browser, such as Ripple for Chrome. Others are standalone tools like Opera Mobile Classic Emulator, shown in Figure 6-2 or the Android Emulator (part of the Android SDK).

 Download the Opera emulator (*http://www.opera.com/developer/ mobile-emulator*), or access Ripple for Chrome at the Google Web Store (*http://bit.ly/1JazB96*). An excellent resource for discovering emulators is the Emulator page at "Breaking the Mobile Web" (*http:// www.mobilexweb.com/emulators*).

A variation for testing mobile applications is a simulator, which simulates some of the environment but doesn't fully emulate it at the hardware level. An example of a simulator is Apple's iOS Simulator.

Figure 6-2. Snapshot of Opera Mobile Classic Emulator emulating my cellphone

If you're more interested in testing how the client interface works in different browsers and different environments, then you'll want to look for a cross-browser testing service (BrowserStack (*http://www.browserstack.com/*) or Sauce Labs (*https://saucelabs.com/ home*)), or an application like Ghostlab (*http://vanamco.com/ghostlab/*) (demonstrated in Figure 6-3). You might also consider automated testing services, where you create a script that's automatically run (Selenium is an example). The key is to look for a service or tool that provides interactive testing—not one that is primarily used to check out the design of the page in different environments. One advantage to some of these tools is they provide testing in both browser and mobile environments. The disadvantage is cost: either a one-time cost for an application, or a monthly or annual fee for a service. The only tool that didn't have a price tag attached is IE NetRenderer (*http://netrender er.com/*), which allows you to test your website in every variation of IE, from versions 5.5 through 11.

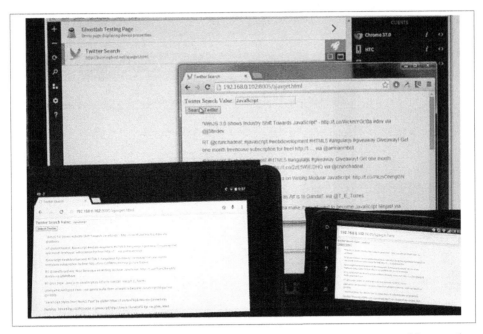

Figure 6-3. Ghostlab Demonstration Photo: one computer, one tablet, and a smartphone

One of the services I have used is BrowserStack. It, like most of the other tools and services, provides a trial period for testing the service. In addition, it also works with testing environments, such as QUnit, demonstrated earlier in the chapter.

BrowserStack offers a variety of services, including screenshots of your site across several devices—desktop or mobile. From a client-side JavaScript developer's perspective, the service we're most interested in is the Live testing, where we can pick an OS and a browser and test our client application, directly. Figure 6-4 demonstrates running an application in Safari on OS X—an environment I don't have access to.

Figure 6-4. Testing an app on Safari in OS X using Browserstack

BrowserStack also provides automated cloud-testing of JavaScript applications. The testing is free for open source software, and available for a fee for commercial and non-open source testing. You can incorporate automated testing with various tools, such as Yeti and TestSwarm. However, it's primarily focused on testing Node.js applications.

See Also

I'm covering the Web APIs for mobile development in Chapter 18, and the frameworks and tools in Chapter 15. Integrating testing into a modular development with Node.js is covered in Chapter 12.

6.4. Performance Testing Different Coding Techniques

Problem

In JavaScript there are, typically, multiple ways you can code a solution. The problem then becomes determining which of the different ways performs best across different environments.

Solution

One approach is to use a performance testing tool, such as jsPerf, to try out the different approaches and then proceed accordingly.

For instance, in Recipe 2.9, I wanted to determine which had better performance—using an anonymous function or a named function—when passed as a callback function in an Array method. In jsPerf, I set up an array of string elements and created the named function, rpl(), in the Preparation code section:

```
var charSet = ["**","bb","cd","**","cc","**","dd","**"];
```

```
function rpl (element) {
    return (element !== "**");
};
```

My first test case was using the anonymous function:

```
var newArray = charSet.filter(function(element) {
    return (element !== "**");
});
```

My second test case was using the named function:

```
var newArray = charSet.filter(rpl);
```

Running the test in various browsers, shown in Figure 6-5, demonstrated that the anonymous function was the better-performing alternative.

Figure 6-5. Results of running two test cases in jsPerf

Discussion

There are variations of performance testing, from the simple *alternative testing* demonstrated in the solution, to complex, involved *load testing* of entire systems. These types of testing aren't used to discover whether there are bugs in the code, or if the code meets use requirements—unit testing should find the former, and some form of user compliance testing finds the latter.

Performance testing is specifically for finding the best, most efficient approach to creating your application, and then making sure it meets the demands placed on it when running at peak usage.

> JsPerf (*http://jsperf.com/*) is built on Benchmark.js, which is also available for separate use (*http://benchmarkjs.com/*). The test case in the solution can be accessed at *http://jsperf.com/anony*. There are numerous performance and load testing tools to use with Node.js applications. One I've used is Selenium (*http://www.seleniumhq.org/*).

Another approach to performance testing is *profiling*. Most browser debuggers have a built-in profiling capability. As an example, the popular Firebug debugger for Firefox has profiling built in and available with the click of the "Profile" button, shown in Figure 6-6. Once you turn profiling on, you can run your user compliance tests as a way of generating good usage statistics, and then click the "Profile" button again. Firebug then generates a listing of functions called any time for them to respond.

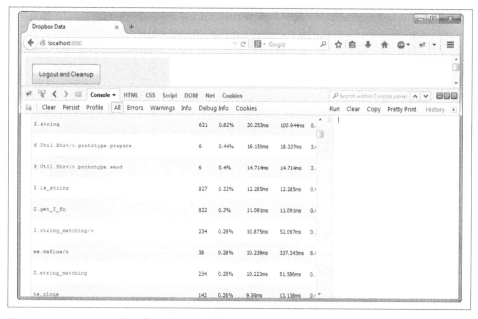

Figure 6-6. An example of Firebug profiling in Firefox

Chrome also has extensive profiling capability, shown in Figure 6-7. To use it, open up the JavaScript Console, click the Profiles tab, and then start whichever profiling type you want to start. After you've used your application for some time, click the Profiles "Stop" button and view the results.

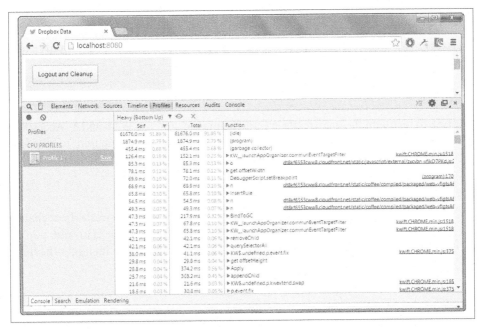

Figure 6-7. An example of profiling in Chrome

 You do want to make sure all of your browser extensions are disabled when you run a profiling tool in your browser, as these will impact the results. In fact, you want to eliminate or minimize *any* extension when you're testing your code.

Extra: About That Use of jsPerf

jsPerf is a fun tool to use, and can be very informative. However, there are issues associated with the tool that can impact the reliability of its tests. One such is the JIT (Just-In-Time) compiler optimizations, which can influence the results. Unless you're really familiar with what's happening with the JavaScript engine, you don't know if your tests results have been skewed because of optimizations.

The creator of jsPerf, Mathias Bynens, discusses some of the issues of benchmarking in "Bulletproof JavaScript Benchmarks" (*http://bit.ly/1GVRN2x*). Vyacheslav Egorov gave a talk on the subject, available on YouTube (*http://bit.ly/1yHXEs1*).

As an aside, an interesting article, "Optimization Killers" (*http://bit.ly/1GVS31j*), discusses coding techniques that *kill* optimization.

6.5. Highlighting Errors Accessibly

Problem

You want to highlight form field entries that have incorrect data, and you want to ensure the highlighting is effective for all web page users.

Solution

Use CSS to highlight the incorrectly entered form field, and use WAI-ARIA (Accessible Rich Internet Applications) markup to ensure the highlighting is apparent to all users:

```
[aria-invalid] {
  background-color: #ffeeee;
}
```

For the fields that need to be validated, assign a function to the form field's onchange event handler that checks whether the field value is valid. If the value is invalid, pop up an alert with information about the error at the same time that you highlight the field:

```
document.getElementById("elemid").onchange=validateField;
...
function validateField() {

  // check for number
  if (isNaN(this.value)) {
    this.setAttribute("aria-invalid, "true");
    generateAlert("You entered an invalid value for A. Only numeric values
    such as 105 or 3.54 are allowed");
  }
}
```

For the fields that need a required value, assign a function to the field's onblur event handler that checks whether a value has been entered:

```
document.getElementById("field").onblur=checkMandator;
...
function checkMandatory() {
  // check for data
  if (this.value.length == 0) {
    this.setAttribute("aria-invalid", "true");
    generateAlert("A value is required in this field");
  }
}
```

If any of the validation checks are performed as part of the form submission, make sure to cancel the submission event if the validation fails.

Discussion

The WAI-ARIA (Accessible Rich Internet Applications) provides a way of marking certain fields and behaviors in such a way that assistive devices do whatever is the equivalent behavior for people who need these devices. If a person is using a screen reader, setting the `aria-attribute` attribute to `true` (or adding it to the element) should trigger a visual warning in the screen reader—comparable to a color indicator doing the same for people who aren't using assistive technologies.

 Read more on WAI-ARIA at the Web Accessibility Initiative at the W3C (*http://www.w3.org/WAI/intro/aria*). I recommend using NV Access (*http://www.nvaccess.org/*), an open source, freely available screen reader, for testing whether your application is responding as you think it should with a screen reader.

In addition, the `role` attribute can be set to several values of which one, "alert", triggers a comparable behavior in screen readers (typically saying out the field contents).

Providing these cues are essential when you're validating form elements. You can validate a form before submission and provide a text description of everything that's wrong. A better approach, though, is to validate data for each field as the user finishes, so they're not left with a lot of irritating error messages at the end.

As you validate the field, you can ensure your users know exactly which field has failed by using a visual indicator. They shouldn't be the only method used to mark an error, but they are an extra courtesy.

If you highlight an incorrect form field entry with colors, avoid those that are hard to differentiate from the background. If the form background is white, and you use a dark yellow, gray, red, blue, green, or other color, there's enough contrast that it doesn't matter if the person viewing the page is color blind or not. In the example, I used a darker pink in the form field.

I could have set the color directly, but it makes more sense to handle both updates—setting `aria-invalid` and changing the color—with one CSS setting. Luckily, CSS *attribute selectors* simplify our task in this regard.

In addition to using color, you also need to provide a text description of the error, so there's no question in the user's mind about what the problem is.

How you display the information is also an important consideration. None of us really like to use alert boxes, if we can avoid them. Alert boxes can obscure the form, and the only way to access the form element is to dismiss the alert with its error message. A better approach is to embed the information in the page, near the form. We also want to ensure the error message is available to people who are using assistive technologies, such as a screen reader. This is easily accomplished by assigning an ARIA `alert role` to the element containing the alert for those using screen readers or other AT devices.

One final bonus to using `aria-invalid` is it can be used to discover all incorrect fields when the form is submitted. Just search on all elements where the attribute is present and if any are discovered, you know there's still an invalid form field value that needs correcting.

Example 6-1 demonstrates how to highlight an invalid entry on one of the form elements, and highlight missing data in another. The example also traps the form submit, and checks whether there are any invalid form field flags still set. Only if everything is clear is the form submission allowed to proceed.

Example 6-1. Providing visual and other cues when validating form fields

```
<!DOCTYPE html>
<head>
<title>Validating Forms</title>
<style>
[aria-invalid] {
    background-color: #ffeeee;
}

[role="alert"]
{
  background-color: #ffcccc;
  font-weight: bold;
  padding: 5px;
  border: 1px dashed #000;
}

div
{
  margin: 10px 0;
  padding: 5px;
  width: 400px;
  background-color: #ffffff;
}
</style>
</head>
<body>

<form id="testform">
    <div><label for="firstfield">*First Field:</label><br />
        <input id="firstfield" name="firstfield" type="text" aria-required="true"
        required />
    </div>
    <div><label for="secondfield">Second Field:</label><br />
        <input id="secondfield" name="secondfield" type="text" />
    </div>
    <div><label for="thirdfield">Third Field (numeric):</label><br />
```

```
        <input id="thirdfield" name="thirdfield" type="text" />
     </div>
     <div><label for="fourthfield">Fourth Field:</label><br />
        <input id="fourthfield" name="fourthfield" type="text" />
     </div>

     <input type="submit" value="Send Data" />
  </form>

  <script>

    document.getElementById("thirdfield").onchange=validateField;
    document.getElementById("firstfield").onblur=mandatoryField;
    document.getElementById("testform").onsubmit=finalCheck;

    function removeAlert() {

      var msg = document.getElementById("msg");
      if (msg) {
        document.body.removeChild(msg);
      }
    }

    function resetField(elem) {
      elem.parentNode.setAttribute("style","background-color: #ffffff");
      var valid = elem.getAttribute("aria-invalid");
      if (valid) elem.removeAttribute("aria-invalid");
    }

    function badField(elem) {
      elem.parentNode.setAttribute("style", "background-color: #ffeeee");
      elem.setAttribute("aria-invalid","true");
    }

    function generateAlert(txt) {

      // create new text and div elements and set
      // Aria and class values and id
      var txtNd = document.createTextNode(txt);
      msg = document.createElement("div");
      msg.setAttribute("role","alert");
      msg.setAttribute("id","msg");
      msg.setAttribute("class","alert");

      // append text to div, div to document
      msg.appendChild(txtNd);
      document.body.appendChild(msg);
    }

    function validateField() {

      // remove any existing alert regardless of value
```

```
    removeAlert();

    // check for number
    if (!isNaN(this.value)) {
      resetField(this);
    } else {
      badField(this);
      generateAlert("You entered an invalid value in Third Field. " +
                    "Only numeric values such as 105 or 3.54 are allowed");
    }
  }

  function mandatoryField() {

    // remove any existing alert
    removeAlert();

    // check for value
    if (this.value.length > 0) {
      resetField(this);
    } else {
      badField(this);
      generateAlert("You must enter a value into First Field");
    }
  }

  function finalCheck() {

    removeAlert();
    var fields = document.querySelectorAll("[aria-invalid='true']");
    if (fields.length > 0) {
      generateAlert("You have incorrect fields entries that must be fixed " +
                    "before you can submit this form");
      return false;
    }
  }

</script>

</body>
```

If either of the validated fields is incorrect in the application, the aria-invalid attribute is set to true in the field, and an ARIA role is set to alert on the error message, as shown in Figure 6-8. When the error is corrected, the aria-invalid attribute is removed, as is the alert message. Both have the effect of changing the background color for the form field.

Figure 6-8. Highlighting an incorrect form field

Notice in the code that the element wrapping the targeted form field is set to its correct state when the data entered is correct, so that when a field is corrected it doesn't show up as inaccurate or missing on the next go-round. I remove the existing message alert regardless of the previous event, as it's no longer valid with the new event.

When the form is submitted, the application uses the `querySelectorAll()` method call to check for all instances of `aria-invalid` set to `true`, and rejects the submission until these are corrected, as shown in Figure 6-9:

```
var badFields = document.querySelectorAll("[aria-invalid='true']");
```

You can also disable or even hide the correctly entered form elements, as a way to accentuate those with incorrect or missing data. However, I don't recommend this approach. Your users may find as they fill in the missing information that their answers in other fields are incorrect. If you make it difficult for them to correct the fields, they're not going to be happy with the experience—or the company, person, or organization providing the form.

Another approach you can take is to only do validation when the form is submitted. Many built-in libraries operate this way. Rather than check each field for mandatory or correct values as your users tab through, you only apply the validation rules when the form is submitted. This allows users who want to fill out the form in a different order to do so without getting irritating validation messages as they tab through. This approach is a friendlier technique for those people using a keyboard, rather than a mouse, to tab through the form. Or you can use a mix of both: field-level validation for correct data type and format, form-level validation for required values.

Figure 6-9. Attempting to submit a form with inaccurate form field entries

Using JavaScript to highlight a form field with incorrect and missing data is only one part of the form submission process. You'll also have to account for JavaScript being turned off, which means you have to provide the same level of feedback when processing the form information on the server, and providing the result on a separate page.

It's also important to mark if a form field is required ahead of time. Use an asterisk in the form field label, with a note that all form fields with an asterisk are required. Use the aria-required attribute to ensure this information is communicated to those using assistive devices. I also recommend using the HTML5 required attribute when using aria-required.

See Also

In Recipe 17.1 I cover form validation libraries and modules to simplify form validation. I also touch on using HTML5's declarative form validation techniques.

6.6. Creating an Accessible Automatically Updated Region

Problem

You have a section of a web page that is updated periodically, such as a section that lists recent updates to a file, or one that reflects recent Twitter activity on a subject. You want to ensure that when the page updates, those using a screen reader are notified of the new information.

Solution

Use WAI-ARIA *region* attributes on the element being updated:

```
<ul id="update" role="log" aria-alive="polite" aria-atomic="true"
aria-relevant="additions">
</ul>
```

Discussion

A section of the web page that can be updated after the page is loaded, and without direct user intervention, calls for WAI-ARIA Live Regions. These are probably the simplest ARIA functionality to implement, and they provide immediate, positive results. And there's no code involved, other than the JavaScript you need to create the page updates.

Recipe 8.8 updates the web page based on the contents of a text file on the server that the application retrieves using Ajax.

I modified the code that polls for the updates to check how many items have been added to the unordered list after the update. If the number is over 10, the oldest is removed from the page:

```
// process return
function processResponse() {
   if(xmlhttp.readyState == 4 && xmlhttp.status == 200) {
     var li = document.createElement("li");
     var txt = document.createTextNode(xmlhttp.responseText);
     li.appendChild(txt);
     var ul = document.getElementById("update");
     ul.appendChild(li);

     // prune top of list
     if (ul.childNodes.length > 10) {
       ul.removeChild(ul.firstChild);
     }

   } else if (xmlhttp.readyState == 4 && xmlhttp.status != 200) {
     console.log(xmlhttp.responseText);
```

```
        }
    }
```

With this change, the list doesn't grow overly long.

I made one more change, adding the ARIA roles and states to the unordered list that serves as the updatable live region:

```
<ul id="update" role="log" aria-live="polite" aria-atomic="false"
    aria-relevant="additions s">
```

From left to right: the `role` is set to `log`, because I'm polling for log updates from a file, and only displaying the last 10 or so items. Other options include `status`, for a status update, and a more general `region` value, for an undetermined purpose.

The `aria-live` region attribute is set to `polite`, because the update isn't a critical update. The `polite` setting tells the screen reader to voice the update, but not interrupt a current task to do so. If I had used a value of `assertive`, the screen reader would interrupt whatever it is doing and voice the content. Always use `polite`, unless the information is critical.

The `aria-atomic` is set to `false`, so that the screen reader only voices new additions, based on whatever is set with `aria-relevant`. It could get very annoying to have the screen reader voice the entire set with each new addition, as would happen if this value is set to `true`.

Lastly, the `aria-relevant` is set to `additions`, as we don't care about the entries being removed from the top. This setting is actually the default setting for this attribute, so, technically, it isn't needed. In addition, AT devices don't have to support this attribute. Still, I'd rather list it than not. Other values are `removals`, `text`, and `all` (for all events). You can specify more than one, separated by a space.

This WAI-ARIA–enabled functionality was probably the one that impressed me the most. One of my first uses for Ajax, years ago, was to update a web page with information. It was frustrating to test the page with a screen reader (JAWS, at the time) and hear nothing but silence every time the page was updated. I can't even imagine how frustrating it was for those who needed the functionality.

Now we have it, and it's so easy to use. It's a win-win.

See Also

See Recipe 8.8 for more of the code for the live update. Hopefully your code is clean, unit and performance tested, functioning, and accessible. But that's only half the job of preparing your code for production use. Chapter 12 dives into how to make sure your code—whether browser-based or a Node application—works in today's modular environments.

## CHAPTER 7

Creating and Using JavaScript Libraries

You need to know what JavaScript can do, which is why this book primarily features native JavaScript examples. For the most part, though, you'll use libraries and/or frameworks to create your applications, because these essential tools make your job so much easier.

This chapter takes a look at finding that perfect library, as well as using libraries for tasks that are complex or mundane. It looks at incorporating the popular jQuery library into your application, as well as how to use some of the various jQuery *plug-ins*—libraries built on top of the jQuery framework.

But the Web does not live by jQuery alone. There are other libraries, such as Underscore.js, providing a host of useful utilities. And there are special-purpose libraries created for specific business needs. We focus so much on developing the UI (user interface) that we forget that libraries can help with basic math and date functionality, as well as provide handy UI functionality, such as managing keystrokes.

No matter how many good libraries there are, though, sometimes you can't find what you need, or what you need is specific to your own application(s). Then you need to create your own code—from scratch, or based on existing libraries—and do so in such a way that it can be used again and again (and is easily maintained, as well as clean, and, hopefully, bug free).

7.1. Finding the Perfect Library

Problem

You need functionality in your application, and you're pretty sure someone somewhere must have already created it. So, other than using a search engine, how can you find good modules, libraries, and tools?

Solution

Look for resource sites that not only provide a listing of libraries, modules, and tools, but also provide information about their use, their popularity, and how active the support is for them.

Discussion

First of all, don't knock search engines for finding good JavaScript source. By using Google's Search tools and restricting results to the past year, I can easily find recent and up-to-date code, as well as interesting newcomers that haven't yet achieved a high level of popularity.

Still, you're also just as likely to run into pages of Stack Overflow results rather than a library when searching for JavaScript functionality, so another option when looking for a new library is to search popular script resources sites.

GitHub is a good resource for JavaScript libraries, modules, and tools, and you'll also be able to see at a glance if the code is being maintained and how popular it is. You can search for specific functionality, or you can use the GitHub Explore page (*https://github.com/explore*) to find new and interesting GitHub projects by category. I especially recommend the Data Visualization category (*http://bit.ly/1yHY4ia*).

Micro.js (*http://microjs.com/#*) is a site featuring a small set of what it calls *microframeworks*. These are smaller, more purposed JavaScript libraries, all displayed in a fun little site.

JSDB.io (*http://www.jsdb.io/*) calls itself "the definitive source of the best JavaScript libraries, frameworks, and plugins," and it is an excellent resource. Again, just search for the general type of functionality you need, such as `canvas chart`, and then peruse the results. The results even give you an approval percentage, and the returned page also provides information such as GitHub watchers, average time between commits, average forks, and average number of contributors.

7.2. Testing for Features with Modernizr.load

Problem

You're using newer technologies, and you want to make sure the client can support the technologies before you load them.

Solution

You can use a library such as Modernizr to handle basic HTML5/CSS differences between browsers. But you can also use a companion tool, `Modernizr.load`, to test to see if an existing technology is supported.

As an example, if you want to incorporate touch events in your application, you can use Modernizr to test whether they're supported in an environment and only load the application script if they are. In the following code, the application is testing to see if the *touch events*, covered in Chapter 18, are supported. If they are, the application script is loaded:

```
Modernizr.load({
  test: Modernizr.touch,
  yep : 'touchtest.js'
});
```

Discussion

Modern browser makers are highly competitive, which means that most of the modern technologies we want to use are already part of the browser your user is most likely using. Unfortunately, we can't take it as given that *every* user is using the most modern browser, and that's where a concept like *feature detection* enters.

Years ago, when testing for browser differences, we'd check browser versions because browser companies didn't release new versions all that often. The idea of doing this nowadays, when some of the companies seemingly release a new version every week, is ludicrous. Feature detection is a way of guaranteeing that the environment will support your application, regardless of browser version or client.

Feature detection can be tedious, though, and tricky. That's where a feature detection tool like `Modernizr.load` comes in. It comes with a set of feature detection tests already built in, as demonstrated in the solution. And you can use `Modernizer.load` plugins to check for others, or even create your own.

To use `Modernizr.load`, go to the Modernizr site (*http://modernizr.com/*), check the features you want to test and/or support, and the site builds a custom library. To use the library, include the script in the page (in the head element, preferably after your style elements), and then include the links to your test scripts.

You can also use the software to load a *polyfill* library to manage differences:

```
Modernizr.load({
  test: Modernizr.websockets,
  nope : 'websockets.js'
});
```

You can list multiple JavaScript files, separated by commas, for both the yep and nope properties.

7.3. Going Beyond the Math Object's Capability

Problem

The Math object provides good, basic mathematical functionality, but lacks advanced or business-specific math functionality that you need. In addition, Math does everything in floating point, and you need functions that work to a higher degree of precision.

Solution

Use a library that expands on the Math object's capability. Examples of these libraries and their usage are covered in the discussion.

Discussion

Most of our math functionality is satisfied by the built-in Math object. However, there are instances where what it provides, or doesn't provide, leaves gaps. That's where a small but powerful set of Math libraries and/or modules comes in. I'll cover some options in this section.

Math.js

The Math.js library can be installed using npm or Bower, downloaded directly from its website (*http://mathjs.org/*), or accessed via content delivery network (CDN). It can be used in the browser, or in Node applications. It provides a set of functions to perform operations, such as add() and multiply(), that have the added advantage of being chainable:

```
var result = math.select(9)
               .add(3)
               .subtract(6)
               .multiply(23)
               .done(); // get value

console.log(result); //{ value: 138 }
```

It also provides functionality to parse a mathematical expression, with its own version of eval():

```
var exp = "4 + 3  * 10 / 8";
console.log(math.eval(exp)); // 7.75
```

In addition, it supports matrices. For example, to create a [3,3] matrix:

```
var m = math.matrix([[4,3,2],[6,6,8],[7,4,5]]);
console.log(m.valueOf()); //[ [ 4, 3, 2 ], [ 6, 6, 8 ], [ 7, 4, 5 ] ]
```

Note that the matrix arrays are contained within an outer array. Use the following to create a zero-filled matrix:

```
var z = math.zeros(2,2);
console.log(z.valueOf()); // [ [ 0, 0 ], [ 0, 0 ] ]
```

Most of the Math.js functions require the valueOf() or done() function to actually get the value of the operation, as noted in the code snippets.

Math.js also provides support for BigNumbers, numbers that have arbitrary precision, as well as complex numbers, with both real and imaginary parts:

```
var b = math.complex('4 - 2i');
b.re = 5;
console.log(b.valueOf()); // 5 - 2i
```

Accounting

There are several libraries and modules for providing accounting capability, but arguably the most popular is Accounting.js, maintained by Open Exchange Rates (whose currency conversion API is introduced in Recipe 13.1). Like many other libraries, it can be downloaded from its main site (*http://openexchangerates.github.io/accounting.js/*), accessed via CDN (*http://bit.ly/1z9AWtG*), or installed using npm:

```
npm install accounting
```

You can use Accounting.js to format a number into a currency format:

```
var options = {
        symbol : "$",
        decimal : ".",
        thousand: ",",
        precision : 2,
        format: "%s%v"
};

// Example usage:
var m = accounting.formatMoney(45998307);
console.log(m);// $45,998,307.00
```

You can also format entire columns of numbers:

```
var list = [[456, 12, 3], [99, 23,3],[667,902,12]];
var c = accounting.formatColumn(list);
console.log(c);[ [ '$456.00', '$ 12.00', '$  3.00' ],
  [ '$99.00', '$23.00', '$ 3.00' ],
  [ '$667.00', '$902.00', '$ 12.00' ] ]
```

The formatting isn't all U.S. dollar–based either:

```
var p = accounting.formatMoney(4899.49, "€", 2, ".", ",");
console.log(p); // €4.899,49
```

The Accounting.js functionality isn't extensive, but what it does, it does well.

Advanced Mathematics and Statistics

A popular advanced math module in Node is Numbers (*http://www.numbersjs.info/*), installed as:

```
npm install numbers
```

You can also download or install it on the client using Bower.

The library provides advanced calculus functions, matrix math, and even some statistics. From the documentation:

```
numbers.statistic.mean(array);
numbers.statistic.median(array);
numbers.statistic.mode(array);
numbers.statistic.standardDev(array);
numbers.statistic.randomSample(lower, upper, n);
numbers.statistic.correlation(array1, array2);
```

I'll leave it for the more mathematically inclined to explore all the functionality.

See Also

Using npm to install Node modules is covered in Recipe 12.6. Working with Bower is covered in Recipe 12.11, and CDNs are discussed in Recipe 7.13.

7.4. Finding the Number of Days Between Two Dates

Problem

You can create two different dates with the Date object, but you can't easily find the number of days between them.

Solution

Use the date library Moment.js to access the more advanced datetime functions. The following solution shows how to find the number of days between two dates using this library:

```
var deadline = moment('October 1, 2014');
var t = moment();

var df = deadline.diff(t, 'days');
console.log(df); // 37 days
```

Discussion

The Moment.js library can be used in Node via npm, or in the browser—either downloaded, via Bower or Require.js, or linking directly to the CDN:

```
<script src="//cdnjs.cloudflare.com/ajax/libs/moment.js/2.8.1/moment.min.js">
</script>
```

The Date object does not provide any technique to easily find differences between two dates. Not so with Moment.js. In the solution, I could easily discover how many days there were between two dates. And in the following snippet, I created a Date when this was written, and added seven days:

```
var t = moment();
console.log(t.format("dddd, MMMM Do YYYY, h:mm:ss a")); // formatted date

t.add(7, 'days');
console.log(t.format("dddd, MMMM Do YYYY, h:mm:ss a")); // date 7 days in future
```

The Moment.js library is an excellent example of a small, well-purposed JavaScript library fulfilling a real need.

7.5. Using an External Library: Building on the jQuery Framework

Problem

You want to create application-specific libraries without having to create your own library of reusable routines.

Solution

Use one of the JavaScript libraries, such as jQuery or Underscore, to provide the basic functionality you need, but isolate the use so that you can swap libraries if needed.

Discussion

There are good reasons for using an existing JavaScript library such as jQuery. One is that the code has been robustly tested by several people. Another is that you can tap into a community of support when you run into problems in your applications. jQuery is also extensible, with a wealth of plugins you can incorporate, as well as the ability to create your own. Then there's the time-saving aspect, as jQuery takes over managing the tedious bits of your application.

I'm focusing primarily on jQuery because it is the library incorporated into most of the applications I use. It's also small, specific, modular, and uncomplicated. However, there are other good general-purpose and extensible libraries, depending on your needs and preferences.

 You can access both a minified version of jQuery (*http://jquery.com/*) and an uncompressed developer version. You can also access jQuery through GitHub (*https://github.com/jquery/jquery*), or link directly to the CDN version (*https://code.jquery.com/jquery-2.1.1.min.js*).

To use jQuery, include a link to the library before providing links to your own or other, secondary libraries. If using the CDN, use the following:

```
<script src="//code.jquery.com/jquery-2.1.1.min.js"></script>
```

A basic starting page that jQuery provides is the following, where the jQuery script is downloaded, and included in the web page's body:

```
<!doctype html>
<html>
<head>
  <meta charset="utf-8" />
  <title>Demo</title>
</head>
<body>
  <script src="jquery.js"></script>
  <script>
    // Your code goes here.
  </script>
</body>
</html>
```

If you are placing the scripting block in the body, consider putting it at the end, making it easier to discover. There are several application-specific libraries that are dependent on jQuery, so you may want to check if they provide it as part of their own installation.

One aspect of jQuery that differs from most of the examples in this book is that jQuery's starting point for script is not window.onload, as used for many applications. Instead, the jQuery library provides a page start routine that waits for DOM elements to be loaded, but does not wait for images or other media to finish loading. This beginning point is called the *ready event*, and looks like the following:

```
$(document).ready(function() {
  ...
});
```

The code snippet demonstrates a couple of other things about jQuery. First, notice the dollar sign element reference: $(document). In jQuery, the dollar sign ($) is a reference to the main jQuery class, and acts as a selector for all element access in the application. If you're working with jQuery, use the jQuery selector rather than your own element access, because the jQuery selector comes with prepackaged functionality essential for jQuery to operate successfully.

The syntax you use when querying for page elements is the same as the syntax for the `querySelector()` and `querySelectorAll()` methods, described in Chapter 5. It's based on CSS selector syntax for accessing a named element, such as the following:

```
#divOne{
   color: red;
}
```

Using jQuery to access a `div` element with an `id` of `divOne` looks like this:

```
$("#divOne").click(function() {
   console.log("element clicked");
});
```

This code snippet returns a reference to the `div` element identified by `divOne`, and then attaches a function to the element's `onclick` event handler that prints out a message.

The code also demonstrates another fundamental aspect of jQuery—it makes heavy use of *method chaining*. Method chaining is a way of appending methods one to another. In the code, instead of returning a reference to the `div` element and then attaching the event handler function to it, you attach the event handler directly to the element request.

There is extensive documentation and tutorials on using jQuery, so I'll leave any further exploration of jQuery for an off-book exercise. However, I did want to cover one important aspect of using jQuery—or any framework library with your own applications.

The key to making these work now and in the future is to wrap the library use in such a way that you can swap one library out for another, without having to recode your applications—or, at least, minimize the amount of recoding you would have to do.

Instead of using the jQuery ready event, create your own so you don't build a higher-level dependency on jQuery. Instead of using jQuery methods directly in your business logic, use your own objects and methods, and call the jQuery methods within these. By providing a layer of abstraction between the implementation of your application's business logic and the external framework library, if someday you stumble upon Frew, the Wonder Library, you can swap out jQuery (or another library or framework) and build on Frew.

When I wrote the first edition of the *JavaScript Cookbook*, the big libraries at the time were Prototype.JS and jQuery. Since then, Prototype.JS hasn't been updated since 2012. This is why you want to isolate which library you use: if it's no longer being supported, you can swap to another if necessary. It may seem like jQuery will be around forever, but things change.

Of course, some frameworks really do require a commitment, so if you go with this approach, make sure that your choice has an active community and lively support.

See Also

jQuery Cookbook by Cody Lindley (O'Reilly) is an excellent book that provides a comprehensive overview and detailed how-tos for jQuery. "How jQuery Works" (*https://learn.jquery.com/about-jquery/how-jquery-works/*) is a good introduction into using jQuery.

7.6. Using a jQuery Plugin

Problem

You've made use of jQuery in all of your applications, but it doesn't support some functionality you need, such as sliding an element in from the side of the web page, or providing a color animation.

Solution

Use a jQuery UI plugin to provide the additional functionality. In Example 7-1, I'm using the jQuery UI Toggle plugin to show and hide a block of text based on a button clicked event. The effect I'm using is `fold`, which creates a nice paper fold effect as the content is shown. I'm also starting with the block hidden with the `style` setting on the element, with a value of `display: none`.

Example 7-1. Showing and hiding a block of text using a jQuery UI effect

```html
<!doctype html>
<html lang="en">
<head>
<meta charset="utf-8">
<title>jQuery fold demo</title>
<link rel="stylesheet"
      href="//code.jquery.com/ui/1.11.1/themes/smoothness/jquery-ui.css">
<style>
#extra {
  width: 600px;
  height: 200px;
  background-color: floralwhite;
  padding: 10px;
  margin-bottom: 20px;
}
</style>
<script src="//code.jquery.com/jquery-1.10.2.js"></script>
<script src="//code.jquery.com/ui/1.11.1/jquery-ui.js"></script>
</head>
<body>
<div id="extra" style="display: none">Lorem ipsum dolor sit amet, consectetur ad
ipiscing elit. Integer in erat semper, condimentum erat nec, porttitor ipsum. Ma
uris id erat luctus, finibus quam a, luctus est. Morbi id metus magna. Sed inter
```

dum vel arcu sed accumsan. Etiam quis ultrices elit. Maecenas efficitur in orci
a efficitur. Duis id elit commodo, malesuada lorem nec, aliquet lacus. Praesent
sit amet laoreet eros, eu pulvinar libero. Sed vel dolor ac orci congue vulputat
e. Donec pulvinar risus magna, non feugiat sem aliquet eget. Nullam viverra vive
rra nunc et rutrum. Sed sed tellus a lorem porta vestibulum vel ac lacus. Suspen
disse potenti. Curabitur ac tristique lorem, sed ullamcorper odio. Mauris at acc
umsan lacus. Pellentesque at faucibus neque, nec aliquet mauris.</div>

```
<button id="choice">Show additional info</button>
<script>
$("#choice").click(function() {
  $( "#extra" ).toggle( "fold" , {horizFirst: true});
});
</script>
</body>
</html>
```

Discussion

jQuery is a slim library providing core functionality that allows us to manipulate the
DOM simply and easily. To keep it slim, any additional functionality is added via plugins,
each of which are created to work within the jQuery infrastructure.

The jQuery UI is a set of plugins and is probably one of the better known jQuery extensions. As the name implies, we can use it to create a nice variety of visual effects to
add some liveliness to the page—and without having to spend days coding the effect.

In the solution, the code links to a stylesheet, as well as two JavaScript libraries: the
primary jQuery library, and the jQuery UI. The stylesheet ensures that the effects meet
our expectations, as the jQuery UI plugins are all involved with appearance.

 The jQuery plugins website (*http://plugins.jquery.com/*) provides a
search engine to look for useful plugins. In addition, they're also
tagged, so you can browse among the plugins specific to whatever is
your interest: UI, Ajax, forms, etc. Each plugin provides whatever
instruction is needed to get the plugin to work.

Extra: Why Not Just Use HTML5 and CSS3 for Managing Visual Effects?

Some of the functionality in jQuery and the plugins is now implemented *declaratively*
in HTML5 and CSS3. Declarative functionality is the ability to specify what we want,
and it just happens. Instead of having to code a transition, we declare it in CSS and trust
that the browser handles the transition properly.

The following CSS modifies the *extra* div element in Example 7-1. Now, when the
mouse cursor is over the element, it shrinks until disappearing completely. Move the
mouse cursor out, and it transitions back to its full size:

```
#message {
  width: 600px;
  height: 200px;
  background-color: floralwhite;
  padding: 10px;
  margin-bottom: 20px;
    -webkit-transition:width 2s, height 2s, background-color 2s,
    -webkit-transform 2s;
    transition:width 2s, height 2s, transform 2s;
}
#message:hover {
    -webkit-transform:scale(0);
    transform:scale(0);
}
```

The advantage to this approach is it works even if JavaScript is turned off. And the browser developers can optimize the transition effect—increasing both the efficiency and the overall appearance of the effect. It seems like a win-win.

The limitation to using CSS3/HTML5 is trying to trigger the effect based on the button's click event. In addition, you don't have complete control over appearance or effect. This is particularly true with HTML5 elements.

If you're using the new HTML5 input elements, such as date, the browser creates the appropriate container, but you'll find that the container's appearance can differ dramatically from browser to browser. Firefox just provides a field, while Opera pops up a calendar picker when you click in the field. The color input pops up the system color picker in Firefox and Chrome, but an odd drop-down color picker in Opera.

If it's important for appearance and behavior to be consistent across all agents and in all environments, depending on the declarative power of HTML5 and CSS3 is probably not going to be the best option. They can be a useful addition, but not a complete replacement.

Extra: Plugin? Or Plug-in?

I use both "plug-in" and "plugin" in the book. The proper word usage is *plug-in*, hyphenated, but as you'll notice, many communities (e.g., the jQuery community) use *plugin* without hyphenation. Eventually, I expect *plugin* without the hyphenation to become the standard.

Ultimately, though, we all know what we're talking about, so use whatever is comfortable for you, or whatever maps to what the community uses.

See Also

The world of jQuery is large. In Recipe 17.1, I use jQuery to demonstrate one method of validating forms. jQuery also supports a nice, touch-enabled mobile interface system called jQuery Mobile. It's demonstrated in "Extra: Adding jQuery Mobile Support to a Cordova Android App" on page 556.

7.7. Handling Keyboard Shortcuts with Mousetrap

Problem

You need to provide support for keyboard shortcuts, but coding for these is exceedingly tedious.

Solution

Use a standalone library, such as Keypress, or a jQuery plugin, like jQuery.hotkeys.

Keypress is very simple to use. Just drop in the library, and set up the shortcuts or key combinations you want to capture. You can capture simple combos, or more complex sequences:

```
<!DOCTYPE html>
<html lang="en">
<head>
<meta charset="utf-8">
<title>Keypress</title>
<script src="keypress.js"></script>
</head>
<body>
  <div id="message">Press shift-r or press a b c </div>

<script>
  var message = document.getElementById("message");
  var listener = new window.keypress.Listener();
  listener.simple_combo("shift r", function() {
        message.innerHTML = "Pressed shift r";
      });
  listener.sequence_combo("a b c", function() {
        message.innerHTML = "you know your ABCs";
      });
</script>

</body>
</html>
```

If you're using jQuery, then you can use the jQuery.hotkeys plugin as follows:

```
<!doctype html>
<html lang="en">
<head>
<meta charset="utf-8">
<title>jQuery hotkeys</title>
<script src="//code.jquery.com/jquery-1.10.2.js"></script>
```

```
<script src="jquery.hotkeys.js"></script>

<script type="text/javascript">
 $(document).ready(function() {
   $(document).on('keydown',null,'shift+r', function() {
       $('#message').html('you pressed shift r');
   });
   $(document).bind('keydown', 'ctrl+a', function() {
       $('#message').html('Pressed ctrl+a');
   });
 });
</script>
</head>
<body>
<div id="message"></div>
</body>
</html>
```

Discussion

Capturing keystrokes and shortcut combinations isn't a complex task, but it is tedious, which makes it ideal for a library.

Two popular libraries for keyboard shortcut and key tracking are Mousetrap and the one demonstrated in the solution, Keypress. I went with Keypress because it looks to be more actively maintained than Mousetrap—an important consideration when picking a library. In addition, Keypress supports more sophisticated keyboard actions I found to be useful.

Keypress is very easy to use, as the solution demonstrated. There are three simple methods to use:

- `simple_combo`: For the typical two-key shortcut, such as Ctrl+a
- `counting_combo`: Takes two arguments, the key sequence, and a counter
- `sequence_combo`: Takes a sequence of keys

The `counting_combo()` function is a handy bit of code. It takes a two-key combination, such as Tab+space, or Ctrl+a. As long as you continue holding down the first key, the counter increases for key press on the second key. It makes a great way to cycle through tabs, or highlight paragraphs in a row, or whatever action cycling through a collection.

Any key combination can be a *modifier* in Keypress. Typically, modifiers would be combinations like Alt+q, Ctrl+a, or Shift+r. The combinations begin with one of the three:

- Ctrl
- Shift
- Tab

Keypress basically allows you to define your shortcut to be whatever you want it to be, which is extensible, but use such freedom with caution: we're creatures of habit, and we like our shortcuts to be familiar.

If you need something even more complicated, there's register_combo() that takes an object specifying any number of properties associated with the key action. In the following code, register_combo() specifies both key up and key down functions, as well as setting the is_unordered to true. This property allows me to type Alt+m and m+Alt, equally:

```
listener.register_combo( {
        "keys": "alt m",
        "on_keydown": function() {
            message.innerHTML = "alt m down";
        },
        "on_keyup": function() {
            message.innerHTML = "alt m up";
        },
        "is_unordered": true
    });
}
```

There are several other properties you can set, detailed in the library's documentation. Lastly, if you want to register several shortcuts at one time, use register_many():

```
var scope = this;
var many = listener.register_many([
        {
          "keys": "alt b",
          "on_keydown": function() {
              message.innerHTML = "alt b";
          },
          "this": scope
        },
        {
          "keys": "alt c",
          "on_keydown": function() {
              message.innerHTML = "alt c";
          },
          "this": scope
    }]);
```

The scope of the object is specifically set to the window via the `this` property.

You can also unregister any key combination with:

- unregister_combo(*shift r*)
- unregister_many(name of variable)
- reset: Resets all combinations

There are also opportunities to pause the keyboard capturing when the cursor is in an input field or in other circumstances. Keypress works equally on its own or in combination with JQuery.

If you prefer to use a jQuery plugin, though, then jQuery.hotkeys (*https://github.com/ jeresig/jquery.hotkeys*) is probably for you, as demonstrated in the solution. Note, though, that its functionality is limited compared to Keypress. However, if you're only interested in creating traditional shortcuts, then the plugin fits your needs.

To use, simply map the key combination using jQuery's `on()`/`off()` syntax, or you can use the plugins own `bind()`/`unbind()` methods.

7.8. Utilizing the Utility Library Underscore

Problem

You want a simple-to-use, basic utility library that can be used with your applications or in combination with other more complex frameworks like jQuery.

Solution

Use the increasingly ubiquitous Underscore.js library. It can be downloaded, installed using npm or Bower, or accessed via CDN:

```
<script src="//cdnjs.cloudflare.com/ajax/libs/underscore.js/1.7.0/underscore.js">
</script>
```

In Recipe 3.8, I demonstrated memoization with a Fibonacci. With Underscore.js, my job is greatly simplified:

```
var fibonacci = _.memoize(function(n) {
  return n < 2 ? n: fibonacci(n - 1) + fibonacci(n - 2);
});

console.log(fibonacci(10)); // 55
```

Discussion

Underscore.js provides various functions categorized as:

- Collections
- Arrays
- Functions
- Objects
- Utility
- Chaining

Underscore.js enhances existing JavaScript capability, but does so without extending the prototype object, which could make the library incompatible with other libraries or your own application.

The utility's functionality is accessible via the underscore (_) character, hence the name. However, if you use it with another library that also uses the underscore, you can remove the conflict:

```
var underscore = _.noConflict();
```

The solution demonstrated the _.memoize() functionality. The following code demonstrates just a sampling of some of the other functionality:

```
// flatten a multidimensional array
var ary = _.flatten([1, ['apple'], [3, [['peach']]]]);
console.log(ary); // [1, "apple", 3, "peach"]

// filter an object based on an array of blacklisted keys
var fltobj = _.omit({name: 'moe', age: 50, userid: 'moe1'}, 'userid');

console.log(fltobj); // [object Object] { age: 50, name: "moe'}

// escape a string for insertion into HTML
var str = _.escape("<div>This & that and 'the other'</div>");

console.log(str); // "&lt;div&gt;This &amp; that and
                  //    &#x27;the other&#x27;&lt;/div&gt;"
```

 Underscore.js is documented at *http://underscorejs.org/*. The GitHub repository is at *https://github.com/jashkenas/underscore*.

7.9. Packaging Your Code

Problem

You want to package your code for reuse in your own projects, and possible reuse by others.

Solution

If your code is in one big file, look for opportunities to extract reusable functionality into self-contained objects in a separate library.

If you find you have a set of functions you repeat in all of your applications, consider packaging them for reuse via an object literal. Transform the following:

```
function getElem(identifier) {
    return document.getElementById(identifier);
}

function stripslashes (str) {
    return str.replace(/\\/g, '');
}

function removeAngleBrackets(str) {
    return str.replace(/</g,'&lt;').replace(/>/g,'&gt;');
}
```

to:

```
var jscbObject = {

    // return element
    getElem : function (identifier) {
        return document.getElementById(identifier);
    },

    stripslashes : function(str) {
        return str.replace(/\\/g, '');
    },

    removeAngleBrackets: function(str) {
        return str.replace(/</g,'&lt;').replace(/>/g,'&gt;');
    }
};
```

Discussion

We can't find everything we need in external libraries. On rare occasions, there isn't a library that provides the basic functionality we need, or you need to extend an existing library. In addition, our business requirements are unique and requires their own

JavaScript functionality. Both types of code can be packaged up into libraries, either to make them easier to use in our applications, or to share with the world.

There is some fundamental restructuring you need to perform on the code in order to neatly package it into a library. In the solution, I've taken three functions in the global space and converted them into three methods on one object. Not only does this reduce the clutter in the global space, but it helps prevent clashes with similar-sounding function names in other libraries.

Even as global functions, though, they're a step up from code that's hardcoded to a specific use. For instance, if your code has the following to access a `style` property from an element:

```
// get width
var style;
var elem = div.getElementById("elem");

if (elem.currentStyle) {
  style = elem.currentStyle["width"];
} else if (document.defaultView &&
          document.defaultView.getComputedStyle) {
  style = document.defaultView.getComputedStyle(elem,null)
          .getPropertyValue("width");
}
```

Repeating this code in more than one function in your application can quickly bloat the size of the JavaScript, as well as make it harder to read. Package the code by extracting it into a reusable function, and eventually into a new member of your library object literal:

```
var jscbObject = {

    // get stylesheet style
    getStyle : function (obj, styleName) {
        if (obj.currentStyle) {
           return obj.currentStyle[styleName];
        } else if (document.defaultView &&
               document.defaultView.getComputedStyle) {
           return
           document.defaultView.getComputedStyle(obj,null)
            .getPropertyValue(styleName);
        }
        return undefined;
    },
  ...
}
```

As you split your code into libraries of reusable objects, look for an opportunity to collect your code into layers of functionality.

Before the advent of jQuery and other very nice user interface libraries, I had one library, *bb.js*, that provided basic functionality such as event handling, accessing generic style elements, and processing keyboard events. I had another library, *mtwimg.js*, providing image handling in a web page, similar to what the library Lightbox 2 provides, but on a much smaller scale. My image handling library is built on my general library, so that I don't have to repeat the functionality in both libraries, but I also keep my *bb.js* library small, and focused.

 Download Lightbox 2 (*http://lokeshdhakar.com/projects/lightbox2/*), or access it via the GitHub page (*https://github.com/lokesh/lightbox2/*).

When I created a third library, *accordion.js*, which created automatic accordion widgets (also sometimes called collapsible sections), it was also built on the *bb.js* generic library, considerably reducing the development time. More importantly, if I eventually decide to drop support for my generic library in favor of another externally developed library, such as jQuery, though the internal functionality in *accordion.js* and *mtwimg.js* has to change, the web pages that use both don't, because the latter two libraries' outward-facing functionality isn't impacted. This is a concept known as *refactoring*: improving the efficiency of your code without affecting the external functionality.

Oh, and while you're at it: document your code. Though you may provide a minified version of your code for production use, consider providing a *nonminified*, well-documented version of your JavaScript libraries so that others can learn from your code, the same as you're able to learn from theirs.

See Also

You can take your code a step further by wrapping the functionality in an Immediately-Invoked Function Expression (IIFE), covered in Recipe 7.10. Cleaning up your code, testing it, and packaging it for easy reuse are also the first steps you need to take to *modularize* your code. The concept of JavaScript modularization, as well as tools to assist you in modularizing your code for both internal and external use, are covered in Chapter 12.

7.10. Adding Support for Private Data Members

Problem

You've discovered reusable functionality and created an object with the functionality defined as object methods. However, you also need to add support for private data members, too.

Solution

One approach to ensuring a data member isn't exposed to public access is to redefine the object as a function with publicly exposed methods or data objects that use the private data or methods. If we redefined the functionality of the object in Recipe 7.9, modifying the string methods to use a replacement string, we could store the replacement string as private data:

```
var StrManipulate = function() {
    var replacementText = "**";

    this.replaceSlashes = function(str) {
      return str.replace(/\\/g, replacementText);
    };

    this. replaceAngleBrackets = function(str) {
      return str.replace(/</g,replacementText).replace(/>/g,replacementText);
    };
};
```

And create a new instance of the object:

```
var strObj = new StrManipulate();
console.log(strObj.replaceAngleBrackets("<html>")); // "**html**"
```

However, if we don't want to use a declared function, or abandon our use of an object, we can encapsulate that object in an IIFE:

```
(function() {

  var replacementStr = "**";

  this.jscb = {

  // return element
  getElem : function (identifier) {
     return document.getElementById(identifier);
  },

  replaceSlashes : function(str) {
     return str.replace(/\\/g, replacementStr);
  },
```

```
    replaceAngleBrackets: function(str) {
      return str.replace(/</g,replacementStr).replace(/>/g,replacementStr);
    }
  };
})();
```

Discussion

A simple function-to-object conversion is easier on the global namespace than separate functions, but a *one-off* object of this nature has disadvantages, including an inability to add private data accessible by all of the object methods.

One approach is to convert the object to a declared function and expose all of the methods, but not the data, via `this`, as shown in the example. For years, this was the approach to use when creating libraries.

However, a more future-proof solution, which is also more elegant and efficient, is to use an IIFE to encapsulate the object's methods and data. This approach creates a *singleton*—a single object—rather than an object that's instantiated. It also allows you to use either a function as the core of the library object, or an object, as shown in the solution.

You can even ensure that the object is a singleton. I adapted the object created in the solution into a true singleton, following the Singleton implementation in Addy Osmani's *Learning JavaScript Design Patterns*. Example 7-2 shows the new implementation, and a test case. The main difference is that a singleton implementation is created with `init()`, which is called when the `getInstance()` function is called. If the instance already exists, though, the original instance is returned—a new instance is not created, as the strict equality (===) tests demonstrates.

Example 7-2. Converting library object into Singleton

```
var jscbSingleton = (function() {

  var instance;

  function init() {
    var replacementStr = "**";

    return {

      // return element
      getElem : function (identifier) {
        return document.getElementById(identifier);
      },

      replaceSlashes : function(str) {
        return str.replace(/\\/g, replacementStr);
      },
```

```
      replaceAngleBrackets: function(str) {
        return str.replace(/</g,replacementStr).replace(/>/g,replacementStr);
      }
    };
  }

  return {

    // Get the Singleton instance if one exists
    // or create one if it doesn't
    getInstance: function () {

      if ( !instance ) {
        instance = init();
      }

      return instance;
    }

  };
})();

var jscb = jscbSingleton.getInstance();
var jscb2 = jscbSingleton.getInstance();

console.log(jscb === jscb2); // true

var str = jscb.replaceAngleBrackets("<html>");
console.log(str);
```

There are no absolutes when it comes to creating a reusable library or utility object. I demonstrated a couple of approaches in this and the last few sections, but they're just a start. The best way to determine how to implement your library object is to examine existing ones. I suggest taking a look at the source code for jQuery and Underscore, both of which were covered earlier in the chapter, and Lightbox 2, which I mentioned in Recipe 7.9—all of these can be discovered in GitHub.

7.11. Minify Your Library

Problem

You want to compactly package your code for wider distribution.

Solution

After you've optimized your library code and tested it thoroughly through unit testing, compress it with a JavaScript optimizer.

Discussion

Once you've created your library, optimized it for efficiency, and run it through your unit testing, you're ready to prep your code for production use.

One preparation is to compress the JavaScript as much as possible, so the file is small and loads quickly. JavaScript compression is handled through *minify* applications you can find online, such as the well-known and interestingly named UglifyJS. Why Uglify? Because when you compress your JavaScript, it becomes an incomprehensible jumble of densely packed characters.

To use Uglify, you can either cut and paste your JavaScript into the UglifyJS website page, provide the URL for your JavaScript library, or use the command-line tool.

 Access UglifyJS at *http://marijnhaverbeke.nl/uglifyjs*.

The result of running the tool is a mess, like the following:

```
function timerEvent(){4==xmlhttp.readyState&&populateList(),timer=
setTimeout(timerEvent,3e3)}function populateList(){var a=
"http://burningbird.net/text.txt";xmlhttp.open("GET",a,!0),
xmlhttp.onreadystatechange=processResponse,xmlhttp.send(null)}
function processResponse(){if(4==xmlhttp.readyState&&200==xmlhttp.status)
{var a=document.createElement("li"),
b=document.createTextNode(xmlhttp.responseText);
a.appendChild(b);var c=document.getElementById("update");c.appendChild(a),
c.childNodes.length>10&&c.removeChild(c.firstChild)}else 4==
xmlhttp.readyState&&200!=xmlhttp.status&&console.log(xmlhttp.responseText)}
var xmlhttp=new XMLHttpRequest,timer;window.onload=function()
{populateList(),timerEvent()};
```

The purpose of a minification tool is to compress the text so it requires less bandwidth and loads faster. Some would say the lack of readability is a perk.

See Also

See Recipe 6.2 for more on unit testing.

7.12. Hosting Your Library

Problem

You want to *open source* your code, but you don't want to have to maintain the libraries on your own server.

Solution

Use one of the source code sites to host your code, and provide the tools to manage collaboration with other developers.

Discussion

One of the beautiful things about JavaScript is that many of the libraries and applications are open source, which means that not only are they typically free to use, but you can also adapt the library with your innovations, or even collaborate on the original. I strongly encourage open sourcing your libraries as much as possible. However, unless you have the resources to mount a public-facing source code control system, you'll want to use one of the sites that provide support for open source applications.

One source code host is Google Code (*http://code.google.com/hosting/*), which contains a simple user interface to start a new project and upload code. You can choose between two version control software systems (Subversion and Mercurial), as well as one of a host of open source licenses.

There is a wiki component to each project where you can provide documentation, as well as a way to provide updates for those interested in the project. The site also provides issue-tracking software for people to file bugs in addition to a download link and a separate link for source code.

The SVG-enabling software SVGWeb is hosted in Google Code. Figure 7-1 shows the front page for the project and the links to all of the secondary support pages, including the Wiki, Downloads, Issues, Source, and so on.

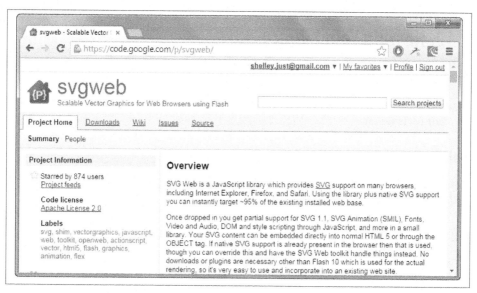

Figure 7-1. SVGWeb hosted at Google Code

There is no charge for hosting an application on Google Code.

Another very popular host for open source projects is GitHub. Unlike Google Code, there are limits to what is supported for a free account on the service, but JavaScript libraries should not tax these limits. You shouldn't incur any costs, as long as your projects are open source and publicly available. However, there is a fee if you want to use the service for a private collaboration with several others.

As with Google Code, GitHub supports source code control and collaboration from several people, including records of issues, downloads, a wiki support page, and a nice graphs page that provides graphics of language support, usage, and other interesting indicators.

The very popular jQuery library is hosted on GitHub, as shown in Figure 7-2, though you can download jQuery from its own domain. Node and most Node modules are also hosted by GitHub.

Figure 7-2. The GitHub page for the jQuery library

Source Forge (*http://sourceforge.net/*) used to be the place to host your open source software in the past. However, the site blocks access to certain countries listed in the United States Office of Foreign Assets Control sanction list, and has fallen out of favor with many open source developers.

GitHub is based on Git, an open source, source code control system. You typically install Git locally and manage your project in GitHub via Git. There are Git client applications for Linux, Windows, and Mac OS X.

The Git site (*http://git-scm.com/*) provides extensive documentation, including a very nice interactive tutorial for learning how the system works. GitHub also provides solid documentation in using the service.

Git is usually accessed via the command line. When setting it up, the first thing you'll do is introduce yourself to it—providing a name that is used to label all commits:

```
git config --global user.name "name"
```

Next, you'll need to sign up for a GitHub account, providing an email you'll use with Git to connect your local environment with the hub:

```
git config --global user.email "email address"
```

At this point, you can do a variety of tasks, including setting up a repository, as well as participating in other GitHub-hosted projects.

See Also

As I mentioned in the text, there is good documentation associated with Git and GitHub, but I also recommend *Version Control with Git, 2nd Edition* by Jon Loeliger and Matthew McCullough (O'Reilly).

7.13. Serving Code from a CDN

Problem

You've created a module or library and want to make it available for others to use. You're providing it for download, but you also want to provide a link to the code allowing people to directly link it—a concept known as *hotlinking*. However, you don't want to host the source on your own server because you're concerned about up-time, availability, and performance.

Solution

Use a content delivery network (CDN)—sometimes referred to as a content distribution network—to host your module/library. In addition, encourage developers to link to the module/library using a *protocol-less URL* or *protocol-relative URL*, in order to prevent unnecessary browser or user agent warnings:

```
//somedomain.com/somescript.js
```

Discussion

The first time you access a web page or application that incorporates a JavaScript file, the browser or other user agent typically caches the results. The browser pulls up the cached library the next time you access the file, making the access that much faster. The ability to take advantage of browser caching is just one of the reasons why hosting popular JavaScript libraries on a CDN makes sense. Others are ensuring access even if your server goes down (or goes away), as well as preventing an unnecessary burden on your own server. After all, when you provide a link to a JavaScript file to download, people will link the script directly (as the jQuery folks discovered (*http://bit.ly/1C8gZEU*)).

There are various CDNs, and which one you use is dependent on cost, availability, and company preference. Google provides CDN service (*https://developers.google.com/speed/libraries/*) for popular script libraries, but hosting libraries is by invitation only. jQuery uses MaxCDN (*http://www.maxcdn.com/*), but it is a commercial service. In fact, most CDNs are commercial, with only a few, such as cdnjs (*http://cdnjs.com/*), providing a free service.

Once you do decide on a CDN, when you provide links for developers, you'll also want to encourage the use of *protocol-less* or a *protocol-relative* URL:

```
//somedomain.com/library.js
```

This is because the browser or user agent will use the same protocol used to access the web page with all the protocol-less links, which means the resource is accessed with a compatible protocol. If you've ever accessed a script or file with "http://" in a web page that you've accessed with, "https://", then you're familiar with the annoying warning you can get in a browser such as Internet Explorer.

 I believe it was Paul Irish who first wrote about the protocol-relative URL (*http://bit.ly/1yHYB3N*).

7.14. Convert Your Library to a jQuery Plug-in

Problem

You want to convert your library methods and functions into a jQuery plug-in for use by others.

Solution

If your plug-in has one or more separate functions that do not need to participate in the jQuery chain, create a function on the fn property:

```
$.fn.setColor = function(color) {
    this.css("color", color);
};
```

If you want your method to participate in the jQuery chain, assign your method to the fn property and then return the original jQuery object:

```
$.fn.increaseWidth = function() {
    return this.each(function() {
        var width = $(this).width() + 10;
        $(this).width(width);
    });
};
```

If your function uses the jQuery dollar sign function ($) and you're concerned that the library could be used with other libraries that make use of $, wrap your function in an anonymous function:

```
;(function($) {
    $.fn.flashBlueRed = function() {
        return this.each(function() {
            var hex = rgb2hex($(this).css("background-color"));
            if (hex == "#0000ff") {
                $(this).css("background-color", "#ff0000");
            } else {
                $(this).css("background-color", "#0000ff");
            }
        });
    };
})(jQuery);
```

Discussion

It's relatively simple to create a jQuery plug-in once you understand the nuances of the jQuery plugin infrastructure.

If you're interested in creating a jQuery method that can be used with a jQuery selector and participate in the jQuery chain, you'll use syntax such as the following, which sets the function to the fn property, and returns the original jQuery object:

```
$.fn.increaseWidth = function() {
    return this.each(function() {
        var width = $(this).width() + 10;
        $(this).width(width);
    });
};
```

However, if you want to make use of the dollar sign function ($) within the code, but still have the plug-in work within a multiple library setting, wrap the method in an anonymous function:

```
;(function($) {
    $.fn.flashBlueRed = function() {
        return this.each(function() {
            var hex = rgb2hex($(this).css("background-color"));
            if (hex == "#0000ff") {
                $(this).css("background-color", "#ff0000");
            } else {
                $(this).css("background-color", "#0000ff");
            }
        });
    };
})(jQuery);
```

Notice the following line in both examples:

```
   return this.each(function () {
```

This code is necessary to allow the method to work on whatever is returned by the selector, regardless of whether it's a single item or a group of items. The line begins the code block that includes your actual method code.

 Check out the semicolon (;) just before the anonymous function. I picked this trick up from Cody Lindley in *jQuery Cookbook* (O'Reilly). Putting the semicolon before the anonymous function ensures that the function won't break if another plugin forgets to terminate a method or function with a semicolon.

If you're only interested in adding a jQuery function that isn't part of the jQuery chain, use the jQuery function syntax:

```
$.fn.setColor = function(color) {
    this.css("color", color);
};
```

Once you have created your plug-in code, package it in a separate file; to use the code, all someone has to do is create a `script` reference to include the plugin source following the jQuery script.

7.15. Safely Combining Several Libraries in Your Applications

Problem

You want to incorporate more than one external library, as well as your own, into one application without each stepping all over the others.

Solution

The safest approach for using multiple libraries is to pick ones that are all based on the same framework, such as using only libraries based on jQuery, the framework used in earlier recipes.

If that strategy doesn't work, make sure the libraries all use good programming practices, and none are overriding functionality or event handling provided by the others.

Discussion

Regardless of library purpose, there are fundamental rules governing the behavior of libraries that must be followed. Well-designed libraries do not do things like this:

```
window.onload=function() {...}
```

I use the DOM Level 0 `window.onload` event handler with some of the examples in the book because it's quick, simple, and doesn't add a lot of code to the sample. However, if you have one library that uses the old DOM Level 0 event handling, it overwrites the event capturing utilized by the other libraries and your own application. Well-designed libraries don't use DOM Level 0 event handling. Well-designed libraries also namespace all of their functionality. You won't find the following in a well-defined library:

```
function foo() { ... }
function bar() { ... }
```

Each function like this ends up in the global space, which increases the likelihood of clashes with other libraries, and your own applications. Well-designed libraries typically use an anonymous function, ensuring no clash with whatever is exposed to the global space:

```
(function() {
   var root = this;

   ...

   if (typeof define === 'function' && define.amd) {
    define('underscore', [], function() {
      return _;
    });
   }
}).call(this);
```

A library that plays well with other libraries and applications will not extend existing objects via the `prototype` object. Yes, I know it's a wonderful way of extending objects, and fundamental to JavaScript, but you can't control one library from overriding another if both are extending the `prototype` property for the same object. Besides, if the framework and external libraries you use don't extend existing objects via the `prototype`, this leaves you free to play in your application.

Come to that, library builders should never assume that their library is the only one used in a project.

Well-designed libraries provide event hooks so that you can hook into the library at the points where it performs a major action. In Recipe 7.14, the jQuery plug-in described in the solution provided event handler hooks you can use to provide your own functionality before or after the plug-in's validation routine.

Well-designed libraries provide good documentation of all of the publicly exposed bits, including methods, properties, and events. You shouldn't have to guess how to use the library, or examine minute portions of the code, in order to figure out what you need to do.

The Underscore.js library, covered earlier, provides a wonderfully annotated version of the source code (*http://underscorejs.org/docs/underscore.html*)—a concept that should be mandatory for all library developers.

Well-designed libraries are thoroughly tested, and provide a way to report bugs and view existing bugs. Test code should be accessible wherever it's hosted. If there's a major security problem with an existing library, you need to know about it. If there are minor bugs, you need to know about these, too.

Well-designed libraries provide nonminified, original source code. This isn't essential —just helpful, and something I look for in a library.

It goes without saying that a good library is one actively maintained, but it can't hurt to repeat this assertion. An even better library is one that's open sourced, and maintained by a community of users, who hopefully play well together—or is one you can maintain on your own, if the original maintainer can no longer do so.

To summarize:

- A good library does not use DOM Level 0 event handling.
- A well-defined library uses an anonymous function to wrap its functionality and doesn't pollute the global namespace.
- A well-defined library introduces few global objects.
- Libraries that play well with others provide event hooks. Well-behaved libraries also don't extend existing objects via the `prototype` property.
- Solid libraries are well-tested, and provide these tests as deliverables.
- Stable libraries are actively maintained, and preferably, open sourced.
- Secure libraries provide documentation of known bugs and problems, and a way to report on any bugs and problems you find.
- Usable libraries are well-documented. Bandwidth-friendly libraries are optimized and compressed, though you can always compress the library yourself.
- Confident libraries aren't built on the assumption that no other library will be used.

For the most part, you should be able to find what you need and have it work with your preferred framework. Be cautious if a library requires you to add a new framework, that needs to coexist with another framework. However, most well-built framework libraries *could* work with others.

As an example of framework coexistence, if you use jQuery, you can use another framework library, such as Underscore or Mootools. The use of global namespaces should prevent name clashes. The only exception to the namespace rule is the dollar sign ($) function, which can be used in other libraries. You can override the $ by adding the following, after all the libraries have been loaded:

```
var $j = jQuery.noConflict();
```

Once you add this code, instead of:

```
$("#elem").fadeOut('slow');
```

use:

```
$j("#elem").fadeOut('slow');
```

You can use most well-made framework libraries together, but there is tremendous overlap in functionality between the libraries, and this overlap in functionality comes with a cost: bandwidth to download the libraries. Try to avoid using more than one framework library at a time. Find the one you like, and be prepared to commit to it for some time to come.

See Also

The jQuery web page documenting how to use the framework with other libraries is at *http://bit.ly/1x63fEe*.

## CHAPTER 8

Simplified Client-Server Communication and Data

The oldest client-server communication technique is Ajax, and it's still the most widely used. In a nutshell, the procedure consists of preparing a request to the web server, typically as a *POST* or *GET* request, making the request, and assigning a callback function to process the result. In the callback function, server responses are tested until a successful response is received and the result is processed—either an acknowledgment is made that the request was successful (POST), or the returned results are processed (GET).

The data that passes between the client and server can be simple text, or it can be formatted as XML or JSON. The latter is becoming the increasingly popular choice, with most server-side technologies providing APIs that generate and consume JSON.

 This chapter focuses on Ajax, only, as well as basic processing of text, XML, and JSON data. Chapter 14 covers other, more leading-edge client-server communication techniques.

8.1. Handling an XML Document Returned via an Ajax Call

Problem

You need to prepare your Ajax application to deal with data returned in XML.

Solution

First, ensure the application can handle a document with an XML MIME type:

```
    if (window.XMLHttpRequest) {
        xmlHttpObj = new XMLHttpRequest();
        if (xmlHttpObj.overrideMimeType) {
            xmlHttpObj.overrideMimeType('application/xml');
        }
    }
```

Next, access the returned XML document via the XHMLHttpRequest's responseXML property, and then use the DOM methods to query the document for data:

```
    if (xmlHttpObj.readyState == 4 && xmlHttpObj.status == 200) {
        var citynodes = xmlHttpObj.responseXML.getElementsByTagName("city");
        ...
    }
```

Discussion

When an Ajax request returns XML, it can be accessed as a document object via the XMLHttpRequest object's responseXML property. You can then use DOM methods to query the data and process the results.

If the server-side application is returning XML, it's important that it return a MIME type of text/xml, or the responseXML property will be null. If you're unsure whether the API returns the proper MIME type, or if you have no control over the API, you can override the MIME type when you access the XMLHttpRequest object:

```
    if (window.XMLHttpRequest) {
        xmlHttpObj = new XMLHttpRequest();
        if (xmlHttpObj.overrideMimeType) {
            xmlHttpObj.overrideMimeType('application/xml');
        }
    }
```

The overrideMimeType() is not supported with versions of IE older than IE11, nor is it supported in the first draft for the W3C XMLHttpRequest specification. Because of this uncertain support, if you want to use responseXML, it's better to either change the server-side application so that it supports the application/xml MIME type, or convert the text into XML using the following cross-browser technique:

```
    if (window.DOMParser) {
        parser=new DOMParser();
        xmlResult = parser.parserFromString(xmlHttpObj.responseText,
        "text/xml");
    } else {
        xmlResult = new ActiveXObject("Microsoft.XMLDOM");
        xmlResult.async = "false"
        xmlResult.loadXML(xmlHttpObj.responseText);
    }
    var stories = xmlResult.getElementsByTagName("story");
```

Parsing XML in this way adds another level of processing. It's better, if possible, to return the data formatted as XML from the service. Example 8-2 in Recipe 8.2 demonstrates a complete application page processing an XML document.

See Also

The W3C specification for `XMLHttpRequest` can be found at *http://www.w3.org/TR/XMLHttpRequest/*.

8.2. Extracting Pertinent Information from an XML Tree

Problem

You want to access individual pieces of data from an XML document.

Solution

Use the same DOM methods you use to query your web page elements to query the XML document. For example, the following will get all elements that have a *resource* tag name:

```
var resources = xmlHttpObj.responseXML.getElementsByTagName("resource");
```

Discussion

When you have a reference to an XML document, you can use the DOM methods to query any of the data in the document. It's not as simple as accessing data from a JSON object, but it's vastly superior to extracting data from a large piece of just plain text.

To demonstrate working with an XML document, Example 8-1 contains a Node.js (commonly referred to simply as *Node*) application that returns XML containing three resources. Each `resource` contains a `title` and a `url`.

It's not a complicated application or a complex XML result, but it's sufficient to generate an XML document. Notice that a MIME type of `text/xml` is given in the header, and the `Access-Control-Allow-Origin` header value is set to accept queries from all domains (*). Because the Node application is running at a different port than the web page querying it, we have to set this value in order to allow cross-domain requests.

 Node is covered in Chapter 11, and the details for Example 8-1 are covered in Recipe 11.2. Cross-domain requests are covered in more detail in Recipe 15.1.

Example 8-1. Node.js server application that returns an XML result

```
var http = require('http'),
    url = require('url');
var XMLWriter = require('xml-writer');

// start server, listen for requests
var server = http.createServer().listen(8080);
server.on('request', function(req, res) {

  var xw = new XMLWriter;

  // start doc and root element
  xw.startDocument().startElement("resources");

  // resource
  xw.startElement("resource");
  xw.writeElement("title","Ecma-262 Edition 6");
  xw.writeElement("url",
  "http://wiki.ecmascript.org/doku.php?id=harmony:specification_drafts");
  xw.endElement();

  // resource
  xw.startElement("resource");
  xw.writeElement("title","ECMA-262 Edition 5.1");
  xw.writeElement("url",
  "http://www.ecma-international.org/publications/files/ECMA-ST/Ecma-262.pdf");
  xw.endElement();

   // resource
  xw.startElement("resource");
  xw.writeElement("title", "ECMA-402");
  xw.writeElement("url",
  "http://ecma-international.org/ecma-402/1.0/ECMA-402.pdf");
  xw.endElement();

  // end resources
  xw.endElement();

  res.writeHeader(200, {"Content-Type": "application/xml",
  "Access-Control-Allow-Origin": "*"});
  res.end(xw.toString(),"utf8");
});
```

Most Ajax calls process plain text or JSON, but there's still a need for processing XML. SVG is still XML, as is MathML, XHTML, and other markup languages. In the solution, a new XMLHttpRequest object is created to handle the client-server communication. If you've not used Ajax previously, the XMLHttpRequest object's methods are:

- open: Initializes a request. Parameters include the method (GET, POST, DELETE, or PUT), the request URL, whether the request is asynchronous, and a possible username and password. By default, all requests are sent asynchronously.

- setRequestHeader: Sets the MIME type of the request.

- send: Sends the request.

- sendAsBinary: Sends binary data.

- abort: Aborts an already sent request.

- getResponseHeader: Retrieves the header text, or null if the response hasn't been returned yet or there is no header.

- getAllResponseHeaders: Retrieves the header text for a multipart request.

The communication is opened using object's open() method, passing in the HTTP method (GET), the request URL (the Node application), as well as a value of true, signaling that the communication is asynchronous (the application doesn't block waiting on the return request). If the application is password protected, the fourth and fifth optional parameters are the username and password, respectively.

I know that the application I'm calling is returning an XML-formatted response, so it's not necessary to override the MIME type (covered in Recipe 8.1).

In the application, the XMLHttpRequest's onReadyStateChange event handler is assigned a callback function, getData(), and then the request is sent with send(). If the HTTP method had been POST, the prepared data would have been sent as a parameter of send().

In the callback function getData(), the XMLHttpRequest object's readyState and status properties are checked (see Example 8-2). Only when the readyState is 4 and status is 200 is the result processed. The readyState indicates what state the Ajax call is in, and the value of 200 is the HTTP OK response code. Because we know the result is XML, the application accesses the XML document via the XMLHttpRequest object's responseXML property. For other data types, the data is accessed via the response property, and responseType provides the data type (*arrayBuffer*, *blob*, *document*, *json*, *text*). Not all browsers support all data types, but all modern browsers do support XML and at least arrayBuffer, JSON, and text.

Example 8-2. Application to process resources from returned XML

```
<!DOCTYPE html>
<html>
<head>
  <title>Stories</title>
  <meta charset="utf-8" />
</head>
```

```
<body>
  <div id="result">
  </div>
<script type="text/javascript">

  var xmlHttpObj;

  // ajax object
  if (window.XMLHttpRequest) {
    xmlRequest = new XMLHttpRequest();
  }

  // build request
  var url = "http://shelleystoybox.com:8080";
  xmlRequest.open('GET', url, true);
  xmlRequest.onreadystatechange = getData;
  xmlRequest.send();

  function getData() {
    if (xmlRequest.readyState == 4 && xmlRequest.status == 200) {
      try {
        var result = document.getElementById("result");
        var str = "<p>";

        // can use DOM methods on XML document
        var resources =
         xmlRequest.responseXML.getElementsByTagName("resource");

        // process resources
        for (var i = 0; i < resources.length; i++) {
          var resource = resources[i];

          // get title and url, generate HTML
          var title = resource.childNodes[0].firstChild.nodeValue;
          var url = resource.childNodes[1].firstChild.nodeValue;
          str += "<a href='" + url + "'>" + title + "</a><br />";
        }

        // finish HTML and insert
        str+="</p>";
        result.innerHTML=str;
      } catch (e) {
        console.log(e.message);
      }
    }
  }
</script>

</body>
</html>
```

When processing the XML code, the application first queries for all resource elements, returned in a nodeList. The application cycles through the collection, accessing each resource element in order to access the title and url, both of which are child nodes. Each is accessed via the childNodes collection, and their data, contained in the node Value attribute, is extracted.

The resource data is used to build a string of linked resources, which is output to the page using innerHTML. Instead of using a succession of childNodes element collections to walk the trees, I could have used the Selectors API to access all URLs and titles, and then traversed both collections at one time, pulling the paired values from each, in sequence:

```
var urls = xmlRequest.responseXML.querySelectorAll("resource url");
var titles = xmlRequest.responseXML.querySelectorAll("resource title");

for (var i = 0; i < urls.length; i++) {
    var url = urls[i].firstChild.nodeValue;
    var title = titles[i].firstChild.nodeValue;
    str += "<a href='" + url + "'>" + title + "</a><br />";
}
```

I could have also used getElementsByTagName against each returned resource element —any XML DOM method that works with the web page works with the returned XML.

The try...catch error handling should catch any query that fails because the XML is incomplete.

 The document returned in responseXML has access to the standard DOM APIs, but not the HTML DOM APIs. For the most part, this shouldn't be a problem, as most of the functionality you'll use is based on the standard DOM APIs. An example of the DOM API is the getElementsByTagName() method used in the solution. An example of the HTML DOM is when you access elements from a form, or use the write() method. This book rarely uses the HTML DOM API.

See Also

The DOM methods are covered in Chapter 5. For more on the differences between the standard DOM and the HTML DOM, check out the W3C DOM specification page (*http://www.w3.org/DOM/DOMTR*). The JavaScript (ECMAScript) binding for each specification demonstrates how to access the DOM using script.

8.3. Parsing and Automatically Modifying JSON

Problem

You want to safely create a JavaScript object from JSON. You also want to replace the numeric representation of true and false (1 and 0, respectively) with their Boolean counterparts (true and false).

Solution

Parse the object with the JSON built-in capability added to browsers via ECMAScript 5. To transform the numeric values to their Boolean counterparts, create a *reviver* function:

```
var jsonobj = '{"test" : "value1", "test2" : 3.44, "test3" : 0}';
var obj = JSON.parse(jsonobj, function (key, value) {
   if (typeof value == 'number') {
     if (value == 0) {
       value = false;
     } else if (value == 1) {
       value = true;
     }
   }
   return value;
   });

console.log(obj.test3); // false
```

Discussion

To figure out how to create JSON, think about how you create an object literal and just translate it into a string (with some caveats).

If the object is an array:

```
var arr = new Array("one","two","three");
```

the JSON notation would be equivalent to the literal notation for the array:

```
["one","two","three"];
```

Note the use of double quotes ("") rather than single, which are not allowed in JSON.

If you're working with an object:

```
var obj3 = {
   prop1 : "test",
   result : true,
   num : 5.44,
   name : "Joe",
   cts : [45,62,13]};
```

the JSON notation would be:

```
{"prop1":"test","result":true,"num":5.44,"name":"Joe","cts":[45,62,13]}
```

Notice in JSON how the property names are in quotes, but the values are only quoted when they're strings. In addition, if the object contains other objects, such as an array, it's also transformed into its JSON equivalent. However, the object *cannot* contain methods. If it does, an error is thrown. JSON works with data only.

The JSON static object isn't complex, as it only provides two methods: `stringify()` and `parse()`. The `parse()` method takes two arguments: a JSON-formatted string and an optional `reviver` function. This function takes a key/value pair as parameters, and returns either the original value or a modified result.

In the solution, the JSON-formatted string is an object with three properties: a string, a numeric, and a third property, which has a numeric value but is really a Boolean with a numeric representation—0 is false, 1 is true.

To transform all 0, 1 values into `false`, `true`, a function is provided as the second argument to `JSON.parse()`. It checks each property of the object to see if it is a numeric. If it is, the function checks to see if the value is 0 or 1. If the value is 0, the return value is set to `false`; if 1, the return value is set to `true`; otherwise, the original value is returned.

The ability to transform incoming JSON-formatted data is essential, especially if you're processing the result of an Ajax request or JSONP response. You can't always control the structure of the data you get from a service.

 There are restrictions on the JSON: strings must be double quoted, and there are no hexadecimal values and no tabs in strings.

See Also

See Recipe 8.4 for a demonstration of `JSON.stringify()`. For more on the allowable syntax for JSON, I recommend the original JSON page (*http://json.org/*).

8.4. Converting an Object to a Filtered/Transformed String with JSON

Problem

You need to convert a JavaScript object to a JSON-formatted string for posting to a web application. However, the web application has data requirements that differ from your client application.

Solution

Use the JSON.stringify() method, passing in the object as first parameter and providing a transforming function (a *replacer*) as the second parameter:

```
function convertBoolToNums(key, value) {
  if (typeof value == 'boolean') {
    if (value)
      value = 1;
    else
      value = 0;
  }
  return value;
};


var obj = {test : "value1",
           test2 : 3.44,
           test3 : false};

var jsonstr = JSON.stringify(obj, convertBoolToNums, 3);

console.log(jsonstr); // '{ "test" : "value1", "test2" : 3.44, "test3" : 0}'
```

Discussion

The JSON.stringify() method takes three parameters: the object to be transformed into JSON, an optional function or array used either to transform or filter one or more object values, and an optional third parameter that defines how much and what kind of whitespace is used in the generated result.

In the solution, a function is used to check property values, and if the value is a Boolean, converts false to 0, and true to 1. The function results are transformed into a string if the return value is a number or Boolean. The function can also act as a filter: if the returned value from the function is null, the property/value pair is removed from the JSON.

You can also use an array rather than a function. The array can contain strings or numbers, and is a *whitelist* of properties that are allowed in the result. The following code:

```
var whitelist = ["test","test2"];

var obj = {"test" : "value1", "test2" : 3.44, "test3" : false};
var jsonobj = JSON.stringify(obj, whitelist, '\t');
```

Would result in a JSON string including the object's *test* and *test2* properties, but not the third property (*test3*), The resulting string is also *pretty-printed* using a tab (\t) this time, instead of the three spaces used in the solution:

```
{
    "test": "value1",
    "test2": 3.44
}
```

The last parameter controls how much whitespace is used in the result. It can be a number representing the number of spaces or a string. If it is a string, the first 10 characters are used as whitespace. If I use the following:

```
var jsonobj = JSON.stringify(obj, whitelist, "***");
```

the result is:

```
{
***"test": "value1",
***"test2": 3.44
}
```

As mentioned earlier, the tab (\t) generates the standard *pretty-print* for JSON.

See Also

See Recipe 8.3 for a discussion on `JSON.parse()`.

8.5. Making an Ajax Request to Another Domain (Using JSONP)

Problem

You want to query for data using a web service API, such as the Rotten Tomatoes API, or the Flicker API. However, the Ajax *same-origin* security policy prevents cross-domain communication.

Solution

One approach is to use JSONP (*JSON with padding*) to work around the security issues.

First, you create a new `script` element, making the URL the endpoint for the API method call. The following creates a `script` element with a call to Flickr's photo search API method:

```
function addScript( url) {
   var script = document.createElement('script');
   script.type="text/javascript";
   script.src = url;
   document.getElementsByTagName('head')[0].appendChild(script);
}
```

The URL looks like the following, including a request to return the data formatted as JSON, and providing a callback function name. The `api_key` is generated by Flickr, and the `user_id` is the unique user identifier, the *NSID*, for your account. Note this isn't the same as the username.

 Easily find the `user_id` using the idGettr web service (*http://idgettr.com/*).

I'm asking for the first page of results for a given user:

```
http://api.flickr.com/services/rest/?method=flickr.photos.search&user_id=xxx
&api_key=xxx&page=1&format=json&jsoncallback=processPhotos
```

When the `script` tag is created, the request to Flickr is made, and because I passed in the request for a JSON-formatted result and provided a callback function name, that's how the return is provided. The following is a basic callback function that just displays the results to the `console`:

```
function processPhotos(obj) {
  photos = obj.photos.photo;
  var str = '';
  photos.forEach(function(photo) {
    str+=photo.title + '<br /> ';
  });
  document.getElementById('result').innerHTML = str;
}
```

Discussion

Ajax works within a protected environment that ensures we don't end up embedding dangerous text or code into a web page because of a call to an external application (which may or may not be secure). The downside to this security is that we can't directly access services to external APIs. Instead, we have to create a server-side proxy application because server applications don't face the cross-domain restriction.

One workaround is to use JSONP, demonstrated in the solution. Instead of using XMLHttpRequest, we convert the request URL into one that we can attach to a script's src attribute, because the script element does not follow the same-origin policy.

If the service is amenable, it returns the data formatted as JSON, even wrapping it in a callback function. When the script is created, it's no different than if the function call is made directly in our code, and we've passed an object as a parameter. We don't even have to worry about converting the string to a JavaScript object. The callback's argument is a JSON object.

The photos are returned in pages, and you can repeat the calls as many times as you want to get as many photos as you need, changing the page number with each call. Example 8-3 contains a simple, working example of using JSONP to access information from Flickr. Just remember to use your own API key and NSID.

Example 8-3. Using JSONP to circumvent cross-domain restrictions and processing the result

```
<!DOCTYPE html>
<html>
<head>
  <meta charset="utf-8">
  <title>JSONP</title>
</head>
<body>
  <div id="result">
  </div>
<script >
function addScript( url) {
  var script = document.createElement('script');
  script.src = url;
  document.getElementsByTagName('head')[0].appendChild(script);
}

addScript('https://api.flickr.com/services/rest/?method=flickr.photos.search
&user_id=NSID&api_key=yourapikey&page=1&format=json&jsoncallback=processPhotos');


// assign photos globally, call first to load
function processPhotos(obj) {
  photos = obj.photos.photo;
  var str = '';
  photos.forEach(function(photo) {
    str+=photo.title + '<br /> ';
  });
  document.getElementById('result').innerHTML = str;
}
</script>
</body>
</html>
```

It's a clever trick, but should only be used with caution. Even with secure services such as Flickr, there is the remote possibility that someone could find a way to inject JavaScript into the data via the client-side application for the service, which can cause havoc in the application.

See Also

The Flickr API and development environment is documented at *https://www.flickr.com/ services/api/*. I also access the Flickr services in Recipe 13.1.

A more modern solution to the problem of cross-domain service access is to use cross-origin resource sharing (CORS). I discuss and demonstrate this capability in Recipe 15.1.

8.6. Processing JSON from an Ajax Request

Problem

You want to format Ajax data as JSON, rather than text or XML.

Solution

Create and initiate the Ajax request the same as for an XML or text data request. In this code, the service is a Node application, accessible at port 8080:

```
// ajax object
if (window.XMLHttpRequest) {
    httpRequest = new XMLHttpRequest();
}

// build request
var url = "http://shelleystoybox.com:8080";
httpRequest.open('GET', url, true);
httpRequest.onreadystatechange = getData;
httpRequest.send();
```

In the function to process the response, use the JSON object's `parse()` method to convert the returned text into a JavaScript object:

```
function getData() {
  if (httpRequest.readyState == 4 && httpRequest.status == 200) {
    try {

      // Javascript function JSON.parse to parse JSON data
      var jsonObj = JSON.parse(httpRequest.responseText);
      console.log(jsonObj.list[0].name);
    } catch (e) {
      console.log(e.message);
    }
```

```
        }
    }
```

The key to sending JSON in response to an Ajax request is to use whatever language's version of the `JSON.stringify()` method to convert the object into a JSON-formatted string. In the following Node application, we can use the Node version of JSON to format the data. The MIME type for the data is also set to `application/json`:

```
var http = require('http');

// start server, listen for requests
var server = http.createServer().listen(8080);
server.on('request', function(req, res) {

    var titleList = {
        "list" : [
          { "id": "id1",
            "name": "Title One"
          },
          { "id": "id12",
            "name": "Another Value"
          },
          { "id": "id20",
            "name": "End of the Road"
          },
          { "id": "id24",
            "name": "One More"
          }
        ],
        "totalRecords": 4
    };
  res.writeHeader(200, {"Content-Type": "application/json", "Access-Control-All
ow-Origin": "*"});
    res.end(JSON.stringify(titleList));
});
```

Example 8-4 contains the script for a client to process the data by printing out each value to the console.

Example 8-4. Processing JSON data from an Ajax request

```
var httpRequest;

// ajax object
if (window.XMLHttpRequest) {
   httpRequest = new XMLHttpRequest();
}

// build request
var url = "http://shelleystoybox.com:8080";
httpRequest.open('GET', url, true);
httpRequest.onreadystatechange = getData;
httpRequest.send();
```

```
function printData(element) {
  console.log(element.name);
}

function getData() {
  if (httpRequest.readyState == 4 && httpRequest.status == 200) {
    try {

        // Javascript function JSON.parse to parse JSON data
        var jsonObj = JSON.parse(httpRequest.responseText);
        jsonObj.list.forEach (function(element) {
            console.log(element.name);
            });

    } catch (e) {
      console.log(e.message);
    }
  }
}
```

8.7. Populating a Selection List from the Server

Problem

Based on a user's actions with another form element, you want to populate a selection list with values.

Solution

Capture the change event for the form element:

```
document.getElementById("nicething").onchange=populateSelect;
```

In the event handler function, make an Ajax call with the form data:

```
var url = "nicething.php?nicething=" + value;
xmlhttp.open('GET', url, true);
xmlhttp.onreadystatechange = getThings;
xmlhttp.send(null);
```

In the Ajax result function, populate the selection list:

```
if(xmlhttp.readyState == 4 && xmlhttp.status == 200) {
  var select = document.getElementById("nicestuff");
  select.length=0;
  var nicethings = xmlhttp.responseText.split(",");
  for (var i = 0; i < nicethings.length; i++) {
    select.options[select.length] =
      new Option(nicethings[i],nicethings[i]);
  }
```

```
            select.style.display="block";
     } else if (xmlhttp.readyState == 4 && xmlhttp.status != 200) {
        document.getElementById('nicestuff').innerHTML =
            'Error: Search Failed!';
     }
```

Discussion

One of the more common forms of Ajax is to populate a `select` or other form element
based on a choice made by the user. Instead of populating a `select` element with many
options, or building a set of 10 or 20 radio buttons, you can capture the user's choice in
another form element, query a server application based on the value, and build the other
form elements based on the value—all without leaving the page.

Example 8-5 demonstrates a simple page that captures the change event for radio buttons within a `fieldset` element, makes an Ajax query with the value of the selected
radio button, and populates a selection list by parsing the returned option list. A comma
separates each of the option items, and new options are created with the returned text
having both an option label and option value. Before populating the `select` element,
its length is set to 0. This is a quick and easy way to truncate the `select` element—
removing all existing options, and starting fresh.

Example 8-5. Creating an on-demand select Ajax application

```
<!DOCTYPE html>
<head>
<title>On Demand Select</title>
<style>
#nicestuff
{
  display: none;
  margin: 10px 0;
}
#nicething
{
  width: 400px;
}
</style>
</head>
<body>
<form action="backuppage.php" method="get">
  <p>Select one:</p>
  <fieldset id="nicething">
     <input type="radio" name="nicethings" value="bird" />
     <label for="bird">Birds</label><br />

     <input type="radio" name="nicethings" value="flower" />
     <label for="flower">Flowers</label><br />

     <input type="radio" name="nicethings" value="sweets" />
```

```
      <label for="sweets">Sweets</label><br />

      <input type="radio" name="nicethings" value="cuddles" />
      <label for="cuddles">Cute Critters</label>
    </fieldset>
    <input type="submit" id="submitbutton" value="get nice things" />
    <select id="nicestuff"></select>
</form>
<script>

var xmlhttp;

function populateSelect() {

  var value;

  var inputs = this.getElementsByTagName('input');
  for (var i = 0; i < inputs.length; i++) {
    if (inputs[i].checked) {
      value = inputs[i].value;
      break;
    }
  }

  // prepare request
  if (!xmlhttp) {
    xmlhttp = new XMLHttpRequest();
  }
  var url = "nicething.php?nicething=" + value;
  xmlhttp.open('GET', url, true);
  xmlhttp.onreadystatechange = getThings;
  xmlhttp.send(null);
}

// process return
function getThings() {
   if(xmlhttp.readyState == 4 && xmlhttp.status == 200) {
     var select = document.getElementById("nicestuff");
     select.length=0;
     var nicethings = xmlhttp.responseText.split(",");
     for (var i = 0; i < nicethings.length; i++) {
       select.options[select.length] =
          new Option(nicethings[i], nicethings[i]);
     }
     select.style.display="block";
   } else if (xmlhttp.readyState == 4 && xmlhttp.status != 200) {
     alert("No items returned for request");
   }
}

document.getElementById("submitbutton").style.display="none";
document.getElementById("nicething").onclick=populateSelect;
```

```
</script>

</body>
```

The form does have an assigned `action` page, and a submit button that's hidden when the script is first run. These are the backup if scripting is turned off. The application is also *old school*—text-based data that you can either append directly to the page (if formatted as HTML), or parse using the String functions. JSON is nice, but there's always room for just plain text.

The example uses a PHP application to populate the selection list. It could also be a Node application if you want to use JavaScript in both the client and server:

```php
<?php

//If no search string is passed, then we can't search
if(empty($_REQUEST['nicething'])) {
  echo "No State Sent";
} else {
  //Remove whitespace from beginning & end of passed search.
  $search = trim($_REQUEST['nicething']);
  switch($search) {
    case "cuddles" :
      $result = "puppies,kittens,gerbils";
      break;
    case "sweets" :
      $result = "licorice,cake,cookies,custard";
      break;
    case "bird" :
      $result = "robin,mockingbird,finch,dove";
      break;
    case "flower" :
      $result = "roses,lilys,daffodils,pansies";
      break;
    default :
      $result = "No Nice Things  Found";
      break;
  }

  echo $result;
}
?>
```

Progressively building form elements using Ajax or another communication technique isn't necessary in all applications, but it is a great way to ensure a more effective form in cases where the data can change, or the form is complex.

8.8. Using a Timer to Automatically Update the Page with Fresh Data

Problem

You want to display entries from a file, but the file is updated frequently.

Solution

Use Ajax and a timer to periodically check the file for new values and update the display accordingly.

The Ajax we use is no different than any other Ajax request. We'll use a GET, because we're retrieving data. We put together the request, attach a function to the onreadysta techange event handler, and send the request:

```
var xmlhttp;

// prepare and send XHR request
function populateList() {
    var url = 'text.txt'; // change to full url to prevent caching problems
    xmlhttp.open('GET', url, true);
    xmlhttp.onreadystatechange = processResponse;
    xmlhttp.send(null);
}
```

In the code that processes the response, we just place the new text into a new unordered list item and append it to an existing ul element:

```
// process return
function processResponse() {
    if(xmlhttp.readyState == 4 && xmlhttp.status == 200) {
        var li = document.createElement("li");
        var txt = document.createTextNode(xmlhttp.responseText);
        li.appendChild(txt);
        document.getElementById("update").appendChild(li);
        setTimeout(populateList,15000);
    } else if (xmlhttp.readyState == 4 && xmlhttp.status != 200) {
        console.log(xmlhttp.responseText);
    }
}
```

The new part is the addition of the setTimeout() in the code. It triggers the entire process again in 15 seconds.

The process is started by creating the xmlHttpRequest object in the Window load event handler, and then calling populateList() the first time:

```
window.onload=function() {
  xmlhttp = new XMLHttpRequest();
  populateList();
}
```

Discussion

The fact that we're doing a direct request on a static text file might be new, but remember that a GET request is more or less the same as the requests we put into the location bar of our browsers. If something works in the browser, it should successfully return in an Ajax GET request…within reason.

The key to using timers with Ajax calls is to make sure that the last call is completed before making the next. By adding the call to setTimeout() at the end of the Ajax call, we trigger the timer when we know an outstanding request isn't being processed. We can also put in a check for the request status, and cancel the timer event altogether if we're concerned about hitting a failing service, over and over again.

When I ran the application that included the solution code, I changed the text file by using the Unix echo command:

```
$ echo "This is working" > text.txt
```

And then watched as the text showed up on the page, as shown in Figure 8-1.

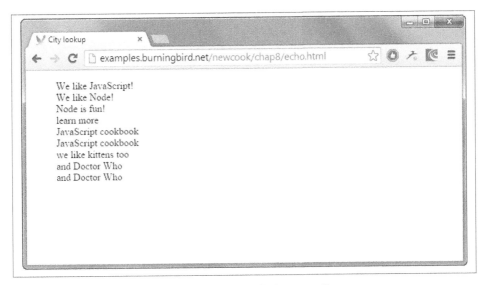

Figure 8-1. Demonstration of updates from polled Ajax calls

If you're planning to use this form of polling with another service, like the Twitter API, be aware that you can get kicked off if you're considered abusive of the service. Check to see if there are restrictions for how often you can access a service using the API.

 Depending on the browser, you may run into caching issues if you access the *text.txt* file locally. Providing a full URL should prevent this from occurring.

See Also

An example of accessing Twitter's API from a Node application is in Recipe 13.7.

A more viable approach to updating client data based on changes in the server is using WebSockets, covered in Recipe 15.5. However, if you want to keep all your processes in the client, the use of a timer is effective.

## CHAPTER 9

Creating Media Rich, Interactive Web Effects

Pretty pictures. Cool videos. Sound!

The Web of the future will be a richer place with the new and improved innovations ready to use. Our old friends SVG and Canvas are getting new life and generating new interest. Added to them are the new video and audio elements included in HTML5, and the near-future potential of 3D graphics.

Best of all, none of these innovations requires any kind of proprietary plug-in—they're all becoming integrated with all your browser clients, including those on your smartphones and tablets, as well as your computers.

 This chapter assumes you have some familiarity with the Canvas element, as well as SVG. A brief tutorial or introduction should be sufficient. I recommend the Mozilla Developer Network Canvas Tutorial (*http://mzl.la/1zG4ME5*) and the W3C's SVG Primer (*http://bit.ly/1zG4NrA*). MDN also has several good introductions to working with SVG.

9.1. Creating a Dynamic Line Chart in Canvas

Problem

You want to display a line chart in your web page, but the data changes over time, and you want to dynamically update it.

Solution

Use the `canvas` element and the `path` method to create the chart. When the data changes, update the chart:

```
var array1 = [[100,100], [150, 50], [200,185],
              [250, 185], [300,250], [350,100], [400,250],
              [450, 100], [500,20], [550,80], [600, 120]];

var imgcanvas = document.getElementById("imgcanvas");

if (imgcanvas.getContext) {
  var ctx = imgcanvas.getContext('2d');


  // rect one
  ctx.strokeRect(0,0,600,300);

  // line path
  ctx.beginPath();
  ctx.moveTo(0,100);
  for (var i = 0; i < array1.length; i++) {
    ctx.lineTo(array1[i][0], array1[i][1]);
  }
  ctx.stroke();
}
```

Discussion

Canvas paths are the way to create arbitrary shapes in Canvas. After getting the canvas context, `ctx`, the path is begun with a call to `ctx.beginPath()`, which begins a new Canvas path. The next line of code is `ctx.moveTo`, which moves the drawing "pen" to a beginning location, but without drawing. From that point, several `lineTo()` calls are made using an array of paired values representing the x,y location for each line endpoint.

After the path has been defined, it's drawn. We're not creating a closed path, so I'm not using `ctx.closePath()`, which would draw all the defined lines and then attempt to draw a line from the ending point to the beginning point. Instead, I'm drawing the line given the points that have been defined, using `ctx.stroke()`.

The appearance of the drawing is influenced by two Canvas settings: `strokeStyle` and `fillStyle`. The `strokeStyle` setting sets the color for the outline of a drawing, while the `fillStyle` does the same for the drawing filling:

```
ctx.strokeStyle="black";
ctx.fillStyle="#ff0000;
```

Any CSS setting will do, or you can use a CanvasGradient or CanvasPattern. You can use the `rgba` setting to add transparency:

```
ctx.fillStyle="rgba(255,0,0,0.5)";
```

You can also use the `globalAlpha` setting to set the transparency for any drawing that follows:

```
ctx.globalAlpha = 0.2;
```

You can further control the appearance of the drawing outline by changing the stroke's line width:

```
ctx.line
```

To dynamically update the chart, you can incorporate timers, and either replace the path (by creating an entirely new context, which would erase the old), or add the new line chart to the same chart. Example 9-1 shows a web page that creates the line in the solution and then creates two others, each drawn after a short period of time using timers. The colors for the stroke path are changed between lines.

Example 9-1. Using timers to dynamically update a line chart

```
<!DOCTYPE html>
<head>
<title>Canvas Chart</title>
<meta charset="utf-8" />

</head>
<body>
<canvas id="imgcanvas" width="650" height="350">
<p>Include an image that has a static representation of the chart</p>
</canvas>

<script>

  var points = [[[100,100], [150, 50], [200,185],
               [250, 185], [300,250], [350,100], [400,250],
               [450, 100], [500,20], [550,80], [600, 120]],

               [[100,100], [150, 150], [200,135],
               [250, 285], [300,150], [350,150], [400,280],
               [450, 100], [500,120], [550,80], [600, 190]],

               [[100,200], [150, 100], [200,35],
               [250, 185], [300,10], [350,15], [400,80],
               [450, 100], [500,120], [550,80], [600, 120]]];

  var colors = ['black','red','green'];

  var imgcanvas = document.getElementById("imgcanvas");

  if (imgcanvas.getContext) {

    var ctx = imgcanvas.getContext('2d');
```

```
// rectangle wrapping line chart
ctx.strokeRect(0,0,600,300);

points.forEach(function(element, indx, arry) {
  setTimeout(function() {

    // set up beginning
    ctx.beginPath();
    ctx.moveTo(0,100);

    ctx.strokeStyle = colors[indx];

    for (var i = 0; i < element.length; i++) {
      ctx.lineTo(element[i][0], element[i][1]);
    }

    ctx.stroke();

  }, indx * 5000);

});
}
</script>

</body>
```

Figure 9-1 shows the line chart after all three lines have been drawn.

There are other path methods: `arc()`, to draw curves, and `quadraticCurveTo()` and `bezierCurveTo()`, to draw quadratic and bezier curves. All of these methods can be combined in one path to create complex images.

See Also

All modern browsers support the Canvas element and 2D API. Mozilla provides a solid Canvas tutorial (*https://developer.mozilla.org/en/Canvas_tutorial*).To ensure the Canvas examples work with older versions of Internet Explorer (8.0 and older), you can use the ExplorerCanvas (*http://code.google.com/p/explorercanvas/*) library.

Figure 9-1. Canvas drawing from Example 9-1 using the path method

Extra: Simplify Your Canvas Charts Using a Library

It doesn't have to be difficult to create a chart using Canvas from scratch, but why walk the steps taken by others? There are several excellent libraries that can simplify not only chart making but other Canvas effects.

Over 50 libraries for chart making are listed in a TechSlides Page (*http://bit.ly/ 1zG5mBP*), including the increasingly popular D3, which I'll cover in Recipe 16.1. Most of the libraries are freely available, though some do charge a fee for commercial use.

One of the libraries, Highcharts (*http://www.highcharts.com/*), even provides demonstrations that you can edit in jsFiddle, making it easy to try out the library's capability. It's dependent on jQuery, reducing the code to an absurdly simple level. As an example, one of the demonstrations is for a very professional line chart, with plot lines and labels, as shown in Figure 9-2. Yet the code to create this example is equivalent to that in the following code block, which I modified to feature my own locations and temperature metric, which you can try yourself at jsFiddle (*http://jsfiddle.net/Lm3xvy74/*):

```
$(function () {
        $('#container').highcharts({
            title: {
                text: 'Monthly Average Temperature',
                x: -20 //center
```

```
            },
            subtitle: {
                text: 'Source: Weather.com',
                x: -20
            },
            xAxis: {
                categories: ['Jan', 'Feb', 'Mar', 'Apr', 'May', 'Jun',
                    'Jul', 'Aug', 'Sep', 'Oct', 'Nov', 'Dec']
            },
            yAxis: {
                title: {
                    text: 'Temperature (°F)'
                },
                plotLines: [{
                    value: 0,
                    width: 1,
                    color: '#808080'
                }]
            },
            tooltip: {
                valueSuffix: '°F'
            },
            legend: {
                layout: 'vertical',
                align: 'right',
                verticalAlign: 'middle',
                borderWidth: 0
            },
            series: [{
                name: 'Seattle, WA',
                data: [47,51,55,59,65,70,75,75,70,60,52,47]
            }, {
                name: 'Grand Isle, VT',
                data: [27,31,40,54,67,76,81,79,71,57,45,33]
            }, {
                name: 'St. Louis, MO',
                data: [40,45,55,67,77,85,89,88,81,69,56,43]
            }]
        });
    });
```

Not only is the plotted chart professional looking, it's zoomable, which means you can move your mouse cursor over the chart to examine the plot points in detail. That level of interactivity isn't necessarily trivial in Canvas, because one of the downsides to Canvas is the fact that you can't attach event handlers to the individual elements of Canvas—only to the Canvas area itself. Not being able to attach an event to individual elements means that you'll have to keep track of where the mouse is, and what's underneath it at any point in time.

Thankfully, you can attach event handlers to SVG elements, as demonstrated in Recipe 9.2.

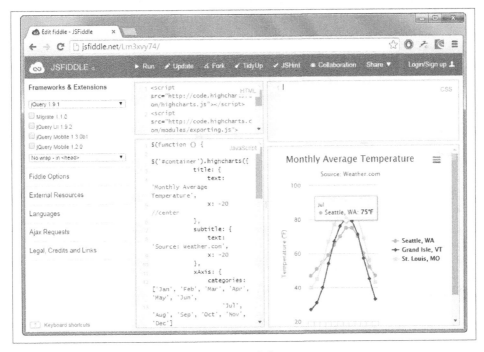

Figure 9-2. Line graph with interactive zoomability

9.2. Adding JavaScript to SVG

Problem

You want to add JavaScript to an SVG file or element.

Solution

JavaScript in SVG is included in `script` elements, just as with HTML, except with the addition of CDATA markup surrounding the script in case XHTML-sensitive characters, such as < and >, are used (Example 9-2).

The DOM methods are also available for working with the SVG elements.

Example 9-2. Demonstration of JavaScript within an SVG file

```
<?xml version="1.0" encoding="UTF-8" standalone="no"?>
<svg xmlns="http://www.w3.org/2000/svg"
xmlns:xlink="http://www.w3.org/1999/xlink" width="600" height="600">
  <script type="text/ecmascript">
    <![CDATA[
```

```
        // set element onclick event handler
        window.onload=function () {

            var square = document.getElementById("square");

            // onclick event handler, change circle radius
            square.onclick = function() {
                var color = this.getAttribute("fill");
                if (color == "#ff0000") {
                    this.setAttribute("fill", "#0000ff");
                } else {
                    this.setAttribute("fill","#ff0000");
                }
            }
        }
    ]]>
  </script>
  <rect id="square" width="400" height="400" fill="#ff0000"
    x="10" y="10" />
</svg>
```

Discussion

As the solution demonstrates, SVG is XML, and the rules for embedding script into XML must be adhered to. This means providing the script type within the script tag, as well as wrapping the script contents in a CDATA block. If you don't have the CDATA section, and your script uses characters such as < or &, your page will have errors, because the XML parser treats them as XML characters, not script.

There is some drive to treat SVG as HTML, especially when the SVG is inline in HTML documents. That's what Chrome does. Still, it's better to be safe than sorry, and follow XML requirements.

The DOM methods, such as document.getElementById(), aren't HTML specific; they're usable with any XML document, including SVG. What's new is the SVG-specific fill attribute, an attribute unique to SVG elements, such as rect.

If namespaces were used with any of the elements in the file, then the namespace version of the DOM methods (discussed previously in "Extra: Namespace Variation" on page 112), would have to be used.

The code in the solution is a standalone SVG file, with a *.svg* extension. If we were to embed the SVG within an HTML file, as shown in Example 9-3, the color-changing animation would work the same. The CDATA section is removed because all modern browsers understand the SVG is now in an HTML context. If the file is XHTML, though, add them back.

Example 9-3. SVG element from Example 9-2, embedded into an HTML page

```
<!DOCTYPE html>
<html>
<head>
<title>Accessing Inline SVG</title>
<meta charset="utf-8">
</head>
<body>
<svg width="600" height="600">
  <script>

      // set element onclick event handler
      window.onload=function () {

          var square = document.getElementById("square");

          // onclick event handler, change circle radius
          square.onclick = function() {
             var color = this.getAttribute("fill");
             if (color == "#ff0000") {
                this.setAttribute("fill","#0000ff");
             } else {
                this.setAttribute("fill","#ff0000");
             }
          }
      }
  </script>
  <rect id="square" width="400" height="400" fill="#ff0000"
 x="10" y="10" />
</svg>
</body>
</html>
```

Chrome, Safari, Opera, and Firefox all support SVG, including SVG in HTML. IE supports SVG after version 9.

 To learn more about SVG, in general, I recommend *SVG Essentials, Second Edition* by J. David Eisenber (O'Reilly).

Extra: Using SVG Libraries

There aren't quite as many libraries for working with SVG as there are for working with Canvas, but the ones that exist are very handy. One of the most popular is the D3 library, covered in Chapter 17. Three other popular libraries include the granddaddy of the SVG libraries, Raphaël (*http://raphaeljs.com/*), and the newer Snap.svg (*http://snapsvg.io/*) and SVG.js (*http://www.svgjs.com/*). All three can simplify SVG creation and animation. You can even use Raphaël in both jsBin and jsFiddle, as shown in Figure 9-3. The following code snippet shows an example of using Raphaël:

```
// Creates canvas 320 × 200 at 10, 50
var paper = Raphael(10, 50, 320, 400);

// Creates circle at x = 150, y = 140, with radius 100

var circle = paper.circle(150, 140, 100);
// Sets the fill attribute of the circle to red (#f00)
circle.attr("fill", "#f0f");

// Sets the stroke attribute of the circle to white
circle.attr("stroke", "#ff0");
```

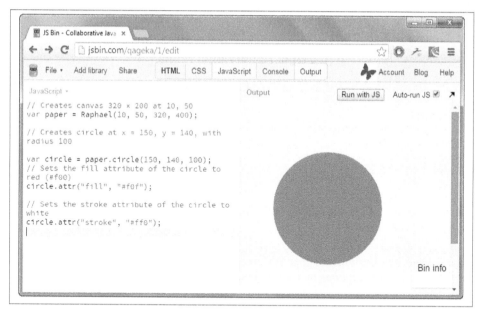

Figure 9-3. Using Raphaël in jsBin

9.3. Accessing SVG from Web Page Script

Problem

You want to modify the contents of an SVG element from script within the web page.

Solution

If the SVG is embedded directly in the web page, access the element and its attributes using the same functionality you would use with any other web page element:

```
var square = document.getElementById("ssquare");
square.setAttribute("width", "500");
```

However, if the SVG is in an external SVG file embedded into the page via an `object` element, you have to get the document for the external SVG file in order to access the SVG elements. The technique requires object detection because the process differs by browser:

```
// set element onclick event handler
window.onload=function () {

    var object = document.getElementById("object");
    var svgdoc;

    try {

       svgdoc = object.contentDocument;
    } catch(e) {
      try {

         svgdoc = object.getSVGDocument();

       } catch (e) {
          alert("SVG in object not supported in your environment");
       }
    }

    if (!svgdoc) return;

    var square = svgdoc.getElementById('square');
    square.setAttribute("width", "500");
```

Discussion

The first option listed in the solution accesses SVG embedded in an HTML file. You can access SVG elements using the same methods you've used to access HTML elements.

The second option is a little more involved, and depends on retrieving the document object for the SVG document. The first approach tries to access the contentDocument property on the object. If this fails, the application then tries to access the SVG document using getSVGDocument(). Once you have access to the SVG document object, you can use the same DOM methods you would use with elements native to the web page.

Example 9-4 shows the second way to add SVG to a web page, and how to access the SVG element(s) from script in HTML.

Example 9-4. Accessing SVG in an object element from script

```
<!DOCTYPE html>
<head>
<title>SVG in Object</title>
<meta charset="utf-8" />
</head>
<body>
<object id="object" data="rect.svg"
style="padding: 20px; width: 600px; height: 600px">
<p>No SVG support</p>
</object>
<script type="text/javascript">

  var object = document.getElementById("object");
  object.onload=function() {
      var svgdoc;

      // get access to the SVG document object
      try {

          svgdoc = object.contentDocument;
      } catch(e) {
        try {

            svgdoc = object.getSVGDocument();

          } catch (e) {
            alert("SVG in object not supported in your environment");
          }
      }

      if (!svgdoc) return;
      var r = svgdoc.rootElement;

      // get SVG element and modify
      var square = svgdoc.getElementById('square');
      square.onclick = function() {

          var width = parseFloat(square.getAttribute("width"));
          width-=50;
          square.setAttribute("width",width);
          var color = square.getAttribute("fill");
          if (color == "blue") {
              square.setAttribute("fill","yellow");
```

```
                square.setAttribute("stroke","green");
        } else {
                square.setAttribute("fill","blue");
                square.setAttribute("stroke","red");
        }
    }
  }
</script>

</body>
```

In addition to the different approaches to get the SVG document, you also have to handle browser differences in how the onload event handler works. Firefox and Opera fire the onload event handler for the window after all the document contents have loaded, including the SVG in the object element. However, Safari and Chrome, probably because of the shared core, fire the window.onload event handler before the SVG has finished loading.

In the example code, the object is accessed in script after it has loaded; the object.on load event handler is then accessed to get the SVG document and assigned the function to the onclick event handler.

9.4. Integrating SVG and the Canvas Element in HTML

Problem

You want to use the canvas element and SVG together within a web page.

Solution

One option is to embed both the SVG and the canvas element directly into the HTML page, and then access the canvas element from script within SVG:

```
<!DOCTYPE html>
<head>
<title>Canvas and SVG</title>
<meta charset="utf-8" />
</head>
<body>
<canvas id="myCanvas" width="400px" height="100px">
    <p>canvas item alternative content</p>
</canvas>

  <svg id="svgelem" height="400">
    <title>SVG Circle</title>
    <script type="text/javascript">
      window.onload = function () {
          var context =
```

```
        document.getElementById("myCanvas").getContext('2d');

        context.fillStyle = 'rgba(0,200,0,0.7)';
        context.fillRect(0,0,100,100);
      };
    </script>
    <circle id="redcircle" cx="100" cy="100" r="100" fill="red" stroke="#000" />
  </svg>
</body>
```

Or you can embed the canvas element as a foreign object directly in the SVG:

```
<!DOCTYPE html>
<html>
<head>
<title>Accessing Inline SVG</title>
<meta charset="utf-8">
</head>
<body>
<svg id="svgelem" height="400" width="600">
   <script type="text/javascript">
      window.onload = function () {
         var context2 = document.getElementById("thisCanvas").getContext('2d');

         context2.fillStyle = "#ff0000";
         context2.fillRect(0,0,200,200);
       };
   </script>

   <foreignObject width="300" height="150">
      <canvas width="300" height="150" id="thisCanvas">
         alternate content for browsers that do not support Canvas
      </canvas>
   </foreignObject>
   <circle id="redcircle" cx="300" cy="100" r="100" fill="red" stroke="#000" />
  </svg>
</body>
</html>
```

Discussion

When the SVG element is embedded into the current web page, you can access HTML elements from within the SVG. However, you can also embed elements directly in SVG, using the SVG foreignObject element. This element allows us to embed XHTML, MathML, RDF, or any other XML-based syntax.

 At the time this was written, IE didn't support foreignObject in SVG.

In both solutions, I was able to use getElementById(). However, if I want to manipulate the elements using other methods, such as getElementsByTagName(), I have to be careful about which version of the method I use. For instance, I can use getElementsByTag Name() for the outer canvas element, but I would need to use the namespace version of the method, getElementsByTagNameNS, if the contained object is XML, such as RDF/XML. Because the embedded object in the solution is HTML5, a namespace wasn't necessary.

Once you have the canvas context, use the element like you would from script within HTML: add rectangles, draw paths, create arcs, and so on.

Extra: Canvas? Or SVG?

Why would you use Canvas over SVG, or SVG over Canvas? The canvas element is faster in frame-type animations. With each animation, the browser only needs to redraw the changed pixels, not re-create the entire scene. However, the advantage you get with the canvas element animation lessen when you have to support a variety of screen sizes, from smartphone to large monitor. SVG scales beautifully.

Another advantage to SVG is that it figures in rich data visualizations with the assistance of powerful libraries, covered in Chapter 17. But then, Canvas is used with 3D systems, such as WebGL, also covered in Chapter 17.

But why choose one over the other? One use of SVG and Canvas together is to provide a fallback for the canvas element: the SVG writes to the DOM and persists even if JavaScript is turned off, while the canvas element does not.

9.5. Running a Routine When an Audio File Begins Playing

Problem

You want to provide an audio file and then pop up a question or other information when the audio file begins or ends playing.

Solution

Use the HTML5 audio element:

```
<audio id="meadow" controls>
   <source src="meadow.mp3" type="audio/mpeg3"/>
   <source src="meadow.ogg" type="audio/ogg" />
   <source src="meadow.wav" type="audio/wav" />
   <p><a href="meadow.wav">Meadow sounds</a></p>
</audio>
```

and capture either its play event (playback has begun) or ended event (playback has finished):

```
var meadow = document.getElementById("meadow");
meadow.addEventListener("ended", aboutAudio);
```

then display the information:

```
function aboutAudio() {
  var info = 'This audio file is a recording from Shaw Nature Reserve';
  var txt = document.createTextNode(info);
  var div = document.createElement("div");
  div.appendChild(txt);
  document.body.appendChild(div);
}
```

Discussion

HTML5 added two media elements: audio and video. These simple-to-use controls provide a way to play audio and video files without having to use Flash.

In the solution, the audio element's controls Boolean attribute is set, so the controls are displayed. The element has three source children elements, providing support for three different types of audio files: WAV, MP3, and Ogg Vorbis. The use of the source element allows different browsers to find the format (codec) that they support. For the example, the browser support is:

- Firefox accepts either the WAV or Ogg Vorbis. It also accepts MP3, but uses the underlying operating system support to do so, rather than providing its own.
- Opera supports WAV and Ogg Vorbis, but not MP3.
- Chrome supports WAV, MP3, and Ogg Vorbis.
- Safari supports MP3 and WAV.
- IE supports the MP3.

A link to the WAV file is provided as a fallback, which means people using browsers that don't support audio can still access the sound file. I could have also provided an object element, or other fallback content.

 The Mozilla Developer Network has a comprehensive table (*http://mzl.la/1DS3rPL*) with audio and video codec support for the various browsers.

The media elements come with a set of methods to control the playback, as well as events that can be triggered when the event occurs. In the solution, the ended event is captured and assigned the event handler `aboutAudio()`, which displays a message about the file after the playback is finished. Notice that though the code is using a DOM Level 0 event handler with the window load event, it's using DOM Level 2 event handling with the `audio` element. Browser support is erratic with this event handler, so I strongly recommend you use `addEventListener()`. However, `onended` does seem to work without problems when used directly in the element:

```
<audio id="meadow" src="meadow.wav" controls onended="alert('All done')">
  <p><a href="meadow.wav">Meadow sounds</a></p>
</audio>
```

It's interesting to see the appearance of the elements in all of the browsers that currently support them. There is no standard look, so each browser provides its own interpretation. You can control the appearance by providing your own playback controls and using your own elements/CSS/SVG/Canvas to supply the decoration.

See Also

See Recipe 9.6 for a demonstration of using the playback methods and providing alternative visual representations for the new media elements, as well as providing a different form of fallback.

9.6. Controlling Video from JavaScript with the video Element

Problem

You want to embed video in your web page, without using Flash. You also want a consistent look for the video control, regardless of browser and operating system.

Solution

Use the HTML5 `video` element:

```
<video id="meadow" poster="purples.jpg" >
  <source src="meadow.m4v" type="video/mp4"/>
  <source src="meadow.ogv" type="video/ogg" />
</video>
```

You can provide controls for it via JavaScript, as shown in Example 9-5. Buttons are used to provide the video control, and text in a `div` element is used to provide feedback on time during the playback.

Example 9-5. Providing a custom control for the HTML5 video element

```
<!DOCTYPE html>
<head>
<title>Meadow Video</title>
<script>
<style>
  video {
    border: 1px solid black;
  }
</style>

window.onload=function() {

  // events for buttons
  document.getElementById("start").addEventListener("click",startPlayback);
  document.getElementById("stop").addEventListener("click",stopPlayback);
  document.getElementById("pause").addEventListener("click",pausePlayback);

  // setup for video playback
  var meadow = document.getElementById("meadow");
  meadow.addEventListener("timeupdate",reportProgress);

  // video fallback
  var detect = document.createElement("video");
  if (!detect.canPlayType) {
    document.getElementById("controls").style.display="none";
  }
}

// start video, enable stop and pause
// disable play
function startPlayback() {
  var meadow = document.getElementById("meadow");
  meadow.play();
  document.getElementById("pause").disabled=false;
  document.getElementById("stop").disabled=false;
  this.disabled=true;
}

// pause video, enable start, disable stop
// disable pause
function pausePlayback() {
  document.getElementById("meadow").pause();
  this.disabled=true;
  document.getElementById("start").disabled=false;
  document.getElementById("stop").disabled=true;
}

// stop video, return to zero time
// enable play, disable pause and stop
function stopPlayback() {
  var meadow = document.getElementById("meadow");
```

```
    meadow.pause();
    meadow.currentTime=0;
    document.getElementById("start").disabled=false;
    document.getElementById("pause").disabled=true;
    this.disabled=true;
}

// for every time divisible by 5, output feedback
function reportProgress() {
    var time = Math.round(this.currentTime);
    var div = document.getElementById("feedback");
    div.innerHTML = time + " seconds";
}

</script>

</head>
<body>
<video id="meadow" poster="purples.jpg" >
    <source src="meadow.m4v" type="video/mp4"/>
    <source src="meadow.ogv" type="video/ogg" />
</video>
<div id="feedback"></div>
<div id="controls">
<button id="start">Play</button>
<button id="stop">Stop</button>
<button id="pause">Pause</button>
</controls>
</body>
```

Discussion

The new HTML5 video element, as with the HTML5 audio element, can be controlled with its own built-in controls, or you can provide your own, as shown in Example 9-5. The media elements support the following methods:

- play: Starts playing the video
- pause: Pauses the video
- load: Preloads the video without starting play
- canPlayType: Tests if the user agent supports the video type

The media elements don't support a stop method, so the code emulates one by pausing video play and then setting the video's currentTime attribute to 0, which basically resets the play start time.

I also used currentTime to print out the video time, using Math.round to round the time to the nearest second, as shown in Figure 9-4.

Figure 9-4. Playing a video using the video control, displaying the number of seconds of video

The video control is providing two different video codecs: H.264 (*.mp4*), and Ogg Theora (*.ogv*). Firefox, Opera, and Chrome support Ogg Theora, but Safari and IE only support the H.264-formatted video. However, by providing both types, the video works in all of the browsers that support the video element.

The video and audio controls are inherently keyboard-accessible. If you do replace the controls, you'll want to provide accessibility information with your replacements. The video control doesn't have built-in captioning, but work is underway to provide the API for captioning.

The video playback functionality demonstrated in the solution works, as is, with video that isn't encrypted. If the video (or audio) file is encrypted, considerably more effort is necessary so that the video plays, making use of the new HTML 5.1 W3C Encrypted Media Extensions (EME).

The W3C Encrypted Media Extensions working draft can be seen at *http://www.w3.org/TR/encrypted-media/*. EME is implemented in certain versions of IE11 (*http://bit.ly/1DS5umQ*), Chrome, and Opera, and Mozilla has announced implementation in Firefox.

9.7. Adding Filter Effects to Video via Canvas

Problem

You're interested in not only playing video in your web page but also playing modified versions of the video, such as one that has been grayscaled, or manipulated in some way.

Solution

Use HTML5 video with the Canvas element, playing the video to a *scratch* Canvas element:

```
function drawVideo() {
    var videoObj = document.getElementById("videoobj");

    // if not playing, quit
    if (videoObj.paused || videoObj.ended) return false;

    // draw video on canvas
    var canvasObj = document.getElementById("canvasobj");
    var ctx = canvasObj.getContext("2d");
    ctx.drawImage(videoObj,0,0,480,270);

    ...
    setTimeout(drawVideo,20);
}
```

You can then add the ability to capture the image data using the Canvas element's `getImageData()`, modify the image data with whatever filter you want, and then play the image data to a second, visible Canvas element:

```
var pData = ctx.getImageData(0,0,480,270);

// grayscale it and set to display canvas
pData = grayScale(pData);
ctx2.putImageData(pData,0,0);
```

Discussion

The best thing about all the new HTML5 media elements is how you can use them together. Using video and Canvas, you can not only provide custom controls, you can also provide custom video filters, too.

The new CSS filter capability can be used with the Video element to create any variation of blurred, or colored, or other effect. However, not all browsers currently support it—only the Webkit-based browsers, such as Chrome, Opera, and Safari. Firefox does have plans to implement the filters in the future. The W3C specification for the filters can be found at *http://www.w3.org/TR/filter-effects-1/*.

To play a video in a Canvas element, we'll need to add both elements to the web page:

```
<video id="videoobj" controls width="480" height="270">
  <source src="videofile.mp4" type="video/mp4" />
  <source src="videofile.webm" type="video/webm" />
</video>
<canvas id="canvasobj" width="480" height="270"></canvas>
```

Both the canvas and video elements are the same width and height.

To draw the video onto the canvas, we're going to use the Canvas drawImage(). There are several variations of parameters we could use with this method, but the signature we're interested in is the following:

```
void drawImage(
  in nsIDOMElement image,
  in float dx,
  in float dy,
  in float dw,
  in float dh
);
```

These parameters are:

- image: A reference to a Canvas element, an img element, or a Video element
- dx: *x* coordinate of the top-left corner of the source image
- dy: *y* coordinate of the top-left corner of the source image
- dw: Width of the source image (can be scaled)
- dh: Height of the source image (can be scaled)

Example 9-6 demonstrates a first pass at an application to modify the video playing the Canvas element. It just takes what's showing in the video and plays it, as is, in the Canvas. The application uses setTimeout() to test whether the video is still playing and grabs the video every 20 milliseconds, which is fast enough to provide smooth playback for human perceptions. There is a timeupdate event handler for the Video element, but it's only invoked every 200 milliseconds (per the W3C specification on the media elements), which is way too slow for our purposes.

Example 9-6. A first cut at drawing video data to a canvas element

```
<!DOCTYPE html>
<head>
<title>Play video in canvas</title>
    <meta charset="utf-8" />
    <script>
      window.onload=function() {
         document.getElementById("videoobj").
                addEventListener("timeupdate", drawVideo, false);
      }
      function drawVideo() {
        var videoObj = document.getElementById("videoobj");
        var canvasObj = document.getElementById("canvasobj");
        var ctx = canvasObj.getContext("2d");
        ctx.drawImage(videoObj,0,0);
        }
    </script>
</head>
<body>
    <video id="videoobj" controls width="480" height="270">
        <source src="videofile.mp4" type="video/mp4" />
        <source src="videofile.webm" type="video/webm" />
    </video>
    <canvas id="canvasobj" width="480" height="270"></canvas>
</body>
```

In the code, during each time out event, the video is tested to see if it's still playing before it's grabbed and displayed in the Canvas element. The application works in all modern browsers.

The next step is to modify the video data before it's streamed to the Canvas element. For the example, I'm going to do a crude modification of the original video to simulate how a person could perceive the video if they suffered from a form of color blindness known as *protanopia*. This type of color blindness is one of the most common, and those who have it can't perceive red light. I say "crude" because a much more accurate representation is so computationally expensive that the playback visibly stutters.

I used values from a web page (*http://bit.ly/1DS6lnB*) that's now on-ly accessible via the Internet Archive. I tested variations of the different color blind values against online tools and the accuracy is close enough to give a good approximation of what an individual experiences—without blowing the app up.

A more accurate JavaScript function to demonstrate color blindness is Color.vision.simulate (*http://bit.ly/1yHYOE2*). There are also on-line color blindness simulators; the two I tested are ASP.Net Color Blindness simulator (*http://bit.ly/1yHYQM8*) and the Etre Color Blindness Simulator (*http://bit.ly/1yHYR2L*). I took screenshots of the video at various points and then ran the comparison.

To modify the video playback, we need two things: the function to modify the data, and a *scratch* canvas object used to capture the video data, as it is, and then serve as our intermediate in the transformation. We need a scratch Canvas element because we're using the Canvas element's `getImageData()` to access the actual video data, and `putImageData()` to play the video data after it has been manipulated.

The `getImageData()` function returns an object consisting of three values: the width, the height, and the image data as a `Uint8ClampedArray` typed array.

The `getImageData()` method originally returned the data as a CanvasPixelArray. However, the folks at the W3C have deprecated CanvasPixelArray in favor of a `Uint8ClampedArray` typed array.

The canvas pixel data is sent to the filter, which does its conversion and then returns the data, as shown in Example 9-7.

Example 9-7. Video with applied color blind filter, playing side by side with original

```
<!DOCTYPE html>
<head>
<title>Protanopia</title>
  <meta charset="utf-8" />
  <script>

    // Protanopia filter
    function protanopia(pixels) {
      var d = pixels.data;
      for (var i=0; i<d.length; i+=4) {
        var r = d[i];
        var g = d[i+1];
        var b = d[i+2];

        //convert to an approximate protanopia value
```

```
            d[i] = 0.567*r + 0.433*g;
            d[i+1] = 0.558*r + 0.442*g;
            d[i+2] = 0.242*g + .758*b;
        }
      return pixels;
    }
    // event listeners
    window.onload=function() {
      document.getElementById("videoobj").
            addEventListener("play", drawVideo, false);
    }

    // draw the video
    function drawVideo() {
      var videoObj = document.getElementById("videoobj");

      // if not playing, quit
      if (videoObj.paused || videoObj.ended) return false;

      // create scratch canvas
      var canvasObj = document.getElementById("canvasobj");
      var bc = document.createElement("canvas");
      bc.width=480;
      bc.height=270;

      // get contexts for scratch and display canvases
      var ctx = canvasObj.getContext("2d");
      var ctx2 = bc.getContext("2d");

      // draw video on scratch and get its data
      ctx2.drawImage(videoObj, 0, 0, 480, 270);
      var pData = ctx2.getImageData(0,0,480,270);

      // grayscale it and set to display canvas
      pData = protanopia(pData);
      ctx.putImageData(pData,0,0);

      setTimeout(drawVideo,20);
    }
  </script>
</head>
<body>
  <video id="videoobj" controls width="480" height="270">
    <source src="videofile.mp4" type="video/mp4" />
    <source src="videofile.webm" type="video/webm" />
  </video>
  <canvas id="canvasobj" width="480" height="270"></canvas>
</body>
```

Figure 9-5 shows a screenshot of the filter in action with the video, "Big Buck Bunny," beloved by video developers everywhere for its generous Creative Commons license.

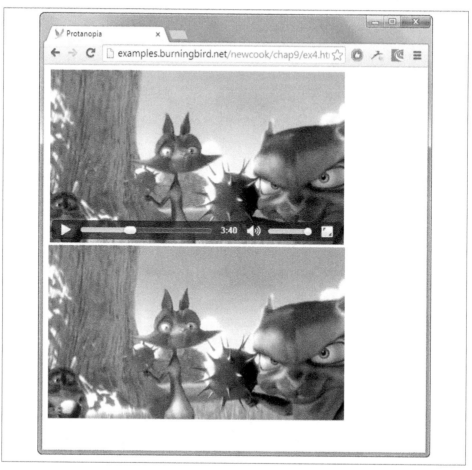

Figure 9-5. Screenshot of filter effect

## PART II

JavaScript, All Blown Up

The JavaScript in this section of the book breaks out of the boundaries of the browser, introduces new built-in objects, works with new and interesting forms of data, and encompasses complex frameworks. In this section, we learn not to reinvent the wheel, to embrace the mobile environment, and to integrate a plethora of new tools into our development effort.

## CHAPTER 10

The New ECMAScript Standard Objects

In Part I, we examined the objects that have been a part of JavaScript from the beginning: the global object (window in the browser), Object, String, Number, Boolean, Math, Date, Array, and Function. Beginning with ECMAScript 6, also known as *ECMAScript Next* and ES 6, we now have new constructs: Map, WeakMap, Set, WeakSet, Symbol, Class, Proxy, and Promise.

Though it's technically not an object, I also decided to include a discussion of let in this chapter. I wanted to demonstrate to you the difficulties with handling cross-browser differences for a new language construct, such as let, yield, const, and others, as compared to how we can handle the differences for objects.

For the most part, you can manage browser differences for object support using a poly-fill. I recommend using Paul Miller's ES 6 Shim (*https://github.com/paulmillr/es6-shim*). You can also use Google's Traceur, covered in Recipe 10.8.

If you're concerned about which browser or environment currently supports what objects, the following are a list of references that can help you discover this information:

- The ECMAScript 6 Compatibility Table (*http://kangax.github.io/compat-table/es6/*)
- Addy Osmani's "Tracking ECMAScript 6 Support" (*http://addyosmani.com/blog/tracking-es6-support/*)
- ECMAScript 6 Support in Mozilla (*http://mzl.la/1xN8JHB*)
- Microsoft's "What's New in JavaScript" (*http://bit.ly/1xN8KeN*)
- Chromium Dashboard: What We're Up To (*http://www.chromestatus.com/features*)

Even if you use a polyfill or other tool, you'll need to test your use of ES 6 features in *every* target browser if you plan on using them in production.

10.1. Using let in Your Browser Application

Problem

You're interested in using let in your browser application, but aren't sure which browsers support it (or other ECMAScript functionality), or what you need to do to get it to work.

Solution

Support for ECMAScript 6 functionality, such as let, can be difficult to determine, and may require setting flags, specifying JavaScript version numbers, or using specialized polyfills or other tools. Unfortunately, not all approaches are compatible across all the modern browsers. The support for let is a perfect example of fractured ES 6 support across browsers.

To use let in Firefox, you have to give a version number with the script tag:

```
<script type="application/javascript;version=1.7">
  if (true) {
    let i = 'testing let';
    console.log(i);
  }

  if (typeof i != 'undefined'){
    console.log(i);
  } else {
    console.log('undefined');
  }
</script>
```

In Firefox, the console output is what we would expect:

```
testing let
undefined
```

To get the same result in Internet Explorer 11, your HTML document *must* be HTML5, which means using the following DOCTYPE:

```
<!DOCTYPE html>
```

This puts IE 11 into *edge mode*, where many ES 6 features are supported. Unfortunately, IE 11 ignores any script block with a type of `application/javascript;version=1.7`, so you'll have to remove the `type` setting for the script to work.

The same applies to Chrome. Chrome supports `let` if you remove Firefox's peculiar use of `type` and if you enable the `chrome://flags/#enable-javascript-harmony` flag. In addition, you *must* also use *strict mode*, so the code needs to be modified to:

```
<script>

  'use strict';

  if (true) {
    let i = 'testing let';
    alert(i);
  }

  if (typeof i != 'undefined'){
    alert(i);
  } else {
    alert('undefined');
  }
</script>
```

This code snippet also works for IE, but not Firefox. The code also works in Opera if you enable the same Chrome Harmony flag (copy and paste the above flag URI into the location bar for Opera and click "Enable").

Safari doesn't, at this time, support `let`.

Discussion

The `let` keyword allows JavaScript developers to define block-level variables, rather than global variables or variables in a function block. An example is given in the solution, where the variable `i` is only available within the conditional block, but is `undefined` outside the block.

JavaScript developers have pushed for the concept of `let` longer than most additions to ECMAScript 6, but its use in production applications must be restricted because of the difficulty to support it, as was demonstrated in the solution. Yes, you can support it across browsers, but only when flags are set, and even then, Firefox doesn't currently support a syntax that works for Chrome, IE, and Opera, and Safari is missing, altogether.

 By the time you read this, Firefox may have dropped its versioning syntax.

The same holds for many of the ES 6 new language constructs: if the construct requires setting a browser flag, you have to assume your end user hasn't set it so you can't depend on it. This differs from supporting the new ES objects (covered in the rest of this chapter) because it's easier to emulate a new object using a polyfill, than it is to emulate a new language construct.

Even a translator-compiler (*transpiler*), such as Google's Traceur, can only convert let into var, because there is no current workaround for the concept of let. Running the solution code snippet in the Traceur REPL (read-evaluate-print) (*http://google.github.io/traceur-compiler/demo/repl.html#*) results in the following:

```
$traceurRuntime.ModuleStore.getAnonymousModule(function() {
  "use strict";
  'use strict';
  if (true) {
    var i = 'testing let';
    alert(i);
  }
  if (typeof i != 'undefined') {
    alert(i);
  } else {
    alert('undefined');
  }
  return {};
});
//# sourceURL=traceured.js
```

In this case, the workaround is worse than not having a workaround, because var does *not* result in the same behavior as the use of let. The resulting print-out for the Traceur version is:

```
testing let
testing let
```

The variable i is printed out twice, as it is defined in the code outside the conditional block—the variable is no longer scoped to the block.

See Also

Read more about Microsoft's Edge mode in Document Modes are Deprecated (*http://bit.ly/1xN9ujP*). Microsoft also provides a JavaScript compatibility table that lists Edge Mode support (*http://bit.ly/1xN9y33*).

To peek under the covers regarding let (and other new ES 6 language constructs) in Firefox, check out a related Bugzilla bug specific to the use of let (*http://mzl.la/1xN9BvX*). To go even deeper into the inner workings of the ES 6 specification, you might also want to explore the concept of *temporal dead zones* related to let and const, beginning with "Performance concern with let/const" (*http://bit.ly/1xN9z7e*).

Recipe 10.8 has more on incorporating Traceur into your browser apps. Using `let` in Node is covered in Recipe 11.4.

10.2. Creating a Collection of Non-Duplicated Values

Problem

You want to create a collection of unique values.

Solution

Use the new ECMAScript 6 Set object to create the collection:

```
var col1 = new Set();
col1.add("apple");
col1.add("oranges");
console.log(col1.size); // 2
```

Discussion

Before ECMAScript 6, the only object JavaScript provided for collections was the Array. It's been very useful, but has its limitations: one glaring example is lack of ability to enforce uniqueness of collection members without having to do some computationally expensive processing.

To ensure a unique value in an Array, before you add the new member, you'd have to see if it was already in the Array by checking it against all existing members. No amount of fancy new Array methods is going to make this simpler.

The Set handles uniqueness for us. If you try to add the same value multiple times, it's added the first time and the rest of the additions are just ignored:

```
col1.add("banana");
col1.add("banana"); // ignored
col1.add("banana"); // yup, still ignored
```

The Set also has a clean way of removing members, without having to use the `splice()` method:

```
col1.delete("banana"); // OK, all gone
```

To discover whether the Set has a specific value, use the `has()` method:

```
col1.has("banana"); // false, it was removed
col1.has("apple"); // true
```

You can also iterate through the members:

```
col1.forEach(function(value) {
  console.log(value);
});
```

as well as convert a Set to an Array using the new ES 6 *spread* operator:

```
var arr = [...col1];
console.log(arr[1]); // oranges
```

If the browser supports the spread operator, of course. The spread operator allows for expansion in place. Instead of specifying each member of the set when assigning to the new array, the spread operator performs a one-to-one assignment, until all members of the expanded object are exhausted. It can be used in array literals, as demonstrated in the code snippet, or it can be used with function arguments:

```
functionName(...iterableObj)
```

Returning to Set, you can also create a set from an array literal with the following syntax:

```
var col2 = new Set(['one','two','three']);
console.log(col2.size); // 3
```

And if you want to get rid of all the Set members, use `clear()`:

```
col1.clear();
console.log(col1.size); // 0
```

Unlike some other JavaScript functionality, the Set does not do any type coercion. If you add 5 and "5", both will be added and treated as two distinct Set members. Think of how *strict equality* works: the only time Set won't add a member is if they are strictly equal.

Advanced

A Set collection can consist of any number of object types, including objects. And that includes well-known objects, functions, even other Sets:

```
var mySet = new Set();

mySet.add(window);
mySet.add(function() { console.log("whoa");});

var mySet2 = new Set();
mySet2.add('test');
mySet2.add(5);
mySet2.add(true);

mySet.add(mySet2);

mySet.forEach(function(value) {
  console.log(value.toString());
});
```

The output from this code snippet is:

```
[object Window]
function () { console.log("whoa");}
[object Set]
```

There's also a variation of Set that accepts *only* objects, and that's WeakSet. The entire reason for this second object is that references to objects contained in the collection are *weakly held*. When there is no other reference to the object in the collection, it can be *garbage collected*. The advantage to using WeakSet is that it helps prevent memory leaks. However, because of their nature, you can't enumerate through the collection members with a WeakSet, like you can with Set.

10.3. Creating Unique Key/Value Pairs with Uniquely Different Keys

Problem

You want to create a set of key/value pairs, but not all of the keys are strings.

Solution

Use the new Map object:

```
var myMap = new Map();

myMap.set("value1", "this is value");
myMap.set(3, "another value");

myMap.set(NaN, "isn't this interesting");

myMap.set(window, "really now");

console.log(myMap.get("value1")); // this is a value
console.log(myMap.get(NaN)); // isn't this interesting
console.log(myMap.get(3)); // another value
console.log(myMap.get(window)); // really now
```

Discussion

Prior to ES 6, you could create key/value pairs by creating an Object using a specialized syntax (to avoid default values), and adding each key and value to the new object:

```
var newObj = Object.create(null, {
        prop1: {
            value: undefined,
            enumerable: true,
            writable: true,
            configurable: true
```

```
          },
          prop2: {
            value: undefined,
            enumerable: true,
            writable: true,
            configurable: true
          }
     });

newObj.prop1 = "first";
newObj.prop2 = "second";
newObj.prop3 = "third"; // added third prop

console.log(newObj.prop1); // first
console.log(newObj.prop2); // second
```

Using Object.create() with null as the first parameter ensures that the object doesn't inherit the Object prototype, and the only properties are those specifically added. If you didn't care about creating a completely clean object, you could also use an object literal:

```
var newObj = { prop1: "first", prop2: "second"};
```

One limitation with using objects as a way of mapping key/value pairs, other than having to ensure they're created without an existing prototype, is that keys are strings. Even when it seems as if our use of non-string values is acceptable:

```
newObj.NaN = 'hey, it works!';
```

What happens is the NaN is really converted into a string representation of NaN:

```
for (var prop in newObj) {
  console.log(prop); // NaN prints out as "NaN"
}
```

In addition, trying to assign a property such as a function, or a number, throws an error:

```
newObj.5 = 'no way';
```

```
newObj.function() {} = 'Seriously?';
```

However, functions, numbers, strings, objects...all of these are allowable with a Map, as demonstrated in the solution.

Use set() to add new key/value pairs, and delete() to remove those no longer needed:

```
myMap.set('mykey',100);
myMap.delete('mykey');
```

And use clear() to clear all collection members.

Unlike object properties, it's simple to discover how many key/value pairs a Map contains:

```
console.log(myMap.size); // 3
```

And you can easily traverse through both keys and values:

```
// iterating through both key an value
for (var [key, value] of myMap) {
  console.log(key + " = " + value);
}

// iterating through keys
for (var key of myMap.keys()) {
  console.log(key);
}

// iterating through values
for (var value of myMap.values()) {
  console.log(value);
}

// using forEach
myMap.forEach(function(value) {
  console.log(value);
});
```

All the traversals use *iterators*, except for forEach(). The first example uses an implicit entries() method that returns an object with an array of [key, value] pairs, allowing us to access both in the loop. The entries(), keys(), and values() function all return iterators, which also means we can use the following syntax with each:

```
var mapIter = myMap.keys();

console.log(mapIter.next().value); // "value1"
console.log(mapIter.next().value); // 3
console.log(mapIter.next().value); // NaN
```

 Iterators are discussed in more detail in Recipe 10.5.

You can also discover if a specific key is contained in a Map collection with has():

```
myMap.set(23,'value');
console.log(myMap.has(23)); // true
```

The solution demonstrates using NaN as a key value. As the Mozilla Developer Network entry on Map notes, while NaN is technically not equivalent to itself, when used as a key, it is equivalent:

```
myMap.set(NaN, 'nada');
```

```
var id = Number('not a number');

console.log(myMap.get(id)); // 'nada'
```

When all is said and done, though, you may want to just forgo using NaN as a key.

Advanced

As with Sets, Map keys and values can be objects, as well as scalar values. This includes the built-in objects, such as window. But the objects must be exactly equal—they can't be equivalent. In the following code snippet, two object literals, an array, and window are used to set members in the Map. The code tries to access the Array object's value using another equivalent array literal, but it doesn't work. Only when I use the exact same object (whether through the original variable, or a new one assigned the object), can the application access the value:

```
var b = {first: 'apple', second: 'pear'};
var c = {first: '5', second: '1'};
var d = [1,2,3,4];
var e = b;

var myMap = new Map();

myMap.set(b, 'first');
myMap.set(c, 'second');
myMap.set(d, 'array');
myMap.set(window,'global');

console.log(myMap.get(window)); // 'global'
console.log(myMap.get([1,2,3,4])); // undefined
console.log(myMap.get(d)); // 'array'
console.log(myMap.get(e)); // 'first'
```

There is also another new object, WeakMap, that functions in a similar manner to Map, except the collection only accepts object keys, and the object keys are held weakly, and therefore can be garbage collected. This means the WeakMap collection can't be enumerated, but does help prevent unexpected and unwanted memory leaks.

10.4. Creating Absolutely Unique Object Property Keys

Problem

You want to create unique object property keys that you're absolutely confident will remain unique and won't clash.

Solution

Use the ECMAScript 6 Symbol to create the unique key:

```
var uniqueId = Symbol();
var newObj = {};
newObj[uniqueId] = 'No two alike';
console.log(newObj[uniqueId]); // 'No two alike'
var uniqueId2 = Symbol('one');
var uniqueId3 = Symbol('one');
```

Discussion

Symbol is one of those new additions with ECMAScript 6 that you didn't know you needed until you saw it. We've become rather adept over the years at dealing with not having the capability to create unique identifiers. But being adept at working around a gap in a language isn't the same as having the language flexibly move to fill in the gap.

In the solution, a new identifier, uniqueId, is created to act as property identifier. Even if some other library wanted to use the exact same identifier, the two uses can't clash because the new identifier would just be returned when making the call to Symbol, even with the same optional string, as demonstrated with the second and third unique identifiers.

Symbol can also be used to create a set of enumerated values:

```
var green = Symbol();
var red = Symbol();

function switchLight(light) {
   if (light === green) {
      console.log("Turning light red");
      light = red;
   } else {
      console.log("Turning light green");
      light = green;
   }
   return light;
}

var light = green;

light = switchLight(light);
light = switchLight(light);
```

Instead of creating a number or string variables and then assigning values (and having to perform type checking as well as value checking when the value is evaluated), you can just create a new enumerated identifier.

Symbol is not like String or Number, in that you don't create a new instance of an object using new. You call it as a Function, and the new identifier is returned.

At the time this was written, only Chrome and Firefox Nightly supported Symbol. Exercise caution when using it.

10.5. Iterating Through Tasks Made Easy

Problem

You want to iterate over a set of tasks, but not all at the same time, and not all within the same expression.

Solution

Use an *iterator*, a new ES 6 protocol:

```
function makeIterator(array){
    var nextIndex = 0;
    return {
      next: function(){
          return nextIndex < array.length ?
              {value: array[nextIndex++], done: false} :
              {done: true};
      }
    }
}

var tasks = [{"task": function() {
                    console.log('hello from a');
                }},
             {"task": function() {
                    console.log('hello from b');
                }}];

var taskRunner = makeIterator(tasks);

taskRunner.next().value.task();
taskRunner.next().value.task();
```

It has the following results:

```
hello from a
hello from b
```

Discussion

The ES 6 *iterator* isn't a new object or construct, but an implementation strategy, or protocol. It's not a new syntax, like *spread*, or a new built-in, like Map. As long as an existing object can support some specific characteristics, it can be used as an iterator. In the solution, a function is called, and returns an iterator over an array of functions.

The makeIterator() function accepts an array as argument and returns an object with one property: next(). This property is used to iterate over the array contents, but iteration doesn't require a loop, and we don't have to maintain the state of each array access via incremented index variable.

Each successive next() returns the next value in the array. Because each array value is a function, it can then be invoked.

As an example, consider an online help system that walks the user through steps. As they complete each step, they hit the Enter key, and your code calls up the next data/function using next(). The application isn't blocking, as it would in a loop, and you don't have to maintain an array counter as a global variable.

When the list is complete, the done variable is set to true. So to make the implementation safer, you could use the following:

```
var taskRunner = makeIterator(tasks);

var task = taskRunner.next();
console.log(task);
if (!task.done) task.value.task();

task = taskRunner.next();
console.log(task);
if (!task.done) task.value.task();

task = taskRunner.next();
console.log(task);
if(!task.done) task.value;
```

which prints out:

```
{ value: { task: [Function] }, done: false }
hello from a
{ value: { task: [Function] }, done: false }
hello from b
{ done: true }
```

10.6. Creating Functions that Gracefully Yield

Problem

It's simple to break out of a function with return, but you want to be able to get back into the function at that point in the future, and then have it resume.

Solution

Use an ES 6 *generator function*:

```
function* taskRunner() {
   console.log('doing something');
   yield function () {
     console.log('hello from a');
   };
   console.log('doing something after a');
   yield function() {
     console.log('hello from b');
   }
   console.log('doing something after b');
}

var tasks = taskRunner();

tasks.next().value();
tasks.next().value();
tasks.next();
```

which results in:

```
doing something
hello from a
doing something after a
hello from b
doing something after b
```

Discussion

As already noted, it's easy to break out of a JavaScript function. Just type in a `return` statement and you're done. But what if you want to get back into the function at that exact point, and have it continue?

Couldn't be done, or at least not without embedded event handlers and callbacks and such, until ES 6 brought us *generators*: functions that can be entered and exited and that remember their state.

The solution demonstrates iterating over a set of tasks, each preceded by a `yield` statement with a function expression, though any expression works. Mozilla demonstrates a function generator by providing code for a neverending counter. In this case, the expression is a number incrementation:

```
function* idMaker(){
   var index = 0;
   while(true)
       yield index++;
}

var gen = idMaker();
```

```
console.log(gen.next().value); // 0
console.log(gen.next().value); // 1
console.log(gen.next().value); // 2
```

See Also

The Node community has been especially interested in generators because they can be used to prevent *callback hell*. Node is covered in Chapter 11, but you can read more about using generators in Node in Arunoda Susiripala's "JavaScript Generators and Preventing Callback Hell" (*http://bit.ly/1xNbvg6*).

Generators also figure heavily in Koa (*http://koajs.com/*), a lightweight alternative to the popular Express Node framework.

10.7. Implementing Just-in-Time Object Behavioral Modifications with Proxies

Problem

You want to attach behavior to an object, such as ensuring proper data types for values or log when an object changes, but you want to do so transparently.

Solution

Use the ES 6 Proxy to attach the desired behavior to the targeted action. To ensure that only given properties are set on an object and that a number property for an object is given an actual number, not a string or other value that can't be converted to a number, use a Proxy to test the value when it's set on the object:

```
function propChecker(target) {

    return Proxy(target, {
        set: function(target, property, value) {
            if (property == 'price') {
                if (typeof value != 'number') {
                    throw new TypeError("price is not a number");
                } else if (value <= 0) {
                    throw new RangeError("price must be greater than zero");
                }
            } else if (property != 'name') {
                throw new ReferenceError("property '" + property + "' not valid");
            }
            target[property] = value;
        }
    });
}
```

```
function Item() {

    return propChecker(this);
}

try {

    var keyboard = new Item();

    keyboard.name = "apple"; // OK

    keyboard.type = "red delicious"; // throws ReferenceError

    keyboard.price = "three dollars"; // throws TypeError

    keyboard.price = -1.00; // throws RangeError

} catch(err) {
    console.log(err.message);
}
```

Discussion

The Proxy object wraps an object and can be used to *trap* specific actions, and then provide additional or alternative behaviors based on both the actions and the object's data at the time of the action. The Mozilla Developer Network documentation for the object refers to the capability as *meta-programming API*.

In the solution, because we want to modify what happens when properties are set on the target object, and the target objects are themselves instances, the proxy of the object is returned, rather than the object directly, in the constructor. This is accomplished by passing this as the target object for the Proxy call, and then defining a handler function, propChecker, for the object.

 Proxy has undergone considerable change over time and is currently only implemented in Firefox. Note that some code examples for Proxy use Proxy.create(). This has been deprecated in favor of just calling Proxy.

In the handler, we're only interested in altering the semantics of the *set* operation. The function used to handle the operation is passed the target object, the property, and the new property value. In the function, the code tests to see if the property being set is price, and if so, it then checks to see if it's a Number. If it isn't, a TypeError is thrown. If it is, then the value is checked to make sure it's greater than zero. If it's not, then a RangeError is thrown.

Finally, the property is checked to see if it's name, instead. If it isn't, the final error, a ReferenceError, is thrown. If none of the error conditions is triggered, then the property is assigned the value.

Based on all of this, new instances of the target object can only have the two properties set, and the numeric property must be a number greater than zero.

 The solution is based, in part, on a code sample created by Nicholas Zakas (*http://bit.ly/1xNbPLF/*), and repurposed, with thanks.

Proxy supports a considerable number of traps, which I've listed in Table 10-1. The table lists the API trap, followed by the parameters the handler function expects, expected return value, and how it's triggered. These are all pulled directly from the Harmony documentation, as it's the most current listing at this time. The important point to keep in mind is that each of these is a *trap* that you can trigger and redefine the semantics of.

Table 10-1. Proxy traps

Proxy trap	Function parameters	Expected return value	How the trap is triggered
getOwnPropertyDescriptor	target, name	desc or undefined	Object.getOwnPropertyDescriptor(proxy,name)
getOwnPropertyNames	target	string	Object.getOwnPropertyNames(proxy)
getPrototypeOf	target	any	Object.getPrototypeOf(proxy)
defineProperty	target, name, desc	boolean	Object.defineProperty(proxy,name,desc)
deleteProperty	target, name	boolean	Object.deleteProperty(proxy,name)
freeze	target	boolean	Object.freeze(target)
seal	target	boolean	Object.seal(target)
preventExtensions	target	boolean	Object.preventExtensions(proxy)
isFrozen	target	boolean	Object.isFrozen(proxy)
isSealed	target	boolean	Object.isSealed(proxy)
isExtensible	target	boolean	Object.isExtensible(proxy)
has	target, name	boolean	name in proxy
hasOwn	target, name	boolean	({}).hasOwnProperty.call(proxy,name)
get	target, name, receiver	any	receiver[name]
set	target, name, value, receiver	boolean	receiver[name] = val
enumerator	target	iterator	for (name in proxy) (iterator should yield all enumerable own and inherited properties)

Proxy trap	Function parameters	Expected return value	How the trap is triggered
keys	target	string	Object.keys(proxy) (return array of enumerable own properties only)
apply	target, thisArg, args	any	proxy(...args)
construct	target, args	any	new proxy(...args)

Proxies can also wrap JavaScript built-in objects, such as Arrays, or even the Date object. In the following code, a proxy is used to redefine the semantics of what happens when the code accesses an array. The get passes the target, name, and receiver to the proxy handling function. The value of the array at the given index is checked and if it's a value of zero (0), a value of false is returned; otherwise, a value of true is returned:

```
var handler = {
    get: function(arry, indx){
      if (arry[indx] === 0) {
        return false;
      } else {
        return true;
      }

    }
};

var arr = [1,0,6,1,1,0];
var a = new Proxy(arr, handler);

console.log(a[2]); // true
console.log(a[0]); // true
console.log(a[1]); // false
```

The array value at an index of 2 is not zero, so true is returned. The same is true for the value at an index of zero. However, the value at the index of 1 is zero, so false is returned.

This behavior holds anytime this array proxy is accessed.

Object properties can be accessed as array elements, so we can't always assume that the index value is numeric. However, the accuracy of the proxy handler in this case is the same: if the value at the given index is exactly equivalent to a numeric value of zero (0), false is returned; otherwise, true is returned.

10.8. Creating a True Class and Extending It (with a Little Help from Traceur)

Problem

JavaScript's ability to emulate a class using functions and the `prototype` is all well and good, but you want a more conventional class.

Solution

Use the ES 6 *class*.

The class is created with the `class` keyword, providing a constructor to instantiate the object. You can then include additional functionality to suit your needs. To extend the class, use the `extends` keyword, and in the subclass's constructor, invoke the super class constructor. You'll need to do the same within any function that's shared in both classes:

```
class Book {
    constructor(title, author, pubdate) {
      this.title = title;
      this.author = author;
      this.pubdate = pubdate;
    }
    getBook() {
      return this.author + " published " + this.title + " in " + this.pubdate;
    }
}

class TypedBook extends Book {
    constructor(title, author, pubdate, type) {
      super.constructor(title, author, pubdate);
      this.type = type;
    }
    getBook() {
      return super.getBook() + " - category: " + this.type;
    }
    getType() {
      return this.type;
    }
}

var bookA = new TypedBook("Winning Small", "Sally Author", 2012, "history");
console.log(bookA.getBook());
// Sally Author published Winning Small in 2012 - category: history
console.log(bookA.getType()); // history
```

Discussion

The new class functionality in ECMAScript 6 is actually quite clean, and relatively simple to understand. As the solution demonstrates, all you need to do is define the superclass, provide a constructor() and whatever additional functionality you want, and then define any subclasses. The important point to remember is to invoke the superclass functions in the constructor and in any subclass functions shared between both.

The tricky part is trying the class functionality out before it's implemented in the browsers. At the time this was written, no browser had implemented the class functionality. Instead, I used Google Traceur to test out the code.

If you've not used Traceur previously, you'll need to include a reference to the main Traceur JavaScript file, and to the associated Bootstrap script file that triggers the Traceur compile that generates the code necessary to make the functionality work. You can download both files, or link directly to the Google Code files:

```
<script src="https://google.github.io/traceur-compiler/bin/traceur.js">
</script>
<script src="https://google.github.io/traceur-compiler/src/bootstrap.js">
</script>
```

If you also want to take advantage of the ES 6 experimental features, add the following script block:

```
<script>
      traceur.options.experimental = true;
</script>
```

Next, include the class JavaScript in another script block, but instead of using text/javascript for type, you must use module in order to trigger the Traceur functionality. Example 10-1 has a complete page with all that's necessary to get the classes to work.

Example 10-1. Using Traceur to emulate the ECMAScript 6 class

```
<!DOCTYPE html>
<html>
<head>
  <meta charset="utf-8">
  <title>ECMAScript 6 class</title>
<script src="https://google.github.io/traceur-compiler/bin/traceur.js"></script>
<script src="https://google.github.io/traceur-compiler/src/bootstrap.js"></script>
</head>
<body>
<script type="module">

  class Book {
    constructor(title, author, pubdate) {
      this.title = title;
      this.author = author;
      this.pubdate = pubdate;
```

```
      }
    getBook() {
      return this.author + " published " + this.title + " in " + this.pubdate;
    }
  }


  class TypedBook extends Book {
      constructor(title, author, pubdate, type) {
        super.constructor(title, author, pubdate);
        this.type = type;
      }
      getBook() {
        return super.getBook() + " - category: " + this.type;
      }

      getType() {
        return this.type;
      }
  }

  var bookA = new TypedBook("Winning Small", "Sally Author", 2012, "history");

  // Sally Author published Winning Small in 2012 - category: history
  console.log(bookA.getBook());

  // history
  console.log(bookA.getType());
</script>
</body>
</html>
```

To better understand what Traceur does to your code, you can copy and paste just the script into the Traceur REPL (read-evaluate-print) tool (*http://google.github.io/traceur-compiler/demo/repl.html#*). The results for the class code are as follows:

```
$traceurRuntime.ModuleStore.getAnonymousModule(function() {
  "use strict";
  var Book = function Book(title, author, pubdate) {
    this.title = title;
    this.author = author;
    this.pubdate = pubdate;
  };
  ($traceurRuntime.createClass)(Book, {getBook: function() {
      return this.author + " published " + this.title + " in " + this.pubdate;
    }}, {});
  var TypedBook = function TypedBook(title, author, pubdate, type) {
    $traceurRuntime.superCall(this, $TypedBook.prototype, "constructor",
    [title, author, pubdate]);
    this.type = type;
  };
  var $TypedBook = TypedBook;
```

```
($traceurRuntime.createClass)(TypedBook, {
  getBook: function() {
    return
    $traceurRuntime.superCall(this, $TypedBook.prototype, "getBook", []) +
    " - category: " + this.type;
  },
  getType: function() {
    return this.type;
  }
}, {}, Book);
var bookA = new TypedBook("Winning Small", "Sally Author", 2012, "history");
console.log(bookA.getBook());
console.log(bookA.getType());
return {};
});
//# sourceURL=traceured.js
```

In many cases, the resulting behavior of the new ES 6 code and the compiled alternative are equivalent, but as covered earlier in the chapter, in Recipe 10.1, such a happy result isn't guaranteed.

10.9. Using Promises for Efficient Asynchronous Processing

Problem

You want to have your code do something based on the success or failure of an asynchronous operation.

Solution

One option is to use the new native Promise object. A classic use for Promise in a client application is to use it with an Ajax call:

```
<!DOCTYPE html>
<html lang="en">
  <head>
    <meta charset="utf-8">
    <title>Promises</title>
    <script>
      var test = new Promise(function(resolve, reject) {
        var req = new XMLHttpRequest();

        req.open('GET', 'http://examples.burningbird.net:8124');
        req.onload = function () {
          if (req.status == 200) {
            resolve(req.response);
          } else {
            reject(req.statusText);
```

```
          }
        };

        req.onerror = function() {
          reject("network error");
        };

        req.send();
      });

    test.then(
        function(response) {
          console.log("Response is ", response);
        }, function (error) {
          console.error("Request failed: ", error);
        });
    </script>
  </head>
  <body>
  </body>
</html>
```

Discussion

In the solution, a Promise is created and assigned to a variable. The Promise encapsulates an Ajax call to a server application. Instead of assigning a function name to the XMLHttpRequest's onload event handler, the function is defined within the Promise, so it has access to the resolve() and reject() functions, passed as parameters to the Promise.

If the Ajax request is successful, the resolve() Promise function is called; otherwise, the reject() function is called.

Once the Promise has been defined, it's invoked by chaining the Promise's then() function call to the variable. The first parameter to then() is the function that handles a successful event; the second is a function handling an unsuccessful event.

If you compare the solution to the typical Ajax application, such as the one demonstrated in Example 8-2 in Chapter 8, you'll notice one missing component: no callback. There is no assignment of a traditional callback function to onreadystatechange:

```
xmlRequest.onreadystatechange = getData;
```

There is no testing for HTTP status or errors. Instead, an ES 6 promise is used with the HTTP request, with a status of 200 *resolving* the promise, sending the HTTP response to the resolving function, and anything else *rejecting* the promise, with HTTP status Text sent to the function.

The E6 Promise allows us to assign handlers to the two possible states of a pending request: resolved or rejected. The Promise, and the contained HTTP request, is invoked with then( ), with two parameters: the resolving function, and the rejecting function.

In the earlier incarnations of Node, the developers originally intended to use the concept of a *promise* to provide asynchronous access, rather than the last argument callback that exists today. I believe this was a good decision, though many folks disagreed with it. I feel the callback is more intuitively obvious solution, but those that disagree state that the callback concept fails in more complex situations, where nested callbacks cause additional complexity.

 There are solutions to complex, nested callbacks in Node, as I detail in Recipe 11.8.

The interest in promises persisted and now their implementation is being incorporated into existing and future versions of JavaScript.

See Also

Marc Harter discusses using generators and promises with Node application in "Managing Node.js Callback Hell with Promises, Generators and Other Approaches" (*http://bit.ly/1xNcL2Cs/*). James Coglan wrote a thoughtful piece on why Node's callback choice was in error in "Callbacks are imperative, promises are functional: Node's biggest missed opportunity" (*http://bit.ly/1xNcNHZ*).

A variation of the solution that creates a reusable function utilizing a Promise for an Ajax call is discussed in HTML5 Rocks article "JavaScript Promises" (*http://www.html5rocks.com/en/tutorials/es6/promises/*) by Jake Archibald. Note there is limited browser support for the Promise at this time, but the HTML5 Rocks article lists out various polyfills you can use to achieve the same effect in all browsers.

## CHAPTER 11

Node: JavaScript on the Server

The dividing line between "old" and "new" JavaScript occurred when Node.js (referred to primarily as just Node) was released to the world. Yes, the ability to dynamically modify page elements was an essential milestone, as was the emphasis on establishing a path forward to new versions of ECMAScript, but it was Node that really made us look at JavaScript in a whole new way. And it's a way I like—I'm a big fan of Node and server-side JavaScript development.

 I won't even attempt to cover all there is to know about Node on an introductory level in one chapter, so I'm focusing primarily on the interesting bits for the relative newbie. For more in-depth coverage, I'm going to toot my own horn and recommend my book, *Learning Node* (O'Reilly).

At a minimum, this chapter does expect that you have Node installed in whatever environment you wish, and are ready to jump into the solution examples.

11.1. Responding to a Simple Browser Request

Problem

You want to create a Node application that can respond to a very basic browser request.

Solution

Use the built-in Node HTTP server to respond to requests:

```
// load http module
var http = require('http');

// create http server
```

```
http.createServer(function (req, res) {

  // content header
  res.writeHead(200, {'content-type': 'text/plain'});

  // write message and signal communication is complete
  res.end("Hello, World!\n");
}).listen(8124);

console.log('Server running on 8124/');
```

Discussion

The simple text message web server response to a browser request is the "Hello World" application for Node. It demonstrates not only how a Node application functions, but how you can communicate with it using a fairly traditional communication method: requesting a web resource.

Starting from the top, the first line of the solution loads the http module using Node's require() function. This instructs Node's modular system to load a specific library resource for use in the application—a process I'll cover in detail in Chapter 12. The http module is one of the many that comes, by default, with a Node installation.

Next, an HTTP server is created using http.createServer(), passing in an anonymous function, known as the RequestListener with two parameters. Node attaches this function as an event handler for every server request. The two parameters are *request* and *response*. The request is an instance of the http.IncomingMessage object and the response is an instance of the http.ServerResponse object.

The http.ServerResponse is used to respond to the web request. The http.Incoming Message object contains information about the request, such as the request URL. If you need to get specific pieces of information from the URL (e.g., query string parameters), you can use the Node url utility module to parse the string. Example 11-1 demonstrates how the query string can be used to return a more custom message to the browser.

Example 11-1. Parsing out query string data

```
// load http module
var http = require('http');

// create http server
http.createServer(function (req, res) {

  // get query string and parameters
  var query = require('url').parse(req.url,true).query;

  // content header
  res.writeHead(200, {'content-type': 'text/plain'});
```

```
// write message and signal communication is complete
var name = query.first ? query.first : "World";

  res.end("Hello, " + name + "!\n");
}).listen(8124);

console.log('Server running on 8124/');
```

A URL like the following:

```
http://shelleystoybox.com:8124/?first=Reader
```

results in a web page that reads "Hello, Reader!"

Notice in the application that I used `require()` in the code, and chained methods directly on the returned module object. If you're using an object multiple times, it makes sense to assign it a variable at the top of the application. However, if you're only using the module object once, it can be more efficient to just load the object in place, and then call the methods directly on it. In the code, the `url` module object has a `parse()` method that parses out the URL, returning various components of it (`href`, `protocol`, `host`, etc.). If you pass `true` as the second argument, the string is also parsed by another module, `querystring`, which returns the query string as an object with each parameter as an object property, rather than just returning a string.

In both the solution and in Example 11-1, a text message is returned as page output, using the `http.ServerResponse end()` method. I could also have written the message out using `write()`, and then called `end()`:

```
  res.write("Hello, " + name + "!\n");
  res.end();
```

The important takeaway from either approach is you *must* call the response `end()` method after all the headers and response body have been sent.

Chained to the end of the `createServer()` function call is another function call, this time to `listen()`, passing in the port number for the server to listen in on. This port number is also an especially important component of the application.

Traditionally, port 80 is the default port for most web servers (that aren't using HTTPS, which has a default port of 443). By using port 80, requests for the web resource don't need to specify a port when requesting the service's URL. However, port 80 is also the default port used by our more traditional web server, Apache. If you try to run the Node service on the same port that Apache is using, your application will fail. The Node application either must be standalone on the server, or run off a different port.

I cover how to run both Node and Apache seemingly on port 80 at the same time in Recipe 11.10.

You can also specify an IP address (host) in addition to the port. Doing this ensures that people make the request to a specific host, as well as port. Not providing the host means the application will listen for the request for any IP address associated with the server. You can also specify a domain name, and Node resolves the host.

There are other arguments for the methods demonstrated, and a host of other methods, but this will get you started. Refer to the Node documentation for more information.

See Also

Node documentation can be found at *http://nodejs.org/api/*.

11.2. Serving Up Formatted Data

Problem

Instead of serving up a web page or sending plain text, you want to return formatted data, such as XML, to the browser.

Solution

Use Node module(s) to help format the data. For example, if you want to return XML, you can use a module to create the formatted data:

```
var XMLWriter = require('xml-writer');

var xw = new XMLWriter;

// start doc and root element
xw.startDocument().startElement("resources");

// resource
xw.startElement("resource");
xw.writeElement("title","Ecma-262 Edition 6");
xw.writeElement("url","http://wiki.ecmascript.org/doku.php?id=harmony:specific
ation_drafts");

// end resource
xw.endElement();
```

```
// end resources
xw.endElement();
```

Then create the appropriate header to go with the data, and return the data to the browser:

```
// end resources
xw.endElement();

res.writeHeader(200, {"Content-Type": "application/xml", "Access-Control-Allow
-Origin": "*"});
res.end(xw.toString(),"utf8");
```

Discussion

Web servers frequently serve up static or server-side generated resources, but just as frequently, what's returned to the browser is formatted data that's then processed in the web page before display.

In Chapter 8, in Recipe 8.2 we examined one use of data formatted as XML that's generated by a Node application on the server and then processed using the DOM API in the browser. Parts of the server application have been excerpted out for the solution.

There are two key elements to generating and returning formatted data. The first is to make use of whatever Node library to simplify the generation of the data, and the second is to make sure that the header data sent with the data is appropriate for the data.

In the solution, the `xml-writer` module is used to assist us in creating proper XML. This isn't one of the modules installed with Node by default, so we have to install it using npm, the Node Package Manager:

```
npm install xml-writer
```

This installs the `xml-writer` module in the local project directory, in the /node-modules subdirectory. To install the module globally, which makes it available for all projects, use:

```
npm install xml-writer -g
```

Then it's just a simple matter of creating a new XML document, a root element, and then each resource element, as demonstrated in the solution. It's true, we could just build the XML string ourselves, but that's a pain. And it's too easy to make mistakes that are then hard to discover. One of the best things about Node is the enormous number of modules available to do most anything we can think of. Not only do we not have to write the code ourselves, but most of the modules have been thoroughly tested and actively maintained.

It's important to understand that not all Node modules are actively maintained. When you look at a module in GitHub, check when it was last updated, and whether there are any old, unresolved issues. You may not want to use a module that's no longer being actively updated. However, if you do like a module that's not being actively maintained, you can consider forking it and maintaining the fork, yourself.

Once the formatted data is ready to return, create the header that goes with it. In the solution, because the document is XML, the header content type is set to `application/xml` before the data is returned as a string.

See Also

Using npm to install and manage Node modules is covered in Recipe 12.6.

11.3. Reading and Writing File Data

Problem

You want to read from or write to a locally stored file.

Solution

Node's filesystem management functionality is included as part of the Node core, via the `fs` module:

```
var fs = require('fs');
```

To read a file's contents, use the `readFile()` function:

```
var fs = require('fs');

fs.readFile('main.txt', {encoding: 'utf8'},function(err,data) {
  if (err) {
    console.log("Error: Could not open file for reading\n");
  } else {
    console.log(data);
  }
});
```

To write to a file, use `writeFile()`:

```
var fs = require('fs');

var buf = "I'm going to write this text to a file\n";
fs.writeFile('main2.txt', buf, function(err) {
  if (err) {
```

```
      console.log(err);
    } else {
      console.log("wrote text to file");
    }
  });
```

The `writeFile()` function overwrites the existing file. To append text to the file, use `appendText()`:

```
var fs = require('fs');

var buf = "I'm going to add this text to a file";
fs.appendFile('main2.txt', buf, function(err) {
    if (err) {
      console.log(err);
    } else {
      console.log("appended text to file");
    }
  });
```

Discussion

Node's filesystem support is both comprehensive and simple to use. To read from a file, use the `readFile()` function, which supports the following parameters:

- The filename, including the operating system path to the file if it isn't local to the application
- An options object, with options for `encoding`, as demonstrated in the solution, and `flag`, which is set to *r* by default (for reading)
- A callback function with parameters for an error and the read data

In the solution, if I didn't specify the encoding in my application, Node would have returned the file contents as a raw buffer. Since I did specify the encoding, the file content is returned as a string.

The `writeFile()` and `appendFile()` functions for writing and appending, respectively, take parameters similar to `readFile()`:

- The filename and path
- The string or buffer for the data to write to the file
- The options object, with options for `encoding` (*w* as default for `writeFile()` and *a* as default for `appendFile()`) and `mode`, with a default value of 438 (0666 in Octal)
- The callback function, with only one parameter: the error

The options value of mode is used to set the file's *sticky* and *permission* bits, if the file was created because of the write or append. By default, the file is created as readable and writable by the owner, and readable by the group and the world.

I mentioned that the data to write can be either a buffer or a string. A string cannot handle binary data, so Node provides the Buffer, which is capable of dealing with either strings or binary data. Both can be used in all of the filesystem functions discussed in this section, but you'll need to explicitly convert between the two types if you want to use them both.

For example, instead of providing the *utf8* encoding option when you use write File(), you convert the string to a buffer, providing the desired encoding when you do:

```
var fs = require('fs');

var str = "I'm going to write this text to a file";
var buf = new Buffer(str, 'utf8');
fs.writeFile('mainbuf.txt', str, function(err) {
  if (err) {
    console.log(err);
  } else {
    console.log("wrote text to file");
  }
});
```

The reverse—that is, to convert the buffer to a string—is just as simple:

```
var fs = require('fs');

fs.readFile('main.txt', function(err,data) {
  if (err) {
    console.log(err.message);
  } else {
    var str = data.toString();
    console.log(str);
  }
});
```

The Buffer toString() function has three optional parameters: encoding, where to begin the conversion, and where to end it. By default, the entire buffer is converted using the *utf8* encoding.

The readFile(), writeFile(), and appendFile() functions are *asynchronous*, meaning the won't wait for the operation to finish before proceeding in the code. This is essential when it comes to notoriously slow operations such as file access. There are synchronous versions of each: readFileSync(), writeFileSync(), and appendFile Sync(). I can't stress enough that you should *not* use these variations. I only include a reference to them to be comprehensive.

Advanced

Another way to read or write from a file is to use the open() function in combination with read() for reading the file contents, or write() for writing to the file. The advantages to this approach is more finite control of what happens during the process. The disadvantage is the added complexity associated with all of the functions, including only being able to use a buffer for reading from and writing to the file.

The parameters for open() are:

- Filename and path
- Flag
- Optional mode
- Callback function

The same open() is used with all operations, with the *flag* controlling what happens. There are quite a few flag options, but the ones that interest us the most at this time are:

- r: Opens the file for reading; the file must exist
- r+: Opens the file for reading and writing; an exception occurs if the file doesn't exist
- w: Opens the file for writing, truncates the file, or creates it if it doesn't exist
- wx: Opens the file for writing, but fails if the file *does* exist
- w+: Opens the file for reading and writing; creates the file if it doesn't exist; truncates the file if it exists
- wx+: Similar to w+, but fails if the file exists
- a: Opens the file for appending, creates it if it doesn't exist
- ax: Opens the file for appending, fails if the file exists
- a+: Opens the file for reading and appending; creates the file if it doesn't exist
- ax+: Similar to a+, but fails if the file exists

The mode is the same one mentioned earlier, a value that sets the *sticky* and *permission* bits on the file if created, and defaults to 0666. The callback function has two parameters: an error object, if an error occurs, and a *file descriptor*, used by subsequent file operations.

The read() and write() functions share the same basic types of parameters:

- The open() methods callback file descriptor
- The buffer used to either hold data to be written or appended, or read

- The offset where the input/output (I/O) operation begins
- The buffer length (set by read operation, controls write operation)
- Position in the file where the operation is to take place; *null* if the position is the current position

The callback functions for both methods have three arguments: an error, bytes read (or written), and the buffer.

That's a lot of parameters and options. The best way to demonstrate how it all works is to create a complete Node application that opens a brand new file for writing, writes some text to it, writes some more text to it, and then reads all the text back and prints it to the console. Since open() is asynchronous, the read and write operations have to occur within the callback function. Be ready for it in Example 11-2, because you're going to get your first taste of a concept known as *callback hell*.

Example 11-2. Demonstrating open, read, and write

```
var fs = require('fs');

fs.open('newfile.txt', 'a+',function(err,fd){
   if (err) {
      console.log(err.message);
   } else {
      var buf = new Buffer("The first string\n");
      fs.write(fd, buf, 0, buf.length, 0, function(err, written, buffer) {
         if (err) {
            console.log(err.message);
         } else {
            var buf2 = new Buffer("The second string\n");
            fs.write(fd, buf2, 0, buf2.length, 0,
                           function(err, written2, buffer) {
               if (err) {
                  console.log(err.message);
               } else {
                  var length = written + written2;
                  var buf3 = new Buffer(length);
                  fs.read(fd, buf3, 0, length, 0,
                        function( err, bytes, buffer) {
                     if(err) {
                        console.log(err.message);
                     } else {
                        console.log(buf3.toString());
                     }
                  });
               }
            });
         }
      });
   }
});
```

To find the length of the buffers, I used length, which returns the number of bytes for the buffer. This value doesn't necessarily match the length of a string in the buffer, but it does work in this usage.

That many levels of indentation can make your skin crawl, but the example demonstrates how open(), read(), and write() work. These combinations of functions are what's used within the readFile(), writeFile(), and appendFile() functions to manage file access. The higher level functions just simplify the most common file operations.

 See Recipe 11.8 for a solution to all that nasty indentation.

11.4. Using let and Other ES 6 Additions in Node

Problem

You want to use some of the new ECMAScript 6 functionality, such as let in your Node application, but they don't seem to work.

Solution

You'll need to use two command-line options when you run the Node application: harmony, to add in support for whatever ECMAScript Harmony features are currently implemented, and use-strict to enforce strict JavaScript processing:

```
node --harmony --use-strict open.js
```

Or you can trigger strict mode by adding the following line as the first in the application:

```
'use strict';
```

Discussion

Internally, Node runs on V8, Google's open source JavaScript engine. You might assume that the engine implements most if not all of the newest cutting-edge JavaScript functionality, including support for let. And it is true that Google has implemented much of the newest JavaScript functionality.

However, some of the newer functionality isn't available to a Node application unless you specify the harmony command-line option, similar to having to turn the option on in your browser. You can find this and other options by typing the following at the command line:

```
man node
```

Once the --harmony option has been given, you can use let instead of var. However, you must also use *strict mode* to use let, either by providing the command-line flag, or using use strict in the application:

```
'use strict';

let fs = require('fs');

fs.readFile('main.txt', {encoding: 'utf8', flag: 'r+'},function(err,data) {
   if (err) {
      console.log(err.message);
   } else {
      console.log(data);
   }
});
```

 Recipe 10.1 discusses using let in the browser.

Node's parent company, Joyent, maintains a GitHub page (*http://bit.ly/1xNhKR1*) listing all of the new ECMAScript 6 (Harmony) features currently implemented in V8. It also lists out the flags you can use to utilize all, or a subset, of the features.

11.5. Interactively Trying Out Node Code Snippets with REPL

Problem

You can test JavaScript code snippets in jsFiddle or jsBin, but what about Node's server-based code snippets?

Solution

Use Node's REPL (read-evalute-print-Loop), an interactive command-line version of Node that can run any code snippet.

To use REPL, type node at the command line without specifying an application to run. If you wish, you can also specify a flag, like --harmony, to use the ECMAScript 6 functionality:

```
$ node --harmony
```

You can then specify JavaScript in a simplified emacs (sorry, no vi) line-editing style. You can import libraries, create functions—whatever you can do within a static application. The main difference is that each line of code is interpreted instantly:

```
> var f = function(name) {
... console.log('hello ' + name);
```

```
... }
undefined
> f('world');
hello world
undefined
```

When you're finished, just exit the program:

```
> .exit
```

Discussion

REPL can be started standalone or within another application if you want to set certain features. You type in the JavaScript as if you're typing in the script in a text file. The main behavioral difference is you might see a result after typing in each line, such as the undefined that shows up in the runtime REPL.

But you can import modules:

```
> var fs = require('fs');
```

And you can access the global objects, which we just did when we used require().

The undefined that shows after typing in some code is the return value for the execution of the previous line of code. Setting a new variable and creating a function are some of the JavaScript that returns undefined, which can get quickly annoying. To eliminate this behavior, as well as make some other modifications, you can use the REPL.start() function within a small Node application that triggers REPL (but with the options you specify).

The options you can use are:

- prompt: Changes the prompt that shows (default is >)
- input: Changes the input readable stream (default is process.stdin, which is the standard input)
- output: Changes the output writable stream (default is process.stdout, the standard output)
- terminal: Set to true if the stream should be treated like a TTY, and have ANSI/ VT100 escape codes written
- eval: Function used to replace the asynchronous eval() function used to evaluate the JavaScript
- useColors: Set to true to set output colors for the writer function (default is based on the terminal's default values)
- useGlobal: Set to true to use the global object, rather than running scripts in a separate context

---

- `ignoreUndefined`: Set to `true` to eliminate the `undefined` return values
- `writer`: The function that returns the formatted result from the evaluated code to the display (default is the `util.inspect` function)

An example application that starts REPL with a new prompt, ignoring the undefined values, and using colors is:

```
var net = require("net"),
    repl = require("repl");

var options = {
   prompt: '-- ',
   useColors: true,
   ignoreUndefined: true,
};

repl.start(options);
```

Both the `net` and `repl` modules are necessary. The options we want are defined in the `options` object and then passed as parameter to `repl.start()`. When we run the application, REPL is started but we no longer have to deal with undefined values:

```
# node reciple11-5.js
-- var f = function (name) {
... console.log('hello ' + name);
... }
-- f('world');
hello world
```

As you can see, this is a much cleaner output without all those messy `undefined` print outs.

Extra: Wait a Second, What global Object?

Caught that, did you?

One difference between JavaScript in Node and JavaScript in the browser is the global scoping. In a browser, when you create a variable outside a function, using `var`, it belongs to the top-level global object, which we know as `window`:

```
var test = 'this is a test';
console.log(window.test); // 'this is a test'
```

This has been a bit of a pain, too, as we get namespace collisions among all our older libraries.

In Node, each module operates within its own separate context, so modules can declare the same variables, and they won't conflict if they're all used in the same application.

However, there are objects accessible from Node's `global` object. We've used a few in previous examples, including `console`, the Buffer object, and `require()`. Others include some very familiar old friends: `setTimeout()`, `clearTimeout()`, `setInterval()`, and `clearInterval()`.

11.6. Getting Input from the Terminal

Problem

You want to get input from the application user via the terminal.

Solution

Use Node's Readline module.

To get data from the standard input, use code such as the following:

```
var readline = require('readline');

var rl = readline.createInterface({
  input: process.stdin,
  output: process.stdout
});

rl.question(">>What's your name?  ", function(answer) {
  console.log("Hello " + answer);
  rl.close();
});
```

Discussion

The Readline module provides the ability to get lines of text from a readable stream. You start by creating an instance of the Readline interface with `createInterface()` passing in, at minimum, the readable and writable streams. You need both, because you're writing prompts, as well as reading in text. In the solution, the input stream is `process.stdin`, the standard input stream, and the output stream is `process.stdout`. In other words, input and output are from, and to, the command line.

The solution used the `question()` function to post a question, and provided a callback function to process the response. Within the function, `close()` was called, which closes the interface, releasing control of the input and output streams.

You can also create an application that continues to listen to the input, taking some action on the incoming data, until something signals the application to end. Typically that something is a letter sequence signaling the person is done, such as the word *exit*. This type of application makes use of other Readline functions, such as `setPrompt()` to change the prompt given the individual for each line of text, prompt(), which prepares the input area, including changing the prompt to the one set by setPrompt(), and write(), to write out a prompt. In addition, you'll also need to use event handlers to process events, such as line, which listens for each new line of text.

Example 11-3 contains a complete Node application that continues to process input from the user until the person types in *exit*. Note that the application makes use of process.exit(). This function cleanly terminates the Node application.

Example 11-3. Access numbers from stdin until the user types in exit

```
var readline = require('readline');
var sum = 0;

var rl = readline.createInterface({
  input: process.stdin,
  output: process.stdout
});

console.log("Enter numbers, one to a line. Enter 'exit' to quit.");

rl.setPrompt('>> ');
rl.prompt();

rl.on('line', function(input) {
   input = input.trim();
   if (input == 'exit') {
      rl.close();
      return;
   } else {
     sum+= Number(input);
   }
   rl.prompt();
});

// user typed in 'exit'
rl.on('close', function() {
   console.log("Total is " + sum);
   process.exit(0);
});
```

Running the application with several numbers results in the following output:

```
Enter numbers, one to a line. Enter 'exit' to quite.
>> 55
>> 209
>> 23.44
>> 0
>> 1
>> 6
>> exit
Total is 294.44
```

I used `console.log()` rather than the Readline interface `write()` to write the prompt followed by a new line, and to differentiate the output from the input.

11.7. Working with Node Timers and Understanding the Node Event Loop

Problem

You need to use a timer in a Node application, but you're not sure which of Node's three timers to use, or how accurate they are.

Solution

If your timer doesn't have to be precise, you can use `setTimeout()` to create a single timer event, or `setInterval()` if you want a reoccurring timer:

```
setTimeout(function() {}, 3000);

setInterval(function() {}, 3000);
```

Both function timers can be canceled:

```
var timer1 = setTimeout(function() {}, 3000);
clearTimeout(timer1);

var timer2 = setInterval(function() {}, 3000);
clearInterval(timer2);
```

However, if you need more finite control of your timer, and immediate results, you might want to use `setImmediate()`. You don't specify a delay for it, as you want the callback to be invoked *immediately* after all I/O callbacks are processed but before any `setTimeout()` or `setInterval()` callbacks:

```
setImmediate(function() {});
```

It, too, can be cleared, with `clearImmediate()`.

Discussion

Node, being JavaScript based, runs on a single thread. It is *synchronous*. However, input/output (I/O) and other native API access either runs *asynchronously* or on a separate thread. Node's approach to managing this timing disconnect is the *event loop*.

In your code, when you perform an I/O operation, such as writing a chunk of text to a file, you specify a callback function to do any post-write activity. Once you've done so, the rest of your application code is processed. It doesn't wait for the file write to finish. When the file write has finished, an event signaling the fact is returned to Node, and pushed on to a queue, waiting for process. Node processes this event queue, and when it gets to the event signaled by the completed file write, it matches the event to the callback, and the callback is processed.

As a comparison, think of going into a deli and ordering lunch. You wait in line to place your order, and are given an order number. You sit down and read the paper, or check your Twitter account while you wait. In the meantime, the lunch orders go into another queue for deli workers to process the orders. But each lunch request isn't always finished in the order received. Some lunch orders may take longer. They may need to bake or grill for a longer time. So the deli worker processes your order by preparing your lunch item and then placing it in an oven, setting a timer for when it's finished, and goes on to other tasks.

When the timer pings, the deli worker quickly finishes his current task, and pulls your lunch order from the oven. You're then notified that your lunch is ready for pickup by your order number being called out. If several time-consuming lunch items are being processed at the same time, the deli worker processes them as the timer for each item pings, in order.

All Node processes fit the pattern of the deli order queue: first in, first to be sent to the deli (thread) workers. However, certain operations, such as I/O, are like those lunch orders that need extra time to bake in an oven or grill, but don't require the deli worker to stop any other effort and wait for the baking and grilling. The oven or grill timers are equivalent to the messages that appear in the Node event loop, triggering a final action based on the requested operation.

You now have a working blend of synchronous and asynchronous processes. But what happens with a timer?

Both setTimeout() and setInterval() fire after the given delay, but what happens is a message to this effect is added to the event loop, to be processed in turn. So if the event loop is particularly cluttered, there is a delay before the the timer functions' callbacks are called:

> It is important to note that your callback will probably not be called in exactly (delay) milliseconds. Node.js makes no guarantees about the exact timing of when the callback will fire, nor of the ordering things will fire in. The callback will be called as close as possible to the time specified.
>
> — Node Timers documentation

For the most part, whatever delay happens is beyond the kin of our human senses, but it can result in animations that don't seem to run smoothly. It can also add an odd effect to other applications.

In Recipe 16.3, I created a scrolling timeline in SVG, with data fed to the client via WebSockets. To emulate real-world data, I used a three-second timer and randomly generated a number to act as a data value. In the server code, I used `setInterval()`, because the timer is reoccurring:

```
var app = require('http').createServer(handler)
  , fs = require('fs');
var ws = require("nodejs-websocket");

app.listen(8124);

// serve static page
function handler (req, res) {
  fs.readFile(__dirname + '/drawline.html',
  function (err, data) {
    if (err) {
      res.writeHead(500);
      return res.end('Error loading drawline.html');
    }
    res.writeHead(200);
    res.end(data);
  });
}

// data timer
function startTimer() {
  setInterval(function() {
    var newval = Math.floor(Math.random() * 100) + 1;
    if (server.connections.length > 0) {
      console.log('sending ' + newval);
      var counter = {counter: newval};
      server.connections.forEach(function(conn, idx) {
        conn.sendText(JSON.stringify(counter), function() {
          console.log('conn sent')
        });
      });
    }
  },3000);
}


// websocket connection
var server = ws.createServer(function (conn) {
  console.log('connected');
  conn.on("close", function (code, reason) {
    console.log("Connection closed")
  });
}).listen(8001, function() {
    startTimer(); }
);
```

I included `console.log()` calls in the code so you can see that the timer event in comparison to the communication responses. When the `setInterval()` function is called,

---

it's pushed into the process. When its callback is processed, the WebSocket communications are also pushed into the queue.

The solution uses `setInterval()`, one of Node's three different types of timers. The `setInterval()` function has the same format as the one we use in the browser. You specify a callback for the first function, provide a delay time (in milliseconds), and any potential arguments. The timer is going to fire in three seconds, but we already know that the callback for the timer may not be immediately processed.

The same applies to the callbacks passed in the WebSocket `sendText()` calls. These are based on Node's Net (or TLS, if secure) sockets, and as the `socket.write()` (what's used for `sendText()`) documentation notes:

> The optional callback parameter will be executed when the data is finally written out—this may not be immediately.

> — Node Net documentation

If you set the timer to invoke immediately (giving zero as the delay value), you'll see that the data sent message is interspersed with the communication sent message (before the browser client freezes up, overwhelmed by the socket communications—you don't want to use a zero value in the application again).

However, the timelines for all the clients remain the same because the communications are sent within the timer's callback function, *synchronously*, so the data is the same for all of the communications—it's just the callbacks that are handled, seemingly out of order.

Earlier I mentioned using `setInterval()` with a delay of zero. In actuality, it isn't exactly zero—Node follows the HTML5 specification that browsers adhere to, and "clamps" the timer interval to a minimum value of four milliseconds. While this may seem to be too small of an amount to cause a problem, when it comes to animations and time-critical processes the time delay can impact the overall appearance and/or function.

To bypass the constraints, Node developers utilized Node's `process.nextTick()` instead. The callback associated with `process.nextTick()` is processed on the next event loop go around, usually before any I/O callbacks (though there are constraints, which I'll get to in a minute). No more pesky four millisecond throttling. But then, what happens if there's an enormous number of recursively called `process.nextTick()` calls?

To return to our deli analogy, during a busy lunch hour, workers can be overrun with orders and so caught up in trying to process new orders that they don't respond in a timely manner to the oven and grill pings. Things burn when this happens. If you've ever been to a well-run deli, you'll notice the counter person taking the orders will assess the kitchen before taking the order, tossing in some slight delay, or even taking on some of the kitchen duties, letting the people wait just a tiny bit longer in the order queue.

The same happens with Node. If `process.nextTick()` were allowed to be the spoiled child, always getting its way, I/O operations would get starved out. Node uses another value, `process.maxTickDepth`, with a default value of 1000 to constrain the number of `process.next()` callbacks that are processed before the I/O callbacks are allowed to play. It's the counter person in the deli.

In more recent releases of Node, the `setImmediate()` function was added. This function attempts to resolve all of the issues associated with the timing operations and create a happy medium that should work for most folks. When `setImmediate()` is called, its callback is added after the I/O callbacks, but before the `setTimeout()` and `setInterval()` callbacks. We don't have the four millisecond tax for the traditional timers, but we also don't have the brat that is `process.nextTick()`.

To return one last time to the deli analogy, `setImmediate()` is a customer in the order queue who sees that the deli workers are overwhelmed with pinging ovens, and politely states he'll wait to give his order.

However, you do *not* want to use `setImmediate()` in the scrolling timeline example, as it will freeze your browser up faster than you can blink.

11.8. Managing Callback Hell

Problem

You want to do something such as check to see if a file is present, and if so open it and read the contents. Node provides this functionality, but to use it asynchronously, you end up with nested code (noted by indentations) in the code that makes the application unreadable and difficult to maintain.

Solution

Use a module such as Async. For instance, in Example 11-2 we saw definitely an example of nested callbacks, and this is a fairly simple piece of code: open a file, write two lines to it, and then read them back and output them to the console:

```
var fs = require('fs');

fs.open('newfile.txt', 'a+',function(err,fd){
    if (err) {
        console.log(err.message);
    } else {
        var buf = new Buffer("The first string\n");
        fs.write(fd, buf, 0, buf.length, 0, function(err, written, buffer) {
```

```
              if (err) {
                console.log(err.message);
              } else {
                var buf2 = new Buffer("The second string\n");
                fs.write(fd, buf2, 0, buf2.length, 0,
                                    function(err, written2, buffer) {
                  if (err) {
                    console.log(err.message);
                  } else {
                    var length = written + written2;
                    var buf3 = new Buffer(length);
                    fs.read(fd, buf3, 0, length, 0,
                            function( err, bytes, buffer) {
                      if(err) {
                        console.log(err.message);
                      } else {
                        console.log(buf3.toString());
                      }
                    });
                  }
                });
              }
            });
          }
        });
```

Notice the messy indentation for all the nested callbacks. We can clean it up using Async:

```
var fs = require('fs');
var async = require('async');

async.waterfall([
  function openFile(callback) {
    fs.open('newfile.txt', 'a+',function (err, fd){
      callback(err,fd);
    });
  },
  function writeBuffer(fd, callback) {
    var buf = new Buffer("The first string\n");
    fs.write(fd, buf, 0, buf.length, 0, function(err, written, buffer) {
      callback(err, fd, written);
    });
  },
  function writeBuffer2(fd, written, callback) {
    var buf = new Buffer("The second string\n");
    fs.write(fd, buf, 0, buf.length, 0, function(err, written2, buffer){
      callback(err, fd, written, written2);
    });
  },
  function readFile(fd, written, written2, callback) {
    var length = written + written2;
    var buf3 = new Buffer(length);
    fs.read(fd, buf3, 0, length, 0, function(err, bytes, buffer) {
```

```
          callback (err, buf3.toString());
      });
    }
], function (err, result) {
    if (err) {
      console.log(err);
    } else {
      console.log(result);
    }
});
```

Discussion

Async is a utility module that detangles the *callback spaghetti* that especially afflicts Node developers. It can now be used in the browser, as well as Node, but it's particularly useful with Node.

Node developers can install Async using npm:

```
npm install async
```

 To access the source for the browser, go to the module's GitHub page (*https://github.com/caolan/async*).

Async provides functionality that we're now finding in native JavaScript, such as map, filter, and reduce. However, the functionality I want to focus on is its asynchronous control management.

The solution used Async's waterfall(), which implements a series of tasks, passing the results of prior tasks to those next in the queue. If an error occurs in any task, when the error is passed in the callback to the next task, Async stops the sequence and the error is processed.

Comparing the older code and the new Async-assisted solution, the first task is opening a file for writing. In the older code, if an error occurs, it's printed out. Otherwise, a new Buffer is created and used to write a string to the newly opened file. In the Async version, though, the functionality to create the file is embedded in a new function openFile(), included as the first element in an array passed to the waterfall() function. The openFile() function takes one parameter, a callback() function, which is called once the file is opened, in the fs.open() callback function and takes as parameters the error object and the *file descriptor*.

The next task is to write a string to the newly created file. In the old code, this happens *directly* in the callback function attached to the fs.open() function call. In the Async version, though, writing a string to the file happens in a new function, added as second task to the `waterfall()` array. Rather than just taking a callback as argument, this function, `writerBuffer()`, takes the file descriptor `fd` returned from `fs.open()`, as well as a callback function. In the function, after the string is written out to the file using `fs.write()`, the number of bytes written is captured and passed in the next callback, along with the error and file descriptor.

The following task is to write out a second string. Again, in the old code, this happens within the callback function, but this time, the first `fs.write()`'s callback. At this time, we're looking at the third nested callback in the old code, but in the Async version, the second written string operation is just another task and another function in the `water fall()` task array. The function, `writeBuffer2()`, accepts the file descriptor, the number of bytes written out in the first write task, and, again, a callback function. Again, it writes the new string out and passes the error, file descriptor, the bytes written out in the first write, and now the bytes written out on the second to the callback function.

In the old code within the fourth nested callback function (this one for the second `fs.write()` function), the count of written bytes is added and used in a call to `fs.read()` to read in the contents of the newly created file. The file contents are then output to the console.

In the Async modified version, the last task function, `readFile()`, is added to the task array and it takes a file descriptor, the two writing buffer counts, and a final callback as parameters. In the function, again the two byte counts are added and used in `fs.read()` to read in the file contents. These contents are passed, with the error object, in the last callback function call.

The results, or an error, are processed in the `waterfall()`'s own callback function.

Rather than a callback nesting four indentations deep, we're looking at a sequence of function calls in an array, with an absolute minimum of callback nesting. And we could go on and on, way past the point of what would be insane if we had to use the typical nested callback.

I used `waterfall()` because this control structure implies a series of tasks, each implemented in turn, and each passing data to the next task. It takes two arguments: the task array and a callback with an error and an optional result. Async also supports other control structures such as `parallel()`, for completing tasks in parallel; `compose()`, which creates a function that is a composition of passed functions; and `series()`, which accomplishes the task in a series but each task doesn't pass data to the next (as happens with `waterfall()`.

11.9. Accessing Command-Line Functionality Within a Node Application

Problem

You want to access command-line functionality, such as ImageMagick, from within a Node application.

Solution

Use Node's `child_process` module. For example, if you want to use ImageMagick's `identify`, and then print out the data to the console, use the following:

```
var spawn = require('child_process').spawn,
    imcmp = spawn('identify',['-verbose', 'osprey.jpg']);

imcmp.stdout.on('data', function (data) {
  console.log('stdout: ' + data);
});

imcmp.stderr.on('data', function (data) {
  console.log('stderr: ' + data);
});

imcmp.on('exit', function (code) {
  console.log('child process exited with code ' + code);
});
```

Discussion

The `child_process` module provides four methods to run command-line operations and process returned data:

- `spawn(command, [args], [options])`: This launches a given process, with optional command-line arguments, and an `options` object specifying additional information such as cwd to change directory and uid to find the user ID of the process.

- `exec(command, [options], callback)`: This runs a command in a shell and buffers the result.

- `execFile(file, [args],[options],[callback])`: This is like `exec()` but executes the file directly.

- `fork(modulePath, [args],[options])`: This is a special case of `spawn()`, and spawns Node processes, returning an object that has a communication channel built in. It also requires a separate instance of V8 with each use, so use sparingly.

The child_process methods have three streams associated with them: stdin, stdout, and stderr. The spawn() method is the most widely used of the child_process methods, and the one used in the solution. From the solution top, the command given is the ImageMagick identify command-line application, which can return a wealth of information about an image. In the *args* array, the code passes in the --verbose flag, and the name of the image file. When the data event happens with the child_pro cess.stdout stream, the application prints it to the console. The data is a Buffer that uses toString() implicitly when concatenated with another string. If an error happens, it's also printed out to the console. A third event handler just communicates that the child process is exiting.

If you want to process the result as an array, modify the input event handler:

```
imcmp.stdout.on('data', function (data) {
    console.log(data.toString().split("\n"));
});
```

Now the data is processed into an array of strings, split on the new line within the identify output.

If you want to *pipe* the result of one process to another, you can with multiple child processes. If, in the solution, I want to pipe the result of the identify command to grep, in order to return only a subset of the information, I can do this with two different spawn() commands, as shown in Example 11-4.

In the code, the resulting data from the identify command is written to the stdin input stream for the grep command, and the grep's data is then written out to the console.

Example 11-4. Spawning two child processes to pipe the results of one command to another

```
var spawn = require('child_process').spawn,
    imcmp = spawn('identify',['-verbose', 'fishies.jpg']),
    grep = spawn('grep', ['Resolution']);

imcmp.stdout.on('data', function (data) {
    grep.stdin.write(data);
});

imcmp.stderr.on('data', function (data) {
    console.log('stderr: ' + typeof data);
});

grep.stdout.on('data', function (data) {
    console.log('grep data: ' + data);
});

grep.stderr.on('data', function (data) {
    console.log('grep error: ' + data);
```

```
});
imcmp.on('close', function (code) {
  console.log('child process close with code ' + code);
  grep.stdin.end();
});

grep.on('close', function(code) {
  console.log('grep closes with code ' + code);
});
```

In addition, the application also captures the `close` event when the streams terminate (not necessarily when the child processes exit). In the `close` event handler for the `identify` child process, the `stdin.end()` method is called for `grep` to ensure it terminates.

The result of running the application on the test image is:

```
child process close with code 0
grep data:    Resolution: 240x240
    exif:ResolutionUnit: 2
    exif:XResolution: 2400000/10000
    exif:YResolution: 2400000/10000

grep closes with code 0
```

Note the order: the original `identify` child process stream terminates once its data is passed to the `grep` command, which then does its thing and prints out the target data (the photo resolution). Then the `grep` command's `close` event is processed.

Instead of using a child process, if you have either GraphicsMagick or ImageMagick installed, you can use the gm (*http://aheckmann.github.io/gm/*) Node module for accessing the imaging capability. Just install it as:

```
npm install gm
```

Of course, you can still use the child process, but using the GraphicsMagick module can be simpler.

Extra: Using Child Processes with Windows

The solution demonstrates how to use child processes in a Linux environment. There are similarities and differences between using child processes in Linux/Unix, and using them in Windows.

In Windows, you can't explicitly give a command with a child process; you have to invoke the Windows `cmd.exe` executable and have it perform the process. In addition, the first flag to the command is `/c`, which tells `cmd.exe` to process the command and then terminate.

Borrowing an example from *Learning Node* (O'Reilly), in the following code, the `cmd.exe` command is used to get a directory listing, using the Windows `dir` command:

```
var cmd = require('child_process').spawn('cmd', ['/c', 'dir\n']);

cmd.stdout.on('data', function (data) {
    console.log('stdout: ' + data);
});

cmd.stderr.on('data', function (data) {
    console.log('stderr: ' + data);
});

cmd.on('exit', function (code) {
    console.log('child process exited with code ' + code);
});
```

11.10. Running Node and Apache on the Same Port

Problem

You want your users to be able to access your Node application without having to specify a port number. You can run it at port 80, but then your Node application is in conflict with your Apache web server.

Solution

There are a couple of options you can use to run Node and Apache seemingly on port 80 at the same time. One is to use nginx, as a *reserve proxy* for both Apache and Node. A reverse proxy intercepts a web request and routes it to the correct service. Using a reverse proxy, you can start Node on a different port address, and when the reverse proxy gets a request for the Node application, it properly routes it to the appropriate port.

Another option is to use either Node as the reverse proxy to Apache, or Apache as a reverse proxy to Node. In the discussion, I cover the steps to using Apache as a reverse proxy for a Node application.

Discussion

We take our server infrastructures for granted when we're developing traditional web server applications. Node, though, changes all the rules, and we're having to become more familiar with how it all holds together.

For instance, traditional web servers are listening on a specific port, though we don't use a port number in our URLs. However, they're listening on port 80, which is the default port when you're using Hypertext Transfer Protocol (HTTP).

If you're using Apache and attempt to start a Node web service on port 80, it will fail. If Apache isn't running, you can still run into problems starting your Node application on port 80, because you're doing so without administrative (root) privileges. You'll get an EACCES error ("permission denied") because starting an application on a port less than 1024 requires root privileges.

So you might try to then run the application using sudo, which allows you to run an application as root:

```
sudo node app.js
```

Chances are if you do have root privileges your application will start. But it also increases the vulnerability of your server. Very few applications are *hardened* enough to run with *root privileges* and that includes Apache, which actually spawns a worker thread running as a nonprivileged user to respond to all web requests.

There are options for running Apache and a Node application on the same server and seemingly both on port 80. One popular option is to use Nginx (pronounced as "Engine X") as a *reverse proxy* for both Apache and the Node application. Another is to use a separate server for the Node application, which isn't an impossible solution considering how affordable Virtual Private Servers (VPS) have become.

 Another option for Node application deployment is to use a cloud server or other third-party service that enables Node Hosting. Among some of the Node deployment services are Joyent (*https://www.joyent.com/*), host company for Node, Nodejitsu (*https://www.nodejitsu.com/*), and Codeship (*https://www.codeship.io/*).

However, if you're interested in as simple a solution as possible, and the performance requirements for your Node application are such that Apache's single-threaded processing won't be detrimental, you can use Apache as a reverse proxy for your Node application.

A reverse proxy is when the user accesses a specific URL, and the server that receives the request then sends it to the correct application. To use Apache as a reverse proxy for a Node application, you need to ensure that two Apache modules are enabled:

```
sudo a2enmod proxy
sudo a2enmod proxy_http
```

Next, you'll need to configure a virtual host for your Node application. I'm currently running a Ghost weblog (Node-based) on the same server as my main Apache server. The virtual host file I created for this weblog is contained in the following code snippet:

```
<VirtualHost ipaddress:80>
    ServerAdmin myemail
    ServerName shelleystoybox.com
```

```
ErrorLog path-to-logs/error.log
CustomLog path-to-logs/access.log combined

ProxyRequests off

<Location />
        ProxyPass http://ipaddress:2368/
        ProxyPassReverse http://ipaddress:2368/
</Location>
</VirtualHost>
```

You'll need to replace the IP address with your own. Note that the request is proxied to a specific port the Node application is listening to (in this case, port 2368). It's essential that you set `ProxyRequests` to `off`, to ensure forward proxying is turned off. Keeping forward proxying open can allow your server to be used to access other sites, while hiding the actual origins of the request.

Then it's a matter of just enabling the virtual host and reloading Apache:

```
a2ensite shelleystoybox.com
service apache2 reload
```

People can also access the Ghost weblog by directly specifying the port address. The only way to prevent this is to disable direct access to the port from outside the server. In my Ubuntu system, I configured this with an *iptables rule*:

```
iptables -A input -i eth0 -p tcp --dport 2368 -j DROP
```

But unless you *really* need this, use caution when messing around with `iptables`.

Now I can set my Node application to listen in on port 2368, and start the application without root privileges.

The main drawback to using Apache as a reverse proxy for a Node application is that Apache is single-threaded, which can cramp Node's style. If performance is a problem for you, then you should consider the other approaches I outlined earlier.

 Read more about Apache mod_proxy at *http://httpd.apache.org/docs/ 2.2/mod/mod_proxy.html*.

11.11. Keeping a Node Instance Up and Running

Problem

You're in Linux, and you want to start up a Node application, but you also don't want to keep a terminal window open while the application is running.

Solution

Use Forever to ensure the application is restarted if it's ever shut down:

```
forever start  -l forever.log -o out.log -e err.log index.js
```

Discussion

Forever is a CLI (Command-Line Interface) tool that can be used to not only start a Node application, but to ensure the application is restarted if, for some reason, it's shut down.

Install Forever using npm:

```
sudo npm install forever -g
```

Then start your Node application, making use of one or more of Forever's flags. For my Ghost installation, I used:

```
forever start  -l forever.log -o out.log -e err.log index.js
```

The start action is one of the many available with Forever. This action starts the Node application as a Unix *daemon* or background process. It makes use of node.daemon, another Node module that can be used to create Unix daemons.

The command line also makes use of three options:

- -l to create a log file
- -o to log stdout from the script to the specified output file
- -e to log stderr from the script to the specified error file

Some other Forever actions are:

- stop to stop the daemon script
- restart to restart the daemon script
- stopall to stop all scripts
- restartall to restart all scripts
- list to list all running scripts
- logs to list log files for running scripts

Forever will restart the application if it shuts down for whatever reason. However, if the entire system is rebooted, you'll need an additional step, to ensure that Forever is started. For my Node Ghost weblog, I used Ubuntu's Upstart program. To do this, I created a configuration file in */etc/init* named *ghost.conf* with the following text (generalized for the book):

```
# /etc/init/ghost.conf
description "Ghost"

start on (local-filesystems)
stop on shutdown

setuid your-userid
setgid your-grpid

script
    export HOME="path-to-ghost"
    cd path-to-ghost
    exec /usr/local/bin/forever -a -l
        path-to-logfiles/forever.log --sourceDir path-to-ghost index.js

end script
```

When my server reboots, Forever restarts my Ghost weblog's daemon, using the given nonroot user and group IDs.

11.12. Monitoring Application Changes and Restarting

Problems

Development can get rather active, and it can be difficult to remember to restart an application when the code has changed.

Solution

Use the nodemon utility to watch your source code and restart your application when the code changes.

To use, first install nodemon:

```
npm install -g nodemon
```

Instead of starting the application with node, use nodemon instead:

```
nodemon serverapp.js
```

Discussion

The nodemon utility monitors the files within the directory where it was started. If any of the files change, the Node application is automatically restarted. This is a handy way of making sure your running Node application reflects the most recent code changes.

Needless to say, nodemon is *not* a tool you want to use in a production system. You don't want tools to automatically start when a bit of code changes, because the code change may not be production ready. Production systems do better when rollouts are triggered by human intention not accidental software intervention.

If the application accepts values when started, you can provide these on the command line, just as with Node, but precede them with double dashes (--) flag, which signals to nodemon to ignore anything that follows, and pass it to the application:

```
nodemon serverapp.js -- -param1 -param2
```

When started, you should get feedback similar to the following:

```
14 Jul 15:11:40 - [nodemon] v1.2.1
14 Jul 15:11:40 - [nodemon] to restart at any time, enter `rs`
14 Jul 15:11:40 - [nodemon] watching: *.*
14 Jul 15:11:40 - [nodemon] starting `node helloworld.js`
Server running on 8124/
```

If the code changes, you'll see something similar to the following:

```
14 Jul 15:13:42 - [nodemon] restarting due to changes...
14 Jul 15:13:42 - [nodemon] starting `node helloworld.js`
Server running on 8124/
```

If you want to manually restart the application, just type rs into the terminal where nodemon is running. You can also use a configuration file with the utility, monitor only select files or subdirectories, and even use it to run non-Node applications.

The nodemon utility can also be used with Forever, discussed in Recipe 11.11. If the Node application crashes, Forever restarts it, and if the source code for the application changes, nodemon restarts the application. To use the two together, you do need to use the --exitcrash flag, to signal nodemon to exit if the application crashes:

```
forever nodemon --exitcrash serverapp.js
```

You can use this combination in production, but I'm wary of restarting applications automatically when code changes. However, you do have this option with this utility.

11.13. Screen Scraping with Request

Problem

You want to access a web resource from within your Node application.

Solution

Use Request, one of the most popular and widely used Node modules. It's installed with npm:

```
npm install request;
```

and can be used as simply as:

```
var request = require('request');
request('http://oreilly.com', function (error, response, body) {
  if (!error && response.statusCode == 200) {
    console.log(body);
  }
})
```

Discussion

Request provides support for the HTTP methods of GET, POST, DELETE, and PUT.
In the case of GET, if the status indicates success (a status code of 200), you can then
process the returned data (formatted as HTML in this instance) however you would
like.

You can stream the result to a file using the filesystem module:

```
var request = require('request');
var fs = require('fs');

request('http://burningbird.net/flame.png')
  .pipe(fs.createWriteStream('flame.png'));
```

You can also stream a system file to a remote server with PUT, as noted in the module's
documentation:

```
fs.createReadStream('flame.json')
  .pipe(request.put('http://mysite.com/flame.json'))
```

You can also handle multipart form uploading and authentication.

An interesting use of Request is to *scrape* a website or resource and then use other
functionality to query for specific information within the returned material. A popular
module to use for querying is Cheerio, which is a very tiny implementation of jQuery
core intended for use in the server. In Example 11-5, a simple application is created to
pull in all links (a) contained in h2 elements (typical for individual article titles in a main
page) and then list the text of the link to a separate output.

Example 11-5. Screen scraping made easy with Request and Cheerio

```
var request = require('request');
var cheerio = require('cheerio');

request('http://burningbird.net', function (error, response, html) {
  if (!error && response.statusCode == 200) {
    var $ = cheerio.load(html);
    $('h2 a').each(function(i,element) {
        console.log(element.children[0].data);
    });
  }
});
```

After the successful request is made, the HTML returned is passed to Cheerio via the load( ) method, and the result is assigned to a dollar sign variable ($), so we can use the result in a manner we're used to, when using jQuery.

The element pattern of *h2 a* is then used to query for all matches, and the result is processed using the each method, accessing the text for each heading. The output to the console should be the titles of all the articles on the main page of the weblog.

11.14. Creating a Command-Line Utility with Help From Commander

Problem

You want to turn your Node module into a Linux command-line utility, including support for command-line options/arguments.

Solution

To convert your Node module to a Linux command-line utility, add the following line as the first line of the module:

```
#!/usr/bin/env node
```

To provide for command-line arguments/options, including the ever important --help, make use of the Commander module:

```
var program = require('commander');

program
    .version ('0.0.1')
    .option ('-s, --source [website]', 'Source website')
    .option ('-f, --file [filename]', 'Filename')
    .parse(process.argv);
```

Discussion

Converting a Node module to a command-line utility is quite simple. First, add the following line to the module:

```
#!/usr/bin/env node
```

Change the module file's mode to an executable, using CHMOD:

```
chmod a+x snapshot
```

Notice that I dropped the *.js* from the file once I converted it to a utility. To run it, I use the following:

```
./snapshot -s http://oreilly.com -f test.png
```

The command-line utility I created makes use of Phantom to create am image capture of a website. Recipe 16.4 covers the use of Phantom, but for now, Example 11-6 contains the complete code, making use of Commander.

Example 11-6. Making a Screenshot utility constructed of Phantom and Commander

```
#!/usr/bin/env node

var phantom = require('phantom');
var program = require('commander');

program
    .version ('0.0.1')
    .option ('-s, --source [website]', 'Source website')
    .option ('-f, --file [filename]', 'Filename')
    .parse(process.argv);

phantom.create(function (ph) {
  ph.createPage(function (page) {
    page.open(program.source, function (status) {
      console.log("opened " + program.source, status);
      page.render(program.file, function() {
        ph.exit();
      });
    });
  });
});
```

Commander is another favorite Node module of mine, because it provides exactly what we need to create a command-line utility: not only a way to process command-line arguments, but also to handle requests for help with the module using --help. To use it, you just need to specify a version for the utility, and then list out all of the command-line arguments/options. Note that you need to specify which of the options require an argument, and provide an English language description of the purpose of the option. Lastly, call Commander's parse() argument, passing to it the process.argv structure, which contains all of the arguments given on the utility's command line.

Now, you can run the utility with the *short option*, consisting of a dash (-) and a single lowercase alphabetic character:

```
./snapshot -s http://oreilly.com -f test.png
```

Or you can use the *long option*, consisting of a double-dash (--) followed by a complete word:

```
./snapshot --source http://oreilly.com --file test.png
```

And when you run the utility with either -h or --help, you get:

```
Usage: snapshot [options]
```

```
Options:

    -h, --help              output usage information
    -V, --version           output the version number
    -s, --source [website]  Source website
    -f, --file [filename]   Filename
```

Running the following returns the version:

```
./snapshot -V
```

Commander generates all of this automatically, so we can focus on our utility's primary functionality.

 Commander (*https://github.com/visionmedia/commander.js*) can be installed using npm:

```
npm install commander
```

## CHAPTER 12

Modularizing and Managing JavaScript

One of the great aspects of writing Node.js applications is the built-in modularity the environment provides. As demonstrated in Chapter 11, it's simple to download and install any number of Node modules, and using them is equally simple: just include a single `require()` statement naming the module, and you're off and running.

The ease with which the modules can be incorporated is one of the benefits of JavaScript *modularization*. Modularizing ensures that external functionality is created in such a way that it isn't dependent on other external functionality, a concept known as *loose coupling*. This means I can use a Foo module, without having to include a Bar module, because Foo is tightly dependent on having Bar included.

JavaScript modularization is both a discipline and a contract. The discipline comes in by having to follow certain mandated criteria in order for external code to participate in the module system. The contract is between you, me, and other JavaScript developers: we're following an agreed on path when we produce (or consume) external functionality in a module system, and we all have expectations based on the module system.

> ECMAScript 6 provides native support for modules, but the specification is still undergoing change and there is no implementation support yet. There is some support for it in Traceur (*http://bit.ly/ 14RI7K6*), as well as a polyfill (*https://github.com/ModuleLoader/es6-module-loader*), which can at least provide an idea of how they'll be implemented in the future.

Chances are you have used modularized JavaScript. If you have used jQuery with RequireJS or Dojo, you've used modularized JavaScript. If you've used Node, you've used a modular system. They don't look the same, but they work the same: ensuring that functionality developed by disparate parties works together seamlessly. The modular system that RequireJS and Dojo support is the Asynchronous Module Definition

(AMD), while Node's system is based on CommonJS. One major difference between the two is that AMD is asynchronous, while CommonJS is synchronous.

Even if you don't use a formal modular system, you can still improve the performance of script loading with script loaders and using new HTML5 `async` functionality. You can also improve the management of your entire application process using tools such as Grunt, or ensuring your own code is packaged for ease of use and innovation.

 One major dependency on virtually all aspects of application and library management and publication is the use of Git, a source control system, and GitHub, an extremely popular Git *endpoint*. How Git works and using Git with GitHub are beyond the scope of this book. I recommend *The Git Pocket Guide* (O'Reilly) to get more familiar with Git, and GitHub's own documentation (*https://github.com/*) for more on using this service.

12.1. Loading Scripts with a Script Loader

Problem

You need to use several different JavaScript libraries in your web pages, and they're starting to slow the page loads.

Solution

One solution is to use a *script loader* to load your JavaScript files asynchronously and concurrently. Examples of use are documented in the discussion.

Discussion

There are several techniques you can use to load JavaScript files. One is the traditional method of using a script element for each file, and just loading each in turn. The issue that people have had with this approach is the inefficiency of having to access each file individually, the problems that can occur if scripts are loaded out of order (with one script being dependent on another already loaded), and the fact that the entire page is blocked while the scripts load.

Some solutions are to compile all the individual JavaScript files into a single file, which is what the content management system (CMS) Drupal does. This eliminates the multiple file access and even the issues with ordering, but it still leaves us with the fact that the page is blocked from loading until the scripts are loaded.

Script loaders were created to provide a way of loading JavaScript files asynchronously, which means the rest of the page can continue loading while the script is loading. They use *script injection*: creating a `script` element in a script block that loads the JavaScript file, and then appending that block to the page. The *inline* JavaScript is executed asynchronously and does not block the page from loading like the use of the traditional `script` element does.

The code to do so can be similar to the script block shown in the following minimal HTML5 page:

```
<!DOCTYPE html>
<html lang="en">
<head>
<meta charset="utf-8">
<title>title</title>
</head>
<body>
  <script>
    var scrpt = document.querySelector("script");
    var t = document.createElement("script");
    t.src = "test1.js";
    scrpt.parentNode.insertBefore(t,scrpt);
  </script>
</body>
</html>
```

To prevent the variables from cluttering up the global namespace, they can be included in an Immediately-Invoked Function Expression (IIFE):

```
<script>
  (function() {
    var scrpt = document.querySelector("script");
    var t = document.createElement("script");
    t.src = "test1.js";
    scrpt.parentNode.insertBefore(t,scrpt);
  }());
</script>
```

If you need to use a pathname for the script, you can use a protocol-relative URL (sometimes referred to as a *protocol-less URL*) so that the code adapts whether the page is accessed with *http* or *https*:

```
t.src = "//somecompany.com/scriptfolder/test1.js";
```

With this, the client application uses the same protocol (*http* or *https*) used to access the parent page.

Multiple scripts can be loaded into the page using this approach. It can also be used to load CSS files, as well as larger images or other media files. However, we don't have to do the work ourselves: we can use a script loading library, such as HeadJS.

According to the HeadJS documentation, the best approach to including support for the library is to include a link to the library in the `head` element:

```
<html>
  <head>
    <script src="head.min.js"></script>
    <script>
      head.load("file1.js", "file2.js");
    </script>
  </head>
  <body>
    <!-- my content-->

    <script>
      head.ready(function () {
            // some callback stuff
      });
    </script>
  </body>
</html>
```

Note the head.load() function call. All of the script files to be loaded are listed in the function call. In addition, any ready state functionality can be provided in the head.ready() function call.

If you do have JavaScript, you want to load right away; rather than using another script element, you can use a *data-* attribute on the script element loading HeadJS:

```
<script src="head.min.js" data-headjs-load="init.js"></script>
```

Any immediately invoked functionality is then listed in *init.js*.

 HeadJS has other functionality, including assistance for responsive design and browser version support. Read more about setting it up in the set up documentation (*http://bit.ly/1yI09Lc*).

Another script loader with an interesting twist is Basket.js. It also loads JavaScript files asynchronously, but it goes a step further: it caches the script using localStorage, which means if the JavaScript has already been accessed once, a second access loads the JavaScript from cache rather than loading the file again.

Once you include the Basket.js JavaScript file, you can then define the JavaScript files to be loaded:

```
<!DOCTYPE html>
<html lang="en">
  <head>
    <meta charset="utf-8">
    <title>title</title>
  </head>
<body>
  <script src="basket.full.min.js"></script>
```

```
<script>
  basket.require({ url: 'test1.js'},
                 { url: 'test2.js'});
</script>
</body>
</html>
```

If you monitor the page using your browser's debugger/development tools, and reload the page, you'll note that the files aren't accessed again after the first load.

To handle source dependencies, Basket.js returns a *promise* from require(), and the then() callback is executed. You can then list the second JavaScript file in the callback:

```
<script>
    basket.require({ url: 'test2.js'}).then(function() {
        basket.require({ url: 'test1.js'});
    });
</script>
```

Access Basket.js and read how to use it in the library's home page (*http://addyosmani.github.io/basket.js/*).

12.2. Loading Scripts Asynchronously the HTML5 Way

Problem

You're interested in processing scripts asynchronously—not blocking the page from loading while the scripts load—but you have discovered that the *script injection* technique has one problem: the CSS Object Model (CSSOM) blocks inline scripts because these scripts typically operate on the CSSOM. Since the CSSOM doesn't know what the script is going to do, it blocks the script until all of the CSS is loaded. This, then, delays the network access of the script until all CSS files have been loaded.

Solution

Use the new HTML5 async script element attribute instead of script injection:

```
<script src="//cdnjs.cloudflare.com/ajax/libs/mathjs/0.26.0/math.min.js" async>
</script>
<script
src="//cdnjs.cloudflare.com/ajax/libs/backbone.js/1.1.2/backbone-min.js" async>
</script>
```

Discussion

There are two script element attributes: `defer`, which defers script loading until the rest of the page is loaded, and the newest `async`. The latter tells the browser to load the script asynchronously, as the page is being parsed. It only works with external scripts; the page still blocks with inline scripts.

The `async` attribute prevents many of the problems we've had with blocked scripts and having to use tricks such as script injection. The only reason script injection is still being used is there are older versions of browsers, such as IE9 and older, that don't support it.

12.3. Converting Your JavaScript to AMD and RequireJS

Problem

You're interested in taking advantage of modularization and controlled dependencies by converting your libraries to the Asynchronous Module Definition (AMD) format, implemented with RequireJS, but you're not sure where to start and what to do.

Solution

RequireJS is integrated into the following three small JavaScript libraries:

one.js

```
define(function() {
        return {
          hi: function() {
            console.log('hello from one');
          }
        }
});
```

two.js

```
define(function() {
        return {
          hi: function(val) {
            console.log('hello ' + val + ' from two');
          }
        }
});
```

mylib.js

```
require(["./one","./two"],function(one,two) {
        one.hi();
        two.hi('world');
        console.log("And that's all");
});
```

And the web page, *index.html*:

```
<!DOCTYPE html>
<html>
  <head>
    <title>Hello Modularization</title>
    <script data-main="scripts/mylib" src="scripts/require.js"></script>
  </head>
  <body>
    <h1>Stuff</h1>
  </body>
</html>
```

Discussion

Consider the following three very basic JavaScript libraries:

one.js

```
function oneHi() {
  console.log('hello from one');
}
```

two.js

```
function twoHi(val) {
  console.log('hello ' + val + ' from two');
}
```

mylib.js

```
function allThat() {
  oneHi();
  twoHi('world');
  console.log("And that's all");
}
```

They could be included in a simple web page as demonstrated in the following code, assuming all the JavaScript libraries are in a subdirectory named *scripts/*:

```
<!DOCTYPE html>
<html>
  <head>
    <title>Hello Modularization</title>
    <script src="scripts/one.js" type="text/javascript"></script>
    <script src="scripts/two.js" type="text/javascript"></script>
    <script src="scripts/mylib.js" type="text/javascript"></script>
    <script type="text/javascript">
      allThat();
    </script>
  </head>
  <body>
    <h1>Stuff</h1>
```

```
    </body>
</html>
```

And you might expect the application to work, with the messages printed out in the right order. However, if you make a modest change, such as use the `async` attribute with all of the scripts:

```
<script src="scripts/one.js" async type="text/javascript"></script>
<script src="scripts/two.js" async type="text/javascript"></script>
<script src="scripts/mylib.js" async type="text/javascript"></script>
```

You'll be hosed, because the browser no longer blocks program execution, waiting for each script to load, in turn, before going to the next. Other challenges that can occur are that you're using other people's libraries and you don't know the correct order to list the source scripts, or you forget one or more of them. The problem with this common approach from the past is that nothing enforces both order and dependencies. That's where RequireJS comes in.

In the solution, you'll notice two key words: `define` and `require`. The `define` keyword is used to define a module, while `require` is used to list dependencies with a callback function that's called when all dependencies are loaded.

In the solution, two of the libraries are defined as modules, each return a function. The third library, *mylib.js*, declares the two modules as dependencies and in the callback function, invokes the returned module functions. All of this is pulled into the HTML page with the following line:

```
<script data-main="scripts/mylib" src="scripts/require.js"></script>
```

The actual source is the RequireJS library (*http://requirejs.org/*). The custom attribute `data-main` specifies the JavaScript source to load after RequireJS is loaded.

The modules can return more than one function, or can return data objects, functions, or a combination of both:

```
define(function() {
    return {
        value1: 'one',
        value2: 'two',
        doSomething: function() {
            // do something
        }
    }
})
```

Modules can also have dependencies. The following code version of *two.js* creates a dependency on *one.js* in *two.js* and removes it as a dependency in *mylib.js*:

two.js

```
define(['one'], function(one) {
        return {
            hi: function(val) {
                one.hi();
                console.log('hello ' + val + ' from two');
            }
        }
});
```

mylib.js

```
require(["./two"],function(two) {
        two.hi('world');
        console.log("And that's all");
});
```

 Typically after you create your JavaScript files, you'll want to optimize them. RequireJS provides the tools and documentation for optimizing your source at *http://requirejs.org/docs/optimization.html*.

See Also

Your library can still exist as a standard JavaScript library and an AMD-compliant module, as discussed in Recipe 12.9.

12.4. Using RequireJS with jQuery or Another Library

Problem

Your applications uses jQuery (or Underscore.js or Backbone). How can the library fit into the use of RequireJS to manage dependencies?

Solution

If the library can work with AMD (as jQuery can), and you save the jQuery file as *jquery.js* and load it in the same directory as your application JavaScript, you can use the jQuery functionality easily, as shown in the following small code snippet:

```
require(["./jquery"],function($) {
    $('h1').css('color','red');
});
```

However, if the jQuery file is named something else, or you're accessing the library from a CDN, then you'll need to use a RequireJS *shim*:

```
requirejs.config({
  baseUrl: 'scripts/lib',
  paths: {
    jquery: '//ajax.googleapis.com/ajax/libs/jquery/2.1.1/jquery.min'
  },
});
```

Discussion

As the solution demonstrates, if your application code already incorporates jQuery's dollar sign ($) and the jQuery file is local to the script, you can incorporate its use in your application in the same manner used for any other module. The jQuery library can recognize that it's within a RequireJS environment, and respond accordingly. Where things get a little more complicated is if the library is not accessed locally, is accessed from a CDN, or the library doesn't support AMD.

To demonstrate, I modified the source files discussed in Recipe 12.3. The source files are now organized in the following directory structure:

```
www
  app
    main.js
  index.html
  scripts
    app.js
    lib
      one.js
      require.js
      two.js
```

In addition, I removed the `define()` in the source library *two.js*, making it into an *anonymous closure*—an IIFE object that is added to the Window object as two:

```
(function (){
  window.two = this;
  this.hi = function(val) {
    console.log('hello ' + val + ' from two');
  }
}());
```

The *one.js* file still contains the AMD `define()` statement, meaning it requires no special handling to use:

```
define(function() {
    return {
      hi: function() {
          console.log('hello from one');
        }
    }
});
```

The *app.js* file contains a RequireJS `config` block that, among other things, sets a `base Url` for all loaded modules, defines a CDN path for both jQuery and the app subdirectory, and creates a shim for the non-AMD compliant `two`. It also loads the `app/main` module:

```
requirejs.config({
    baseUrl: 'scripts/lib',
    paths: {
        app: '../../app',
        jquery: '//ajax.googleapis.com/ajax/libs/jquery/2.1.1/jquery.min'
    },
    shim: {
        two: {
            exports: 'two'
        }
    }
});

requirejs(["app/main"]);
```

The shim for `two` defines an exported object (an object defined on Window in the browser), since the library doesn't use `define()` to identify the object.

Lastly, the *main.js* module lays out the dependency on jQuery, one, and two, and runs the application:

```
define(["jquery","one","two"],function($,one, two) {
    one.hi();
    two.hi('world');
    console.log("And that's all");
    $('h1').css('color','red');
});
```

If two had been dependent on one of the modules or other libraries, such as one, the dependency would have been noted in the shim:

```
requirejs.config({
    baseUrl: 'scripts/lib',
    paths: {
        app: '../../app',
        jquery: '//ajax.googleapis.com/ajax/libs/jquery/2.1.1/jquery.min'
    },
    shim: {
        two: {
            deps: ['one'],
            exports: 'two'
        }
    }
});
```

If you'd like to make your JavaScript library into an AMD-compliant module, but still allow it to be used in other contexts, you can add a small amount of code to ensure both:

```
(function (){
  window.two = this;
  this.hi =  function(val) {
    console.log('hello ' + val + ' from two');
  }

}());
```

The tiny library is now redesigned into an IIFE. Any private data and methods would be fully enclosed in the closure, and the only public method is exposed by adding it as a property to the object. The object itself is given global access via assignment to the Window property.

A variation on this would be the following, where the exposed methods and data are returned as an object to the assigned variable:

```
var two = (function (){
  return {
    hi: function (val) {
      console.log('hello ' + val + ' from two');
    }
  }

}());
```

The code now meets the *module pattern*, ensuring both public and private data and functions are encapsulated using the closure, and globally accessible methods and data are returned in the object. Another variation of the module pattern is the following:

```
var two = (function() {
  var my = {};
  my.hi = function(val) {
      console.log('hello ' + val + ' from two');
    };
  return my;
}());
```

I modified the original form of the object to make it AMD compliant:

```
(function (){
  window.two = this;
  this.hi =  function(val) {
    console.log('hello ' + val + ' from two');
  }

  if ( typeof define === "function" && define.amd ) {
    define( "two", [], function() {
      return two;
    });
  }
}());
```

The code tests to see if the `define()` function exists. If so, then it's invoked, passing in the name of the exported library object and in the callback, returning the exported library object. This is how a library such as jQuery can work in AMD, but still work in other traditional JavaScript environments.

A variation, using the more established module pattern, is the following:

```
var two = (function (){
    var two = {};

    two.hi =  function(val) {
        console.log('hello ' + val + ' from two');
    }

    if ( typeof define === "function" && define.amd ) {
        define( "two", [], function() {
            return two;
        });
    }

    return two;
}());
```

 jQuery also supports the CommonJS modular system.

12.5. Loading and Using Dojo Modules

Problem

You're interested in using some of the Dojo functionality, but you're not sure how to load the associated modules.

Solution

Dojo has implemented the AMD architecture for its functionality. When you add the main Dojo script to your page, what you're loading is the module loader, rather than all of its various functions:

```
<script src="http://ajax.googleapis.com/ajax/libs/dojo/1.10.0/dojo/dojo.js"
        data-dojo-config="async: true"></script>
```

The library can be accessed at a CDN, as the code snippet demonstrates. The custom data attribute `data-dojo-config` specifies that the Dojo asynchronous AMD loader should be used.

To use the Dojo functionality, specify the dependencies in the `require()` method:

```
<script>
    require([
        'dojo/dom',
        'dojo/dom-construct'
    ], function (dom, domConstruct) {
        var ph = dom.byId("placeholder");
        ph.innerHTML = "Using Dojo";
        domConstruct.create("h1", {innerHTML: "<i>Howdy!</i>"},ph,"before");
    });
</script>
```

Discussion

Dojo is a sophisticated library system providing functionality similar to that provided in the jQuery environment. It does require a little time to become familiar with its implementation of AMD, though, before jumping in.

In the solution, the Dojo asynchronous loader is sourced from a CDN. The solution then imports two Dojo modules: dojo/dom and dojo/dom-construct. Both provide much of the basic DOM functionality, such as the ability to access an existing element by an identifier (dom.byId()), and create and place a new element (domConstruct.create()). To give you a better idea how it all holds together, a complete page example is given in Example 12-1.

Example 12-1. A complete Dojo example accessing one page element and adding another

```
<!DOCTYPE html>
<html>
<head>
  <meta charset="utf-8">
  <title>Dojo</title>
  <script src="http://ajax.googleapis.com/ajax/libs/dojo/1.10.0/dojo/dojo.js"
          data-dojo-config="async: true"></script>
</head>
<body>
  <div id="placeholder"></div>
  <script>
    require([
        'dojo/dom',
        'dojo/dom-construct'
    ], function (dom, domConstruct) {
        var ph = dom.byId("placeholder");
        ph.innerHTML = "Using Dojo";
        domConstruct.create("h1", {innerHTML: "<i>Howdy!</i>"},ph,"before");
    });
  </script>
</body>
</html>
```

Though Dojo is generally AMD-compatible, there's still some funkiness with the implementation that makes it incompatible with a module loader like RequireJS. The *concepts* of a module loader, the `require()` and `define()` functions, and creating a configuration object are the same, but implementation compatibility fails.

Dojo does provide a decent set of tutorials (*http://dojotoolkit.org/documentation/*) to help you understand more fully how the framework operates.

12.6. Installing and Maintaining Node Modules with npm

Problem

You're new to Node. You've installed it, and played around with the core Node modules installed with Node. But now, you need something more.

Solution

The glue that holds the Node universe together is npm, the Node package manager. To install a specific module, use the following on the command line:

```
npm install packagename
```

If you want to install the package globally, so it's accessible from all locations in the computer, use the following:

```
npm install -g packagename
```

When to install locally or globally is dependent on whether you're going to `require()` the module, or if you need to run it from the command line. Typically you install `require()` modules locally, and executables are installed globally, though you don't *have* to follow this typical usage. If you do install a module globally, you might need administrative privileges:

```
sudo npm install -g packagename
```

Discussion

The solution demonstrated the most common use of npm: installing a registered npm module locally or globally on your system. However, you can install modules that are located in GitHub, downloaded as a tar file, or located in a folder. If you type:

```
npm install --help
```

you'll get a list of allowable approaches for installing a module:

```
npm install
npm install <pkg>
```

```
npm install <pkg>@<tag>
npm install <pkg>@<version>
npm install <pkg>@<version range>
npm install <folder>
npm install <tarball file>
npm install <tarball url>
npm install <git:// url>
npm install <github username>/<github project>
```

If your current directory contains a *npm-shrinkwrap.json* or *package.json* file, the dependencies in the files are installed by typing npm install.

 Recipe 12.10 covers the structure and purpose of the *package.json* file.

To remove an installed Node module, use:

```
npm rm packagename
```

The package and any dependencies are removed. To update existing packages, use:

```
npm update [g] [packagename [packagename ...]]
```

You can update locally or globally installed modules. When updating, you can list all modules to be updated, or just type the command to update all locally-installed modules relative to your current location.

12.7. Searching for a Specific Node Module via npm

Problem

You're creating a Node application and want to reuse existing modules, but you don't know how to discover them.

Solution

In most cases, you'll discover modules via recommendations from your friends and co-developers, but sometimes you need something new.

You can search for new modules directly at the npm website (*https://www.npmjs.org/*). The front page also lists the most popular modules, which are worth an exploratory look.

You can also use npm directly to search for a module. For instance, if you're interested in modules that do something with PDFs, run the following search at the command line:

```
npm search pdf
```

Discussion

The npm website (*https://www.npmjs.org/*) provides more than just good documentation for using npm; it also provides a listing of newly updated modules, as well as those modules most depended on. Regardless of what you're looking for, you definitely should spend time exploring these essential modules. In addition, if you access each module's page at npm, you can see how popular the module is, what other modules are dependent on it, the license, and other relevant information.

However, you can also search for modules, directly, using npm.

The first time you perform a search with npm, you'll get the following feedback:

```
npm WARN Building the local index for the first time, please be patient
```

The process can take a fair amount of time, too. Luckily, the index build only needs to be performed the first time you do a search. And when it finishes, you're likely to get a huge number of modules in return, especially with a broader topic such as modules that work with PDFs.

You can refine the results by listing multiple terms:

```
npm search PDF generation
```

This query returns a much smaller list of modules, specific to PDF generation. You can also use a regular expression to search:

```
npm search \/Firefox\\sOS
```

Now I'm getting all modules that reference Firefox OS. However, as the example demonstrates, you have to incorporate escape characters specific to your environment, as I did with the beginning of the regular expression, and the use of \s for white space.

Once you do find a module that sounds interesting, you can get detailed information about it with:

```
npm view node-firefoxos-cli
```

You'll get the *package.json* file for the module, which can tell you what it's dependent on, who wrote it, and when it was created. I still recommend checking out the module's GitHub page directly. There you'll be able to determine if the module is being actively maintained or not. If you access the npm website page for the module, you'll also get an idea of how popular the module is.

12.8. Converting Your Library into a Node Module

Problem

You want to use one of your libraries in Node.

Solution

Convert the library into a Node module. For example, if the library is designed as the following IIFE:

```
(function () {
    var val = 'world';
    console.log('Hello ' + val + ' from two');
}());
```

You can convert it to work with Node by the simple addition of an `exports` keyword:

```
module.exports = (function () {
            return {
              hi: function(val) {
                    console.log('Hello ' + val + ' from two');
                }
            };
        }());
```

You can then use the module in your application:

```
var two = require('./two.js');

two.hi('world');
```

Discussion

Node's module system is based on CommonJS, the second modular system covered in this chapter. CommonJS uses three constructs: `exports` to define what's exported from the library, `require()` to include the module in the application, and `module`, which includes information about the module but also can be used to export a function, directly.

Though the solution maintains the IIFE, it's not really required in the CommonJS environment, because every module operates in its own module space. The following is also acceptable:

```
module.exports.hi = function (val) {
    console.log('hello ' + val + ' from two');
}
```

If your library returns an object with several functions and data objects, you can assign each to the comparably named property on `module.exports`, or you could return an object from a function:

```
module.exports = function () {
        return {
          somedata: 'some data',
          hi: function(val) {
                console.log('Hello ' + val + ' from two');
            }
        };
        };
```

And then invoke the object in the application:

```
var twoObj = require('./two.js');

var two = twoObj();
two.hi(two.somedata);
```

Or you can access the object property directly:

```
var hi = require('./twob.js').hi;

hi('world');
```

Because the module isn't installed using npm, and just resides in the directory where the application resides, it's accessed by the location and name, not just the name.

See Also

In Recipe 12.9, I cover how to make sure your library code works in all of the environments: CommonJS, Node, AMD, and as a traditional JavaScript library.

12.9. Taking Your Code Across All Module Environments

Problem

You've written a library that you'd like to share with others, but folks are using a variety of module systems to incorporate external JavaScript. How can you ensure your library works in all of the various environments?

Solution

The following library with two functions:

```
function concatArray(str, array) {
  return array.map(function(element) {
      return str + ' ' + element;
  });
```

```
}

function splitArray(str,array) {
  return array.map(function(element) {
      var len = str.length + 1;
      return element.substring(len);
  });
}
```

Will work with RequireJS, Node, as a plain script, and CommonJS in the browser when converted to:

```
(function(global) {
    'use strict';

    var bbArray = {};

    bbArray.concatArray = function (str, array) {
            return array.map(function(element) {
              return str + ' ' + element;
            });
        };

    bbArray.splitArray = function (str,array) {
            return array.map(function(element) {
              var len = str.length + 1;
              return element.substring(len);
            });
        };

    if (typeof module != 'undefined' && module.exports) {
      module.exports = bbArray;
    } else if ( typeof define === "function" && define.amd ) {
       define( "bbArray", [], function() {
          return bbArray;
       });
    } else {
      global.bbArray = bbArray;
    }

}(this));
```

Discussion

To ensure your library works in a traditional scripting environment, you should encapsulate your functionality in an IIFE, to minimize leak between private and public functionality and data. You'll also want to limit pollution of the global space:

```
(function(global) {
    'use strict';

    var bbArray = {};
```

```
    bbArray.concatArray = function (str, array) {
          return array.map(function(element) {
            return str + ' ' + element;
          });
    };

    bbArray.splitArray = function (str,array) {
          return array.map(function(element) {
            var len = str.length + 1;
            return element.substring(len);
          });
    };

    global.bbArray = bbArray;

}(this));
```

The object is being used in an environment that may not have access to a window object, so the global object (global in Node, window in the browser) is passed as an argument to the object as this, and then defined as global in the library.

At this point, the library can work as a traditional library in a browser application:

```
<!DOCTYPE html>
<html>
<head>
  <meta charset="utf-8">
  <title>Array test</title>
  <script src="bbarray.js" type="text/javascript">
  </script>
  <script type="text/javascript">
      var a = ['one', 'two', 'three'];
      var b = bbArray.concatArray('number is ',a);
      console.log(b);
      var c = bbArray.splitArray('number is ', b);
      console.log(c);
  </script>
</head>
<body>
</body>
</html>
```

The result is two print outs to the console:

```
[ 'number is  one', 'number is  two', 'number is  three' ]
[ 'one', 'two', 'three' ]
```

Next, we'll add the Node support. We add this using the following lines of code:

```
if (typeof module != 'undefined' && module.exports) {
  module.exports = bbArray;
}
```

This code checks whether the module object is defined and if it is, whether the mod ule.exports object exists. If the tests succeed, then the object is assigned to module.ex ports, no different than defining exported functionality (covered earlier in Recipe 12.8). It can now be accessed in a Node application like the following:

```
var bbArray = require('./bbarray.js');

var a = ['one', 'two', 'three'];
var b = bbArray.concatArray('number is ',a);
console.log(b);
var c = bbArray.splitArray('number is ', b);
console.log(c);
```

Now we add support for CommonJS, specifically RequireJS. From Recipe 12.4, we know to check if define exists, and if so, to add support for RequireJS. After adding this modification, the library module now looks like this:

```
(function(global) {
    'use strict';

    var bbArray = {};

    bbArray.concatArray = function (str, array) {
            return array.map(function(element) {
              return str + ' ' + element;
            });
        };

    bbArray.splitArray = function (str,array) {
            return array.map(function(element) {
              var len = str.length + 1;
              return element.substring(len);
            });
        };


    if (typeof module != 'undefined' && module.exports) {
       module.exports = bbArray;
    } else if ( typeof define === "function" && define.amd ) {
        define( "bbArray", [], function() {
          return bbArray;
        });
    } else {
       global.bbArray = bbAarray;
    }

}(this));
```

The module can now be used in a web application that incorporates RequireJS for module support. Following RequireJS's suggestion that all inline scripts be pulled into a separate file, the JavaScript application to test the library is created in a file named *main.js*:

```
require(["./bbarray"], function(bbArray) {
    var a = ['one', 'two', 'three'];
    var b = bbArray.concatArray('number is ',a);
    console.log(b);
    var c = bbArray.splitArray('number is ', b);
    console.log(c);
});
```

And the web page incorporates the RequireJS script, loaded via CDN:

```
<!DOCTYPE html>
<html>
<head>
  <meta charset="utf-8">
  <title>Array test</title>
  <script src="//cdnjs.cloudflare.com/ajax/libs/require.js/2.1.14/require.min.js"
    data-main="main">
  </script>
</head>
<body>

</body>
</html>
```

Modify the URL for Require.js to match what's available at the CDN when you run the test.

See Also

The example covered in this recipe works in all of our environments but it has one limitation: it's not using any other libraries. So what happens when you need to include libraries?

This is where things can get ugly. We know that CommonJS/Node import dependencies with `require`:

```
var library = require('somelib');
```

While AMD incorporates dependencies in `require` or `define`:

```
define(['./somelib'], function(library) {

// rest of the code
});
```

Not compatible. At all. The workaround for this problem has been either to use Browserify (covered in Recipe 12.12) or to incorporate a *Universal Module Definition* (UMD). You can see examples of a UMD online, and it's covered in detail in Addy Osmani's

"Writing Modular JavaScript with AMD, CommonJS, and ES Harmony" (*http://addyos mani.com/writing-modular-js/*).

12.10. Creating an Installable Node Module

Problem

You've either created a Node module from scratch, or converted an existing library to one that will work in the browser or in Node. Now, you want to know how to modify it into a module that can be installed using npm.

Solution

Once you've created your Node module and any supporting functionality (including module tests), you can package the entire directory. The key to packaging and publishing the Node module is creating a *package.json* file that describes the module, any dependencies, the directory structure, what to ignore, and so on.

The following is a relatively basic *package.json* file:

```
{
  "name": "bbArray",
  "version": "0.1.0",
  "description": "A description of what my module is about",
  "main": "./lib/bbArray",
  "author": {
    "name": "Shelley Powers"
  },
  "keywords": [
    "array",
    "utility"
  ],
  "repository": {
    "type": "git",
    "url": "https://github.com/accountname/bbarray.git"
  },
  "engines" : {
    "node" : ">=0.10.3 <0.12"
  },
  "bugs": {
    "url": "https://github.com/accountname/bbarray/issues"
  },
  "licenses": [
    {
      "type": "MIT",
      "url": "https://github.com/accountname/bbarray/raw/master/LICENSE"
    }
  ],
  "dependencies": {
```

```
      "some-module": "~0.1.0"
   },
   "directories":{
      "doc":"./doc",
      "man":"./man",
      "lib":"./lib",
      "bin":"./bin"
   },
   "scripts": {
      "test": "nodeunit test/test-bbarray.js"
   }
}
```

Once you've created *package.json*, package all the source directories and the *package.json* file as a gzipped tarball. Then install the package locally, or install it in npm for public access.

Discussion

The *package.json* file is key to packaging a Node module up for local installation or uploading to npm for management. At a minimum, it requires a `name` and a `version`. The other fields given in the solution are:

- `description`: A description of what the module is and does
- `main`: Entry module for application
- `author`: Author(s) of the module
- `keywords`: List of keywords appropriate for module
- `repository`: Place where code lives, typically GitHub
- `engines`: Node version you know your module works with
- `bugs`: Where to file bugs
- `licenses`: License for your module
- `dependencies`: Any module dependencies
- `directories`: A hash describing directory structure for your module
- `scripts`: A hash of object commands that are run during module lifecycle

There are a host of other options, which are described at the npm website (*https://www.npmjs.org/doc/files/package.json.html*). You can also use a tool to help you fill in many of these fields. Typing the following at the command line runs the tool that asks questions and then generates a basic *package.json* file:

```
npm init
```

Once you have your source set up and your *package.json* file, you can test whether everything works by running the following command in the top-level directory of your module:

```
npm install . -g
```

If you have no errors, then you can package the file as a gzipped tarball. At this point, if you want to publish the module, you'll first need to add yourself as a user in the npm registry:

```
npm add-user
```

To publish the Node module to the npm registry, use the following in the root directory of the module, specifying a URL to the tarball, a filename for the tarball, or a path:

```
npm publish ./
```

If you have development dependencies for your module, such as using a testing framework like Mocha, one excellent shortcut to ensure these are added to your *package.json* file is to use the following, in the same directory as the *package.json* file, when you're installing the dependent module:

```
npm install -g mocha --save-dev
```

Not only does this install Mocha (discussed later, in Recipe 12.13), this command also updates your *package.json* file with the following:

```
"devDependencies": {
    "grunt": "^0.4.5",
    "grunt-contrib-jshint": "^0.10.0",
    "mocha": "^1.21.4"
}
```

You can also use this same type of option to add a module to dependencies in *package.json*. The following:

```
npm install d3 --save
```

adds the following to the *package.json* file:

```
"dependencies": {
    "d3": "^3.4.11"
}
```

If the module is no longer needed and shouldn't be listed in *package.json*, remove it from the devDependencies with:

```
npm remove mocha --save-dev
```

And remove a module from dependencies with:

```
npm remove d3 --save
```

If the module is the last in either `dependencies` or `devDependencies`, the property isn't removed. It's just set to an empty value:

```
"dependencies": {}
```

npm provides a decent developer guide for creating and installing a Node module (*http://bit.ly/1yI0ihz*). You should consider the use of an *.npmignore* file for keeping stuff *out* of your module. And though this is beyond the scope of the book, you should also become familiar with Git and GitHub, and make use of it for your applications/modules.

Extra: The README File and Markdown Syntax

When you package your module or library for reuse and upload it to a source repository such as GitHub, you'll need to provide how-to information about installing the module/library and basic information about how to use it. For this, you need a README file.

You've seen files named *README.md* or *readme.md* with applications and Node modules. They're text-based with some odd, unobtrusive markup that you're not sure is useful, until you see it in a site like GitHub, where the README file provides all of the project page installation and usage information. The markup translates into HTML, making for readable Web-based help.

The content for the README is marked up with annotation known as Markdown. The popular website Daring Fireball calls Markdown easy to read and write, but "Readability, however, is emphasized above all else." Unlike with HTML, the Markdown markup doesn't get in the way of reading the text.

Daring Fireball also provides an overview of generic Markdown (*http://bit.ly/df-markdown*), but if you're working with GitHub files, you might also want to check out GitHub's Flavored Markdown (*http://bit.ly/1yI0iOz*).

In Recipe 18.5 in Chapter 18, I created a simple Firefox OS mobile app named "Where Am I?" Part of its installation is a *README.md* file that provides information about using the app. The following is a brief excerpt from the file:

```
# Where Am I?

This is a simple demonstration Firefox OS app that uses the Geolocation API
to get the user's current location, and then loads a static map into the page.

## Obtaining

The Where Am I? app is hosted on the web, in a [Burningbird work directory]
```

```
(http://burningbird.net/work/whereami)

## Usage

Import it into the Mozilla WebIDE using the hosted app option, and then run
the app in one or more simulators.
```

When I use a CLI tool like Pandoc (*http://johnmacfarlane.net/pandoc/*), I can covert the
README.md file into readable HTML:

```
pandoc README.md -o readme.html
```

Figure 12-1 displays the generated content. It's not fancy, but it is imminently readable.

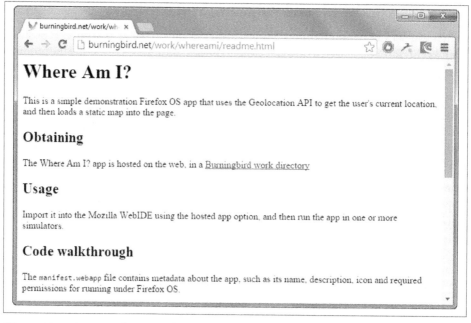

Figure 12-1. Generated HTML from README.md text and Markdown annotation

When you install your source in a site such as GitHub (discussed in Recipe 7.12 in
Chapter 7), GitHub uses the *README.md* file to generate the cover page for the
repository.

12.11. Packaging and Managing Your Client-Side Dependencies with Bower

Problem

You really like how npm manages dependencies and wish there was something comparable for the client.

Solution

Bower can help you manage client dependencies. To use it you must have Node, npm, and support for Git installed on your client or server.

Once your environment is set up, install Bower using npm:

```
npm install -g bower
```

Now, to add packages to the *bower-components* subdirectory, install them with bower:

```
bower install jquery
```

Then you can create a *bower.json* file by typing the following in the root directory of your library or application:

```
bower init
```

The application asks a set of questions and generates a *bower.json* file, which can be used to install the dependencies with another simple command:

```
bower install
```

Discussion

Bower is a way of keeping your script and other dependencies collected and up to date. Unlike npm, it can work with a variety of file extensions, including CSS, images, as well as script. You can use it to install dependencies in *bower-components*, and then access the dependencies directly in your web applications:

```
<script src="path/to/bower_components/d3/d3.min.js"></script>
```

You can package all of your application's dependencies in a *bower.json* file, and reinstall them in a fresh directory with a simple command (in the same directory as the *bower.json* file):

```
bower install
```

To ensure you're using the latest and greatest version of the module and library, update your dependencies:

```
bower update
```

If your application is publicly available on GitHub, you can register its dependencies in Bower by, first, ensuring the *bower.json* file for the application is accurate, you're using semantic versioning (*http://semver.org/*) with your Git tags, your application is publicly available as a Git end point (such as GitHub), and the package name adheres to the *bower.json* specification. Once these dependencies are met, register the application:

```
bower register <package-name> <git-endpoint>
```

If you're wondering why you can't use something like `require` directly with Bower, remember that it's a dependency management tool, just like npm. It's the libraries and infrastructure in place, such as RequireJS, that allows you to use modular AMD or CommonJS techniques.

You can read more about using Bower at the application's website (*http://bower.io/*).

Bower can be used with other tools, such as Grunt, demonstrated later in Recipe 12.14.

12.12. Compiling Node.js Modules for Use in the Browser with Browserify

Problem

Node has a lot of really great modules that you'd really like to use in your browser.

Solution

You can use Browserify to compile the Node module into browser accessible code. If it's one of the Node core modules, many are already compiled into shims that can be used in your browser application.

For instance, if you're interested in using the Node `querystring` module functionality, you create a client JavaScript bundle using the following Browserify command:

```
browserify -r querystring > bundle.js
```

Then use the module in your browser app:

```
<script src="bundle.js" type="text/javascript">
</script>
<script type="text/javascript">
 var qs = require('querystring');

 var str = qs.stringify({ first: 'apple', second: 'pear', third: 'pineapple'})
;
 console.log(str); //first=apple&second=pear&third=pineapple
</script
```

Discussion

Browserify is a tool that basically moves Node functionality to the browser, as long as doing so makes sense. Of course, some functionality won't work (think input/output) but a surprising amount of functionality, including that in Node core, can work in the browser.

Browserify is installed via npm:

```
npm install -g browserify
```

It runs at the command line, as shown in the solution. In the solution, the -r flag triggers Browserify into creating a require() function to wrap the module's functionality, so we can use it in a similar manner in the browser app. The querystring module is one of the many Node core modules already compiled as a shim. The others are:

- assert
- buffer
- console
- constants
- crypto
- domain
- events
- http
- https
- os
- path
- punycode
- querystring
- stream
- string_decoder
- timers
- tty
- url
- util
- vm

- zlib

You can also compile other Node modules into browser code, including your own. As an example, let's say I have the following three Node files:

one.js

```
module.exports = function() {
   console.log('hi from one');
};
```

two.js

```
var one = require ('./one');

module.exports = function(val) {
   one();
   console.log('hi ' + val + ' from two');
};
```

index.js

```
var two = require ('./two');

module.exports = function() {
  two('world');
  console.log("And that's all");
}
```

I compiled it into an *appl.js* file using the following:

```
browserify ./index.js -o ./appl.js
```

Including the library in a web page results in the same three console `log()` function calls as you would see if you ran the original *index.js* file with Node, as soon as the generated script file is loaded.

12.13. Unit Testing Your Node Modules

Problem

You want to know the best way to ensure your module is ready for others to try.

Solution

Add *unit tests* as part of your production process.

Given the following module, named bbarray, and created in a file named *index.js* in the module directory:

```
var util = require('util');
```

```
(function(global) {
    'use strict';

    var bbarray = {};

    bbarray.concatArray = function (str, array) {
        if (!util.isArray(array) || array.length === 0) {
            return -1;
        } else if (typeof str != 'string') {
            return -1;
        } else {
            return array.map(function(element) {
                return str + ' ' + element;
            });
        }
    };
    bbarray.splitArray = function (str,array) {
        if (!util.isArray(array) || array.length === 0) {
            return -1;
        } else if (typeof str != 'string') {
            return -1;
        } else {
            return array.map(function(element) {
                var len = str.length + 1;
                return element.substring(len);
            });
        }
    };
    if (typeof module != 'undefined' && module.exports) {
        module.exports = bbarray;
    } else if ( typeof define === "function" && define.amd ) {
        define( "bbarray", [], function() {
            return bbarray;
        });
    } else {
        global.bbarray = bbaarray;
    }

}(this));
```

Using Mocha, a JavaScript testing framework, and Node's built-in `assert` module, the following unit test (created as *index.js* and located in the project's *test* subdirectory) should result in the successful pass of six tests:

```
var assert = require('assert');
var bbarray = require('../index.js');

describe('bbarray',function() {
    describe('#concatArray()', function() {
        it('should return -1 when not using array', function() {
            assert.equal(-1, bbarray.concatArray(9,'str'));
        });
```

```
it('should return -1 when not using string', function() {
    assert.equal(-1, bbarray.concatArray(9,['test','two']));
});
it('should return an array with proper args', function() {
    assert.deepEqual(['is test','is three'],
                    bbarray.concatArray('is',['test','three']));
});
});
describe('#splitArray()', function() {
    it('should return -1 when not using array', function() {
        assert.equal(-1, bbarray.splitArray(9,'str'));
    });
    it('should return -1 when not using string', function() {
        assert.equal(-1, bbarray.splitArray(9,['test','two']));
    });
    it('should return an array with proper args', function() {
        assert.deepEqual(['test','three'],
                        bbarray.splitArray('is',['is test','is three']));
    });
});
});
```

The result of the test is shown in Figure 12-2, run using npm test.

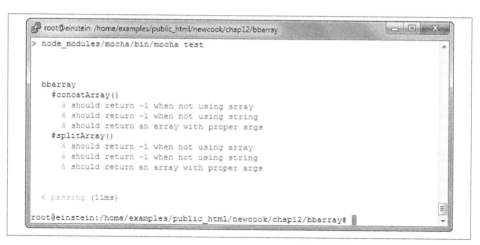

Figure 12-2. Running unit tests based on Node Assert and Mocha

Discussion

Unit testing is one of those development tasks that may seem like a pain when you first start, but can soon become second nature. I don't necessarily agree with the folks that believe we should write the unit tests (*test-driven development*) first, before writing the code. But developing both test and code in parallel to each other should be a goal.

A *unit test* is a way that developers test their code to ensure it meets the specifications. It involves testing functional behavior, and seeing what happens when you send bad arguments—or no arguments at all. It's called unit testing because it's used with individual units of code, such as testing one module in a Node application, as compared to testing the entire Node application. It becomes one part of *integration testing*, where all the pieces are plugged together, before going to *user acceptance testing*: testing to ensure that the application does what users expect it to do (and that they generally don't hate it when they use it).

In the solution, I use two different functionalities for testing: Node's built-in `assert` module, and Mocha, a sophisticated testing framework. My module is simple, so I'm not using some of the more complex Mocha testing mechanisms. However, I think you'll get a feel for what's happening.

To install Mocha, use the following:

```
npm install mocha --save-dep
```

I'm using the `--save-dep` flag, because I'm installing Mocha into the module's Node dependencies. In addition, I modify the module's *package.json* file to add the following section:

```
"scripts": {
    "test": "node_modules/mocha/bin/mocha test"
},
```

The test script is saved as *index.js* in the *test* subdirectory under the project. The following command runs the test:

```
npm test
```

The Mocha unit test makes use of assertion tests from Node's `assert` module.

12.14. Running Tasks with Grunt

Problem

Pulling your Node module together is getting more complex—too complex to manually manage all of the elements.

Solution

Use a task runner like Grunt to manage all the bits for you.

For the following `bbarray` module:

```
var util = require('util');

(function(global) {
```

```
        'use strict';

        var bbarray = {};

        bbarray.concatArray = function (str, array) {
            if (!util.isArray(array) || array.length === 0) {
                return -1;
            } else if (typeof str != 'string') {
                return -1;
            } else {
                return array.map(function(element) {
                  return str + ' ' + element;
                });
            }
        };

        bbarray.splitArray = function (str,array) {
            if (!util.isArray(array) || array.length === 0) {
                return -1;
            } else if (typeof str != 'string') {
                return -1;
            } else {
                return array.map(function(element) {
                  var len = str.length + 1;
                  return element.substring(len);
                });
            }
         };

        if (typeof module != 'undefined' && module.exports) {
           module.exports = bbarray;
        } else if ( typeof define === 'function' && define.amd ) {
            define( 'bbarray', [], function() {
               return bbarray;
            });
        } else {
           global.bbarray = bbaarray;
        }

    }(this));
```

Saved as *bbarray.js* in the root directory, with a Mocha test file:

```
var assert = require('assert');
var bbarray = require('../bbarray.js');

describe('bbarray',function() {
   describe('#concatArray()', function() {
     it('should return -1 when not using array', function() {
        assert.equal(-1, bbarray.concatArray(9,'str'));
     });
     it('should return -1 when not using string', function() {
        assert.equal(-1, bbarray.concatArray(9,['test','two']));
```

```
      });
      it('should return an array with proper args', function() {
         assert.deepEqual(['is test','is three'],
                        bbarray.concatArray('is',['test','three']));
      });
   });
   describe('#splitArray()', function() {
      it('should return -1 when not using array', function() {
         assert.equal(-1, bbarray.splitArray(9,'str'));
      });
      it('should return -1 when not using string', function() {
         assert.equal(-1, bbarray.splitArray(9,['test','two']));
      });
      it('should return an array with proper args', function() {
         assert.deepEqual(['test','three'],
                        bbarray.splitArray('is',['is test','is three']));
      });
   });
});
```

Saved as *index.js* in a *test* subdirectory, the Grunt file is:

```
module.exports = function(grunt) {
   var banner = '/*\n<%= pkg.name %> <%= pkg.version %>';
   banner += '- <%= pkg.description %>\n<%= pkg.repository.url %>\n';
   banner += 'Built on <%= grunt.template.today("yyyy-mm-dd") %>\n*/\n';

   grunt.initConfig({
      pkg: grunt.file.readJSON('package.json'),
      jshint: {
         files: ['gruntfile.js', 'src/*.js'],
         options: {
            maxlen: 80,
            quotmark: 'single'
         }
      },
      uglify: {
         options: {
            banner: banner,
         },
         build: {
            files: {
               'build/<%= pkg.name %>.min.js':
                  ['build/<%= pkg.name %>.js'],
            }
         }
      },
      simplemocha: {
         options: {
            globals: ['assert'],
            timeout: 3000,
            ignoreLeaks: false,
            ui: 'bdd',
```

```
                reporter: 'tap'
            },
            all: { src: ['test/*.js'] }
        }
    });

    grunt.loadNpmTasks('grunt-contrib-jshint');
    grunt.loadNpmTasks('grunt-contrib-uglify');
    grunt.loadNpmTasks('grunt-simple-mocha');

    grunt.registerTask('default',
        ['jshint', 'simplemocha', 'uglify']);
};
```

When the file is saved as *gruntfile.js*, Grunt runs all the tasks defined in the file:

```
grunt
```

Discussion

Grunt is a *task runner*. Its only purpose is to consistently run a series of tasks. It's similar to the old Makefile, but without the decades of musty history.

To use Grunt, install it first:

```
npm install -g grunt-cli
```

Grunt needs to run in the same directory as your application/module's *package.json* file, as it works with the file. You can create either a JavaScript or Coffee-based Grunt file, but I'm focusing on the JS version.

Create the file by using the `grunt-init` CLI, with a given template, or you can use the example file given in the Getting Started Guide (*http://gruntjs.com/getting-started*).

A module needs to run within a certain framework to work with Grunt. Luckily, plugins have been created for many of the commonly used modules, such as the plugins used in the example for JSHint, Uglify, and Mocha. To ensure they're listed in the *package.json* file, they need to be installed using `--save-dev`:

```
npm install grunt-contrib-jshint --save-dev
npm install grunt-simple-mocha --save-dev
npm install grunt-contrib-uglify --save-dev
```

Each plugin also provides instructions about how to modify the Gruntfile to use the plugin and process your files.

Once you have both the *package.json* and *gruntfile.js* files running, the following will install any of the dependencies in the file, and run the Grunt tasks:

```
npm install
grunt
```

The result of running Grunt with the file in the solution is:

```
Running "jshint:files" (jshint) task
>> 1 file lint free.

Running "simplemocha:all" (simplemocha) task
1..6
ok 1 bbarray concatArray() should return -1 when not using array
ok 2 bbarray concatArray() should return -1 when not using string
ok 3 bbarray concatArray() should return an array with proper args
ok 4 bbarray splitArray() should return -1 when not using array
ok 5 bbarray splitArray() should return -1 when not using string
ok 6 bbarray splitArray() should return an array with proper args
# tests 6
# pass 6
# fail 0

Running "uglify:build" (uglify) task
>> Destination build/bbarray.min.js not written because src files were empty.

Done, without errors.
```

There are no files in the *src* directory, but I left the instructions in the Grunt file, for future expansion of the module.

See Also

Read all about Grunt, and check out the available plugins, at the application's website (*http://gruntjs.com/*).

Another popular build system is Gulp (*http://gulpjs.com/*).

## CHAPTER 13

Fun with APIs

An API is a defined interface that acts like a handshake between software components, allowing one component to access another even though the components have been developed separately.

APIs vary widely: from those built into operating systems allowing developers to access OS-specific functionality, to functional APIs that are grouped to allow access to specific types of functionality (in the browser or accessible in the server). APIs are also used to provide a bridge between a client on one machine, to a service or resource on another.

An API isn't a library or module, though both can implement APIs. They're more a contract between developers where the API implementer promises to provide certain functionality, as long as people accessing the functionality play nice (and don't abuse the privilege, in the case of remote services).

In this chapter, we look at APIs in all their glorious forms: how to access, how to create, and how to use.

 A really great resource listing many of the web APIs, or APIs that can be used to allow web applications to access hardware and locally stored data, is the WebAPI page (*https://developer.mozilla.org/en-US/docs/WebAPI*) offered in the Mozilla Developer Network (MDN). The MDN provides a single page resource page (*https://developer.mozilla.org/en-US/docs/Web/Specification_list*) detailing all specifications, in development or stable.

13.1. Accessing JSON-Formatted Data via a RESTful API

Problem

You want to access data formatted as JSON from a service through their API. You need to access the data both in a client and in a Node application, but don't know the best approach to use in both cases.

Solution

One of the simplest approaches for accessing data through an API that supports the principles of Representational State Transfer (REST), and returns data formatted as JSON, is to use jQuery's `getJSON()` function:

```
$.getJSON('http://somedomain.com/latest.json?apid=someid', function(data) {
    // do something with the data now formatted as an object
});
```

In a Node application, the simplest technique for accessing JSON-formatted data from an API is to use `node-rest-client` to access the data:

```
var Client = require('node-rest-client').Client;

var client = new Client();

client.get('http://somedomain.com/latest.json?apid=someid'
        function(data, response) {
            // do something the with data now formatted as an object
});
```

Discussion

A RESTful API is one that is stateless, meaning that each client request contains everything necessary for the server to respond (doesn't imply any stored state between requests); it uses HTTP methods explicitly. It supports a directory-like URI structure, and transfers data formatted a certain way (typically XML or JSON). The HTTP methods are:

- GET: To get resource data
- PUT: To update a resource
- DELETE: To delete a resource
- POST: To create a resource

Because we're focusing on getting data, the only method of interest at this time is GET. And because we're focused on JSON, we're using client methods that can access JSON-formatted data and convert the data into objects we can manipulate in our JavaScript applications.

Let's look at a couple of examples.

The Open Exchange Rate (*https://openexchangerates.org/*) provides an API that we can use to get current exchange rates, name-to-acronym for the different types of currencies, and the exchange rates for a specific date. It has a Forever Free plan (*https://openex changerates.org/signup/free*) that provides limited access to the API without cost—something we should look for in any commercial API service.

It's a very simple matter to make two queries of the system (for current currency rate, and name-to-acronyms), and when both queries finish, to get the acronyms as keys, and use these to look up the long name and rate in the results, printing the pairs out to the console:

```
var moneyAPI1 = "https://openexchangerates.org/api/latest.json?app_id=apid";
var moneyAPI2 = "http://openexchangerates.org/api/currencies.json?app_id=apid";

$.getJSON(moneyAPI1).done(function( data ) {
    $.getJSON(moneyAPI2).done(function(data2) {
        var rates = data.rates;
        var keys = Object.keys(rates);
        for (var i = 0; i < keys.length; i++) {
            var rate = rates[keys[i]];
            var name = data2[keys[i]];
            console.log(name + " " + rate);
        }
    });
});
```

The base currency is "USD" or the U.S. dollar, and a here's a sampling of the results:

```
"Malawian Kwacha 394.899498"
"Mexican Peso 13.15711"
"Malaysian Ringgit 3.194393"
"Mozambican Metical 30.3662"
"Namibian Dollar 10.64314"
"Nigerian Naira 162.163699"
"Nicaraguan Córdoba 26.03978"
"Norwegian Krone 6.186976"
"Nepalese Rupee 98.07189"
"New Zealand Dollar 1.185493"
```

In the code snippet, I use the jQuery done() method to make the next query, and then process both results when both queries are finished. In a production system, we'd cache the results for however long our plan allows (hourly for the free API access).

To demonstrate accessing JSON-formatted data from an API in Node, I'm going to mix it up and use a different API. This time, I'm going to access Flickr's API. The API calls are formed using the same principles. For instance, to search for photos using a text search string with "birds", use:

```
https://api.flickr.com/services/rest/?method=flickr.photos.search&
text=bird&api_key=apikey
```

However, if you want to return search results for a specific person, and formatted as JSON, you'd craft the request as:

```
"https://api.flickr.com/services/rest/?method=flickr.photos.search&
text=bird&user_id=92659632@N05&format=json&api_key=apikey
```

The result is a response formatted as JSON-P, which expects the object to be passed to a function named jsonFlickrAPI(). However, if you want a result crafted purely as JSON, which I do when using node-rest-client, you add another parameter to the query string, nojsoncallback, setting it to a value of *1*:

```
"https://api.flickr.com/services/rest/?method=flickr.photos.search&
text=bird&user_id=92659632@N05&format=json&api_key=apikey&nojsoncallback=1
```

Now, it's just a matter of processing the results. The returned JSON will be an object, photos, with several single properties such as total, pages, and number of items per page given in perpage. The actual photos are in an array of object associated with the property photo, and it contains information such as id, owner, title, whether it's public, and so on. A small Node application that accesses all photos that match a search on "bird" in my account, and that prints out the title for each, is given in the following code snippet:

```
var Client = require('node-rest-client').Client;
var client = new Client();

var flickrapi =
"https://api.flickr.com/services/rest/?method=flickr.photos.search
&text=bird&user_id=92659632@N05&format=json&api_key=apikey&nojsoncallback=1";

client.get(flickrapi, function(data, response) {
    var photos = data.photos.photo;
    photos.forEach(function(elem) {
      console.log(elem.title);
    });
});
```

Simple enough, but one thing I've learned with Node is if there's an API, there's at least one module. A quick search brings up flickrapi (*https://github.com/Pomax/node-flickrapi*), a module to access Flickr. Still, sometimes it's fun to do the down and dirty ourselves.

Access the Flickr API at *https://www.flickr.com/services/api/*.

See Also

The examples didn't need to *escape* the values used as parameters in the API requests, but if you do need to escape values, you can use the built-in `QueryString.escape()` function. It's demonstrated in Recipe 13.6, an application that uses remote API requests made to Google's Map services to provide a movable map.

13.2. Creating a RESTFul API with Restify

Problem

You want to create a RESTful web service, but it doesn't need to provide a browser-friendly interface.

Solution

The Restify Node module is ideal for creating a service that needs to support a REST API, but without having to fuss with templates and other frontend devices.

Once installed, using Restify is as easy as setting up a server, and routing requests:

```
var restify = require('restify');

var server = restify.createServer({name: 'Examples'});
server.use(restify.bodyParser());

server.get('/api/get/:widget', function retrieve(req, res, next) {
   res.send('data is ' + req.params.widget);
   next();
});

server.post('/api/post/', function create(req, res, next) {
   console.log(req.params);
   res.send('created widget ' + req.params.param1);
   return next();
 });

server.listen(8080, function() {
  console.log('%s listening at %s', server.name, server.url);
});
```

Discussion

If you've ever created an application that interacts with an API, like many covered in Chapter 16, then you know that, for the most part, the APIs have no user interface element to them. They're a way to get data from (or send data to) a service, delete existing data, or update data—the Create-Read-Update-Delete (CRUD) of an API. The actual commands translate to HTTP verbs:

- GET: Get the data
- POST: Create new data
- PUT: Update data
- DEL: Remove data

Frameworks like Express work great to provide web pages that people use to interact with the server, but they have an overhead that isn't essential if your main interest is in providing a RESTful API for a data service you're providing (whether externally, or for your own applications). Restify, on the other hand, is specifically geared to supporting an API based on the principles of REST.

As the solution demonstrated, Restify is also quite easy to use. You create a server listening for requests. Based on the URL sent for the request, and the type of HTTP request made, the *router* routes the request to a specific handler, which processes the request. In the solution, the request is processed in a callback function for each handler (one for GET, one for POST). Restify is inherently lean; support for certain functionality is pulled in by plugin. In the solution one plugin is used: `restify.bodyParser`. This plugin will pull out the parameters set with the POST request. I used cURL—a command-line tool to transfer data using one of several protocols (in the example, HTTP)—to test the API:

```
curl --data "param1=value" http://examples.burningbird.net:8080/api/post
```

The resulting response is:

```
"created widget value"
```

If I didn't want to mess with cURL, Restify also provides methods to create a client. To test the POST, I could write a client as follows:

```
var restify = require('restify');

var client = restify.createStringClient({
   url: 'http://examples.burningbird.net:8080'
});

client.post('/api/post', {param1: 'value'}, function(err, req, res, data) {
   console.log(data);
});
```

And the resulting data would be:

```
created widget value
```

Restify provides a JsonClient, a StringClient (demonstrated), and an HttpClient object.

One way to test how this all works is to create a tiny RESTful API supporting GET, POST, PUT, and DEL. To keep it simple, I'm using the save module, which stores the data in memory. The API manages *widgets*, that universally usable demonstration product. The widget data structure is:

- _id: Default identifier
- name: Name of the widget
- cost: Cost of the widget

Example 13-1 contains the complete server application. The code makes use of several Restify objects, to send appropriate messages back to the client. The code also outputs feedback to the console, so you can watch the application as it works.

Example 13-1. A complete though small RESTful API to manage widgets

```
var restify = require('restify');
var widget = require('save')('widget');

var server = restify.createServer({name: 'Examples'});
server.use(restify.fullResponse());
server.use(restify.bodyParser());

// GET
server.get('/api/:widget', function retrieve(req, res, next) {
   widget.findOne({_id: req.params.widget}, function (err, obj) {
      if (err) {
         return next (
            new restify.InvalidArgumentError(JSON.stringify(error.errors)));
      }
      if (obj) {
         res.send(200,obj);
      } else {
         res.send(404);
      }
      return next();
   });
});

// POST
server.post('/api/create', function create(req, res, next) {
   widget.create(req.params, function (err,widget) {
     console.log(widget);
     res.send(201, widget._id);
   });
   return next();
 });
```

```
// PUT
server.put('/api/:id', function(req, res, next) {
    if (req.params.cost === undefined) {
        return next(new
            restify.InvalidArgumentError('cost must be supplied'));
    }
    widget.update({_id: req.params.id, name: req.params.name,
                    cost: req.params.cost},
        function (error, obj) {
            if (error) {
                return next(new
                    restify.InvalidArgumentError(JSON.stringify(error.errors)));
            }
            res.send(200);
            return next();
    });
});

server.del('/api/:id', function (req, res, next) {
    widget.delete(req.params.id, function(err) {
        if (err) {
            console.log(err);
            return next (
                new restify.ResourceNotFoundError(JSON.stringify(err.errors)));
        }
    });
    res.send(200);
    return next();
});

server.listen(8080, function() {
    console.log('%s listening at %s', server.name, server.url);
});
```

To test the application, we can use a command-line utility such as cURL, but it's not the most trivial tool to wrap our heads around. Instead, I made use of a client API that Restify provides. Specifically, I made use of the StringClient object. The test application is in Example 13-2. All it does is create an object (POST), retrieve it (GET), update it (PUT), and finally delete it (DEL).

Example 13-2. Testing a RESTful API using the Restify client API

```
var restify = require('restify');
var assert = require('assert');

var client = restify.createStringClient({
    url: 'http://examples.burningbird.net:8080'
});

function handleError(err) {
    console.log(err);
```

```
    process.exit(1);
}

// POST
client.post('/api/create', {name: 'super gidget', cost: '12.35'},
function(err, req, res, data) {
  if (err)
    return handleError(err);
  if (res.statusCode == '201') {
    console.log('POST id ' + data);

    // GET
    var id = data;
    client.get('/api/' + id, function (err, req, res, data) {
      if (err)
        return handleError(err);
      if (res.statusCode == '200') {
        console.log(data);
        // PUT
        client.put('/api/' + id, {name: 'super gidget', cost: '15,76'},
            function(err, req, res, data) {
              if (err)
                return handleError(err);
              console.log('PUT ' + res.statusCode);

              // DEL
              client.del('/api/' + id, function(err, req, res) {
                 if (err)
                   return handleError(err);
                 console.log('DEL ' + res.statusCode);
                 process.exit(1);
              });
          });
      }
    });
  }
});
```

A little callback spaghetti, but manageable. I also created a simple function to output an error and exit the application.

Running the client against the server the first time results in the following to the server:

```
Examples listening at http://0.0.0.0:8080
Creating 'widget' {"name":"super gidget","cost":"12.35"}
{ name: 'super gidget', cost: '12.35', _id: '1' }
Finding One 'widget' {"_id":"1"} {}
Updating 'widget' {"_id":"1","name":"super gidget","cost":"15,76"}
with overwrite  false
Deleting 'widget' 1
```

And the following to the client:

```
POST id 1
{"name":"super gidget","cost":"12.35","_id":"1"}
PUT 200
DEL 200
```

Running the client several times increments the identifier (id), until the Node API server is shut down, in which case the memory store is released.

See Also

Install Restify and Save using npm:

```
npm install restify
npm install save
```

Restify's documentation is at *http://mcavage.me/node-restify/*, and the Save documentation can be found in its GitHub repository (*https://github.com/serby/save*).

13.3. Enabling a Mobile-Like Notification in the Desktop Browser

Problem

You need a way to notify a user that an event has occurred or a long-running process is finished, even if your web page isn't loaded into the tab that's currently active.

Solution

Use the Web Notifications API.

This API provides a relatively simple technique to pop up a notification window outside of the browser, so that if a person is currently looking at a web page in another tab, she'll still see the notification.

To use a Web Notification, you do need to get permission. In the following code, the Web Notification is wrapped in a request in a timer, to emulate a wait time for the notification. Both are wrapped in a permission request:

```
Notification.requestPermission(function() {

  setTimeout(function() {
    var notification = new Notification('hey wake up',
                      {body: 'your file is done',
                       tag: 'preset'});
  }, 5000);
});
```

Discussion

Mobile environments have notifications that let you know when you received a new Like in Facebook, or a new email in your email client. We don't have this capability in a desktop environment, though some might say this is a good thing.

Still, as we create more sophisticated web applications, it helps to have this functionality when our applications may take a significant amount of time. Instead of forcing people to hang around looking at a "working" icon on our pages, the web page visitor can view other web pages in other tabs, and know she'll get notified when the long-running process is finished.

 The Web Notifications API has gone through a couple of different iterations, and the API is still undergoing work in the W3C. The code in the solution works in the latest versions of Firefox, Safari, and Chrome. However, it doesn't work in IE, or the current stable version of Opera. It also doesn't work with mobile browsers.

In the solution, the first time the code creates a new notification, it gets permission from the web page visitor. If your application is created as a standalone web application, you can specify permissions in the manifest file, but for web pages, you have to ask permission.

Prior to the Notification permission request, you can also test to see if Notification exists, so an error is not thrown if it's not supported:

```
if (window.Notification) {
  Notification.requestPermission(function() {

    setTimeout(function() {
      var notification = new Notification('hey wake up',
                        {body: 'your process is done',
                        tag: 'loader',
                        icon: 'favicon.ico'});
    }, 5000);
  });
}
```

The Notification takes two arguments—a title string and an object with options:

- body: The text message in the body of the notification
- tag: A tag to help identify notifications for global changes
- icon: A custom icon
- lang: Language of notification
- dir: Direction of language

You can also code four event handlers:

- `onerror`
- `onclose`
- `onshow`
- `onclose`

And you can programatically close the notification with `Notification.close()`, though Safari and Firefox automatically close the notification in a few seconds. All browsers provide a window close (*x*) option in the notification.

Extra: Web Notifications and the Page Visibility API

You can combine Web Notifications with the Page Visibility API to set the Notification when the web page visitor isn't in the web page, only.

The Page Visibility API has broad support in modern browsers. It adds support for one event, `visibilitychange`, which is fired when the visibility of the tab page changes. It also supports a couple of new properties—`document.hidden` returns true if the tab page isn't visible and `document.visibilityState`, which has one of the following four values:

- `visible`: When the tab page is visible
- `hidden`: When the tag page is hidden
- `prerender`: The page is being rendered but not yet visible (browser support is optional)
- `unloaded`: The page is being unloaded from memory (browser support is optional)

To modify the solution so that the notification only fires when the tabbed page is hidden, modify the code to the following:

```
if (window.Notification) {
    Notification.requestPermission(function() {

        setTimeout(function() {
         if (document.visibilityState == "hidden") {
          var notification = new Notification('hey wake up',
                    {body: 'your process is done',
                     tag: 'loader',
                     icon: 'favicon.ico'});
         } else {
           document.getElementById("result").innerHTML = 'your process is done';
         }
        }, 5000);
    });
   }
```

Before creating the Notification, the code tests to see if the page is hidden. If it is, then the Notification is created. If it isn't, then a message is written out to the page instead.

13.4. Loading a File Locally in the Browser

Problem

You want to open an ePub XHTML file and output the text to the web page.

Solution

Use the File API in conjunction with the XML DOM parser:

```
function loadFile() {

   // look for the body section of the document
   var parser = new DOMParser();
   var xml = parser.parseFromString(this.result,"text/xml");
   var content = xml.getElementsByTagName("body");

   // if found, extract the body element's innerHTML
   if (content.length > 0) {
      var ct = content[0].innerHTML;
      var title = document.getElementById("bookTitle").value;
      title = "<h2>" + title + "</title>";
      document.getElementById("result").innerHTML = title + ct;
   }
}
```

Discussion

The File API bolts onto the existing input element `file` type, used for file uploading. In addition to the capability of uploading the file to the server via a form upload, you can now access the file directly in JavaScript, and either work with it locally or upload the file using the `XMLHttpRequest` object.

> For more on FileReader, check out MDN's page on the API (*http://mzl.la/1ya0o1k*), and a related tutorial (*http://mzl.la/1ya0qGs*).

There are three objects in the File API:

- `FileList`: A list of files to upload via `input type="file"`
- `File`: Information about a specific file

- `FileReader`: Object to asynchronously upload the file for client-side access

Each of the objects has associated properties and events, including being able to track the progress of a file upload (and provide a custom progress bar), as well as signaling when the upload is finished. The `File` object can provide information about the file, including file size and MIME type. The `FileList` object provides a list of `File` objects, because more than one file can be specified if the input element has the `multiple` attribute set. The `FileReader` is the object that does the actual file upload.

Example 13-3 is an application that uses all three objects in order to upload a file as XML, and embed the XML into the web page. In the example, I'm using it to access uncompressed ePub book chapters. As ePub chapter files are valid XHTML, I can use the built-in XML Parser object, `DOMParser`, to process the file.

Example 13-3. Uploading an ePub XHTML chapter into a web page

```
<!DOCTYPE html>
<head>
<title>ePub Reader</title>
<meta charset="utf-8" />
<style>
#result
{
  width: 500px;
  margin: 30px;
}
</style>
</head>
<body>
  <form>
    <label for="title">Title:</label>
    <input type="text" id="bookTitle" /></br ><br />
    <label for="file">File:</label> <input type="file" id="file" /><br />
  </form>
  <div id="result"></div>

  <script>

    var inputElement = document.getElementById("file");
    inputElement.addEventListener("change", handleFiles, false);

    function handleFiles() {
      var fileList = this.files;
      var reader = new FileReader();
      reader.onload = loadFile;
      reader.readAsText(fileList[0]);
    }

    function loadFile() {
```

```
// look for the body section of the document
var parser = new DOMParser();
var xml = parser.parseFromString(this.result,"text/xml");
var content = xml.getElementsByTagName("body");

// if found, extract the body element's innerHTML
if (content.length > 0) {
  var ct = content[0].innerHTML;
  var title = document.getElementById("bookTitle").value;
  title = "<h2>" + title + "</title>";
  document.getElementById("result").innerHTML = title + ct;
}
    }
  </script>
</body>
```

Figure 13-1 shows the page with the first chapter of the public domain ePub of *Moby Dick*. Note that this is the XHTML file that forms part of the ePub package, not the actual ePub, itself.

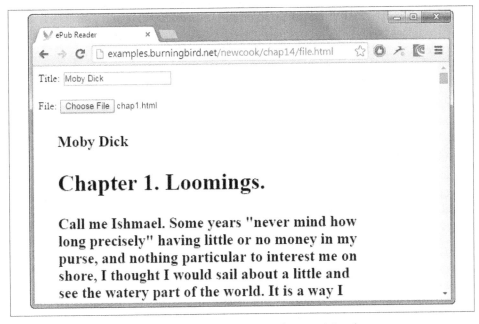

Figure 13-1. Using the File API to read a chapter of an ePub book

The File API is a W3C effort. You can read the latest draft at *http://www.w3.org/TR/FileAPI/*. Read Mozilla's coverage at *http://mzl.la/1ya0qGs*.

13.5. Creating a Mini E-Pub Reader Using Web Workers and the File API

Problem

Your application uploads E-Pub XHTML documents for reading in your web application, but you don't want to block the browser while the file is being processed.

Solution

The solution needs to incorporate two pieces: uploading a file and opening it, and doing all of this in a separate thread so the browser isn't blocked waiting for what could be a time-consuming operation to finish.

See the discussion for the code.

Discussion

In a language such as Java, you can create multiple threads of execution that can operate concurrently. Computers and operating systems have long had the ability to support multiple threads—switching the necessary resources among the threads as needed. Handled correctly, threads can make your application run faster and more efficiently. Multithreaded development also provides the functionality necessary to ensure the threads are synced, so the applications are accurate, too.

In the past, a major difference between JavaScript and these multithreaded programming languages is that JavaScript runs within a single thread of execution. Even when a timer fires, the associated event falls into the same queue as other pending events. This single-execution-thread queue is why you can't absolutely depend on the preciseness of a JavaScript timer. With Web Workers, introduced as one of the W3C WebApps 1.0 specifications, for better or worse, this all changes.

I say "for better or worse" because thread-based development has always been a double-edged sword in most development environments. If they're not properly managed, multithreaded applications can crash and burn rather spectacularly. Web workers differ from most of the other multithreaded environments because the latter gives the developers more control over the creation and destruction of threads. Web workers provide threaded development, but at a higher, hopefully safer level.

To create a web worker, all you need do is call the Worker object constructor, passing in the URI for a script file to run:

```
var theWorker = new Worker("loading.js");
```

You can also assign a function to the web worker's onmessage event handler, and onerror event handler:

```
theWorker.onmessage = handleMessage;
theWorker.onerror = handleError;
```

To communicate with the web worker, use the postMessage method, providing any data it needs:

```
theWorker.postMessage(dataObject);
```

In the web worker, an onmessage event handler receives this message, and can extract the data from the event object:

```
onmessage(event) {
   var data = event.data;
   ...
}
```

If the web worker needs to pass data back, it also calls postMessage. The function to receive the message in the main application is the event handler function assigned to the web worker's onmessage event handler:

```
theWorker.onmessage= handleMessage;
```

The function can extract any data it's expecting from the event object.

One caveat about worker threads, though, is that not all built-in objects or functionality is available *within* a worker thread across all browsers. In Firefox at least, the asynchronous FileReader won't work in a worker thread. Instead, you have to use the synchronous version of the code, FileReaderSync thread, as shown in the worker thread, *loading.js*, created for this application:

```
onmessage = function(event) {

    function handleFile(loadFile) {
      var reader = new FileReaderSync();
      var txt = reader.readAsText(loadFile);
      postMessage(txt);
    }

    var str = handleFile(event.data);

};
```

The reason why the asynchronous version of the function won't work is the global object in a worker is not the same as the global object in a browser application, and FileReader is not one of the objects supported in the thread context. Instead, you have to use FileReaderSync, which, because of its blocking nature, is *only* supported in worker threads. The blocking nature of FileReaderSync isn't an issue with a worker thread because the thread is asynchronous by design.

Mozilla provides a listing of what it supports in worker threads (*http:// mzl.la/1KstRbq*). In my testing, what Firefox supports typically matches what other browsers support, too.

Now we need to use the worker thread. Example 13-4 is the web page that loads a file incorporating a worker thread, printing the contents out to the web page when finished.

Example 13-4. Reading a file using a web worker

```
<!DOCTYPE html>
<head>
<title>ePub Reader</title>
<meta charset="utf-8" />
<style>
#result
{
  width: 500px;
  margin: 30px;
}
</style>
</head>
<body>
  <form>
    <label for="file">File:</label>
    <input type="file" id="file" /><br />
  </form>
  <div id="result"></div>

  <script>

    var inputElement = document.getElementById("file");
    inputElement.addEventListener("change", handleFiles, false);

    function handleFiles() {
      var file = this.files[0];
      var worker = new Worker("loading.js");
      worker.onmessage=loadFile;
      worker.postMessage(file);
    }

    function loadFile(event) {

      // look for the body section of the document
      var parser = new DOMParser();
      var xml = parser.parseFromString(event.data,"text/xml");
      var content = xml.getElementsByTagName("body");

      // if found, extract the body element's innerHTML
      if (content.length > 0) {
```

```
        var ct = content[0].innerHTML;
        document.getElementById("result").innerHTML = ct;
      }
    }

  </script>
</body>
```

Normally with worker threads the script you'd run would be a computationally intensive script, with results that aren't immediately needed. Mozilla's example for web workers demonstrates a script that computes a Fibonacci sequence. My own attempt at a more time consuming process is running a function that reverses an array passed to the worker thread as data. The worker code is listed in Example 13-5, and saved as *reverse.js*.

In the JavaScript library, an `onmessage` event handler function accesses the data from the event object—the array to reverse—and passes it to the reversed array function. Once the function finishes, the web worker routine calls `postMessage`, sending the resulting string back to the main application.

Example 13-5. Using web worker JavaScript to reverse an array and return the resulting string

```
// web worker thread - reverses array
onmessage = function(event) {

    var reverseArray = function(x,indx,str) {
       return indx == 0 ? str :
                   reverseArray(x,--indx,(str+= " " + x[indx]));;
    }

    // reverse array
    var str = reverseArray(event.data, event.data.length, "");

    // return resulting string to main application
    postMessage(str);
};
```

The application that uses the worker is given in Example 13-6. When the application retrieves the uploaded file and extracts the body element, it splits the content into an array based on the space character. The application sends the array through to the reversed array web worker. Once the web worker finishes, the data is retrieved and output to the page.

Example 13-6. The ePub reader in Example 13-3, using a web worker to reverse the content

```
<!DOCTYPE html>
<head>
<title>ePub Reader</title>
<meta charset="utf-8" />
```

```
<style>
#result
{
  width: 500px;
  margin: 30px;
}
</style>
</head>
<body>
  <form>
    <label for="file">File:</label>
    <input type="file" id="file" /><br />
  </form>
  <div id="result"></div>

  <script>

    var inputElement = document.getElementById("file");
    inputElement.addEventListener("change", handleFiles, false);

    function handleFiles() {
      var fileList = this.files;
      var reader = new FileReader();
      reader.onload = loadFile;
      reader.readAsText(fileList[0]);
    }

    function loadFile() {

      // look for the body section of the document
      var parser = new DOMParser();
      var xml = parser.parseFromString(this.result,"text/xml");
      var content = xml.getElementsByTagName("body");

      // if found, extract the body element's innerHTML
      if (content.length > 0) {
        var ct = content[0].innerHTML;
        var ctarray = ct.split(" ");
        var worker = new Worker("reverse.js");
        worker.onmessage=receiveResult;
        worker.postMessage(ctarray);
      }
    }

    function receiveResult(event) {
      document.getElementById("result").innerHTML = event.data;
    }
</script>

</body>
```

As you can see in Figure 13-2, the results are interesting. Not very useful—except they demonstrate that the web worker performs as expected, and quickly, too.

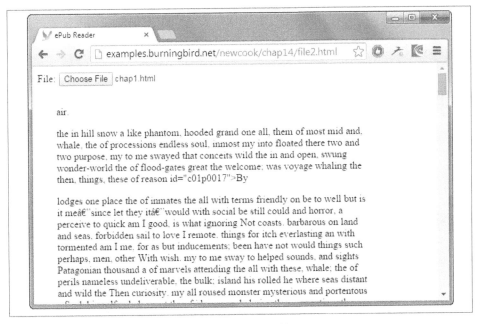

Figure 13-2. Result of reversing the ePub XHTML file contents

13.6. Exploring Google Maps and Other APIS

Problem

Your application needs to incorporate a map, and various map supportive services.

Solution

Use the Google Maps API to add map support to your web page.

In Example 13-7, a form and a space for a map is added to a web page, and the Google Maps API is used to center the map based on the latitude and longitude given in the form.

Example 13-7. Panning the Map based on input values

```
<!DOCTYPE html>
<html>
  <head>
    <style type="text/css">
      #map-canvas {
```

```
            width: 600px;
            height: 400px;
            margin-left: 15px;
        }
        form {
            margin: 15px;
        }
    </style>
    <script type="text/javascript"
        src="https://maps.googleapis.com/maps/api/js?key=yourkey">
    </script>
    <script type="text/javascript">
        var map;
        function initialize() {
            var mapOptions = {
                center: { lat: 38, lng: -90},
                zoom: 5
            };
            map = new google.maps.Map(document.getElementById('map-canvas'),
                mapOptions);

            document.getElementById("runit").onclick=changeMap;
        }

        function changeMap() {
            var long = parseFloat(document.getElementById("long").value);
            var lat = parseFloat(document.getElementById("lat").value);

            map.panTo({lat: lat, lng: long});
            return false;
        }

        google.maps.event.addDomListener(window, 'load', initialize);

    </script>
</head>
<body>
    <form >
        Lat: <input type="text" id="lat" /><br />
        Long: <input type="text" id="long" /><br />
        <button id="runit">Map it!</button>
    </form>

    <div id="map-canvas"></div>
</body>
</html>
```

Figure 13-3 shows the map, centered near where I currently live.

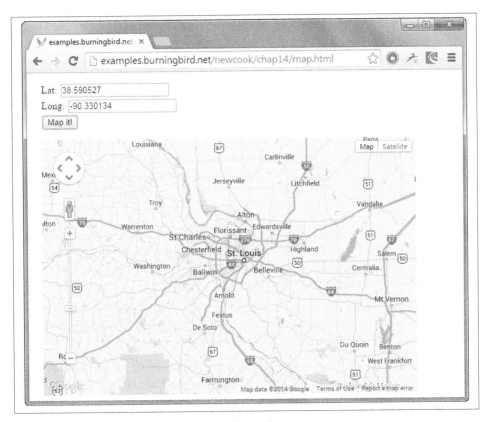

Figure 13-3. Google map centered near where I live

Discussion

Google Maps is the granddaddy of APIs for web applications. Though it has become more functionally rich over the years, it's still relatively simple to use.

Google Maps is one of Google's many APIs available via their Google API Console (*https://code.google.com/apis/console*). To use any of the APIs, you'll need to create a project, but there's no expectations about what you need to do with the project, and unless your application gets a sudden hit of popularity, you'll not be charged for the API use.

As long as you provide free access to the pages utilizing Google APIs, you're generally free to use the APIs without cost. However, if your application gets significant use, such as more than 25,000 Google Maps accesses in a 24-hour window, Google will contact you about potential payment plans. Each Google API has a Terms of Service (TOS), spelling out the API's allowable use.

Once you create a project, you can enable one or more Google APIs for it. The Google Maps app in the solution app uses the Google Maps JavaScript API v3. You'll also have to create an API key, which you can do by clicking the Credentials link in the left sidebar. For browser applications, create a new Client API key and specify the domain that serves up the web page containing the app. Google also provides support for OAuth 2.0, which I cover in Recipe 14.4.

 Google mixes things up from time to time. To ensure you're working with the most current environment, double check the Google documentation for setting up a project, getting an API key, and the API documentation.

There is a also a server-based API key if your Node application is accessing one of Google's server-based APIs, such as the API to Google's Cloud Storage. The Cloud Storage API is one of the APIs that does require payment, and you'll need to set up a billing account if your application is utilizing it.

If you're not sure which Google API to use, you can use Google's API Picker (*http://bit.ly/1ya5FG6*). From this you can tell if you need the JavaScript API I used, the Google Maps Android API v2, the embedded Google Maps API, and so on.

The Android-flavored APIs are generally based in Java, which is the Android development language. If you're creating web applications for Android based in HTML5/CSS/JavaScript, you'll need to look for APIs that are RESTful, using the API techniques covered in the first recipe of this book, or have a JavaScript interface, such as the Map API demonstrated in the solution.

In addition, Google APIs can be client- or server-based. An example is the APIs for Google's *geocoding* services, which takes a full address and returns longitude and latitude for Google Maps markers and positioning. The server API has significant limits on use because the assumption is that the API will be used by a server application that has access to a fixed set of addresses. The server application then processes the geocode request for each address, and then caches the request locally, so the Google service doesn't need to be accessed again.

 All the Google Maps APIs are covered in one set of documents at Google (*https://developers.google.com/maps/*). The server APIs are listed separately (*http://bit.ly/1ya63ED*), including the Google Geocoding API. The client-side geocoding services are part of the Google Maps JavaScript API.

To demonstrate server access to Google APIs, you first need to create a Server API key, providing the IP address for your server. You'll also need to enable the API service (in this case, the Google Maps Geolocation API). The client keys are domain specific, but the server key is IP address specific (including subnet, if appropriate).

The server Geocode API uses SSL to protect the data requests, so all API requests begin with "https". The general format for the request is:

```
http://maps.googleapis.com/maps/api/geocode/output?parameters
```

There are only a finite set of parameters to a request. The `address` is required; the other, optional parameters are:

- `bounds`: Bounding box of viewport within which to prominently bias geocode results
- `key`: The server API key
- `language`: Language for results, defaulting to the language derived from the requesting domain
- `region`: Two character code that can influence results
- `components filter`: If you're using *component filtering*

Instead of specifying an address, you can specify a component, if you're using component filtering (*http://bit.ly/1ya6sXy*).

We're keeping the application as simple as possible, so the only parameters we're using are the address and the API key.

The Node application is a simple web server that takes address requests from a browser client, checks to see if the address has already been processed, and if not, makes a call to the Google service. When it gets the result, it caches it using the Node module `memory-cache`, and then returns the latitude/longitude pair to the client. The next look up for the address comes from the cache, rather than from the Google service.

Install `memory-cache` with npm:

```
npm install memory-cache
```

I am using the `region` parameter in the Google API call, to signal that the API request is coming from the U.S. region. Adjust your copy of the code to your region, accordingly.

In Example 13-8, the call to the Google API happens in the server response end event, rather than the data event, because of the asynchronous nature of both the end event and the Google API client request.

Example 13-8. Accessing Google Geocoding service to get latitude/longitude pairs for an address

```
var http = require("http");
var cache = require("memory-cache");
var Client = require("node-rest-client").Client;
var client = new Client();

var server = http.createServer();
server.on('request', request);
server.listen(8080);

function request(request, response) {
    var address;

    // get address from client
    request.on('data', function(data)
    {
        var addrObj = JSON.parse(data);
        address = require("querystring").escape(addrObj.address);
    });

    // get geo loc
    request.on('end', function()
    {
        response.setHeader("Content-Type", "text/json");
        response.setHeader("Access-Control-Allow-Origin", "*");

        // check if cached
        // if so, return cached results
        var loc = cache.get(address);
        if (loc) {
            console.log(loc);
            response.end(loc);
            return;
        }

        // not cached, look up loc using API
        var api =
        "https://maps.googleapis.com/maps/api/geocode/json?key=yourkey&address="
                + address +
                "&region=us";

        client.get(api, function(data, res) {
            var resultObj = JSON.parse(data);
            location = resultObj.results[0].geometry.location;
            var loc = JSON.stringify(location);
            cache.put(address,loc);
```

```
            response.end(JSON.stringify(location));
        });
    });
}
```

Note the use of the built-in Node module, QueryString, and its escape() method to prepare the address string for use in a REST API call.

To simplify the client, I'm using jQuery to handle the Ajax call. There is a plugin for jQuery specifically for Google Maps, but as this chapter is focused on playing with existing APIs, I'm not using the plugin.

In Example 13-9, the Google Map is loaded with a default location. When a new address is entered into the form, and the button to change the map is clicked, the Ajax call is made to the Node server app, sending along the address. When the Ajax call is returned, map.panTo() is used with the returned latitude/longitude location, and the map is moved.

Example 13-9. The client page to access addresses and reposition the Google map

```
<!DOCTYPE html>
<head>
<title>Map Mover</title>
<meta charset="utf-8" />
   <style>
      #map-canvas {
         width: 600px;
         height: 400px;
         margin-left: 15px;
      }
    form {
      margin-bottom: 20px;
    }
   </style>
   <script type="text/javascript"
      src="https://maps.googleapis.com/maps/api/js?key=yourclientkey">
   </script>

   <script src="https://code.jquery.com/jquery-2.1.1.js"></script>
   <script type="text/javascript">

      var map;
      function initialize() {
        var mapOptions = {
           center: { lat: 38, lng: -90},
           zoom: 8
          };
        map = new google.maps.Map(document.getElementById('map-canvas'),
           mapOptions);

      }
```

```
    google.maps.event.addDomListener(window, 'load', initialize);

    $( document ).ready(function() {
       $("#changemap").click(function(event) {
       event.preventDefault();
       var address = $("#address").val();
       console.log(address);
       $.ajax
          ({
          type: "POST",
          url: "http://examples.burningbird.net:8080",
          crossDomain:true,
          dataType: "json",
          data: JSON.stringify({"address": address})
          }).done(function ( data ) {
             map.panTo(data);
          })
    });
 })
</script>
</head>
<body>
<form>
   <label for="address">Address:</label>
   <input type="text" id="address" name="address" /></br ><br />
   <button id="changemap">Change Map</button>
</form>
<div id="map-canvas"></div>
</body>
```

Figure 13-4 shows the application after a certain book publisher's address is submitted to the application.

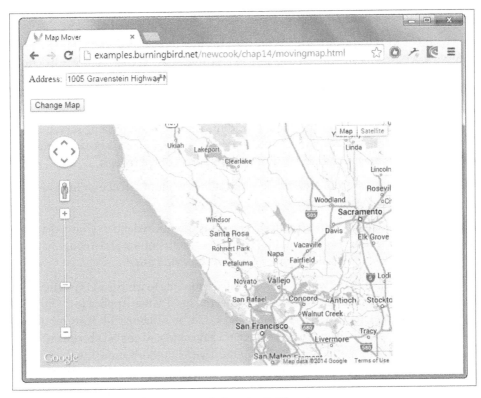

Figure 13-4. Map moved to a magical place in California

See Also

Another way to access latitude and longitude of a current address is using the Geolocation API. It's used in Chapter 18, in Recipe 18.5.

13.7. Accessing Twitter's API from a Node Application

Problem

You're interested in accessing search results and other data from Twitter, without having to get authorization access from any individual user.

Solution

You don't need to get authorization from an individual user if you use Application-Only Authentication, based on OAuth 2.0's Client Credentials Grant.

Details are in the discussion.

Discussion

The world of APIs is no longer the Wild West frontier it once was not that many years ago. Now, API service providers such as Flickr, Twitter, and Facebook place restrictions on API access to keep from being overwhelmed with requests. In addition, many of the services are also requiring OAuth authorization, especially with any requests to modify data, or to access confidential data. Though OAuth 2.0 has simplified the authorization *flow*, it still requires a round-trip for a user to the resource's authorizing server, which requires a frontend to accommodate the user, and support for SSL, because most authorizing servers now require HTTPS at the end points of the request.

The days of API access from server-side applications, without direct user intervention, are increasingly becoming endangered.

Thankfully, there is an OAuth 2.0 pattern, known as Client Credentials Grant, that does still allow server-side access without individual user intervention, and Twitter has provided an implementation called *Application-Only authentication.*

Because we're focusing on Twitter's API, I created a module to wrap the OAuth bits. The code for it, and an explanation of its use, is covered in "Twitter Application-Only and OAuth 2.0 Client Credentials Grant" on page 424, in Chapter 14. The module is `twitreq`, and exposes two functions: `getAuthorization()` and `getTwitterData()`. The `getAuthorization()` method handles all of the Twitter authorization, invoking a callback function returning an error (or null), and an access token. Twitter's Application-Only authentication does still require an access token for each service request.

The `getTwitterData()` method takes, as parameters, the access token, and a service path request. The latter is the key piece of data we're going to focus on. Twitter's Application-Only authentication works with a subset of the REST API that exposes public facing data accessible via a GET. In other words, you can't make updates, change data for an individual user, or use this type of authentication to get information about an individual's personal account. You can determine which API endpoint is available for Application-Only authentication by checking the "Requires authentication?" value in the endpoint's page. If it states "Requires user context", you can't use it with Application-Only authentication.

Filtering out the endpoints that require user context still leaves several very useful endpoints:

- The Search API
- Get the tweets, retweets, and favorites for an individual or group of individuals
- Get the friends/followers for an individual or group of individuals
- Get the lists of a particular user and get the tweets for members of the list

There are rate limits for the API. Twitter has set a limit of 15 requests per 15-minute window for most of the endpoints. The limit is 180 per 15-minute window for search. If you're incorporating the Twitter results into a web application, you can ensure you don't exceed this limit by caching the results in the server or the client. You can also check the status of your rate access using the Twitter REST endpoint of GET applica tion/rate_limit_status. An example of the query with this endpoint is the following, checking rate usage for search:

```
https://api.twitter.com/1.1/application/rate_limit_status.json?resources=search
```

The API results are returned in JSON:

```
{
  "rate_limit_context": {
    "access_token": "786491-24zE39NUezJ8UTmOGOtLhgyLgCkPyY4dAcx6NA6sDKw"
  },
  "resources": {
    "search": {
      "/search/tweets": {
        "limit": 180,
        "remaining": 180,
        "reset": 1403602426
      }
    }
  }
}
```

Twitter maintains a chart of rate limits at *https://dev.twitter.com/rest/ public/rate-limits*.

In this recipe, we'll focus on the Search API. The Search API provides a rich interface for returning a set of tweets (*statuses* in the parlance of Twitter). An example query is the following, which returns all recent tweets featuring the hashtag #rose that are in English:

```
https://api.twitter.com/1.1/search/tweets.json?q=%23rose
&result_type=recent&lang=en
```

The data that's returned is quite extensive. The results of a search returned to an Ajax call in a web page is shown broken out in Firebug in Figure 13-5. And this is only a tiny, graphical snapshot of the available data.

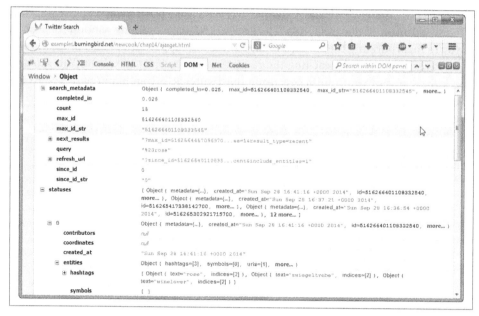

Figure 13-5. Returned Twitter search JSON results, expanded in Firebug

We can refine the results in the server, but it depends on what the client accessing the service is expecting. If the client is expecting all the results, sending all the data isn't a bandwidth breaker. The #rose result size was 43.9 KB, which is less than a typical animated GIF, and we're subjected to them seemingly hundreds of times per day.

The Twitter search incorporates several operators, including the aforementioned hashtag (#). Among some of the operators:

- to:person: Tweets directed at a specific person
- @person: Tweets referencing a specific person
- rose filter:links: Tweets about "rose" with links
- rose :): Tweets featuring "rose" that are positive
- rose -thorn: Tweets featuring "rose" without also including "thorn"

The complete list is included in the Twitter Search documentation.

Time to try out the Twitter Search API. First, you'll need to register an application with Twitter (*https://apps.twitter.com/*). There's no charge, and when you create the new app, you only need to provide the name, description, and the URI of your primary website. You don't need to register a callback URL for this app.

Once you create the app, Twitter assigns it a unique Consumer Key (API Key) and Consumer Secret (API Secret). They're accessible via the application page, and the "Keys and Access Tokens" tab page. You'll need to keep these confidential: they're equivalent to your app's password with Twitter. You'll also need to add them to the code a little later.

To create the Node search server, use the code shown in Example 13-10. The Node server listens for Ajax requests for a client. It parses out the query string using URL.parse() for the request, extracting out the search parameters from the URL.query object. It escapes the result using querystring.escape, and then forms the Twitter search REST endpoint. This gets passed in a call to twitreq.getTwitterData() along with the access token, and a callback function. Change the consumerKey and consumerSecret values to your unique values.

Example 13-10. Twitter Search service in Node

```
var twitreq = require('./twitreq');
var http = require('http');

var consumerKey = 'yourkey';
var consumerSecret = 'yoursecret';

// getting access token from Twitter
twitreq.getAuthorization(consumerKey,
                         consumerSecret, function(err, atoken) {

    if (err) {
        console.log(err);
        return;
    }

    // if authorized, start up HTTP server
    var server = http.createServer(function(req, res) {

        // extract out search query
        var query = require('url').parse(req.url,true).query;
        var search = require('querystring').escape(query.q);

        // forming search path
        var servicePath = '/1.1/search/tweets.json?q=' + search +
                          '&result_type=recent&lang=en';

        // make Twitter request, get results, and return to client
        twitreq.getTwitterData(servicePath, atoken, function(results) {
            res.writeHeader(200, {"Content-Type": "application/json",
                                  "Access-Control-Allow-Origin": "*"});
            res.end(results);
        });
    });
});
```

```
    server.listen(8080);
});
```

The callback function takes the returned results and returns it directly to the client, since it's already formatted as a JSON string.

The client web page contains an input text field and a button, as well as a div element for the results. The user can enter any Twitter search string incorporating operators (or not), and the results are formatted as a list with tweet text and attributed to the Twitter user who posted the tweet.

The results are accessed using Ajax, and parsed using JSON when returned. The array of tweets is an array that's traversed for the individual tweets, and their text, as shown in Example 13-11.

Example 13-11. Web page accessing the Twitter Node service

```html
<!DOCTYPE html>
<head>
<title>Twitter Search</title>
<meta charset="utf-8" />
<style>
   ul {
      width: 600px;
      list-style-type: none;
      margin-left: 50px;
      padding: 0
   }
   li {
      font: 200 14px/1.5 Helvetica, Verdana, sans-serif;
      padding-bottom: 10px;
      color: #606060;
   }
</style>
</head>
<body>
   <label for="one">Twitter Search Value:</label>
   <input type="text" name="one" id="one" /><br />
   <button id="getdata">Search Twitter</button>
   <div id="result"></div>
   <script>
     var httpRequest;

     document.getElementById('getdata')
        .addEventListener('click',getData,false);

     function getData(e) {
        e.preventDefault();

        var search = document.getElementById('one').value;
        if (!search || search.length === 0) return;
        httpRequest = new XMLHttpRequest();
```

```
        search = encodeURIComponent(search);
        var url = "http://shelleystoybox.com:8080/?q=" + search;
        httpRequest.open('GET', url, true);
        httpRequest.onreadystatechange = processData;
        httpRequest.send();
    }

    function processData() {
        if (httpRequest.readyState == 4 && httpRequest.status == 200) {

            var tweets = JSON.parse(httpRequest.responseText);
            var str = '<ul>';
            tweets.statuses.forEach(function(tweet) {
                str += '<li>' + tweet.text + ' via '
                    + '@' + tweet.user.screen_name + '</li>';
            });
            str += '</ul>';
            document.getElementById('result').innerHTML = str;
        }
    }
</script>
</body>
```

The data we're pulling from the results are the tweets, available at `tweets.statuses`, and the tweet text and Twitter user from the individual tweets: `tweet.text` and `tweet.user.screen_name`. The data is listed as list items in an unordered list.

The result of running a Twitter search for references to "#JavaScript" is shown in Figure 13-6.

It's relatively simple to change the search endpoint to other endpoints, or even expand the application to map endpoints to routes: `/search/` or `/status/:id/`.

See Also

The mechanics of OAuth (both 1.0 and 2.0) are covered in Recipe 14.4, and the code behind the OAuth modules created for this recipe's example is covered in "Twitter Application-Only and OAuth 2.0 Client Credentials Grant" on page 424. An example of full read/write access to the Twitter API, using OAuth 1.0, is provided in "Full Read/ Write Authorization with the Twitter API and OAuth 1.0" on page 427.

Accessing Twitter's API using Twitter's implementation is discussed in "Application-Only Authentication" (*https://dev.twitter.com/oauth/application-only*), and the API used in this recipe is covered in "The Search API" (*https://dev.twitter.com/rest/public/ search*).

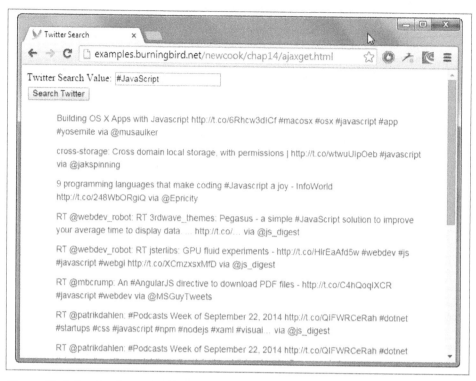

Figure 13-6. Result of running Twitter search for #JavaScript

## CHAPTER 14

JavaScript Frameworks

"Framework" is an overloaded term, used to represent anything from simple libraries and data schemas, to fullblown content systems. In this chapter, when I use the word "framework," I'm using it to represent a class of software created to implement a class of applications, though each specific application is unique.

For today's JavaScript developer, a framework can vary from a complete server-side (or client-based) database application, to authorizations systems, and so on. A framework differs from a standard library or module because the framework is meant to provide all of the underlying infrastructure necessary to solve a complete and typically complex task.

Many of the frameworks—in both the client and the server—are based on a specific paradigm: MVC, or the Model-View-Controller paradigm. MVC is based on a three-way architecture for applications where data, business rules, and the functions to maintain both are represented by the Model, the user interface is the View, and the Controller is the communication between the two. A well-represented variation of the MVC is one where the services of the Controller are merged into that of the View, leading us to reclassify MVC as MV*—encompassing systems that break out the Controller as well as those that don't.

The client-side frameworks, such as AngularJS, support a popular programming paradigm frequently associated with the Single Page Application, or SPA. The basis for these types of applications is that all functionality is implemented within one page that is dynamically updated, as needed, rather than refreshed. Think Gmail, Dropbox, or Git-Hub, and you have an SPA. It's the basis for a comparison site of client-side frameworks, the TodoMVC.

But developers don't live by MVC/SPAs alone. Frameworks can also provide the infrastructure for a more finite functionality, such as authorization (OAuth). In addition, newer technologies such as Web Components allow us to package UI and behavior into reusable components, which can then be used with other framework tools, or on their own.

14.1. Using the Express-Generator to Generate an Express Site

Problem

You're interested in using Express to manage your server-side data application, but you don't want to manage all the bits yourself.

Solution

There are multiple Node frameworks you can use to create server-side applications, but the most popular and widely used is Express. To kickstart your Express application, use the Express-Generator, otherwise known as Express(1). Express(1) is a command-line tool that generates the skeleton infrastructure of a typical Express application.

First, create a working directory where the tool can safely install a new application subdirectory. Next, install Express(1), globally:

```
npm install -g express-generator
```

If you prefer not to install Express(1) globally, you can specify a path to the application. However, installing it globally is the simpler option.

Next, generate the Express application shell. I'll get into the details of the choices made for the application in the discussion, but for now, use the following:

```
express --css stylus tada
```

Express(1) creates a new directory with several subdirectories, some basic files to get you started, and a *package.json* file with all of the dependencies. To install the dependencies, change to the newly created directory and type:

```
npm install
```

Once all of the dependencies are installed, run the application using the following:

```
npm start
```

You can now access the generated Express application, using your IP address or domain and port 3000, the default Express port.

Discussion

Express provides an MVC framework based on Node and with support for multiple templating engines and CSS preprocessors. In the solution, the options I chose for the example application are Jade as the template engine (the default), and Stylus as the CSS preprocessor (plain CSS is the default). Though Express from scratch enables a wider selection, Express(1) supports only the following template engines:

- `express --ejs`: Adds support for the EJS template engine
- `express --hbs`: Adds support for the Handlebar template engine
- `express --hogan`: Adds support for the Hogan.js template engine

Express(1) also supports the following CSS preprocessors:

- `express --css less`: Support for Less
- `express --css stylus`: Support for Stylus
- `express --css compass`: Support for Compass

Not specifying any CSS preprocessor defaults to plain CSS.

 Read more on template engines and preprocessors in "Extra: Working with Templates" on page 393.

Express(1) also assumes that the project directory is empty. If it isn't, force the Express generator to generate the content by using the `-f` or `--force` option.

The newly generated subdirectory has the following structure (disregarding `node_mod ules`):

```
app.js
/bin
    www
/package.json
/public
    /images
    /javascripts
    /stylesheets
        style.css
        style.styl
/routes
    index.js
    users.js
/views
    error.jade
    index.jade
    layout.jade
```

The *app.js* file is the core of the Express application. It includes the references to necessary libraries:

```
var express = require('express');

var path = require('path');
var favicon = require('serve-favicon');
var logger = require('morgan');
var cookieParser = require('cookie-parser');
var bodyParser = require('body-parser');

var routes = require('./routes/index');
var users = require('./routes/users');
```

It also creates the Express app with the following line:

```
var app = express():
```

Next, it establishes Jade as the view engine by defining the `views` and `view engine` variables:

```
app.set('views', path.join(__dirname, 'views'));
app.set('view engine', 'jade');
```

The *middleware* calls are loaded, next, with `app.use()`. Middleware is functionality that sits between the raw request and the routing, processing specific types of requests. The rule for the middleware is if a path is not given as first parameter, it defaults to a path of /, which means the middleware functions are loaded with the default path. In the following generated code:

```
// uncomment after placing your favicon in /public
//app.use(favicon(__dirname + '/public/favicon.ico'));
app.use(logger('dev'));
app.use(bodyParser.json());
app.use(bodyParser.urlencoded({ extended: false }));
app.use(cookieParser());
app.use(require('stylus').middleware(path.join(__dirname, 'public')));
app.use(express.static(path.join(__dirname, 'public')));
```

The first several middleware are loaded with every app request. Among the middleware includes support for a *favicon.ico* for the application, support for development logging, as well as parsers for both JSON and *urlencoded* bodies. It's only when we get to the Stylus and `static` entries that we see assignment to specific paths: the Stylus middleware and static file request middleware are loaded when requests are made to the `public` directory.

The routing is handled next:

```
app.use('/', routes);
app.use('/users', users);
```

The top-level web request (/) is directed to Node module, `routes`, while all user requests (/users) get routed to the `users` module.

What follows is the error handling. First up is 404 error handling when a request is made to a nonexistent web resource:

```
app.use(function(req, res, next) {
    var err = new Error('Not Found');
    err.status = 404;
    next(err);
});
```

Next comes the server error handling, for both production and development:

```
// error handlers

// development error handler
// will print stacktrace
if (app.get('env') === 'development') {
    app.use(function(err, req, res, next) {
        res.status(err.status || 500);
        res.render('error', {
            message: err.message,
            error: err
        });
    });
}

// production error handler
// no stacktraces leaked to user
app.use(function(err, req, res, next) {
    res.status(err.status || 500);
    res.render('error', {
        message: err.message,
        error: {}
    });
});
```

By default, Express is set up to run in *development mode*. To change the application to *production mode*, you need to set an *environment variable*, NODE-ENV to "production". In Linux, the following could be used:

```
export NODE_ENV=production
```

The last line of the generated file is the `module.exports` for the `app`.

In the *routes* subdirectory, the default routing is included in the *index.js* file:

```
var express = require('express');
var router = express.Router();

/* GET home page. */
router.get('/', function(req, res) {
```

```
      res.render('index', { title: 'Express' });
  });

  module.exports = router;
```

What's happening in the file is the Express router is used to route any HTTP GET requests to / to a callback where the request response receives a view rendered for the specific resource page. This is in contrast to what happens in the *users.js* file, where the response receives a text message rather than a view:

```
  var express = require('express');
  var router = express.Router();

  /* GET users listing. */
  router.get('/', function(req, res) {
    res.send('respond with a resource');
  });

  module.exports = router;
```

What happens with the view rendering in the first request? There are three Jade files in the *views* subdirectory: one for error handling, one defining the page layout, and one, *index.jade*, that renders the page. The *index.jade* file contains:

```
  extends layout

  block content
    h1= title
    p Welcome to #{title}
```

It extends the *layout.jade* file, which contains:

```
  html
    head
      title= title
      link(rel='stylesheet', href='/stylesheets/style.css')
    body
      block content
```

The *layout.jade* file defines the overall structure of the page, regardless of content, including a reference to an automatically generated CSS file. The block content setting defines where the location of the content is placed. The format for the content is defined in *index.js*, in the equivalently named block content setting.

The two Jade files define a basic web page with an h1 element assigned a title variable, and a paragraph with a welcome message. Figure 14-1 shows the default page.

Figure 14-1. The Express generated web page served up in Chrome

Figure 14-1 shows that the page isn't especially fascinating, but it does represent how the pieces are holding together: the application router routes the request to the appropriate route module, which directs the response to the appropriate rendered view, and the rendered view uses data passed to it to generate the web page. If you make the following web request:

```
http://yourdomain.com:3000/users
```

you'll see the plain text message, rather than the rendered view.

A basic application generated by Express(1) contains routes and views, but it isn't an MVC application. There is no data persistence and the router is not the same as a controller. These two components will need to be implemented in order for the application to be a fully featured MVC application.

Extra: Working with Templates

The template system used in the solution, Jade, is a succinct language that specifies HTML page constructs, and allows us to map the data to these constructs. A good example is the following, which creates a web page listing out *widgets*, the programming world's favorite example subject:

```
extends layout

block content
  table
    caption Widgets
      if widgets.length
        tr
```

```
        th SN
        th Name
        th Price
        th Description
        th
        th
    each widget in widgets
        if widget
            include row
```

What this little block of code does is, first of all, include in the content of another Jade file (*layout.jade*), which contains the general layout for each web page in the application. Then it defines a block of content consisting of a table with several columns, each headed by their own table header (th). The table rows are where the data passed to the template engine get integrated into the page. Jade provides a looping construct of the form:

```
each element in array of objects
```

Where each object in the array is processed. If there is a row, then another Jade file provides the processing of the data for that row, accessing the data from each object:

```
tr
    td #{widget.sn}
    td #{widget.name}
    td $#{widget.price.toFixed(2)}
    td #{widget.desc}
    td
        a(href='/widgets/edit/#{widget.sn}') Edit
    td
        a(href='/widgets/#{widget.sn}') Delete
```

Recipe 14.2 covers how to convert the generated Express site into a simple MVC, incorporting the Jade files just covered; but for now, let's continue with a discussion about templates.

The whole purpose of the template is to provide the structure for presentation of the data, without having to hard code in the data—allowing us to isolate the generation of the views, from the generation of the data.

Jade is only one template system available. Another popular one is EJS, where the data is embedded directly into the HTML structure, in a manner very similar to what we do with PHP in a CMS such as Drupal:

```
var html = "<h1>"+data.title+"</h1>"
html += "<ul>"
for(var i=0; i<data.supplies.length; i++) {
    html += "<li><a href='supplies/"+data.supplies[i]+"'>"
    html += data.supplies[i]+"</a></li>"
}
html += "</ul>"
```

The structure is different, but the concepts are the same—a controller renders the view, passing whatever data is needed for the view:

```
res.render('widgets/index', {title : 'Widgets', widgets : docs});
```

And the view then incorporates the data into the page structure.

Templates are available in both servers and client applications, though the integration may differ between the two environments, as we'll see later in Recipe 14.3.

 Read more about EJS at its website (*http://embeddedjs.com/*), and Jade at its website (*http://jade-lang.com/*). They're not the only template engines available. A comparison of various engines is available at *http://paularmstrong.github.io/node-templates/*.

Extra: Wait…What About Stylus?

In the basic Express application, I incorporated support for Jade as template engine, but I also incorporated Stylus. So, what's Stylus and where does it fit into all of this?

Stylus is a *CSS Preprocessor*—a way of writing CSS without the excess verbage. With Stylus, we can drop colons, semicolons, and braces. We can also incorporate functions and *mixins* to dynamically modify the CSS, not to mention conditionals, interations, and other programmatic constructs that would cause massive breakage in our CSS files. Stylus then takes all of this, and generates nice, clean, legal CSS.

In the generated Express app, this:

```
body
  padding: 50px
  font: 14px "Lucida Grande", Helvetica, Arial, sans-serif
a
  color: #00B7FF
```

becomes this:

```
body {
  padding: 50px;
  font: 14px "Lucida Grande", Helvetica, Arial, sans-serif;
}
a {
  color: #00b7ff;
}
```

This is not a complicated example, but it does demonstrate a little of what Stylus does.

There is more than one CSS preprocessor—I suggest checking out Less (*http://lesscss.org/*) and Sass (*http://sass-lang.com/*), in addition to Stylus (*http://bit.ly/1yI0Fc7*). Google Chrome's DevTools allows you to live edit the CSS preprocessor files (*http://bit.ly/1yacjw2*) and view the results immediately.

14.2. Converting a Generated Express Site into a Basic MVC App

Problem

The generated Express site is a great start, but where do you begin to turn it into an MVC application?

Solution

When demonstrating something new, a favorite subject is the *widget*, and I'll use the widget to demonstrate how to covert the generated Express site into an MVC.

To start, consider Table 14-1, which defines the actions necessary to maintain an application based on MVC.

Table 14-1. REST/route/CRUD mapping for maintaining widgets

HTTP verb	Path	Action	Used for
GET	/widgets	index	Displaying widgets
GET	/widgets/new	new	Returning the HTML form for creating a new widget
POST	/widgets	create	Creating a new widget
GET	/widgets/:id	show	Displaying a specific widget
GET	/widgets/edit/:id/	edit	Returning the HTML for editing a specific widget
PUT	/widgets/:id	update	Updating a specific widget
DELETE	/widgets/:id	destroy	Deleting a specific widget

The key to implementing these actions is that the user interface is implemented separately from the operations on the data to maintain the underlying model. The thing that controls how it all works together is the controller. This infrastructure reflects the concept of *separation of concerns*, specifically, MVC. The actual solution is embedded in the discussion.

Discussion

The Express basic router can be considered a "controller" because it directs views based on URLs, as well as supplying rudimentary data. But the generated Express application reflects only the "VC" in MVC, and weakly, at that. The missing element is the Model, which we'll have to create from scratch.

However, even after we add support for a Model, the controlling code doesn't make sure the right data gets to the right view, or the right action performs the right database updates. We need to replace the controller with something more sophisticated.

Lastly, the simple Jade files generated by the Express application don't implement any of the user interface components we need, and we'll have to create those ourselves.

When finished, Figure 14-2 shows the interaction between the three components, as implemented in the MVC used in this recipe.

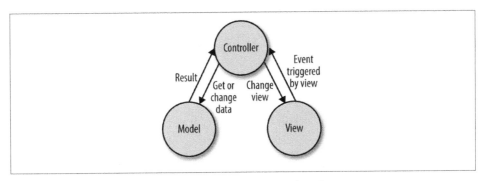

Figure 14-2. Diagram of MVC structure implemented in this section

To start, we'll modify the generated Express directory structure to the following:

```
app.js
bin
    www
controllers
model
package.json
public
    images
    javascripts
    stylesheets
    widgets
routes
    index.js
views
    error.jade
    index.jade
    layout.jade
    widgets
```

The new additions are the *widgets* subdirectories in both *views* and *public*, the *controllers* and *model* subdirectories, and the removal of the *users.js* routing file.

Next, we'll need to map the different routes laid out in Table 14-1 to the appropriate controller. The simplest approach is a separate file that takes the Express app object, and the name of the data object, and maps the routes accessed as verbs on the app to the appropriate controller function. Example 14-1 shows the complete code, saved in *map-routecontroller.js*, to maintain the widgets data store.

Example 14-1. Mapping routes to controllers

```
exports.mapRoute = function(app, prefix) {

    prefix = '/' + prefix;

    var prefixObj = require('./controllers' + prefix);

    // index
    app.get(prefix, prefixObj.index);

    // add
    app.get(prefix + '/new', prefixObj.new);

    // show
    app.get(prefix + '/:sn', prefixObj.show);

    // create
    app.post(prefix + '/create', prefixObj.create);

    // edit
    app.get(prefix + '/edit/:sn/', prefixObj.edit);

    // update
    app.put(prefix + '/:sn', prefixObj.update);

    // delete
    app.delete(prefix + '/:sn', prefixObj.destroy);
};
```

The module is imported into the primary *app.js* file:

```
var map = require('./maproutecontroller');
```

And the mapping is completed with the following code:

```
var prefixes = ['widgets'];

// map route to controller
prefixes.forEach(function(prefix) {
    map.mapRoute(app, prefix);
});
```

Notice that the code could allow for updates to multiple data objects: just add the other data objects to the prefixes array. Speaking of which, before we code the controller, we need to add in the data store. This example uses MongoDB, an open source *document database*. If you've not used MongoDB before, this is a rather abrupt introduction to the database, but thankfully MongoDB requires very little setup code.

 Installation instructions and preliminary setup instructions can be found at the MongoDB website (*http://www.mongodb.org/*). I recommend "Introduction to MongoDB" (*http://bit.ly/1yI1pOb*) and "What is a Document Database" (*http://bit.ly/1yI1q4H*).

The Node module that gives us access to MongoDB is Mongoose (*http://mongoo sejs.com/*). It's installed with:

```
npm install mongoose --saved
```

The `--saved` flag ensures the module dependency is added to the Express application's *package.json* file.

Once Mongoose is imported into the *app.js* file, a connection to the database is made with the URL *mongodb://127.0.0.1/WidgetDB*. The connection is to the MongoDB located in the localhost, and to the database named `WidgetDB`. The first time it's accessed, MondoDB creates the database.

The application is using Node's `process` object to capture the `exit` event, when the application is terminated. In the `exit` event handler, the MongoDB connection is closed. Example 14-2 contains the complete code for the *app.js* file. It's the same generated *app.js* file covered in Recipe 14.1, with the addition of the controller and database code, and one more module, `method-override`, discussed later in this section.

Example 14-2. Complete code for app.js, including router/controller mapping and database connection

```
var express = require('express');
var map = require('./maproutecontroller');
var mongoose = require('mongoose');

// middleware
var path = require('path');
var favicon = require('serve-favicon');
var logger = require('morgan');
var cookieParser = require('cookie-parser');
var bodyParser = require('body-parser');
var methodOverride = require('method-override');

var routes = require('./routes/index');

var app = express();

// view engine setup
```

```
app.set('views', path.join(__dirname, 'views'));
app.set('view engine', 'jade');

// uncomment after placing your favicon in /public
//app.use(favicon(__dirname + '/public/favicon.ico'));
app.use(logger('dev'));
app.use(bodyParser.json());
app.use(bodyParser.urlencoded({ extended: false }));
app.use(cookieParser());
app.use(require('stylus').middleware(path.join(__dirname, 'public')));
app.use(express.static(path.join(__dirname, 'public')));

// override with POST having ?_method=PUT or DELETE
app.use(methodOverride('_method'))

app.use('/', routes);

// MongoDB
mongoose.connect('mongodb://127.0.0.1/WidgetDB');

mongoose.connection.on('open', function() {
    console.log('Connected to Mongoose');
});

var prefixes = ['widgets'];

// map route to controller
prefixes.forEach(function(prefix) {
  map.mapRoute(app, prefix);
});

// catch 404 and forward to error handler
app.use(function(req, res, next) {
    var err = new Error('Not Found');
    err.status = 404;
    next(err);
});

// error handlers

// development error handler
// will print stacktrace
if (app.get('env') === 'development') {
    app.use(function(err, req, res, next) {
        res.status(err.status || 500);
        res.render('error', {
            message: err.message,
            error: err
        });
    });
}
```

```
// production error handler
// no stacktraces leaked to user
app.use(function(err, req, res, next) {
    res.status(err.status || 500);
    res.render('error', {
        message: err.message,
        error: {}
    });
});

module.exports = app;

process.on('exit', function(code) {
    mongoose.disconnect();
});
```

Now it's time to code the model. In a file named *widget.js* in the *model* subdirectory, the Mongoose Schema object is accessed, and used to create a Widget schema. The Widget schema creates a data object that can be used to interface with the widget database:

```
var mongoose = require('mongoose');

var Schema = mongoose.Schema;

// create Widget model
var widgetSchema = new Schema({
    sn : {type: String, require: true, trim: true, unique: true},
    name : {type: String, required: true, trim: true},
    desc : String,
    price : Number
});

var Widget = mongoose.model('Widget', widgetSchema);
```

The rest of the file's code defines the external interface for the data store. The functions created are used to list all of the widgets (`listWidgets`), get one specific widget (`getWidget`), create a widget (`createWidget`), delete the widget (`deleteWidget`), and update the widget (`updateWidget`). Most of the functions are dependent on data passed to them by the still-to-be-coded controller, and all take a callback function as last parameter. That's how the model functions can communicate back with data (and errors) to the controller:

```
exports.widgetDB = {
    createWidget: function (widget, callback) {

        var widgetObj = new Widget(widget);

        widgetObj.save( function(err, data) {
                callback(err,data);
                });
```

```
        },

        listWidgets: function (callback) {
          Widget.find({}, function (err, docs) {
              callback(err,docs);
          });
        },

        getWidget: function(sn, callback) {
          Widget.findOne({sn: sn}, function (err,doc) {
            console.log(err);
            callback(err, doc);
          });
        },

        deleteWidget: function(sn, callback) {
          Widget.remove({sn: sn}, function(err) {
            callback(err);
          });
        },

        updateWidget: function(sn, widget, callback) {
          Widget.update({sn: sn}, widget, function(err) {
            callback(err);
          });
        }
    };
```

Mongoose provides the methods, such as update and remove, to easily communicate with the MongoDB database. The database schema is simple:

- sn: A manually given serial number, so we don't need to depend on the MongoDB automatically generated identifier
- name: Widget name
- desc: A description of the widget
- price: The widget price

The key to finding and manipulating single widgets is the serial number sn.

Now that the model is complete, we can focus on the controller. In the *controller* sub-directory, we create a file, *widgets.js*, containing the controller code. It imports the model object and assigns it to a variable:

```
var widgetDB = require('../model/widget.js').widgetDB;
```

The controller functions are exported individually, and we've already mapped them to routes in *maproutecontroller.js*. Each function does two things: it invokes the appropriate model function to get data or update the database, and it updates the view. When it updates the view, it sends an error message if an error occurs, or it renders a Jade template, sending the template whatever data is retrieved from the database:

```
// index listing of widgets at /widgets/
exports.index = function(req, res) {
    widgetDB.listWidgets(function(err, docs) {
        if (err) {
            res.send(err);
        } else {
            console.log(docs);
            res.render('widgets/index', {title : 'Widgets', widgets : docs});
        }
    });
};

// display new widget form
exports.new = function(req, res) {
    var filePath = require('path')
                    .normalize(__dirname + "/../public/widgets/new.html");
    res.sendFile(filePath);
};

// add a widget
exports.create = function(req, res) {

    var widget = {
      sn : req.body.widgetsn,
      name : req.body.widgetname,
      price : parseFloat(req.body.widgetprice),
      desc: req.body.widgetdesc};

    widgetDB.createWidget(widget, function(err,data) {
        if (err) {
            res.send(err);
        } else {
            console.log(data);
            res.render('widgets/added', {title: 'Widget Added', widget: widget});
        }
    });
};


// show a widget
exports.show = function(req, res) {
    var sn = req.params.sn;
    widgetDB.getWidget(sn, function(err,doc) {
        if (err)
            res.send('There is no widget with sn of ' + sn);
        else
            res.render('widgets/show', {title : 'Show Widget', widget : doc});
    });
};
```

```
// delete a widget
exports.destroy = function(req,res) {
    var sn = req.params.sn;
    widgetDB.deleteWidget(sn, function(err) {
      if (err) {
        res.send('There is no widget with sn of ' + sn);
      } else {
        console.log('deleted ' + sn);
        res.send('deleted ' + sn);
      }
    });

};


// display edit form
exports.edit = function(req, res) {
    console.log(req.params);
    var sn = req.params.sn;
    console.log(sn);
    widgetDB.getWidget(sn, function(err, doc) {
      console.log(doc);
      if(err)
        res.send('There is no widget with sn of ' + sn);
      else
        res.render('widgets/edit', {title : 'Edit Widget', widget : doc});
    });
};

// update a widget
exports.update = function(req,res) {
  var sn = req.params.sn;
  var widget = {
      sn : sn,
      name : req.body.widgetname,
      price : parseFloat(req.body.widgetprice),
      desc : req.body.widgetdesc};

  console.log(sn);
  console.log(widget);
  widgetDB.updateWidget(sn, widget, function(err) {
      if (err)
        res.send('Problem occured with update' + err)
      else
        res.render('widgets/added', {title: 'Widget Edited', widget : widget})
  });
};
```

Though normally we'd use unit testing and debugging with the application, we're keeping things as simple as possible, and just incorporating console.log() function calls to get access to data and results so we can monitor the app as it's running.

We don't capture statistics, use database security, or other components of a robust application. We don't even check to make sure the
serial number field sn is unique before adding a new product, or
editing an existing one. A more robust application would take another chapter. Or two.

The form to add a new widget is just straight-up HTML, in a file named *new.html*,
located in the *public/widgets* subdirectory:

```
<!doctype html>
<html lang="en">
<head>
 <meta charset="utf-8" />
 <title>Widgets</title>
</head>
<body>
<h1>Add Widget:</h1>

<form method="POST" action="/widgets/create"
enctype="application/x-www-form-urlencoded">

 <p>Widget Serial Number: <input type="text" id="widgetsn" name="widgetsn"
 size="25" required /></p>

 <p>Widget name: <input type="text" name="widgetname"
 id="widgetname" size="25" required/></p>

 <p>Widget Price: <input type="text"
 pattern="^\$?([0-9]{1,3},([0-9]{3},)*[0-9]{3}|[0-9]+)(.[0-9][0-9])?$"
 name="widgetprice" id="widgetprice" size="25" required/></p>

 <p>Widget Description: <br />
 <textarea name="widgetdesc" id="widgetdesc" cols="20"
 rows="5"></textarea>
 <p>

 <input type="submit" name="submit" id="submit" value="Submit"/>
 <input type="reset" name="reset" id="reset" value="Reset"/>
 </p>
 </form>
</body>
```

The last additions are to create the view files. They're located in their own *widgets*
subdirectory under *views*. First come the files to handle the overall page structure. The
header.jade file defines the head element for all of the pages, incorporating a link to the
stylesheet:

```
head
  title #{title}
  meta(charset="utf-8")
```

```
link(type="text/css"
     rel="stylesheet"
     href="/stylesheets/main.css"
     media="all")
```

It's incorporated into the rest of the page layout, in the *layout.jade* file:

```
doctype html
html(lang="en")
  include header
  body
    block content
```

The head template is included in with the Jade include command.

The *added.jade* file isn't creating the form to add a new widget—that's accomplished with a static HTML file named *new.html*, located in the *public/widgets* subdirectory. The *added.jade* template is used to provide feedback of the successful creation of the new widget:

```
extends layout

block content
  h1 #{title} | #{widget.name}
  include widget

ul
  li sn: #{widget.sn}
  li Name: #{widget.name}
  li Price: $#{widget.price.toFixed(2)}
  li Desc: #{widget.desc}
```

The partioning of the template into separate components enables reuse of common components, such as the display of the widget data in a specific format.

The next file is *edit.jade*, which is used to update the widget. It's the most complex template because it incorporates data from the controller, and submits the data for an update. Although the form method states it's a POST, the method-override module, which is included in the *app.js* file, is used to signal that the method is really a PUT:

```
action="/widgets/#{widget.sn}?_method=PUT"
```

It's triggered by the following line, way back in the *app.js* file:

```
// override with POST having ?_method=PUT or DELETE
app.use(methodOverride('_method'))
```

Here is the complete *edit.jade* file:

```
extends layout

block content
  h1 Edit #{widget.name}
  form(method="POST"
```

```
    action="/widgets/#{widget.sn}?_method=PUT"
    enctype="application/x-www-form-urlencoded")
p Widget Name:
    input(type="text"
        name="widgetname"
        id="widgetname"
        size="25"
        value="#{widget.name}"
        required)
p Widget Price:
    input(type="text"
        name="widgetprice"
        id="widgetprice"
        size="25"
        value="#{widget.price}"
        pattern=
        "^\$?([0-9]{1,3},([0-9]{3},)*[0-9]{3}|[0-9]+)(.[0-9][0-9])?$"
        required)
p Widget Description:
    br
    textarea(name="widgetdesc"
        id="widgetdesc"
        cols="20"
        rows="5") #{widget.desc}
p
    input(type="submit"
        name="submit"
        id="submit"
        value="Submit")
    input(type="reset"
        name="reset"
        id="reset"
        value="reset")
```

The *index.jade* file displays a lists of all widgets in the database, with options to edit or delete each:

```
extends layout

block content
  table
    caption Widgets
      if widgets.length
        tr
          th SN
          th Name
          th Price
          th Description
          th
          th
        each widget in widgets
          if widget
            include row
```

It makes use of a *row.jade* template, which displays the widget as cells in a table row:

```
tr
  td #{widget.sn}
  td #{widget.name}
  td $#{widget.price.toFixed(2)}
  td #{widget.desc}
  td
    a(href='/widgets/edit/#{widget.sn}') Edit
  td
    a(href='/widgets/#{widget.sn}') Delete
```

When the option to delete the widget is chosen, the widget is displayed in a separate page, generated from the *show.jade* template, the last of the templates:

```
extends layout

block content
  h1 #{widget.name}
  include widget
  form(method="POST"
      action="/widgets/#{widget.sn}?_method=DELETE"
      enctype="application/x-www-form-urlencoded")
      input(type="submit"
            name="submit"
            id="submit"
            value="Delete Widget")
```

The person is given a chance to decide if he wants to delete this particular widget, and a button to do so.

To start the application, type in:

```
npm start
```

And you're off and running. Access the site as follows, starting with the new form:

```
http://yourdomain.com:3000/widgets/new/
```

How does all of this look? The CSS is simple, so set your expectations accordingly. Figure 14-3 shows the display with three widgets, and Figure 14-4 shows the page to edit an existing widget. Nothing exciting, but it does show that all the pieces are working.

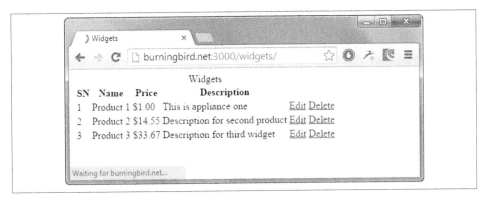

Figure 14-3. *Listing of existing widgets*

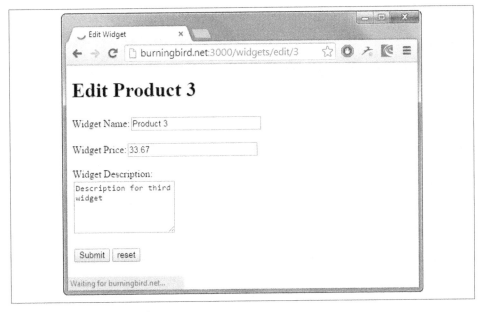

Figure 14-4. *Widget edit form*

Though a very simple application, the Widget is a complete MVC application based on Express.

See Also

If you're unfamiliar with MVC or MV*, I recommend the following resources:

- Jeff Atwood's "Understanding Model-View-Controller" (*http://bit.ly/1IH94gC*)

- Addy Osmani's "Journey Through the JavaScript MVC Jungle" (*http://bit.ly/1IH96oT*)
- The "JavaScript MV* Pattern" chapter in Osmani's book, *Learning JavaScript Design Patterns* (O'Reilly)

14.3. Choosing a SPA Framework: Deconstructing the TodoMVC

Problem

You've been tasked to convert your company website into an SPA—a single-page application. You need to find a framework to use, but there are so many. What should you look for in a framework?

Solution

There are several different frameworks you can choose from when selecting a framework for your new SPA. When determining which to use, check out the documentation for the top tools, read articles comparing the differences, and ask friends and other techies for recommendations.

The most effective approach I've seen, however, for comparing the different frameworks that can support a SPA (or any other MV* application) is the TodoMVC website (*http://todomvc.com/*). At a minimum, you can get a feel for how each framework manages the exact same task.

Discussion

The TodoMVC website has defined a specific type of application, a *to-do list*, and invited developers to create the application using the different MV* frameworks. It's one of the most brilliant ideas I've seen for comparing different architectures, because a to-do list application supports several activities that accentuate architecture comparison:

- Providing a dynamic interface
- An ideal candidate for an SPA architecture
- Requiring data storage and retrieval, but the data is uncomplicated so we can focus on the support without getting bogged down in the data schema (allowing the developers to use localstorage)
- Depends on routing to define activities
- Small and self-contained enough so the examples are simple to review

The TodoMVC folks provide a specification for developers to follow (*http://bit.ly/1IH9MKN*) that's detailed enough to ensure all of the applications meet the same requirements in a similar enough manner to ensure easy comparison.

In this section, I'll briefly cover the ToDo requirements and then examine the submissions for three of the more popular frameworks: AngularJS, Backbone.js, and Ember.js. Note, though, that the site provides ToDo applications from a host of other frameworks, including those for new framework tools as they are developed. Don't feel you have to limit yourself to just these three frameworks.

 The ToDo submissions, and all supporting material, is one big Git-Hub Project (*https://github.com/tastejs/todomvc*), which means you can easily download everything, for perusing and play in your own environment.

The ToDo Requirements

To ensure the apps are easily comparable, the ToDo wranglers have provided a set of programming guidelines. It's basic stuff: use strict mode, run the code through JSHint, indent the code, use semicolons, and so on.

The creators have provided a template for the projects. Following is the directory structure:

```
index.html
bower.json
bower_components/
css
└── app.css
js/
├── app.js
├── controllers/
└── models/
readme.md
```

The project should have a README file and a *bower.json* file, unless having the file conflicts somehow with the application.

 Recipe 12.11 covers Bower, and "Extra: The README File and Markdown Syntax" on page 337 covers README files.

The ToDo List is an SPA, so the only HTML file is the top-level *index.html*. It's also the only file I'm including the complete source for, in Example 14-3, because it's critical for understanding what's happening with each of the framework submissions. The indentation has been removed to accomodate the book page width.

Example 14-3. Complete index.html template from the TodoMVC project

```
<!doctype html>
<html lang="en">
<head>
<meta charset="utf-8">
<title>Template • TodoMVC</title>
<link rel="stylesheet" href="bower_components/todomvc-common/base.css">
<!-- CSS overrides - remove if you don't need it -->
<link rel="stylesheet" href="css/app.css">
</head>
<body>
<section id="todoapp">
<header id="header">
<h1>todos</h1>
<input id="new-todo" placeholder="What needs to be done?" autofocus>
</header>
<!-- This section should be hidden by default and shown when there are todos -->
<section id="main">
<input id="toggle-all" type="checkbox">
<label for="toggle-all">Mark all as complete</label>
<ul id="todo-list">
<!-- These are here just to show the structure of the list items -->
<!-- List items should get the class `editing` when editing and
`completed` when marked as completed -->
<li class="completed">
<div class="view">
<input class="toggle" type="checkbox" checked>
<label>Create a TodoMVC template</label>
<button class="destroy"></button>
</div>
<input class="edit" value="Create a TodoMVC template">
</li>
<li>
<div class="view">
<input class="toggle" type="checkbox">
<label>Rule the web</label>
<button class="destroy"></button>
</div>
<input class="edit" value="Rule the web">
</li>
</ul>
</section>
<!-- This footer should hidden by default and shown when there are todos -->
<footer id="footer">
<!-- This should be `0 items left` by default -->
<span id="todo-count"><strong>1</strong> item left</span>
<!-- Remove this if you don't implement routing -->
<ul id="filters">
```

```
<li>
<a class="selected" href="#/">All</a>
</li>
<li>
<a href="#/active">Active</a>
</li>
<li>
<a href="#/completed">Completed</a>
</li>
</ul>
<!-- Hidden if no completed items are left ↓ -->
<button id="clear-completed">Clear completed (1)</button>
</footer>
</section>
<footer id="info">
<p>Double-click to edit a todo</p>
<!-- Remove the below line ↓ -->
<p>Template by <a href="http://github.com/sindresorhus">Sindre Sorhus</a></p>
<!-- Change this out with your name and url ↓ -->
<p>Created by <a href="http://todomvc.com">you</a></p>
<p>Part of <a href="http://todomvc.com">TodoMVC</a></p>
</footer>
<!-- Scripts here. Don't remove this ↓ -->
<script src="bower_components/todomvc-common/base.js"></script>
<script src="js/app.js"></script>
</body>
</html>
```

Projects could be completed much more quickly and cleanly if all developers were handed annotated HTML files such as this when creating new applications. It's template and requirements in one.

When the ToDo list is empty, the `footer` and `main` blocks should be hidden. ToDos are created from the top, and hitting Enter appends the new item to the list, and clears the input field. There's a "mark all complete" checkbox item that marks all ToDos complete. Each ToDo can be removed, completed, and edited. All ToDos can be removed at once, and the ToDo list is maintained in LocalStorage, so the apps are kept simple and not bogged down in data implementation issues.

The frameworks do require routing (covered in Recipe 14.2). If routing isn't part of the framework tool (it is, for most), then the developer can use Flatiron (*https://github.com/ flatiron/director*), which provides basic routing capabilities regardless of other infrastructure.

ToDo in AngularJS

AngularJS is the Big Daddy in frameworks. It's one of the most popular, and most widely used. It is a complete MVC framework, and is sponsored by Google, which adds to overall stability of the project.

To explore AngularJS and the ToDo, I focused on the Optimized AngularJS project.

 The AngularJS ToDo page (*http://todomvc.com/architecture-examples/angularjs/#/*) lists several links to demos and source. To follow my overview of AngularJS's implementation of the ToDo list, open the source files in GitHub (*http://bit.ly/1IHaB6r*).

AngularJS enhances HTML with a construct that the framework terms *directives*. These are annotations added to existing HTML elements that attach specific behaviors when the application is "compiled"—processed by the framework engine. The ToDo application contains source code for two *custom directives*: todo-escape and todo-focus, both used in the form used to edit each ToDo:

```
form ng-submit="doneEditing(todo)">
<input class="edit" ng-trim="false" ng-model="todo.title"
ng-blur="doneEditing(todo)" todo-escape="revertEditing(todo)"
todo-focus="todo == editedTodo">
</form>
```

The source for the todo-focus is short, sweet, and self-explanatory (an indirect underlying programming constraint for most Framework apps):

```
/*global todomvc */
'use strict';

/**
 * Directive that places focus on the element it is applied to when the
 * expression it binds to evaluates to true
 */
todomvc.directive('todoFocus', function ($timeout) {
    return function (scope, elem, attrs) {
        scope.$watch(attrs.todoFocus, function (newVal) {
            if (newVal) {
                $timeout(function () {
                    elem[0].focus();
                }, 0, false);
            }
        });
    };
});
```

What's the expression? todo == editedToDo when the current ToDo is now the edited ToDo.

There are predefined directives (ones provided with AngularJS) in use in the main section, such as the use of ng-show attached to the outer section element. The ng-show directive controls whether the element and its contents are displayed or not. In the

HTML snippet, the section shows when the `todos.length` is *truthy* (a value greater than zero):

```
<section id="main" ng-show="todos.length" ng-cloak>
<input id="toggle-all" type="checkbox" ng-model="allChecked"
ng-click="markAll(allChecked)">
<label for="toggle-all">Mark all as complete</label>
<ul id="todo-list">
<li ng-repeat="todo in todos | filter:statusFilter track by $index"
ng-class="{completed: todo.completed, editing: todo == editedTodo}">
<div class="view">
<input class="toggle" type="checkbox" ng-model="todo.completed"
ng-change="todoCompleted(todo)">
<label ng-dblclick="editTodo(todo)">{{todo.title}}</label>
<button class="destroy" ng-click="removeTodo(todo)"></button>
</div>
<form ng-submit="doneEditing(todo)">
<input class="edit" ng-trim="false" ng-model="todo.title"
ng-blur="doneEditing(todo)"
todo-escape="revertEditing(todo)" todo-focus="todo == editedTodo">
</form>
</li>
</ul>
</section>
```

Directives are only part of the AngularJS template system. Another system component that appears in the HTML template is *Markup*: double curly brackets, such as {{to do.title}} in the HTML snippet binding expressions to elements. A third system component are the *form controls*, binding view and model, and providing necessary functionality such as data binding. The `ng-model` attribute demonstrates two-way data binding in the HTML snippet.

The specification listed three routes that were mandatory:

- #/ (all - default)
- #/active
- #/completed

They match, naturally enough, a listing of all ToDos that are not complete, a listing of all those that are complete, and the total list.

In the optimized AngularJS app, the routing is handled in the controller implementation, the largest piece of code in the app, located in */controllers/todoControl.js*. The controller method takes, as arguments, a unique name ("TodoCtrl"), and the controller constructor function. It's added to the application's Angular Module, the `to domvc`, so that the controller isn't added to the global space. The Angular Module, which is the container for all the bits, is created in the *app.js* file and consists of one simple line:

```
var todomvc = angular.module('todomvc', []);
```

To return to the controller, its construction function receives four arguments:

- $scope: The execution context for expressions
- $location: The parsed URL and location service
- $filter: Formats expressions for display
- todoStorage: The model

The model itself has two methods: put() and get().

It's quite a clean implementation to walk through, and one can use what's in the example as a way of digging into the extensive AngularJS documentation.

What are some of the pros and cons of AngularJS? The directives are one advantage, providing a way to package reusable chunks of code. So is the simplified support for MVC, as well as the two-way data binding. AngularJS also comes with its own baked-in testing tools. The disadvantages include the fact that is a sophisticated, rather complex system, and has one of the larger code bases. It's not a good choice for smallish applications, but can be definitely worthwhile for larger, more complex websites.

ToDo in Backbone.js

The Backbone.js architecture example ToDo application reflects the simpler infrastructure that is Backbone.js. It's dependent on Underscore, but you don't have to use the Underscore templating system with it. The ToDo app, however, does use Underscore.

The *index.html* page has the following code:

```
<script type="text/template" id="stats-template">
<span id="todo-count"><strong><%= remaining %></strong>
   <%= remaining === 1 ? 'item' : 'items' %> left</span>
<ul id="filters">
<li>
<a class="selected" href="#/">All</a>
</li>
<li>
<a href="#/active">Active</a>
</li>
<li>
<a href="#/completed">Completed</a>
</li>
</ul>
<% if (completed) { %>
<button id="clear-completed">Clear completed (<%= completed %>)</button>
<% } %>
</script>
```

The use of "text/template" is a way of embedding template code that the browser engine ignores. This is the template for the statistics that are displayed at the bottom of the of the ToDo list, as well as links to the different views. In JavaScript, in *views/app-view.js*, the Underscore _template() function is used to compile the template into a function that can be rendered:

```
statsTemplate: _.template($('#stats-template').html()),
```

If you look further down in the Views code, you'll see a render function that basically pulls together all of the view information, including a call to the newly generated statsTemplate function:

```
// Re-rendering the App just means refreshing the statistics -- the rest
// of the app doesn't change.
render: function () {
    var completed = app.todos.completed().length;
    var remaining = app.todos.remaining().length;
    if (app.todos.length) {
        this.$main.show();
        this.$footer.show();
        this.$footer.html(this.statsTemplate({
            completed: completed,
            remaining: remaining
        }));
        this.$('#filters li a')
          .removeClass('selected')
          .filter('[href="#/' + (app.TodoFilter || '') + '"]')
          .addClass('selected');
    } else {
        this.$main.hide();
        this.$footer.hide();
    }
    this.allCheckbox.checked = !remaining;
},
```

The completed and remaining values are derived from the length property on both sets of items, and depending on their value, the footer and main section are displayed (or not), and the values are sent as parameters to statsTemplate for display in the sections marked <%= remaining %> and <%= completed>, as well as used in expressions determining other view characteristics.

The other template in the HTML file is processed in the second view JavaScript file, *todo-view.js*. It renders the ToDo list, as you can imagine, assigning event listeners for all of the relevant events, and so on.

The router code passes on one route, filter triggering a setFilter() function. The function takes one parameter that determines how the collection is filtered. In the Collection JavaScript, the ToDos can be filtered on completed or remaining depending on the value of the ToDo's completed attribute.

The application makes use of an extension, Backbone.localStorage, to manage the model. It's instantiated in the Collections *todo.js* code:

```
localStorage: new Backbone.LocalStorage('todos-backbone'),
```

And then maintained in the Model code:

```
var app = app || {};

(function () {
    'use strict';

    // Todo Model
    // ----------

    // Our basic **Todo** model has `title`, `order`, and `completed` attributes.
    app.Todo = Backbone.Model.extend({
        // Default attributes for the todo
        // and ensure that each todo created has `title` and `completed` keys.
        defaults: {
            title: '',
            completed: false
        },

        // Toggle the `completed` state of this todo item.
        toggle: function () {
            this.save({
                completed: !this.get('completed')
            });
        }
    });

})();
```

The default attribute values for the `title` and `completed` attributes are set for each ToDo, and the only other action is toggling the `completed` attribute.

The advantage to Backbone.js is its community support and small size. Some would say Backbone.js has surpassed AngularJS as the most popular framework, though "popularity" is hard to measure. It is the smallest frameworks that I know of, and requires minimal effort to incorporate. It's also very flexible. The drawbacks to the framework are both its small size and flexibility. You have to develop much of the necessary infrastructure for an application yourself, and this becomes problematic as the project size grows.

ToDo in Ember.js

Ember.js is dependent on jQuery and Handlebars.js for templating, which you can tell as soon as you open the *index.html* file, an excerpt of which follows:

```
<script type="text/x-handlebars" data-template-name="todo-list">
  {{#if length}}
    <section id="main">
      {{#if canToggle}}
        {{input type="checkbox" id="toggle-all" checked=allTodos.allAreDone}}
      {{/if}}
      <ul id="todo-list">
        {{#each}}
          <li {{bind-attr class="isCompleted:completed isEditing:editing"}}>
            {{#if isEditing}}
                {{todo-input type="text" class="edit" value=bufferedTitle
                focus-out="doneEditing" insert-newline="doneEditing"
                  escape-press="cancelEditing"}}
            {{else}}
             {{input type="checkbox" class="toggle" checked=isCompleted}}
             <label {{action "editTodo" on="doubleClick"}}>{{title}}</label>
             <button {{action "removeTodo"}} class="destroy"></button>
            {{/if}}
          </li>
        {{/each}}
      </ul>
    </section>
  {{/if}}
</script>
```

The Handlebars.js template syntax is very identifiable. Instead of using the more generic "text/template" type on the `script` element, Handlebars.js uses "text/x-handlebars". Handlebars.js also more closely matches programming constructs. It is simple, though, to see the data's impact on the views: if the length variable is truthy, process the contained template; if the ToDo is being edited, process this template code; otherwise, process this other; and so on. Very readable.

Like with the AngularJS and the Backbone.js versions, the *app.js* file just creates the overall application. The interesting stuff is in the other files, such as the *router.js* file, which has one of the more identifiable router structure if you've used a framework such as Express (covered earlier in this chapter). Especially when compared to my own version of Express as an MVC app, in Recipe 14.2.

Most of the view work is handled by Handlebars, with the exception of customizing the input element, seemingly to eliminate a redundant text selection problem.

There is a helper file, with some unique code:

```
/*global Ember */
(function () {
    'use strict';

    Ember.Handlebars.helper('pluralize', function (singular, count) {
        /* From Ember-Data */
        var inflector = Ember.Inflector.inflector;
```

```
    return count === 1 ? singular : inflector.pluralize(singular);
  });
})();
```

This is to handle *inflection rules*, so that we get something like "ten items", rather than "ten item", or be forced to use the awkward "ten item(s)". Sure enough, a quick look at the *index.html* file shows us the following:

```
<span id="todo-count"><strong>{{remaining.length}}</strong>
{{pluralize 'item' remaining.length}} left</span>
```

The controller files match the router/controller mapping in the *router.js* file, and is quite easy to follow. An example is the following excerpt, from *todos_controller.js*, when a new ToDo is created:

```
createTodo: function () {
  var title, todo;

  // Get the todo title set by the "New Todo" text field
  title = this.get('newTitle').trim();
  if (!title) {
    return;
  }

  // Create the new Todo model
  todo = this.store.createRecord('todo', {
    title: title,
    isCompleted: false
  });

  todo.save();

  // Clear the "New Todo" text field
  this.set('newTitle', '');
},
```

The store is based on Ember.js DS.Model class, defining the structure (and data types) of the ToDo's fields. The localStorage connection comes in from using the Ember.js *localstorage_adapter.js*. What it does is out of sight, out of mind.

Those who like Ember.js mention its "opinionated" structure, which means it takes care of most of the decision making for you. One could also call this a drawback, as is the fact that though it can emulate an MVC, it isn't a true MVC system. However, the Ember.js team provides excellent documentation, which helps when you're coming up to speed with the framwork.

One concern I've seen expressed frequently about Ember.js is its slowness and memory usage. However, it is one of the newer frameworks and we can assume performance will improve over time.

In Comparison

Out of sight, out of mind is one of the major advantages to using one of the frameworks I've covered in this section: there's some upfront time, but the processing each provides (which we don't have to implement) makes the time worthwhile.

Each framework has its fans, and each has its detractors. These three are also the three most commonly compared, and I'll provide links to some comparisons at the end of the section. AngularJS is the most mature of the frameworks, and arguably, the most popular. It features in the MEAN stack, as in MongoDB-Express-AngularJS-Node.

On the other hand, Ember.js has an infrastructure that could more easily match what we're used to, coming in from an Express background. Backbone.js's goal to minimize its source is a commendable goal—one thing we don't need is bloated code. Because of the basic nature of its implementation, Backbone.js is now the basis of other frameworks, providing expanded functionality. Backbone.js also lets you pick your own template system, but AngularJS and Ember.js seem to have a more smoothly integrated template system.

AngularJS makes use of *promises*, which I touched on in Chapter 11. I'm not as fond of promises as others are, but this may be the kicker for you. Ember.js has put enormous effort into the data model, and also handles much of the functionality, such as back button support, that the other frameworks skipped.

All three frameworks have been used with some major websites, so they're all *hardened* (production and scalability tested).

Of course, they're not the only kids on the block, and it's worth your time to explore the other frameworks at the TodoMVC website.

See Also

For more on SPAs, I suggest:

- Mikito Takada's (mixu) free book, "Single page apps in depth" (*http://bit.ly/1yI1xgK*)
- For more on SPAs in a ASP.NET environment, see "Learn About ASP.NET Single Page Application" (*http://www.asp.net/single-page-application*)
- Manning Publication's book *Single Page Web Applications* (*http://bit.ly/1yI1y4d*)

For comparisons of the three frameworks:

- "AngularJS vs. Backbone.js vs. Ember.js" (*http://bit.ly/1IHcfoE*)
- "A Comparison of Angular, Backbone, CanJS and Ember" (*http://bit.ly/1IHcgZU*)
- "Ember, Angular, and Backbone: Which JavaScript Framework is Right For You?" (*http://bit.ly/1IHcikt*)

- "Evaluation of AngularJS, EmberJS, BackboneJS + MarionetteJS" (*http://bit.ly/ 1IHclwr*)

I also recommend "Journey Through The JavaScript MVC Jungle" (*http://bit.ly/ 1IHcq3a*).

14.4. Working with the OAuth Framework

Problem

You need access to the Dropbox (or Facebook or Twitter) API in your Node application, but it requires authorization. Specifically, it requires OAuth authorization.

Solution

You'll need to incorporate an OAuth client in your application. You'll also need to meet the OAuth requirements demanded by the resource provider.

See the discussion for details.

Discussion

OAuth is an authorization framework used with most popular social media and cloud content applications. If you've ever gone to a site and it's asked you to authorize access to data in (Facebook/Twitter/Dropbox), you've participated in the OAuth authorization *flow*.

There are two versions of OAuth, 1.0 and 2.0, and no, they're not compatible. OAuth 1.0 was based on proprietary APIs developed by Flickr and Google, and was heavily web page focused and didn't gracefully transcend the barrier between web, mobile, and service applications. When wanting to access resources in a mobile phone app, the app would have the user log in to the app in a mobile browser and then copy access tokens to the app—an ugly process guaranteed to fail for most users.

Other criticisms of OAuth 1.0 is that the process required that the authorization server be the same as the resource server, which doesn't scale when you're talking about service providers such as Twitter, Facebook, and Amazon.

OAuth 2.0 presents a simpler authorization process, and also provides different types of authorization (different flows) for different circumstances. Some would say, though, that it does so at the cost of security, as it doesn't have the same demands for encrypting hash tokens and request strings.

Most developers won't have to create an OAuth 2.0 server, and doing so is way beyond the scope of this book, much less this recipe. But it's common for applications to incorporate an OAuth client (1.0 or 2.0), for one service or another, so I'm going to present three different types of OAuth use with two different services: Dropbox and Twitter. First, though, let's discuss the differences between authorization and authentication.

Authorization Isn't Authentication

Authorization is saying to a resource, "I authorize this application to access my resources on your resource server." Authentication is the process of authenticating whether you are, indeed, the person who owns this account and has control over these resources. An example would be if I want to comment on an article at a newspaper's online site. It will likely ask me to log in via some service. If I pick my Facebook account to use as the login, the news site will most likely want some data from Facebook.

The news site is, first, authenticating me as a legitimate Facebook user, with an established Facebook account. In other words, I'm not just some random person coming in and commenting anonymously. Secondly, the news site wants something from me in exchange for the privilege of commenting: it's going to want data about me. Perhaps it will ask for permission to post for me (if I post my comment to Facebook as well as the news site). This is both an authentication and an authorization request.

If I'm not already logged into Facebook, I'll have to log in. Facebook is using my correct application of username and password to authenticate that, yes, I own the Facebook account in question. Once logged in, Facebook asks whether I agree to giving the newspaper site the authorization to access resources it wants. If I agree (because I desperately want to comment on a particular story), Facebook gives the news site the authorization, and there's now a persistent connection from the newspaper to my Facebook account (which you can see in your FB settings). I can make my comment, and make comments at other stories, until I log out or revoke the Facebook authorization.

Of course, none of this implies that Facebook or the news site is actually authenticating who I am. Authentication, in this case, is about establishing that I am the owner of the Facebook account. The only time *real* authentication enters the picture is in a social media context such as Twitter's authenticated accounts for celebrities.

Our development task is made simpler by the fact that software to handle authorization is frequently the same software that authenticates the individual, so we're not having to deal with two different JavaScript libraries/modules/systems. There are also several excellent OAuth (1.0 and 2.0) modules we can use in Node applications. One of the most popular is Passport, and there are extensions for various authorization services created specifically for the Passport system. However, there are also very simple OAuth clients that provide barebones authorization access for a variety of services, and some modules that are created specifically for one service.

Read more about Passport and its various *strategies* supporting different servers at its website (*http://passportjs.org/*). The most popular of the barebones OAuth modules is node-oauth (*http://bit.ly/1yI25Di*), though Simple OAuth 2 (*http://bit.ly/1yI26ao*) is also very popular. Most examples assume the developer is creating an Express application, so you do need to be famliar with Express before reading the OAuth module documentation.

Now, on to the technology.

Twitter Application-Only and OAuth 2.0 Client Credentials Grant

There are few web resources that nowadays provide an API you can access without having some kind of authorization credential. This means having to incorporate a round-trip directive to the end users—asking them to authorize access to their account at the service before the application can access data. The problem is that sometimes all you need is simple read-only access without update privileges, without a frontend login interface, and without having a specific user make an authorizing grant.

OAuth 2.0 accounts for this particular type of authorizing flow with the *Client Credentials Grant*. The diagram for this simplified authorization is shown in Figure 14-5.

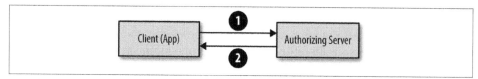

Figure 14-5. The Client Credentials Grant authorization flow

Twitter provides what it calls Application-Only authorization, which is based on OAuth 2.0's Client Credentials Grant. In Recipe 13.7, I used this type of authorization to access Twitter's Search API. We focused on the API in that chapter, but now we'll take a look at the authorization process.

I used the Node module oauth to implement the authorization. It's the most basic of the authorization modules, and supports both OAuth 1.0 and OAuth 2.0 authorization flows. To isolate the Twitter API application from the OAuth bits, I wrapped the OAuth usage with my own module, twitreq, displayed in Example 14-4. It exports two methods: getAuthorization() to get the necessary access token, and getTwitterData() to make the actual API request with the access token.

Example 14-4. The twitreq module code, wrapping OAuth 2.0 authorization

```
var OAuth2 = require('oauth').OAuth2;
var https = require('https');
```

```
var atoken;

// consumer key and secret passed in from client
exports.getAuthorization = function (consumerKey, consumerSecret, callback) {
   var oauth2 = new OAuth2(
      consumerKey,
      consumerSecret,
      'https://api.twitter.com/',
      null,
      'oauth2/token',
      null);

   // signaling a client credentials authorization request
   oauth2.getOAuthAccessToken('', {
      'grant_type': 'client_credentials'},
      function(err, atoken) {
         callback(err,atoken);
      }
   );
};
// can be any Twitter App-only authorization API endpoint
exports.getTwitterData = function (servicePath, atoken, callback) {
   var options = {
      hostname: 'api.twitter.com',
      path: servicePath,
      headers: {
         Authorization: 'Bearer ' + atoken
      }
   };

   https.get(options, function (result) {
      var buffer = '';
      result.setEncoding('utf8');
      result.on('data', function (data) {
         buffer += data;
      });
      result.on('end', function () {
         callback(buffer);
         });
   });
};
```

To use the Twitter authorization API, the client application has to register their application with Twitter. Twitter provides both a *consumer key* and a *consumer secret*. They're passed to the getAuthorization() function, along with a callback function.

In getAuthorization(), a new OAuth2 object is created, passing in:

- Consumer key
- Consumer secret

- API base URI – (API URI minus the query string)
- A value of null signals OAuth to use the default, "/oauth/authorize"
- The access token path
- Null, because we're not using any custom headers

The oauth module takes this data and forms a POST request to Twitter, passing along the consumer key and secret, as well as providing a *scope* for the request. Twitter's documentation provides an example POST request for an access token (line breaks inserted for readability):

```
POST /oauth2/token HTTP/1.1
Host: api.twitter.com
User-Agent: My Twitter App v1.0.23
Authorization: Basic eHZ6MWV2RlM0d0VFUFRHRUZQSEJvZzpMOHFxOVBaeVJn
               NmllS0dFS2hab2xHQzB2SldMdzhpRUo4OERSZHlPZw==
               Content-Type: application/x-www-form-urlencoded;charset=UTF-8
Content-Length: 29
Accept-Encoding: gzip

grant_type=client_credentials
```

The request is sent using SSL, a requirement for OAuth 2.0 (and one I'll get into more detail a little later). The reason why SSL is used is because encryption is not used with the communication as it is with OAuth 1.0.

The response includes the access token (again, line breaks for readability):

```
HTTP/1.1 200 OK
Status: 200 OK
Content-Type: application/json; charset=utf-8
...
Content-Encoding: gzip
Content-Length: 140

{"token_type":"bearer","access_token":"AAAAAAAAAAAAAAAAAAAAAAAAAAAAAAAAAAAA
%2FAAAAAAAAAAAAAAAAAAA%3DAAAAAAAAAAAAAAAAAAAAAAAAAAAAAAAAAAAAAAAAAAA"}
```

The access token has to be used with any of the API requests. There is no further authorization steps, so the process is very simple. In addition, it doesn't require an individual's authorization, so it's not as disruptive to the user.

 Twitter provides wonderful documentation. I recommend reading "Application-Only authentication Overview" (*https://dev.twitter.com/ oauth/application-only*). The oauth module can be installed in the usual way:

```
npm install oauth
```

Full Read/Write Authorization with the Twitter API and OAuth 1.0

Application-Only authentication is great for accessing read-only data, but what if you want to access a user's specific data, or even make a change to her data? Then you'll need the full OAuth authorization. In this section, we'll again use Twitter for the demonstration, because of its use of OAuth 1.0 authorization. In the next, we'll look at OAuth 2.0.

 I refer to it as OAuth 1.0, but Twitter's service is based on OAuth Core 1.0 Revision A (*http://oauth.net/core/1.0a/*). However, it's a lot easier just to say OAuth 1.0.

OAuth 1.0 requires a digital signature. The steps to derive this digital signature, graphically represented in Figure 14-6, and as outlined by Twitter are:

1. Collect the HTTP method and the base URI, minus any query string.

2. Collect the parameters, including the consumer key, request data, nonce, signature method, and so on.

3. Create a signature base string, which consists of the data we've gathered, formed into a string in a precise manner, and encoded just right.

4. Create a signing key, which is a combination of consumer key, and OAuth token secret, again combined in a precise manner.

5. Pass the signature base string and the signing key to an HMAC-SHA1 hashing algorithm, which returns a binary string that needs further encoding.

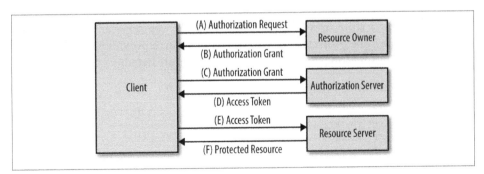

Figure 14-6. OAuth 1.0 authorization flow

You have to follow this process for *every* request. Thankfully, we have modules and libraries that do all of this mind numbing work for us. I don't know about you, but if I

---

had to do this, my interest in incorporating Twitter data and services into my application would quickly wane.

Our friend oauth provides the underlying OAuth 1.0 support, but we don't have to code to it directly this time. Another module, node-twitter-api, has wrapped all of the OAuth pieces, All we need do is create a new node-twitter-api object, passing in our consumer key and secret, as well as the callback/redirect URL required by the resource services, as part of the authorization process. Processing the request object in that URL provides us the access token and secret we need for API access. Every time we make a request, we pass in the access token and secret.

The twitter-node-api module is a thin wrapper around the REST API: to make a request, we extrapolate what the function is from the API. If we're interested in posting a status update, the REST API endpoint is:

```
https://api.twitter.com/1.1/statuses/update.json
```

The twitter-node-api object instance function is statuses(), and the first parameter is the verb, update:

```
twitter.statuses('update', {
        "status": "Hi from Shelley's Toy Box. (Ignore--developing Node app)"
        }, atoken, atokensec, function(err, data, response) {...});
```

The callback function arguments include any possible error, requested data (if any), and the raw response.

A complete example is shown in Example 14-5. It uses the Node core https module for server communication, provides a primitive web page for the user, and then uses another module, route, to handle simple routing. The route is instantiated and then passed to the HTTPS server when created. It will now intercept web requests, looking for matches to process.

Note that the application uses https and not http for web service. OAuth redirect/callback URLs *must* be protected by SSL for most resource providers. "Extra: Setting Up HTTPS for Testing" on page 433 discusses SSL in more detail.

Example 14-5. Twitter app fully authorized via OAuth 1.0

```
var twitterAPI = require('node-twitter-api');
var route = require('router')();
var https = require('https');
var fs = require('fs');
var url = require('url');

var options = {
   key: fs.readFileSync('/home/examples/ssl/server.key'),
   cert: fs.readFileSync('/home/examples/ssl/server.crt')
};
```

```
https.createServer(options, route).listen(443);

var twitter = new twitterAPI({
    consumerKey: 'yourkey',
    consumerSecret: 'yoursecret',
    callback: 'https://yourdomain.com/auth/'
});

var token, tokensec;
var atoken, atokensec;

var menu = '<a href="/post/status/">Say hello</a><br />' +
           '<a href="/get/account/">Account Settings<br />';


route.get('/', function(req, res) {
    twitter.getRequestToken(function(error, requestToken, requestTokenSecret,
      results) {
      if (error) {
          console.log('Error getting OAuth request token : ' + error);
          res.writeHead(200);
          res.end('Error getting authorization' + error);
      } else {
          token = requestToken;
          tokensec = requestTokenSecret;
          res.writeHead(302, {'Location':
          'https://api.twitter.com/oauth/authenticate?oauth_token='
            + requestToken});
          res.end();
      }
    });
});

route.get('/auth/', function(req,res) {
  var url_parts = url.parse(req.url, true);
  var query = url_parts.query;
  twitter.getAccessToken(token, tokensec,query.oauth_verifier,
        function(err, accessToken, accessTokenSecret,results) {
            res.writeHead(200);
            if (err) {
               res.end('problems getting authorization with Twitter' + err);
            } else {
               atoken = accessToken;
               atokensec = accessTokenSecret;
               res.end(menu);
            }
  });
});


route.get('/post/status/', function(req,res) {
    twitter.statuses('update', {
```

```
        "status": "Hi from Shelley's Toy Box. (Ignore--developing Node app)"
      }, atoken, atokensec, function(err, data, response) {
        res.writeHead(200);
        if (err) {
          res.end('problems posting ' + JSON.stringify(err));
        } else {
          res.end('posting status: ' + JSON.stringify(data) + '<br />' + menu);
        }
    });
});

route.get('/get/account/', function(req, res) {
    twitter.account('settings',{},atoken,atokensec,
          function(err,data,response){
          res.writeHead(200);
          if (err) {
            res.end('problems getting account ' + JSON.stringify(err));
          } else {
            res.end('<p>' + JSON.stringify(data) + '</p>' + menu);
          }
    });
});
```

The routes of interest in the app are:

- **/**: Page that triggers a redirect to Twitter for authorization
- **/auth**: The callback or redirect URL registered with the app, and passed in the request
- **/post/status/**: Post a status to Twitter account
- **/get/account/**: Get account information for individual

In each case, the appropriate node-twitter-api function is used:

- **/**: Get a request token and request token secret, using getRequestToken()
- **/auth/**: Get the API access token and token secret, caching them locally, display menu
- **/post/status/**: status() with *update* as first parameter, status, access token and secret, and callback function
- **/get/account/**: account() with *settings* as first parameter, an empty object, since no data is needed for the request, and the access token, secret, and callback

The Twitter authorization page that pops up is displayed in Figure 14-7 and the web page that displays account information for yours truly is displayed in Figure 14-8.

Figure 14-7. Twitter Authorization page, redirected from the recipe app

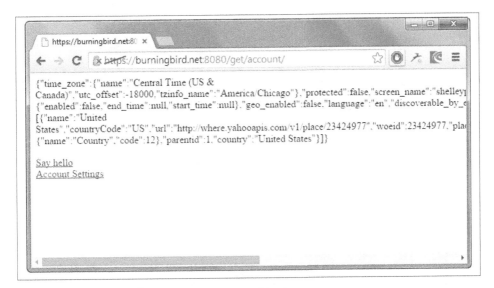

Figure 14-8. Display of Twitter user account data in app

Read more on `node-twitter-api` at its GitHub respository page (*https://github.com/reneraab/node-twitter-api*), and `router` at its GitHub page (*https://github.com/gett/router*). Other libraries provide the same type of functionality at the same level as `node-twitter-api`, but most of them are tightly integrated with Express. Express is a rather heavy tool to use just to demonstrate the target functionality.

Accessing Dropbox using OAuth 2.0 in a Web Page

The popular cloud service Dropbox provides APIs for accessing both its file and data storage cloud services. I covered the data storage components of the service in Recipe 17.7. In this section, I want to focus on its OAuth 2.0 authorization process.

The Dropbox API is utilitizing the Authorization Code Grant OAuth 2.0 flow, diagrammed in Figure 14-9.

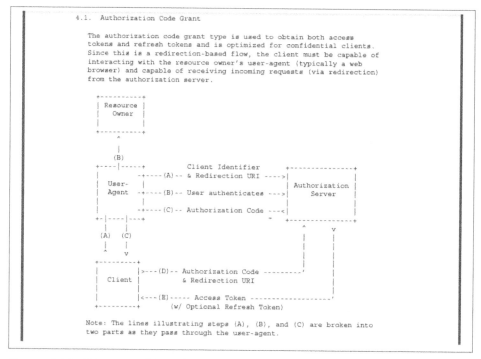

Figure 14-9. Diagram of OAuth 2.0 Authorization Code Grant (source: Oath 2.0 documentation (http://tools.ietf.org/html/rfc6749))

The code for the application created in Chapter 18 is browser-based, using Dropbox's JavaScript SDK for Data Storage. The first step in creating the application was registering it at Dropbox, in order to get the consumer key and secret. However, only the key is used in the client-side application (leaving the secret to remain secret). In the registration process, we also had to register a *redirect URL*, which is *http://localhost: 8080/* for the app.

When the user accesses the page, if he's not already authenticated, he'll click the Dropbox login button. He's redirected to the Dropbox authorization page, where he agrees to authorize Dropbox access to the application. Dropbox redirects him back to the app, using the redirect URL.

What's happening behind the scenes is the client is using the application key to make a request for an authorization token from the Dropbox authorization sever, redirecting the user to the server. When authorized, the user is redirected back to the client, along with the authorization token. The client requests an access token from the authorization server, sending the authorization token and the redirection URL. The authorization server authenticates the client app (application key), validates the authorization key, and ensures the redirect URL sent with the request matches what's registered in the application. If it all works out, the authorization server returns an access token, which can now be used with all future requests.

No digital signature is necessary for the authorization or access token request, but the redirection URL passed with the request had better be identical to that registered to the application, as I discovered when I used:

```
http://localhost:8080
```

rather than:

```
http://localhost:8080/
```

Although it sounds as complicated as OAuth 1.0, it really isn't. Having to use a digital signature and package all of the tokens and data for every request is far more cumbersome than OAuth 2.0's flow, and it doesn't work well with all use cases.

Not all resource services support OAuth 2.0 only, as we noted with Twitter earlier. And the implementations may have interesting quirks. One similarity they all share, though, is the necessity for HTTP server support.

Extra: Setting Up HTTPS for Testing

OAuth is dependent on SSL (Secure Sockets Layer). Some of the resource servers support localhost for development, and *technically* transmissions between the authorization server and the client application doesn't *have* to be protected...but it is. I haven't discovered any service that doesn't require SSL. Eventually you're going to need to set up an HTTPS server. Look on the bright side: by default, the browser assumes an HTTPS server runs on port 443, which means you can have two web services running with default ports on a server at the same time.

HTTPS is dependent on SSL, which is dependent on having a digital certificate. Unless the certificate is signed by a *signing authority* every time someone accesses the server, the browser will put up all sorts of walls trying to keep the end user out. An example is shown in Figure 14-10, when I practically had to arm wrestle Chrome into letting me into my own website.

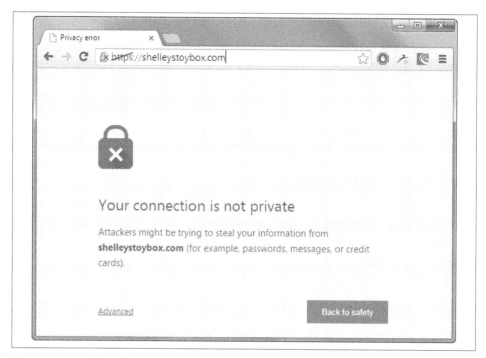

Figure 14-10. The web equivalent of 'ware: there be dragons here

Big problem for publicly accessible sites, but not for development and testing purposes.

Before you set up the HTTPS server, you need a digital certificate. Luckily, there's a *self-signed certificate* that is relatively easy to create. We had to create a self-signed certificate for signing an Android app in Chapter 18, and now we'll create one for HTTPS.

In Windows, in a Command window, I used the following to create a self-signed certificate. The *keytool.exe* file is available as part of the Android SDK:

```
keytool.exe -getkey -v keystore release.keystore -alias MyApp -keyalg RSA
-keysize 2048 -validity 10000
```

In Linux, I used:

```
openssl x509 -req -days 365 -in server.csr -signkey server.key -out server.crt
```

You'll be asked some questions, but the important part is you'll be prompted to set up a password. Remember it, as you'll need it when you start the Node server.

To start up an HTTPS server, rather than HTTP, the application needs to import the https Node core module. An options object has properties named key and cert, which are read in from the *server.key* and *server.cert* generated files, respectively. The options object is passed to the HTTPS server when creating it, as shown in the following code. (The route is a reference to the router object used in the Twitter OAuth 1.0 example, earlier.)

```
var options = {
    key: fs.readFileSync('/home/examples/ssl/server.key'),
    cert: fs.readFileSync('/home/examples/ssl/server.crt')
};

https.createServer(options, route).listen(443);
```

When you run the Node application, you'll be asked for the password you associated with the digital certificate.

Really, if it weren't for the ugly, deliberately scary behavior we hit when accessing a website with a self-signed digital certificate, the whole thing would be a piece of cake. But when it comes to testing and development, we can just ignore the rude messages and focus on developing our apps and testing them.

See Also

For additional reading on OAuth and the differences between OAuth 1 and 2, I recommend the following. As you'll soon discover, there are strong opinions about OAuth:

- "What are the biggest differences between OAuth 1.0 and OAuth 2.0?" (*http://bit.ly/1IHfb4E*)
- "Introducing OAuth 2.0" (*http://bit.ly/1IHffBu*)
- "OAuth 2.0 - The Good, The Bad, & The Ugly" (*http://bit.ly/1IHfhJq*)
- "OAuth 2.0 and the Road to Hell" (*http://bit.ly/1IHfkFf*)
- "Top Differences between OAuth 1.0 and OAuth 2.0 for API Calls" (*http://bit.ly/1IHfxYU*)

And for more on the technology discussed in this section:

- "Google's OAuth 2.0 Playground" (*https://developers.google.com/oauthplayground/*) (give this one a spin for fun)
- node-twitter-api module (*https://github.com/reneraab/node-twitter-api*)
- The Twitter Public APIs (*https://dev.twitter.com/rest/public*)

- "Using OAuth 2.0 for Login" (*http://bit.ly/1IHfnRm*)
- "Implementing Sign in with Twitter Overview" (*http://bit.ly/1IHfsVf*)
- Dropbox Developer Home (*https://www.dropbox.com/developers*)
- Using the (Dropbox) Datastore in JavaScript (*http://bit.ly/1IHfv3m*)

14.5. Extending the Possible with Web Components

Problem

Sometimes you don't need a complete framework ala AngularJS or Express. You just need a component that encapsulates a specific look and feel and behavior and that you can include as easily as you'd include an HTML element.

Solution

If you're willing to work with very new technology, and be dependent on a polyfill, you can consider Web Components. However, use extreme caution if you're considering using them in a production system.

The Web Components consist of a Template, HTML Imports, Shadow DOM, and Custom Elements. Each will be covered in the discussion.

Discussion

Think of a web page widget that's completely self-contained and you have some resemblance to Web Components, but only in the most shallow sense. Web Components, as a term, encompasses several different constructs. In the following sections, I'll cover each, provide examples, discuss polyfills, and what to expect in the future.

 At the time this was written, the examples only worked in Chrome. See the end of the section for a list of polyfills that can help you get Web Components working in other browsers.

Template

The `template` element is now part of the HTML5 specification. Currently it's supported in most modern browsers, except—and this is a biggie—IE.

Within the `template` element we include HTML that we want to group as a whole that isn't instantiated until it is *cloned*. It is parsed when loaded, to ensure it's valid, but it doesn't exist. Yet.

Working with templates is very intuitive. Consider a common practice with today's Ajax applications: taking returned data from a web service and formatting it as an unordered list (ul) (or new paragraph, or table, or whatever). Typically we'd using the DOM methods to query for the existing ul element, create each list item (li) in the list, append text to the item, and append the item to the list.

What if we could cut out some of the steps? We could, with the template. Given the following HTML:

```
<ul id="results">
</ul>

<template id="dataitem">
  <li id="listitem"></li>
</template>
```

This is the JavaScript to add three li elements to the unordered list:

```
if ('content' in document.createElement('template')) {

    var temp = document.getElementById('dataitem');
    var li = temp.content.getElementById('listitem');

    li.textContent = 'first value';

    // Clone the new row and insert it into the table
    var ul = document.getElementById('results');
    var clone = document.importNode(temp.content, true);
    ul.appendChild(clone);

    li.textContent = 'second value';
    clone = document.importNode(temp.content, true);
    ul.appendChild(clone);

    li.textContent = 'third value';
    clone = document.importNode(temp.content, true)
    ul.appendChild(clone);

} else {
    // use traditional approach
}
```

Once we're sure that the user agent supports the technology, we access the template element, access the HTML elements contained in the template that we want to alter, make the alteration, and then *clone* the template using document.importNode(). The first parameter to importNode() is the template's content, the second a boolean indicating whether the descendants of the node also need to be imported.

Once the template is cloned, it's appended to the unordered list using appendChild(). If templates are currently supported in the user agent, an obvious workaround would be to follow the procedure we normally use (create a list item, add text, append to the unordered list).

As I noted, templates are very intuitive, but you might be wondering, what's the point? All we've done is add a lot more code for a process that's already simple.

When you consider adding a table row, which consists of a tr element, and one or more cells (td), then a template begins to make more sense:

```
<template id="tablerow">
   <tr>
     <td></td>
     <td></td>
   </tr>
</template>
```

The process to create this structure in JavaScript requires creating three new elements (a table row and two table cells), adding text to the table cells, appending the cells to the table row, and then appending the table row to the table.

How much simpler is it just to do the following?

```
if ('content' in document.createElement('template')) {
  var temp = document.querySelector('#tablerow');
  var tds = temp.content.querySelectorAll('td');

  tds[0].textContent = 'Washington';
  tds[1].textContent = 'apples';

  var tb = document.getElementsByTagName('tbody');
  var clone = document.importNode(temp.content, true);
  tb[0].appendChild(clone);

  tds[0].textContent = 'Georgia';
  tds[1].textContent = 'peaches';

  clone = document.importNode(temp.content, true);
  tb[0].appendChild(clone);
}
```

Templates are also important for their use in Custom Elements, discussed in "Custom Elements" on page 442, as well as the "Shadow DOM" on page 439.

HTML Imports

A second new Web Component construct is HTML Imports. HTML Imports gives us the ability to include HTML documents in other HTML documents. Yes, we've had this capability with iFrames and Ajax, but these earlier approaches have been kludgy workarounds.

Import an HTML document using the following:

```
<link rel="import" href="src/new.html">
```

If the file included the following HTML:

```
<div id="newbie">
  <ul>
    <li>Value 1</li>
    <li>Value 2</li>
    <li>Value 3</li>
  </ul>
</div>
```

The following JavaScript will clone the HTML and append it to the web page that imports the HTML file:

```
var link = document.querySelector('link[rel="import"]');
var content = link.import;
var el = content.querySelector('#newbie');
document.body.appendChild(el.cloneNode(true));
```

Any other page importing the HTML file can also add the HTML, allowing us to create a chunk of HTML that's now reusable.

But what if the HTML you want to import includes a stylesheet and a `script` element? What happens then?

Let's say the imported `div` element contains a `style` element, such as the following:

```
<div id="newbie">
  <style>
    li { background-color: yellow}
  </style>
</div>
```

If that's the case, when the element is cloned and appended into the importing page, *every* li element in the page would have a yellow background, not just the li elements in the imported HTML.

To apply a style to newly imported elements, we'll need to resort to the next Web Components construct: the Shadow DOM.

Shadow DOM

I can't see Shadow DOM without thinking of the fictional character "The Shadow." What a great character, and appropriate, too. Only The Shadow knew what evil lurked in the minds of men, and only the Shadow DOM knows what lurks in its element's DOM.

Dragging ourselves away from fictional distraction, the Shadow DOM is the most twisty of the Web Components. But intriguing, too.

First, the nonmysterious bits. The Shadow DOM is a DOM, a tree of nodes just like we're used to when we access elements from the document element. The primary difference is that it doesn't exist, not in a way we know a DOM existing. When we create a *shadow root* of an element, then it comes into existence. But then, whatever the element used to have, is gone. That's the key to remember about the Shadow DOM: creating it replaces the element's existing DOM.

 The behavior noted in this chapter related to the Shadow DOM is subject to change without notice. The Shadow DOM—all of the Web Components—are very much a work in progress.

To return to the example demonstrated in "HTML Imports" on page 438, what about providing a stylesheet for the newly added unordered list (ul) and list items (li)? We already know that if we include a stylesheet in the imported div element that wraps the list, the contents are applied to all of the list items in the page.

What we need is to use a Shadow DOM and a template element.

Instead of importing the div element, we'll add it directly to the HTML page. Instead of wrapping the unordered list in a div element in the imported HTML, we'll wrap it in a template, and include a style element for styling the list items:

```
<template id="newcontent">
<style>
  li {
      background-color: yellow;
      font-size: 12pt;
      color: black;
      width: 500px;
      height; 25px;
  }
</style>
<ul>
    <li>Value 1</li>
    <li>Value 2</li>
    <li>Value 3</li>
</ul>
</template>
```

We'll add a link to the imported HTML, and we'll need to access the imported content, but the content we're now importing is a template not the div element:

```
var link = document.querySelector('link[rel="import"]');
var content = link.import;

// get template
var template = content.querySelector('#newcontent');
```

JavaScript is used to get an access to the div element now contained in the imported page, and the createShadowRoot() method is called on it:

```
// create shadow DOM, append template
var div = document.querySelector('#outer');

var shadow = div.createShadowRoot();
```

The template is appended to the div element's Shadow DOM, and the template is
removed:

```
shadow.appendChild(template.content);
template.remove();
```

The entire HTML page is shown in Example 14-6.

Example 14-6. Demonstration of the Shadow DOM

```
<!DOCTYPE html>
<html>
<head>
    <meta charset="UTF-8">
    <title>Web Components</title>

    <!-- Importing Custom Elements -->
    <link rel="import" href="src/new2.html">
</head>
<body>
<ul id="test">
<li>original list</li>
<li>second item</li>
</ul>
<button id="gethtml">Get HTML</button>
<div id="outer"><p>The Shadow DOM doesn't work for you</p></div>
<script>
    document.getElementById('gethtml').addEventListener('click', function() {
      var link = document.querySelector('link[rel="import"]');
      var content = link.import;

      // get template
      var template = content.querySelector('#newcontent');

      // create shadow DOM, append template
      var div = document.querySelector('#outer');

      var shadow = div.createShadowRoot();
      shadow.appendChild(template.content);
      template.remove();
    }, false);

</script>
</div>
</body>
</html>
```

Figure 14-11 displays the web page before the Shadow DOM and template have been applied, and Figure 14-12 displays the page, after.

Figure 14-11. Before the template and Shadow DOM have been applied

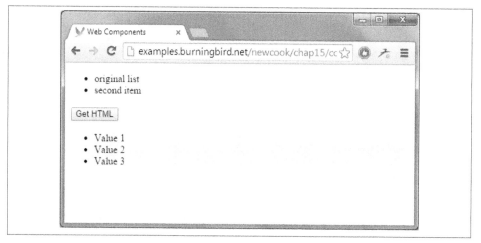

Figure 14-12. After the template and Shadow DOM have been applied

All of these components just demonstrated are useful when creating Custom Elements.

Custom Elements

The Web Components construct that has generated the most interest is the Custom Element. Instead of having to deal with existing HTML elements and their default behaviors and appearance, we create a custom element, package in its styling and behavior, and just attach it to the web page.

An excellent demonstration of creating a Custom Element is a "Hello, World" project (*https://github.com/webcomponents/hello-world-element*) that creates a new custom element named, appropriately enough, `hello-world`:

```
<!DOCTYPE html>
<html>
<head>
    <meta charset="UTF-8">
    <title>&lt;hello-world&gt;</title>

    <!-- Importing Custom Elements -->
    <link rel="import" href="src/hello-world.html">
</head>
<body>

    <!-- Using Custom Elements -->
    <hello-world who="Shelley"></hello-world>

</body>
</html>
```

All of the implementation is in the imported HTML file, reproduced in Example 14-7, with some minor modification from the original. The file starts with a template, which is familiar. It consists of a `template` element wrapping a paragraph (p), which contains a `strong` element and a smiley face :):

```
<template>
    <p>Hello <strong></strong> :)</p>
</template>
```

The file also contains a `script` element, with an IIFE wrapping all of the code, and the `window` and `document` elements passed to the function.

In the function, a reference to the importing HTML document is assigned to a variable (`thatDoc`), while the document related to the script is assigned to `thisDoc`:

```
// Refers to the "importer", which is index.html
var thatDoc = document;

// Refers to the "importee", which is src/hello-world.html
var thisDoc = document.currentScript.ownerDocument;
```

The `template` is accessed and assigned to a variable. The next several lines of code are all related to creating a custom element. Refer to the complete code as we traverse it.

Example 14-7. The hello-world element's definition

```
<template>
    <p>Hello <strong></strong> :)</p>
```

```
    </template>

    <script>
        (function(window,document) {
            // Refers to the "importer", which is index.html
            var thatDoc = document;

            // Refers to the "importee", which is src/hello-world.html
            var thisDoc = document.currentScript.ownerDocument;

            // Gets content from <template>
            var template = thisDoc.querySelector('template').content;

            // Creates an object based in the HTML Element prototype
            var MyElementProto = Object.create(HTMLElement.prototype);

            // Creates the "who" attribute and sets a default value
            MyElementProto.who = 'World';

            // Fires when an instance of the element is created
            MyElementProto.createdCallback = function() {
                // Creates the shadow root
                var shadowRoot = this.createShadowRoot();

                // Adds a template clone into shadow root
                var clone = thatDoc.importNode(template, true);
                shadowRoot.appendChild(clone);

                // Caches <strong> DOM query
                this.strong = shadowRoot.querySelector('strong');

                // Checks if the "who" attribute has been overwritten
                if (this.hasAttribute('who')) {
                    var who = this.getAttribute('who');
                    this.setWho(who);
                }
                else {
                    this.setWho(this.who);
                }
            };

            // Fires when an attribute was added, removed, or updated
            MyElementProto.attributeChangedCallback = function(attr, oldVal, newVal) {
                if (attr === 'who') {
                    this.setWho(newVal);
                }
            };

            // Sets new value to "who" attribute
            MyElementProto.setWho = function(val) {
                this.who = val;
```

```
            // Sets "who" value into <strong>
            this.strong.textContent = this.who;
        };

        // Registers <hello-world> in the main document
        window.MyElement = thatDoc.registerElement('hello-world', {
            prototype: MyElementProto
        });
    })(window, document);
</script>
```

Custom elements inherit from the HTMLElement, and the following code:

```
var MyElementProto = Object.create(HTMLElement.prototype);
```

Creates an instance of the HTMLElement's prototype, to be used to add the who property, as well as a createdCallback() function called when the element is created, and attributeChangedCallback(), called when an attribute is changed. In the created Callback() method, the Shadow DOM is created for the element, and the template is appended to it as a child element. The strong element is queried on the Shadow DOM, and the element's who attribute value is passed to the third method created on the prototype, the setWho() method.

This method just sets the strong element's textContent property to the who attribute's value.

Once all of this is done, the code that makes hello-world into something real happens next:

```
// Registers <hello-world> in the main document
    window.MyElement = thatDoc.registerElement('hello-world', {
        prototype: MyElementProto
});
```

The thatDoc variable is pointing to the document element for the HTML document that's importing the custom element file. The registerElement() method introduces the new element to the document, and returns a constructor for constructing a new instance of the element, assigned to the window element.

All of that, and the page displays the following:

```
Hello Shelley :)
```

with the name in bold text.

It seems like a lot of work, and for a simple element like hello-world it's overkill…until you realize you can use the element everywhere, and that the custom element can do a lot more than output a cute message.

See Also

More on Web Components, and demos:

- WebComponents.org (*http://webcomponents.org/*)
- Custom Elements (*http://customelements.io/*)
- Built with Polymer (*http://builtwithpolymer.org/*)

Currently, only Chrome implements the Web Components natively. If you want to support the constructs in other browsers, you'll need a polyfill. The following are complete web component framework polyfills:

- Google's Polymer (*https://www.polymer-project.org/*)
- Bosonic (*http://bosonic.github.io/*)

You could also consider focusing on a specific component of Web Components, namely Custom Elements. The following are polyfills for Custom Elements:

- Mozilla's X-Tag (*http://x-tags.org/*)
- Mozilla Brick (*http://brick.readme.io/*)
- Polymer's Custom Elements (*https://github.com/Polymer/CustomElements*)

The following three articles by the same author, TJ VanToll, demonstrate both concerns and possibilities about using Web Components now:

- "Why Web Components Aren't Ready for Production... Yet" (*http://bit.ly/1yaxn5v*)
- "An Addendum to Why Web Components Aren't Ready for Production Yet" (*http://bit.ly/1yaxsGg*)
- "Why Web Components Are Ready For Production" (*http://bit.ly/1yaxApa*)

And last, but not least, we couldn't do without HTML5 Rocks, and the site's wonderful articles on the Web Components:

- "HTML Imports" (*http://bit.ly/1yaxJsY*)
- "HTML's New Template Tag" (*http://bit.ly/1yaxRIS*)
- "Shadow DOM 101" (*http://bit.ly/1yaxVIE*)
- "Custom Elements" (*http://bit.ly/1yay0vZ*)

## CHAPTER 15

Advanced Client-Server Communications and Streams

Ajax opened up a world of possibilities for JavaScript developers, and it's rare nowadays that we don't find data being updated *in place* thanks to the technology. But we developers are greedy and we always want more. Thankfully, we have more.

Thanks to the newer Cross-Origin Resource Sharing (CORS), we can now make requests of data and services of other domains as easily as we make those in our own. Perhaps more importantly, we can make requests against our own services running under a different subdomain, or even different port. And we can share data, such as HTTP cookies, too.

We can also indulge in real-time bidirectional communication with Web Sockets, which we can use directly, or assisted by a module such as the popular Socket.IO.

Client-server communication is all about streams, and thanks to the new Node *transform streams*, we can simply and easily transform the data that's communicated. In the past, we could send zipped files to the server, but how about downloading the file, opening it for compression, and then saving the results in a few simple lines of code?

15.1. Allowing Cross-Domain Requests

Problem

You understand how to use Ajax, but the data you need is provided on a server in another domain. When you try to access the data, you got the error shown in Figure 15-1.

Figure 15-1. Error accessing data in another domain with an Ajax request

Solution

The solution to accessing the data on another domain doesn't reside in the client, but in the server. The server application has to enable CORS, Cross-Origin Resource Sharing, in order for your other-domain client to work. Thankfully, doing so in a Node server is extremely easy.

To enable CORS, set the Access-Control-Allow-Origin header value, as demonstrated in the following very simple web server application:

```
var http = require('http');

var server = http.createServer(function(req,res){
  // Set CORS headers
  res.setHeader('Access-Control-Allow-Origin', '*');
  res.writeHead(200);
  res.end("Hello cross-domain");

});

server.listen(8080);
```

Discussion

A security feature of Ajax is the *single domain origin*, which disallows cross-domain access. Originally, all Ajax requests disallowed cross-domain requests, regardless of what the server would allow. However, with the introduction of the XMLHttpRequest Level 2 specification at the W3C, all clients that support Level 2 support CORS by default.

 The CORS Specification (*http://www.w3.org/TR/cors/*) is a W3C Recommendation, and is supported in all of the newer versions of all the major browsers. The different CORS scenarios are covered nicely in the Mozilla Developer Network's HTTP Access Control (CORS) (*http://mzl.la/1B1O4Ch*).

Where the change has to occur now is in the server. All you need do is set the Access-Control-Allow-Origin header value in the server response. Because the solution uses the *wild card*, *, any domain can access the resource. If you want to restrict CORS access to a specific domain, list the domain:

```
res.setHeader('Access-Control-Allow-Origin', 'http://specificdomain.com');
```

Now that your server is set, the client, such as the one in the following code, can access the data:

```
<!DOCTYPE html>
<html lang="en">
<head>
<meta charset="utf-8">
<title>CORS</title>
</head>
<body>
  <div id="result"></div>
  <script type="text/javascript">
    var request = new XMLHttpRequest();

    request.onreadystatechange = function() {
        if (this.readyState == 4) {
          console.log(this.status);
          if (this.status == 200) {
            document.getElementById('result').innerHTML =
              this.responseText;
          }
        }
      }

    request.open('GET','http://burningbird.net:8080/');
    request.send();
  </script>
</body>
</html>
```

See Also

If you want to make sure your cookies go with you when you cross domains, see Recipe 15.4. If you're interested in using verbs other than GET, POST, and HEAD with your Ajax request, learn about *preflighting* in Recipe 15.2. To learn how to send binary data, see Recipe 15.3.

 The XMLHttpRequest Level 2 specification (*http://www.w3.org/TR/XMLHttpRequest2/*) is still in Working Draft status, but has broad support in the newer versions of all the main browsers.

15.2. Implementing a PUT Request in Ajax

Problem

Instead of using GET or POST with your cross-domain Ajax request, you want to signal an update with PUT. But the server doesn't seem to like the action.

Solution

To use a method other than GET, POST, or HEAD, you have to *preflight* your request. As with the cross-domain request covered in Recipe 15.1, the change will need to come from the server. In this case, a server implemented in Node.

To allow the Node server (implemented with the `http` module) to accept methods other than GET, POST, and HEAD, you need to set the `Access-Control-Allow-Methods` header to reflect the HTTP verbs you support:

```
res.setHeader('Access-Control-Allow-Methods', 'GET,PUT,POST,DELETE,OPTIONS');
```

The OPTIONS verb is the one that interests us. When the Ajax request is made with a PUT, the XMLHttpRequest object first sends through the OPTIONS request, to ascertain whether the PUT request is supported on the server. In the server, the code responds to the OPTIONS request by returning a status code of 204, *no content*. The browser then sends through the PUT request, which our application processes:

```
var http = require('http');

var server = http.createServer(function(req,res){
  // Set CORS headers

  res.setHeader('Content-type', 'text/plain');
  res.setHeader('Access-Control-Allow-Origin', '*');
  res.setHeader('Access-Control-Allow-Methods', 'GET,PUT,POST,DELETE,OPTIONS');
  if (req.method.toUpperCase() == "OPTIONS") {
    res.writeHead(204);
    return(res.end());
  }
  var data = '';
  req.on('data', function(chunk) {
    data+=chunk;
  });

  req.on('end', function () {
    console.log('PUT: ' + data);
    res.writeHead(200);
    res.end('PUT ' + data);
  });
});

server.listen(8080);
```

The result of this communication can be seen in Figure 15-2.

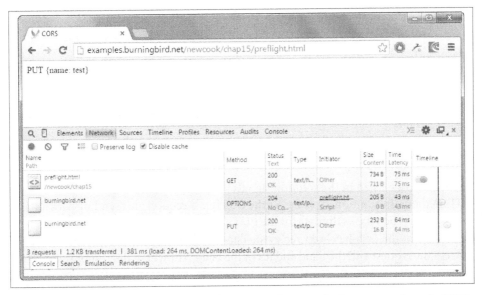

Figure 15-2. Communication between browser and server during a cross-domain PUT

Discussion

Most of our Ajax interactions are GET or POST, but what if it were something else, such as a PUT request? The same security mechanisms that prevented cross-domain requests also restricted the use of any other HTTP method. With the advent of the CORS specification, though, Ajax requests can include PUT and DELETE as well as GET and POST, allowing for truly RESTful applications.

When a method other than the standard is used, that's when *preflighting* comes in. What happens is that the browser first sends an OPTIONS method to the server to determine if the action is allowed. It the action is allowed, the browser sends through the PUT request:

```
<!DOCTYPE html>
<html lang="en">
<head>
<meta charset="utf-8">
<title>CORS</title>
</head>
<body>
  <div id="result"></div>
  <script type="text/javascript">
    var request = new XMLHttpRequest();

    request.onreadystatechange = function() {
```

```
    if (this.readyState == 4) {
      console.log(this.status);
      if (this.status == 200) {
        document.getElementById('result').innerHTML =
        this.responseText;
      }
    }
  }

  request.open('PUT','http://burningbird.net:8080/');
  request.send('{name: test}');
</script>

</body>
</html>
```

The server code listed in the solution signals it will accept both the OPTIONS and the PUT methods. In addition, it processes the OPTIONS request, just sending back a status code of 204. When it gets the data for the PUT, it pops it out and sends it back, as positive feedback that the data has been received. The on event handler for both `data` and `end` process the request and the data, and it's in the `end` event where the response is written back to the client.

Technically, the code doesn't have to respond to the OPTIONS method. However, when it doesn't, then we end up with two `end` events, one for the OPTIONS, and one for the PUT. This mucks up the console logging and feedback response, so I'd rather the code process OPTIONS separately.

 If you're using a framework, such as Express, there is a module, appropriately named CORS, that manages the CORS setup for you. Read more about it on its GitHub repository page (*https://github.com/troy goode/node-cors/*).

Extra: Handling Nonstandard HTTP Request Headers

Preflighting also works if you want to use a nonstandard request header. We're used to a header request like the following, set using a XMLHttpRequest object:

```
request.setRequestHeader('Content-Type', 'application/xml');
```

But something like the following might give us pause:

```
request.setRequestHeader('X-MYWAY', 'ididit');
```

This would give a web server more than pause, unless we specifically allowed for this type of custom header request. In Node, to do so, there is another CORS access control, `Access-Control-Allow-Headers`, that allows us to define which custom header requests will accept:

```
       res.setHeader('Access-Control-Allow-Headers', 'x-myway,content-type');
```

The communication between the client and the server then looks similar to the following, indicating a successful effort:

```
HTTP/1.1 200 OK
Content-Type: text/plain
Access-Control-Allow-Origin: http://examples.burningbird.net
Access-Control-Allow-Headers: X-MYWAY,content-type
Date: Fri, 12 Sep 2014 17:14:23 GMT
Connection: keep-alive
Transfer-Encoding: chunked


OPTIONS / HTTP/1.1
Host: burningbird.net:8080
User-Agent: Mozilla/5.0 (Windows NT 6.1; WOW64; rv:32.0) Gecko/20100101 Firefox/32.0
Accept: text/html,application/xhtml+xml,application/xml;q=0.9,*/*;q=0.8
Accept-Language: en-US,en;q=0.5
Accept-Encoding: gzip, deflate
Origin: http://examples.burningbird.net
Access-Control-Request-Method: GET
Access-Control-Request-Headers: content-type,x-myway
Connection: keep-alive
```

15.3. Sending Binary Data Through Ajax and Loading into an Image

Problem

You want to get a server-side image through Ajax as binary data.

Solution

Getting binary data via Ajax is a matter of setting the responseType to *blob* and then manipulating the data when returned. In the solution, the data is then converted and loaded into an img element:

```
<!DOCTYPE html>
<html lang="en">
<head>
<meta charset="utf-8">
<title>CORS blob</title>
</head>
<body>
  <img id="result" />
  <script type="text/javascript">
    var request = new XMLHttpRequest();

    request.open('GET','burningbird.png', true);
    request.responseType = "blob";
```

```
    var img = document.getElementById("result");
    request.onload=function(event) {
      var blob = request.response;
      img.src = URL.createObjectURL(blob);
    };
    request.send(null);

    img.onload=function(e) {
      URL.revokeObjectURL(this.src);
    };
    </script>

</body>
</html>
```

Discussion

Another benefit of the CORS specification is support for binary data (also known as *typed arrays*) in Ajax requests. The key requirement to a binary request is to set the responseType to one of the following:

- arraybuffer
- blob

The data that is received is accessed via the response property in the XMLHttpRequest object, as one of the following data types (consistent with the responseType setting):

- ArrayBuffer: Fixed-length raw binary data buffer
- Blob: File-like immutable raw data

In the solution, I used the URL.createObjectURL() method to convert the blob to a DOMString (generally mapped to JavaScript String) with the URL of the passed object. The URL is assigned to the img element's src property, as shown in Figure 15-3. Once the image is loaded, the code calls URL.revokeObjectURL() to release the URL.

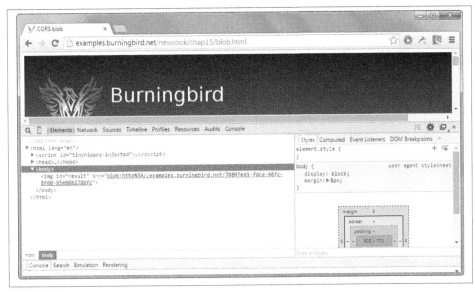

Figure 15-3. Image src set to blob URL returned as binary data in Ajax call

Of course, it would be just as simple to assign the url of the PNG file to the src attribute in the first place. However, the ability to manipulate binary data is a necessity with various technologies, such as Web Workers and WebGL.

See Also

Read more about Web Workers in Recipe 13.5.

15.4. Sharing HTTP Cookies Across Domains

Problem

You want to access a web resource using Ajax in another domain, but you want to send a *credentialed* request, including HTTP cookies and any authentication.

Solution

Changes have to be made in both the client and the server applications to support credentialed requests.

In the client, we have to set the withCredentials property on the XMLHttpRequest object:

```
var request = new XMLHttpRequest();
```

```
request.onreadystatechange = function() {
    if (this.readyState == 4) {
        console.log(this.status);
        if (this.status == 200) {
            document.getElementById('result').innerHTML = this.responseText;
        }
    }
};
request.open('GET','http://burningbird.net:8080/');
request.withCredentials = true;
request.send(null);
```

In the server, the `Access-Control-Allow-Controls` header value must be set to true:

```
var http = require('http');
var Cookies = require('cookies');

var server = http.createServer(function(req,res){
  // Set CORS headers
  res.setHeader('Content-type', 'text/plain');
  res.setHeader('Access-Control-Allow-Origin', 'http://somedomain.com');
  res.setHeader('Access-Control-Allow-Credentials', true);

  var cookies = new Cookies (req, res);
  cookies.set("apple","red");

  res.writeHead(200);
  res.end("Hello cross-domain");

});

server.listen(8080);
```

Discussion

Being able to send HTTP cookies or authentication across domains is another CORS extension, as long as both the client and the server signal agreement. However, there are browser variations that can impact on the success of the application.

In Firefox, I could use a wildcard (*) with the `Access-Control-Allow-Origin`, and my request would be accepted:

```
res.setHeader('Access-Control-Allow-Origin', '*');
```

But the same request would fail in Chrome, as shown in Figure 15-4.

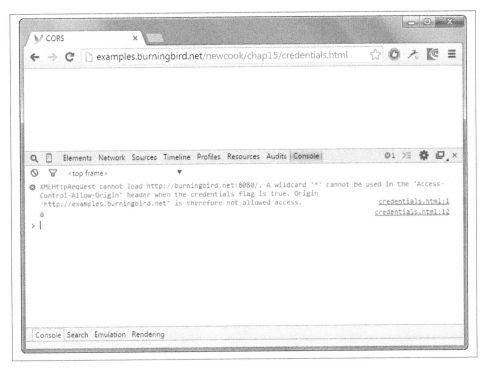

Figure 15-4. Cookie cross-domain request rejected because of domain setting

Changing the header to a specific domain:

```
res.setHeader('Access-Control-Allow-Origin', 'http://examples.burningbird.net');
```

Allows the request to go through, as shown in Figure 15-5.

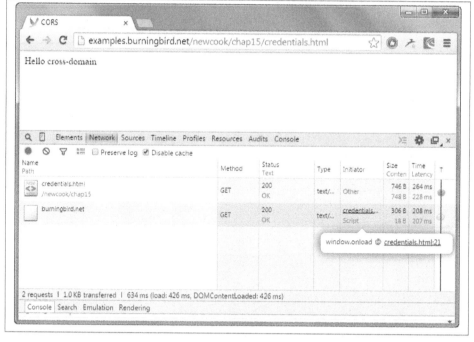

Figure 15-5. Cookie now accessible in cross-domain request after restricting origin

It's best to stick with the more restrictive approach.

15.5. Establishing Two-Way Communication Between Client and Server

Problem

You want to initiate two-way, real-time communication between the Node server and web page client.

Solution

Support bidirectional communication between the client and server by using one of several possible options.

As one example, you can use WebSockets directly in the client, and then a Node module that supports WebSockets in the server. In this solution, I'm using `nodejs-websocket`. Once the server is created, it starts the communication with the client by sending through a JavaScript object with two members: a number counter and a string. The object must be converted to string, first. The code listens for both an incoming message and a close event. When it gets an incoming message, it increments the counter and sends the object:

```
var ws = require("nodejs-websocket");

var server = ws.createServer(function (conn) {

    // object being passed back and forth between
    // client and server
    var counter = {counter: 1, strng: ''};

    // send first communication to client
    conn.sendText(JSON.stringify(counter));

    // on response back
    conn.on('text', function(message) {
        var ct = JSON.parse(message);
        ct.counter = parseInt(ct.counter) + 1;
        if (ct.counter < 100) {
            conn.sendText(JSON.stringify(ct));
        }
    });
    conn.on("close", function (code, reason) {
        console.log("Connection closed")
    });
}).listen(8001);
```

Another popular WebSockets module is ws. As the following code snippet demonstrates, the use is almost identical:

```
var wsServer = require('ws').Server;
var wss = new wsServer({port:8001});
wss.on('connection', (function (conn) {

    // object being passed back and forth between
    // client and server
    var counter = {counter: 1, strng: ''};

    // send first communication to client
    conn.send(JSON.stringify(counter));

    // on response back
    conn.on('message', function(message) {
        var ct = JSON.parse(message);
        ct.counter = parseInt(ct.counter) + 1;
        if (ct.counter < 100) {
            conn.send(JSON.stringify(ct));
        }
    });
}));
```

The client creates a new WebSockets object, passing in the URI for the WebSockets server. Notice the protocol used. When the client gets a message, it converts the message text to an object, retrieves the number counter, increments it, and then uses it in the object's string member. The purpose is to print out every other number, starting with 2. State is maintained between the two by passing the string to be printed out within the message:

```html
<!doctype html>
<html lang="en">
<head>
  <meta charset="utf-8">
  <title>bi-directional communication</title>
  <script type="text/javascript">
    var socket = new WebSocket("ws://shelleystoybox.com:8001");
    socket.onmessage = function (event) {
      var msg = JSON.parse(event.data);
      msg.counter = parseInt(msg.counter) + 1;
      msg.strng+=msg.counter + '-';
      var html = '<p>' + msg.strng + '</p>';
      document.getElementById("output").innerHTML=html;
      socket.send(JSON.stringify(msg));
    };
</script>
</head>
<body>
<div id="output"></div>
</body>
</html>
```

Discussion

Bidirectional communication, also known as *full-duplex* communication, is two-way communication that can occur at the same time. Think of it as a two-way road, with traffic going both ways.

There are numerous ways of handling bidirectional communication, though it's only been in the last year or so that we could use WebSockets. All modern browsers support the WebSockets specification, and as you can see, it's extremely easy to use.

A WebSockets request is actually an HTTP request, with upgrade headers. If the server is capable of understanding the upgrade request, it responds in kind, returning the upgrade headers and establishing a handshake between the two communication end points. You can see the communication happen when you use a debugger that allows you to snoop on the network communication between the client and server, as shown in Figure 15-6.

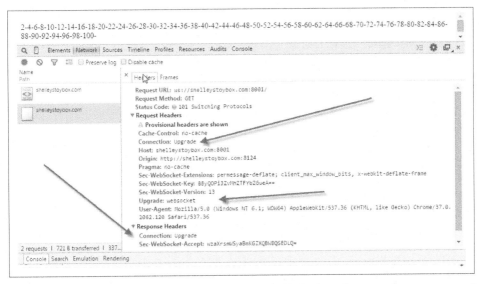

Figure 15-6. WebSockets handshake being established with upgrade request and response

The advantage to WebSockets, other than being unbelievably easy to work with in browsers, is it's able to traverse both proxies and firewalls, something that isn't trivial or even possible with other bidirectional communication techniques such as *HTTP long-polling* or *XHR polling*. And to ensure applications are secure, user agents such as Chrome and Firefox prohibit mixed content (i.e., using both HTTP and HTTPS).

WebSockets supports binary data, as well as text. And as the examples demonstrated, you can transmit JSON by calling `JSON.stringify()` on the object before sending, and `JSON.parse()` on the string in the receiving end.

For more information on WebSockets, check out WebSocket.org (*https://www.websocket.org/index.html*).

If you're using an HTTP server that doesn't speak WebSockets, you can use two servers (one for standard HTTP requests, one for WebSockets), and have them listen on two different ports. Extending this approach to the solution server:

```
var app = require('http').createServer(handler)
  , fs = require('fs');

var ws = require("nodejs-websocket");
```

```
    app.listen(8124);

    function handler (req, res) {
      console.log("if HTTP is required, too");
      fs.readFile(__dirname + '/index.html',
      function (err, data) {
        if (err) {
          res.writeHead(500);
          return res.end('Error loading index.html');
        }
        counter = 1;
        res.writeHead(200);
        res.end(data);
      });
    }

    var server = ws.createServer(function (conn) {

        // object being passed back and forth between
        // client and server
        var counter = {counter: 1, strng: ''};

        // send first communication to client
        conn.sendText(JSON.stringify(counter));

        // on response back
        conn.on('text', function(message) {
            var ct = JSON.parse(message);
            ct.counter = parseInt(ct.counter) + 1;
            if (ct.counter < 100) {
                conn.sendText(JSON.stringify(ct));
            }
        });
        conn.on("close", function (code, reason) {
            console.log("Connection closed")
        });
    }).listen(8001);
```

You can also use a more traditional web server, such as Apache, to handle the web page access, and then just have Node pick up with the WebSockets request. Or use a proxy to correctly transmit requests to the proper server.

There are also Node modules that incorporate support for the HTTP server so only one port is needed. That's how the popular Socket.IO module works. Refactoring the solution server to use Socket.IO:

```
var app = require('http').createServer(handler);
var io = require('socket.io')(app);
var fs = require('fs')

app.listen(8124);
```

```
function handler (req, res) {
  fs.readFile(__dirname + '/index.html',
  function (err, data) {
    if (err) {
      res.writeHead(500);
      return res.end('Error loading index.html');
    }
    res.writeHead(200);
    res.end(data);
  });
}

io.sockets.on('connection', function (socket) {
  var counter = {'counter': 1, 'strng': ''};
  socket.emit('counter', counter);
  socket.on('counter', function (data) {
      data.counter = parseInt(data.counter) + 1;
      if (data.counter < 100) {
          socket.emit('counter', data);
      }
  });
});
```

The key line is:

```
var io = require('socket.io')(app);
```

The Socket.IO server is created and the previously created HTTP server is passed as parameter.

Now, you'd think you could just use WebSockets directly in the client, but no such luck. If you use the the HTTP protocol in the URI (http://), WebSockets complains, but if you send through the WS protocol (ws://), then Socket.IO expresses an immediate and terminal disapproval.

What's happening is that Socket.IO is a polyfill, as well as a service wrapper. To ensure that older clients can use the server, it first connects using long-polling. It is only when the connection succeeds that it attempts to upgrade to WebSockets. Because of this behavior, if you use Socket.IO in the server, you need to use the Socket.IO client:

```
<!doctype html>
<html lang="en">
<head>
  <meta charset="utf-8">
  <title>bi-directional communication</title>
  <script src="//cdn.socket.io/socket.io-1.1.0.js"></script>
  <script>
     var socket = io.connect('http://shelleystoybox.com:8124');
     socket.on('counter', function (data) {
        data.counter = parseInt(data.counter) + 1;
        data.strng+=data.counter + '-';
        var html = '<p>' + data.strng + '</p>';
```

```
        document.getElementById("output").innerHTML=html;
        socket.emit('counter', data);
    });
</script>
</head>
<body>
<div id="output"></div>
</body>
</html>
```

 Check out the Socket.IO website (*http://socket.io/*) for documentation and examples. The module pair also has additional functionality that facilitates creating chat room applications, which is one of the
more popular bidirectional communication end uses.

15.6. Unloading and Zipping Files Using Transform Streams

Problem

Clients can upload files to the server, but you want to compress them as soon as they're
received.

Solution

The solution makes use of the Formidable module to simplify the file uploading, the
Zlib module for compression, and `fs` for reading and writing the data from and to a
file. It's a modification of example code from the Formidable documentation:

```
var formidable = require('formidable');
var http = require('http');
var zlib = require('zlib');
var fs = require('fs');

var gzip = zlib.createGzip();

http.createServer(function(req, res) {
  if (req.url == '/upload' && req.method.toLowerCase() == 'post') {

    // parse a file upload
    var form = new formidable.IncomingForm();
    form.uploadDir = __dirname + '/files';
    form.keepExtensions = false;

    form.parse(req, function(err, fields, files) {
      var wstream = fs.createWriteStream(__dirname + '/files/'
        + files.upload.name + '.gz');
```

```
        var rstream = fs.createReadStream(files.upload.path);
        rstream
          .pipe(gzip)
          .pipe(wstream)
          .on('finish', function() {
              // delete original uploaded file
              fs.unlink(files.upload.path, function(err) {
                if (err) {
                  console.log(err);
                } else {
                    res.writeHead(200, {'content-type': 'text/plain'});
                    res.write('Uploaded and compressed:\n\n');
                    res.end(files.upload.name + '.gz');
                }
              });
          });
    });

    return;
  }

  // show a file upload form
  res.writeHead(200, {'content-type': 'text/html'});
  res.end(
    '<form action="/upload" enctype="multipart/form-data" method="post">'+
    '<input type="text" name="title"><br>'+
    '<input type="file" name="upload" multiple="multiple"><br>'+
    '<input type="submit" value="Upload">'+
    '</form>'
  );
}).listen(8080);
```

Discussion

The Formidable module handles much of the tedious processing required for uploading and saving a file. The `parse()` callback function, called when it's finished, contains information about the location of the uploaded file.

The uploaded file is opened using the `fs createReadStream()` method, compressed using Zlib's `createGzip()`, and then written using `createWriteStream()`, all of which have something in common: they all implement the second-generation Stream `_transform()` method. They're *transform streams*.

A transform stream is a *duplex stream*, which means it can both read and write, rather than being limited to one or the other, as shown in Figure 15-7. As the solution demonstrates, the readable stream ReadStream object created with `createReadStream()` can read the uploaded file, yes, but it can also `pipe()` the data to the next process in the chain, the Gzip object returned with the `createGzip()` method. This object is also capable of both reading and writing to the stream, as it compresses the data in the process.

Figure 15-7. The transform stream pattern

When the Gzip object is finished compressing the data, it pipes the data to the writable WriteStream object. Normally, it's used to write data, but as a transform stream, it can also read the data passed from the Gzip object.

Once finished, the originally uploaded file is deleted, and we're now left with a properly named file.

A file named:

```
somelarge.pdf
```

has become:

```
somelarge.pdf.gz
```

The new file takes up considerably less file space.

Node core modules that support transformation are Zlib, for compression, and cryp to, for encryption. Developers can create their own custom transform streams incorporating their own transforming modules.

15.7. Testing the Performance and Capability of Your WebSockets Application

Problem

You have an application that sends updated information on a frequent basis to every connected client, and you're concerned about performance and how the application will handle the load.

Solution

You'll want to perform both *speed (performance) tests* and *load testing.*

See the discussion for details.

Discussion

Thanks to Node and WebSockets and other bidirectional communication techniques, we no longer have to use timers in web pages to hit servers for new data. The server itself can push the data to all the connected clients whenever the data is fresh. The animated, scrolling timeline in Recipe 16.3 demonstrates just this type of application.

The question then becomes: yes, it's cool, but what does the coolness cost? Is my server going to crash and burn once 10 (100/1,000/10,000) clients connect? Will all the clients get the same response?

The only answer to these questions comes from two types of tests:

- Speed or performance testing: Tests how fast the page loads, especially when the server is under stress
- Load testing: A test that emulates many concurrent clients accessing the page at once

There are services that provide both types of testing, and if you're a large commercial operation and the realibility and performance of your application is critical, I definitely recommend taking advantage of them. Some, like Load Impact (*http://loadimpact.com/*), even provide a decent trial of their product before committing. The result of running a load test in Load Impact is shown in Figure 15-8.

There are also tools you can use that will hit a page concurrently and then print out the load responses for each (or even graph it). Selenium (*http://www.seleniumhq.org/*) is a very popular tool for performance testing.

The Node world also provides tools we can install easily and quickly with npm. They may not have exactly the same polish as the commercial tools, but they're certainly a lot cheaper.

One tool to try is `loadtest`, which is an easier-to-run variation of ApacheBench (aka ab). You need to install it globally:

```
npm install -g loadtest
```

And then you run it from the command line. The following runs 200 requests per second (rps), with a concurrency of 10:

```
loadtest -c 10 --rps 200 http://mysite.com/
```

There are several other options, and ApacheBench is also an alternative that can be good for performance testing. However, the tests don't test the WebSockets connection, because the request to the WebSockets server is contained in JavaScript that's never processed.

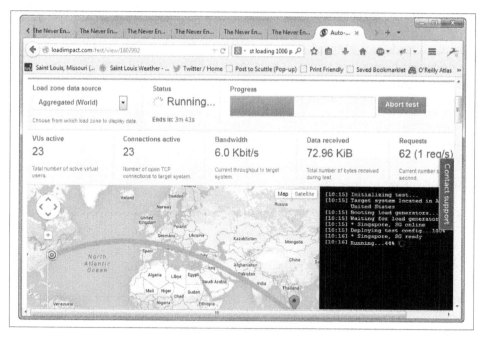

Figure 15-8. Running load test against the scrolling timeline application using Load Impact

Another option is Thor, which is a load tester that's run directly against the WebSockets server:

```
npm install -g thor
```

```
thor --amount 5000 ws://shelleystoybox.com:8001
```

This is an effective way of hammering (ahem) the WebSockets server with connections, but we're still not getting the back and forth communication to *really* test the entire application: front and back. The connections are made, and then dropped as quickly, so it's not really testing the communication as it exists if you and I were to access the application from our browsers. However, used with other tests that actually access the client page and process the WebSockets connection, they can help us determine if performance is going to be an issue with that many demands for connections (note: the app held up).

## CHAPTER 16

Data Visualizations and Client/Server Graphics

Graphics capability with JavaScript has changed significantly in the last few years. Thanks to an increase in support for both SVG and Canvas in the primary browsers and other environments, libraries to support effects related to both have increased in quantity and complexity. And the support doesn't end at the two-dimensional either.

An issue, though, with graphics is that today's hot item typically becomes tomorrow's aged and no longer supported library. A few years back, using the Canvas object to add effects to static images was very big, but libraries that supported such effort aren't receiving the interest they once did and are no longer being actively supported. Even the support for WebGL and 3D, which are only now receiving broader support in browsers, seems to be peaking before it has begun.

However, one area of advanced graphics usage has already transcended the fad stage, and that's data visualization. Being able to present data in a visually compelling manner is never going out of style, and because of the broad support for Canvas, SVG, and WebGL, has a natural fit in the web page. People appreciate getting a graphical representation of data—they like to be able to see the data at a glance. Thankfully, we now have a host of tools and libraries that make data visualization more of a fun and interesting challenge, than the tedious, overly complex job it could be.

Data visualization isn't the only new avenue of creativity for JavaScript developers. Technologies that were once only for the C/C++ developers are now available in JavaScript—both in the client, and in the server. In this chapter, in addition to looking at data visualization techniques, I'm going to touch on accessing server-side graphics tools via Node applications, modifying uploading images, converting graphics to text, and managing web page screen captures.

16.1. Creating an SVG Bar Chart with D3

Problem

You want to create a scalable bar chart, but you're hoping to avoid having to create every last bit of the graphics.

Solution

Use D3 and SVG to create a bar chart bound to a set of data your application provides. Example 16-1 shows a vertical bar chart created using D3 with a given set of data representing the height of each bar.

Example 16-1. SVG bar chart created using D3

```
<!DOCTYPE html>
<html>
<head>
  <meta charset="utf-8">
  <title>SVG Bar Chart using D3</title>
  <style>
   svg {
      background-color: #ff0;
   }
  </style>
  <script src="http://cdnjs.cloudflare.com/ajax/libs/d3/3.4.11/d3.js">
  </script>
</head>
<body>
<script type="text/javascript">
var data = [56, 99, 14, 12, 46, 33, 22, 100, 87, 6, 55, 44, 27, 28, 34];

var height = 400;
var barWidth = 25;

var x = d3.scale.linear()
   .domain([0, d3.max(data)])
   .range([0, height]);

svg = d3.select("body")
   .append("svg")
   .attr("width", data.length * (barWidth +1))
   .attr("height", height);

svg.selectAll("rect")
   .data(data)
   .enter()
   .append("rect")
   .attr("fill","red")
   .attr("stroke","black")
```

```
    .attr("x", function(d,i) {
        return i * (barWidth + 1);
    })
    .attr("y", function(d) {
        return height - (x(d));
    })
    .attr("width", barWidth)
    .attr("height", x)

</script>
</body>
</html>
```

Discussion

D3 isn't a standard graphics tool that creates the shape based on the dimensions you provide. With D3, you give it a set of data, the objects used to visualize the data, and then stand back and let it do its thing. It sounds simple, but to get this data visualization goodness, you do have to properly set it up, and that can be challenging when you first start using the library.

First of all, be aware that D3 makes use of *method chaining* to a maximum degree. Yes, you can invoke methods separately, but it's clearer, cleaner, and more efficient to use the library's chaining support.

In the solution, the first line is the creation of a data set, as an array. D3 expects data points to be in an array, though each element can be an object, as well as a simple value, as shown in the solution. Next, the maximum height of the bar chart is defined, as is the width of each bar. Next, we get into the first use of D3.

 D3 (*http://d3js.org/*), created by Mike Bostock, is a powerful data visualization tool that isn't necessarily something you can pick up and master in a lazy afternoon. However, it is a tool well worth learning, so consider the example in this recipe more of a teaser to get you interested, rather than a definitive introduction.

For a more in-depth primer, I recommend *Getting Started with D3* by Mike Dewar (O'Reilly).

I could have added a static SVG element to the web page, but I wanted to demonstrate how D3 creates an element. By creating the SVG element, we're also getting a reference to it for future work, though we could have used D3 to get a reference to an existing element, which I'll cover a little later in this section. In the code, a reference to the body element is obtained using D3's `select()` method. Once this happens, a new SVG element is appended to the body element via `append()`, and attributes given it via the `attr()` function. The height of the element is already predefined, but the width is equal to multiplying the number of data elements by the bar width (+1, to provide necessary spacing).

Once the SVG element is created, the code uses D3's *scale* functionality to determine the necessary ratio between the element's height and each bar's height, in such a way that the bar chart fills the SVG element, but each bar's height is proportional. It does this by using `scale.linear()` to create a linear scale. According to the D3 documentation, "The mapping is linear in that the output range value *y* can be expressed as a linear function of the input domain value *x*: $y = mx + b$."

The `domain()` function sets the input domain for the scale, while the `range()` sets the output range. In the solution, the value given for the domain is zero to the maximum value in the data set, determined via a call to `max()`. The value given for the range is zero to the height of the SVG element. A function is then returned to a variable that will normalize any data passed to it when called. If the function is given a value equal to the height of the largest data value, the returned value is equal to the height of the element (in this case, the largest data value of 100 returns a scaled value of 400).

The last portion of the code is the part that creates the bars. We need something to work with, so the code calls `selectAll()` with `rect`. There aren't any `rect` elements in the SVG block yet, but we'll be adding them. The data is passed to D3 via the `data()` method, and then the `enter()` function is called. What `enter()` does is process the data and returns placeholders for all the missing elements. In the solution, placeholders for all 15 `rect` elements, one for each bar, are created.

A `rect` element is then appended to the SVG element with `append()`, and the attributes for each are set with `attr()`. In the solution, the `fill` and `stroke` are given, though these could have been defined in the page's stylesheet. Following, the postion for the x attribute, or the lower-left attribute for the bar, is provided as a function, where d is the current datum (data value) and i is the current index. For the x attribute, the index is multiplied by the `barWidth`, plus one (1), to account for spacing.

For the y attribute, we have to get a little tricky. SVG's point of origin is the top-left corner, which means increasing values of y go down the chart, not up. To reverse this, we need to subtract the value of y from the height. However, we can't just do this directly. If the code used the datum passed to it directly, then we'd have a proportional chart with very small, scrunched down bars, as shown in Figure 16-1. Instead we need to use the newly created scale function, x, passing the datum to it.

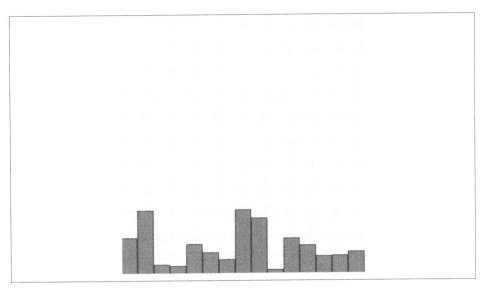

Figure 16-1. Example of a bar chart without each bar's height normalized to fill the given space

The width of each bar is a constant value given in barWidth, and the height is just the scale function variable, which is equivalent to calling the scale function and passing in the datum. All of this creates the chart shown in Figure 16-2.

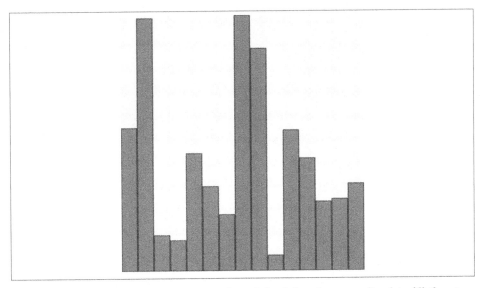

Figure 16-2. Example of a bar chart with each bar's height normalized to fill the given space

Extra: D3 on the Server

The Graphics libraries and tools primarily work in the client, though I do cover generating screenshots with PhantomJS in Recipe 16.4, and cropping images in Recipe 16.6. The reason why most graphics functionality occurs in the client is because the client is where the the graphics are rendered. You can generate the graphics commands to create a Canvas image, but the image has to be rendered in the client.

But you can create the instructions to render the graphics on the server, and in the case of D3, generating the SVG on the server and saving the results to a file, accessible by several clients. There is a Node wrapper for D3, and that, combined with the xmldom library as well as the filesystem modules, is all you need, as shown in Example 16-2.

The D3 commands are identical to those in the solution, except that a rect is used as a background for the bar chart, and the query for the rect elements in the original solution is replaced by a reference to elements with a class name of #rect. We need to do this so the new yellow rect element isn't figured into the solution. It doesn't matter that there are no elements with this class, just as it doesn't matter that no rect exists in the solution.

Then the SVG namespace is added as an attribute to the SVG element. In addition, the SVG is serialized as XML using the xmldom's XMLSerializer().serializeTo String() function. Because the XML elements returned are capitalized and SVG needs lowercase, the toLowerCase() method is chained at the end. The result is then saved to a file.

Example 16-2. Generating SVG on the server and persisting the results to a file

```
var fs = require('fs');
var d3 = require('d3');
var xmldom = require('xmldom');

var data = [56, 99, 14, 12, 46, 33, 22, 100, 87, 6, 55, 44, 27, 28, 34];

var height = 400;
var barWidth = 25;

var x = d3.scale.linear()
    .domain([0, d3.max(data)])
    .range([0, height]);

console.log(x(100)); // returns 400

svg = d3.select("body")
    .append("svg")
    .attr("width", data.length * (barWidth +1))
    .attr("height", height);

svg.append("rect")
    .attr("width", data.length * (barWidth +1))
```

```
    .attr("height", height)
    .attr("z-index", -1)
    .attr("fill", "yellow");

svg.selectAll("#rect")
   .data(data)
   .enter()
   .append("rect")
   .attr("fill","red")
   .attr("stroke","black")
   .attr("x", function(d,i) {
        return i * (barWidth + 1);
   })
   .attr("y", function(d) {
        return height - (x(d));
   })
   .attr("width", barWidth)
   .attr("height", x);

// add the namespace, save to the file
var svgGraph = d3.select('svg')
  .attr('xmlns', 'http://www.w3.org/2000/svg');
var svgXML = (new xmldom.XMLSerializer())
             .serializeToString(svgGraph[0][0]).toLowerCase();

fs.writeFile('chart.svg', svgXML);
```

 With thanks to Rob Ballau (*http://bit.ly/1DZGp5N*) for an earlier version of similar code related to persisting SVG from Node.

See Also

An excellent tutorial on creating a horizonal bar chart is "Let's Make a Bar Chart II" (*http://bost.ocks.org/mike/bar/2/*) by the creator of D3, Mike Bostock.

D3 isn't the only data visualization tool or library you can use, but it is a very flexible and attractive option. CodeGeekz's "30 Best Tools for Data Visualiation" (*http://bit.ly/1DZGw13*) provides an excellent selection of data visualiation tools that also includes a reference to D3.

16.2. Mapping Data Point Variations with a Radar Chart

Problem

You're interested in creating a *radar chart*, which is a way of visualizing *multivariate* or multiple simultaneous data points. But you don't want to try to put something like that together from scratch.

Solution

Use a library like chart.js to create the radar chart.

In Example 16-3, I create a radar chart with seven properties, and three of my favorite snack recipes. Each recipe is judged along the seven properties, allowing me to compare all three recipes across all the seven properties at the same time.

Example 16-3. Charting three different recipes using a radar chart created with chart.js

```
<!DOCTYPE html>
<html>
<head>
  <meta charset="utf-8">
  <title>Radar chart using chart.js</title>
  <script src="Chart.js">
  </script>
</head>
<body>
<canvas id="myChart" width="400" height="400"></canvas>

<script type="text/javascript">
var data = {
    labels: ["Calories","Health","Difficulty","Expense","Taste",
    "Responsible","Time"],
    datasets: [
        {
            label: "Cheddar Cheese Crackers",
            fillColor: "rgba(220,220,220,0.2)",
            strokeColor: "rgba(220,220,220,1)",
            pointColor: "rgba(220,220,220,1)",
            pointStrokeColor: "#fff",
            pointHighlightFill: "#fff",
            pointHighlightStroke: "rgba(220,220,220,1)",
            data: [60, 50, 90, 50, 80, 80, 70]
        },
        {
            label: "Chocolate Chip Cookies",
            fillColor: "rgba(151,187,205,0.2)",
            strokeColor: "rgba(151,187,205,1)",
            pointColor: "rgba(151,187,205,1)",
            pointStrokeColor: "#fff",
```

```
            pointHighlightFill: "#fff",
            pointHighlightStroke: "rgba(151,187,205,1)",
            data: [95, 20, 10, 70, 90, 90, 40]
        },
        {

            label: "Oatmeal Date Cookies",
            fillColor: "rgba(205,205,0,0.2",
            strokeColor: "rgba(151,151,0,1)",
            pointColor: "rgba(151,187,205,1)",
            pointStrokeColor: "#fff",
            pointHighlightFill: "white",
            pointHighlightStroke: "rgba(151,151,0,1)",
            data: [75, 60, 30, 30, 80, 70, 40]
        }
    ]
};

window.onload=function() {
    var ctx = document.getElementById("myChart").getContext("2d");
    var myRadarChart = new Chart(ctx).Radar(data);
}

</script>
</body>
</html>
```

You can see the results in Figure 16-3.

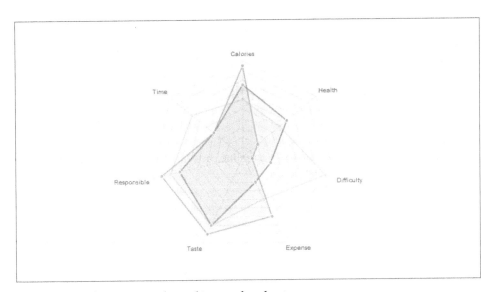

Figure 16-3. Three recipes charted in a radar chart

Discussion

Radar charts are interesting. Unlike a bar chart or line graph, we're less interested in a side-by-side comparison of different properties or points, and more interested in viewing all at once. In addition, as long as we use transparent overlays in our technology, we *can* compare different subjects and easily see how each skews and in what directions. In Figure 16-3, I can see at a glance that my recipe for Cheddar Cheese Crackers takes a significant amount of time, and is much more difficult than my two cookie recipes. I can also see that between the two cookie recipes, the Oatmeal Date trends as a healthier cookie than the Chocolate Chip cookie.

To create a chart like this from scratch in Canvas is not a trivial task, nor is it a unique application of skills. If one person needs to create a radar chart, several need to do so, so it doesn't make sense for everyone to create the same software for the same purpose, which is why charting software is so ubiquitous. The software I used in the example, chart.js, is a top choice because it's actively maintained, provides sophisticated presentation, and is relatively simple to use. It's also extensible, and the documentation includes instructions in how to extend the library.

See Also

There are many different libraries for building charts and graphs. A good resource for discovering them is "50 JavaScript Libraries for Charts and Graphs" (*http://bit.ly/1zG5mBP*). In addition, just searching for "canvas charts" returns a wealth of libraries. The key to discovering the right library is to ensure the software is being actively maintained and that it provides what you need with a minimum of additional cruft, the source is hopefully open and extensible, and whether you have to pay a fee to use the tool.

16.3. Feeding a Scrolling Timeline via WebSocket

Problem

You need to graph changing data to a timeline, but the data is only available on the server.

Solution

Use a combination of graphics with the real-time, bidirectional communication capability of WebSockets.

To demonstrate, the server is quite simple: serving up the primary HTML interface and a WebSockets server that sends a randomly generated value between 0 and 100 every three seconds.

The number generation exists outside of the communication, so that all WebSockets clients get the same data. To manage this, we use setInterval(), set to fire every three seconds to generate the new value. The nodejs-websocket module we're using keeps an array of open connections. The code traverses the array and issues an individual sendText message for each:

```
var app = require('http').createServer(handler)
  , fs = require('fs');
var ws = require("nodejs-websocket");

app.listen(8124);

// serve static page
function handler (req, res) {
  fs.readFile(__dirname + '/drawline.html',
  function (err, data) {
    if (err) {
      res.writeHead(500);
      return res.end('Error loading drawline.html');
    }
    res.writeHead(200);
    res.end(data);
  });
}

function startTimer() {
  setInterval(function() {
    var newval = Math.floor(Math.random() * 100) + 1;
    if (server.connections.length > 0) {
      console.log('sending ' + newval);
      var counter = {counter: newval};
      server.connections.forEach(function(conn, idx) {
        conn.sendText(JSON.stringify(counter), function() {
          console.log('conn sent')
        });
      });
    }
  },1000);
}

// WebSockets connection
var server = ws.createServer(function (conn) {
    console.log('connected');
    conn.on("close", function (code, reason) {
        console.log("Connection closed")
    });
}).listen(8001, function() {
    startTimer(); }
);
```

The console.log() calls are so you can follow the application as it handles new clients. SVG is used for the graphic because we can easily manipulate components within the graphic, to expand a graphic beyond the element's *viewport*, and it's simple to transform the line as it goes beyond the right border of the element:

```html
<!doctype html>
<html lang="en">
<head>
  <meta charset="utf-8">
  <title>The Never Ending Line</title>
  <style>
    #timeline {
        border: 1px solid black;
    }
    path {
        fill: none;
        stroke: maroon;
        stroke-width: 1px;
    }
  </style>
  <script type="text/javascript">
    var counter = 0;
    var x = 0;
    var socket = new WebSocket("ws://shelleystoybox.com:8001");
    socket.onmessage = function (event) {
        var val = JSON.parse(event.data);
        var point = parseInt(val.counter);

        // modify path
        var path = document.getElementById('thepath');
        var d = path.getAttribute('d');
        counter+=10;
        d+= 'L' + counter + ' ' + point;
        path.setAttribute('d',d);

        // now see if path needs moving
        if (counter > 600) {
          x = 600 - counter;
          var translate = 'translate(' + x + ',0)';
          path.setAttribute('transform',translate);
        }
    };

</script>
</head>
<body>
<svg id="timeline" width="600px" height="100px">
  <path id="thepath" d="M0 100" />
</svg>
</body>
</html>
```

Figure 16-4 shows the scrolling timeline loaded in two Chrome windows at different times. As the screenshot demonstrates, both windows are operating on the exact same data.

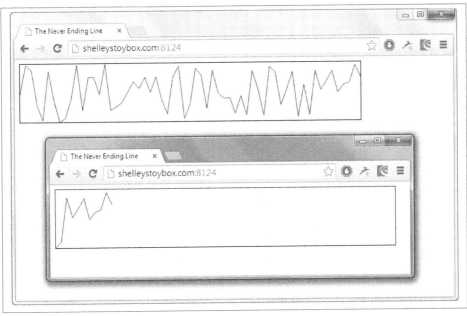

Figure 16-4. The scrolling timeline loaded into two separate windows at different times

Discussion

SVG is ideal for a scrolling timeline for three reasons:

- We can access the path element directly, as well as its attributes
- We can modify the path element's path descriptor attribute d and modify it
- We can move the path easily using a transform when the timeline exceeds the element's *viewport*

Each time the client receives data from the server, it parses out the new y timeline value, calculates a new x value by adding 10 to a running counter, and then adds the new line to command to the end of the path element's d attribute. The attribute is then reset with the newly modified path:

```
d+= 'L' + counter + ' ' + point;
path.setAttribute('d',d);
```

When the counter value exceeds the width of the SVG element (currently at 600 pixels), the path is moved to the left by setting a negative x value (holding y constant, at zero), in a `translate` transform:

```
x = 600 - counter;
var translate = 'translate(' + x + ',0)';
path.setAttribute('transform',translate);
```

The `translate` transformation moves the path. Other transforms can rotate it, scale it, skew it, or perform a combination of all the operations.

> There's more on the SVG `transform` in the Mozilla Developer Network transform page (*http://mzl.la/1DZIsGS*). Be prepared to brush off your matrix mathematics.

This is the ideal type of graphical process for SVG.

The same applies to WebSockets. It was made for this type of action: communicating real-time data to the client without the client having to initiate any action other than just make a connection. And it's so simple to use, in both the client and server.

Because the example is emulating a real-world data situation, the data each of the WebSockets clients receives is exactly the same. If two clients are running concurrently, but one started before the other, once they both hit the 600-pixel mark, their diagrams are identical. This is what we'd expect when working with real data.

Other tweaks we can make to the timeline are adding tick marks, mouse-over data feedback, even the ability to resize the SVG element in order to compress the timeline, or expand it for a clearer view.

See Also

WebSockets are covered in more detail in Recipe 15.5. Recipe 15.7 includes a discussion about performance and stress testing of the application featured in the solution.

I cover Node timers and the event loop in some detail in Recipe 11.7.

One of my favorite timeline implementations is Weather Underground's 10-day Forecast weather timeline. You can see it embedded about halfway down the page in the St. Louis weather page (*http://bit.ly/1DZJX8d*) (or any other weather page). If you mouse over the timeline and inspect the element using Firebug or another tool, you'll see that it's actually using a Canvas element. The especially neat thing it does is expand the timeline when you go from daily to hourly results. Give it a try.

16.4. Generating Screenshots of Generated Web Page Content (PhantomJS)

Problem

You want to add functionality to take screenshots of a web page within your JavaScript application.

Solution

Use a command line, such as PhantomJS, that provides this capability either directly or via Node interface. The following code will take a screenshot of the O'Reilly main website:

```
var phantom = require('phantom');

var pageUrl = "http://oreilly.com";

phantom.create(function (ph) {
   ph.createPage(function (page) {
      page.open(pageUrl, function(status) {
         console.log(status);
         setTimeout(function(){
            page.render('screenshot.png', function(finished){
               console.log('rendering '+pageUrl+' done');
               ph.exit();
            });
         }, 15000);
      });
   });
});
```

Discussion

PhantomJS utilizes WebKit for all of its functionality. It's *headless*, which means it doesn't require a graphical user interface. It can be used for testing in combination with a testing framework, such as Jasmine or Mocha. It can also be used to monitor network traffic, or automate web page applications. The functionality we're interested in, though, is its screen capturing ability. Because PhantomJS is based in WebKit, and WebKit can render web pages, it's a simple step to take screenshots with PhantomJS.

> You can download the application from the PhantomJS website (*http://phantomjs.org/*). Note, though, that the latest from the site may not work well in all environments, including with a Node application. Another approach is to use your system's package installer.

One way to use PhantomJS to generate a screenshot is to create a JavaScript file that provides the screenshot specification, and then run it using the PhantomJS command-line application. Here is an example of a screenshot file:

```
var page = require('webpage').create();
page.open('http://burningbird.net/', function() {
  page.render('bb.png');
  phantom.exit();
});
```

In the JavaScript, the basic `webpage` module is imported and the object created. Then the web page is opened, and when opened, the `render()` method is called to render the web page to a file named *bb.png*. Finally, PhantomJS is exited.

The JavaScript is processed using the PhantomJS command-line tool:

```
phantomjs screen.js
```

This is the simplest screenshot, grabbing the entire page and rendering it to a PNG file. Other supported formats are GIF, JPEG, and PDF; which is used is determined by the file extension. However, you can also set the format via a `render()` options object. You can also specify the quality of the rendered image:

```
page.render('bb.pdf', {'format': 'PDF', 'quality': 100});
```

You can also modify how much of the web page is captured. The default is to make the image large enough to capture all the content in the entire page. Your application can chage the emulated view of the browser when taking the screenshot via the `viewport Size` property. In the following, the viewport is set to 400x800:

```
page.viewportSize = {
    width: 400,
    height: 800
}
```

You can also tell PhantomJS to only rasterize a portion of the web page by using the `clipRect` property:

```
page.clipRect={
  top: 100,
  left: 50,
  width: 100,
  height: 100
}
```

To see the differences these changes can make, Figure 16-5 shows a screenshot of the O'Reilly website using all the default settings, while Figure 16-6 shows a screenshot with both the view port and clipping rectangle set to that in the following JavaScript:

```
var page = require('webpage').create();
page.open('http://oreilly.com', function() {
  page.viewportSize = {
```

```
        width: 800,
        height: 1280
    }
    page.clipRect = {
        top: 50,
        left: 50,
        width: 600,
        height: 600
    }

    page.render('oreilly2.png');
    phantom.exit();
});
```

Figure 16-5. Screenshot of O'Reilly's website using default settings

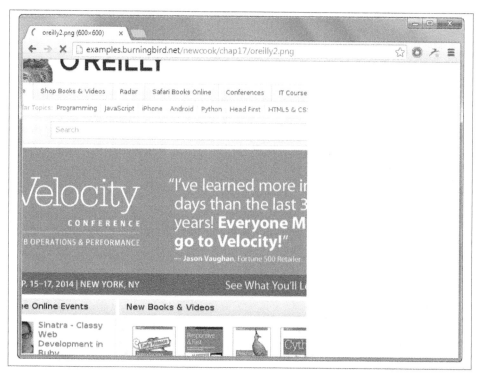

Figure 16-6. Screenshot of O'Reilly's website using set view port and clipping rectangle

If you're saving the rendered image to a PDF, you can control the PDF page size using the `paperSize` property in two different ways. You can specify specific dimensions:

```
page.paperSize = {
    width: '400px',
    height: '500px',
    border: '0px'
}
```

or specific formats:

```
page.paperSize = {
    format: 'letter',
    orientation: 'portrait',
    border: '1cm'
}
```

There are several other PhantomJS options, including command-line options that enable SSL access of the web pages, provide a path for `localStorage` storage, or use a proxy. You can also specify these options in a JSON file.

The PhantomJS `webpage` module functionality can be accessed at *http://phantomjs.org/api/webpage/*. The CLI options are documented at *http://phantomjs.org/api/command-line.html*.

You can use PhantomJS as a Node child process the same as you can use ImageMagick or any other CLI functionality. The npm page for PhantomJS even provides an example you can modify:

```
var path = require('path')
var childProcess = require('child_process')
var phantomjs = require('phantomjs')
var binPath = phantomjs.path

var childArgs = [
  path.join(__dirname, 'phantomjs-script.js'),
  'some other argument (passed to phantomjs script)'
]

childProcess.execFile(binPath, childArgs, function(err, stdout, stderr) {
  // handle results
})
```

This code snippet runs the earlier PhantomJS JavaScript file using this approach:

```
var path = require('path')
var childProcess = require('child_process')
var phantomjs = require('phantomjs')
var binPath = phantomjs.path

var childArgs = [
  path.join(__dirname, 'phantom.js')
]

childProcess.execFile(binPath, childArgs, function(err, stdout, stderr) {
    console.log('stdout: ' + stdout);
    console.log('stderr: ' + stderr);
    if (err !== null) {
      console.log('exec error: ' + err);
    }
})
```

Of course, you still have to create the JavaScript file for PhantomJS to process, but you can also do that in code using Node's file-writing modules. Or create a generic JavaScript file and pass arguments to it specifying web page URL, page sizes, formats, etc., and provide these as child arguments.

There is a PhantomJS-Node bridge module you can install using npm:

```
npm install phantom
```

The key to using the bridge is to remember Node's callback argument structure, and that all functionality that is a separate function call in the command-line files is dependent on callbacks in the Node bridge. In addition, you don't set the properties directly, you have to use the bridge module's set() function, which also utilizes a callback function. If you're thinking this could nest rather quickly, you're right.

The PhantomJS-Node bridge GitHub page (*https://github.com/sgen tle/phantomjs-node*) provides minimal documentation, and the examples are primarily in CoffeeScript. In addition, the results may not be as robust as you'd like.

You'll also need to incorporate a setTimeout() function call, to give enough time for the web page to fully open before rendering. This is because of the module implementation, and isn't required when using PhantomJS via its CLI. A complete example is shown in Example 16-4.

Example 16-4. Complete example using PhantomJS-Node bridge module

```
var phantom = require('phantom');

var pageUrl = "http://oreilly.com";

phantom.create(function (ph) {
    ph.createPage(function (page) {
        page.set('viewportSize', {width:800, height:1200}, function(){
            page.set('clipRect', {top:50,left:50,width:600,height:600}, function(){
                page.open(pageUrl, function(status) {
                    if (status == 'success') {
                        setTimeout(function(){
                            page.render('screenshot.png', function(finished){
                                console.log('rendering '+pageUrl+' done');
                                    ph.exit();
                            });
                        }, 15000);
                    }
                });
            });
        });
    });
});
```

All in all, I recommend using Node's child processes and a generic file and passed arguments, and leave the bridge module for the CoffeeScript fans.

16.5. Converting Graphics to Text (Ocrad.js)

Problem

You want to convert graphical text into plain text.

Solution

Optical Character Recognition (OCR) JavaScript support is somewhat limited, but there are options in both the client and on the server.

In the client, you can use Ocrad.js to convert image data to text:

```javascript
<script src="ocrad.js" type="text/javascript">
</script>
<script type="text/javascript">

   var img = new Image();
   img.addEventListener("load", function() {
      var context = document.createElement('canvas').getContext('2d');
      context.drawImage(img,0,0);

      var imgdata = context.getImageData(0,0,this.width, this.height);

      try {
      var text = OCRAD(imgdata);

      document.getElementById("result").innerHTML = text;
      } catch(err) {
         console.log(err);
      }
   }, false);

   img.src = 'ocrtest.png';

</script>
```

In Node, you can use the Tesseract OCR via a module:

```javascript
var tesseract = require('node-tesseract');
var fs = require('fs');

var myArgs = process.argv.slice(2);

tesseract.process(__dirname + '/' + myArgs[0],function(err, text) {
    if(err) {
       console.log(err);
    } else {
       fs.writeFile(myArgs[1], text, function(err) {
          if(err) {
            console.log(err);
          } else {
```

```
                console.log('Converted text stored in ' + myArgs[1]);
            }
        });
    }
});
```

Run the Node application, passing in the graphical file and the name of the text output file:

```
node ocr.js ocr2.png ocr2.txt
```

Discussion

The client software Ocrad.js is an *Emscripten* of Ocrad, which is a GNU OCR application. Emscripten is a source-to-source compiler that takes compiled C/C++ and converts it into JavaScript. The JavaScript version of Ocrad.js works with a Canvas element, a Context2D instance, or an instance of ImageData. To work with a PNG image, as in the example, we'll need to draw the image to a Canvas element and then get the image data via getImageData(). The best approach is to capture the image's load event, and then perform the conversion in the event handler.

The server software makes use of Tesseract OCR (a respected open source OCR software application) within a Node application. The Node wrapper for the functionality is very easy to use, as demonstrated in the solution, and the results are generally good. The application takes two command-line arguments—the name of the graphic file containing the text, and the name of a text file to write the results to:

```
node ocr.js ocrtest.png ocrtest.txt
```

You can also use Ocrad.js on the server by installing the Ocrad.js Node wrapper, and the Canvas module:

```
npm install ocrad.js
npm install canvas
```

The Ocrad.js GitHub page includes an example for running the software as a Node application:

```
var Ocrad = require('ocrad.js');
var Canvas = require('canvas');
var Image = Canvas.Image;
var fs = require('fs');
fs.readFile(__dirname + '/test.png', function(err, src) {
if (err) {
throw err;
}
var img = new Image();
img.src = src;
var canvas = new Canvas(img.width, img.height);
var ctx = canvas.getContext('2d');
ctx.drawImage(img, 0, 0, img.width, img.height);
```

```
    console.log(Ocrad(canvas));
  });
```

OCR in JavaScript returns erratic results, at best, so set your expectations accordingly. Figure 16-7 demonstrates the results we can get when giving the OCR software a scrap snipped from a court document PDF. Results are best with larger text, with a clean, light colored background, and sans-serif fonts, such as Ariel. If you search for "OCR test images", you can find several good test images you can use when testing your application.

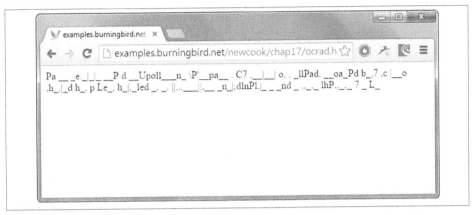

Figure 16-7. Results of running an extract from a PDF file containing a legal document

See Also

Access a demo of Ocrad.js at *http://antimatter15.com/ocrad.js/demo.html*. You can also access the Github page from that URL. The Tesserect OCR Node wrapper can be installed using npm:

```
npm install tesseract-ocr
```

There is also a cloud-based option for OCR, which is intriguing. Read more about it on the ABBYY Cloud OCR SDK website (*http://ocrsdk.com/*).

16.6. Cropping (or Otherwise Modifying) Uploaded Images

Problem

Your application requires the user to upload an image, which is then cropped (or otherwise modified), stored on the server, and made available for use in the application.

Solution

Use ImageMagick to crop or otherwise modify an uploaded image.

There are some client-side technologies you can use, such as JCrop for cropping images in the browser, or tricks associated with Canvas (see Recipe 9.7 for an example) for manipulating images in the client. When you're planning on persisting the image on the server, take advantage of some of the powerful tools available on the server. Specifically, take advantage of ImageMagick.

Example 16-5 displays an application that loads a simple form to upload a photo, uses the imagemagick Node module that wraps ImageMagick to crop the uploaded image, and then loads the cropped image in the feeback page.

Example 16-5. Uploading, cropping, and displaying the cropped image thanks to ImageMagick

```
var formidable = require('formidable');
var http = require('http');
var fs = require('fs');
var im = require('imagemagick');

http.createServer(function(req, res) {
  if (req.url == '/upload' && req.method.toLowerCase() == 'post') {

    // parse a file upload
    var form = new formidable.IncomingForm();
    form.uploadDir = __dirname + '/photos';
    form.keepExtensions = true;

    form.parse(req, function(err, fields, files) {
      var filepath = __dirname + '/photos/' + files.upload.name;
      fs.rename(files.upload.path, filepath, function(err) {
        if (err) {
          res.end(err);
          return;
        }

        // crop the image
        im.convert([filepath, '-crop', '100x100+50+50',
            __dirname + '/cropped/' + 'cropped.' + files.upload.name],
          function(err, metadata) {
            console.log(err);
            res.end(err);
            return;
        });

        res.writeHead(200, {'content-type': 'text/html'});
        res.write('<p>Uploaded and cropped:</p>');
        res.end('<img src="/cropped/cropped.' + files.upload.name + '" />');
      });
```

```
    });

    // display cropped image
  } else if (req.url.indexOf('/cropped') >= 0) {
    var path = require('url').parse(req.url).path;
    fs.readFile(__dirname + path,
      function (err, data) {
        if (err) {
          res.writeHead(500);
          return res.end(req.url);
        }
        res.writeHead(200);
        res.end(data);
      });
  } else {
    // show a file upload form
    res.writeHead(200, {'content-type': 'text/html'});
    res.end(
      '<form action="/upload" enctype="multipart/form-data" method="post">'+
      'Image: <input type="file" name="upload" multiple="multiple"><br><br>'+
      '<input type="submit" value="Upload">'+
      '</form>'
    );
  }
}).listen(8080);
```

Discussion

ImageMagick is a well-known command-line tool to perform an amazing number of operations on images. It supports a small set of basic commands, but the ones that are most commonly used are convert and identify.

The identify command extracts metadata about the image, while convert is the tool that does most of the transformations on the image. Both are accessible as functions by the imagemagick module, installed with:

```
npm install imagemagick
```

The imagemagick module also does a *crop*, but it uses a resize rather than an actual crop. In the solution, I used the general convert method, and then specified the -crop option.

The crop isn't too exciting but does demonstrate the use of ImageMagic in Node. However, you don't have to stay with crop, or with using a library, either. You can also use a child process to run an ImageMagick command. One of my favorites is the following, which creates a Polaroid-like effect of whatever image is passed to the application:

```
var spawn = require('child_process').spawn;

// get photo
var photo = process.argv[2];
```

```
// conversion array
var opts = [
photo,
"-bordercolor", "snow",
"-border", "20",
"-background","grey60",
"-background", "none",
"-rotate", "6",
"-background", "black",
"(", "+clone", "-shadow", "60x4+4+4", ")",
"+swap",
"-background", "none",
"-flatten",
photo + ".png"];

var im = spawn('convert', opts);
```

To convert the photo, run the following command:

```
node polaroid bee2.jpg
```

The result is displayed in Figure 16-8.

Figure 16-8. Photo converted into Polaroid-like effect via Node and ImageMagick

Working with ImageMagick from a Node application is a snap. It's keeping track of all those command-line arguments to create an effect that's hard.

## CHAPTER 17

Data and Persistence

We can animate and interact, stream, play, and render, but we always come back to the data. Data is the foundation on which we build the majority of our JavaScript applications. In Chapter 14, we split data from the view, but in Chapter 16, we twisted them tightly back together again. In Chapter 15, we sent data back and forth between client and server, and in Chapter 13, we manipulated data using a host of APIs. Data and JavaScript, friends forever.

In this chapter, we're going to look at ways we can persist both data and *state* using JavaScript in the client, and on the server. We're also going to take a quick look at validating data before we store it.

17.1. Validating Form Data

Problem

Your web application gathers data from the users using HTML forms. Before you send that data to the server, though, you want to make sure it's well formed, complete, and valid. But you'd really prefer not to have to write code to test the data yourself.

Solution

Form validation is a perfect opportunity to introduce an external library. For a given form, such as the following:

```
<form name="example" action="" method="post">
<fieldset>
    <legend>Example</legend>
    <div>
        <label for="name">Name (required):</label>
        <input type="text" id="name" name="name" value="" />
    </div>
```

```html
    <div>
        <label for="email">Email (required):</label>
        <input type="text" id="email" name="email" value="">
    </div>
    <div>
        <label>Website:</label>
        <input type="text" id="url" name="url" value="">
    </div>

    <div>
        <label>Credit Card:</label>
        <input type="text" id="cc-card" name="cc-card" value="">
    </div>
    <div>
        <label>Expires:</label>
        <input type="text" id="expires" name="expires" value="">
    </div>
    <div>
        <label>CVS:</label>
        <input type="text" id="cvs" name="cvs" value="">
    </div>

    <div>
        <input type="submit" value="Submit">
    </div>
    </fieldset>
</form>
```

You can use a standalone library, such as Validate.js:

```html
<script type="text/javascript">
    var validator = new FormValidator('example', [{
      name: 'name',
      display: 'Name',
      rules: 'required|min_length[10]'
      },
      {
      name: 'email',
      display: 'Email',
      rules: 'required|valid_email'
      },
      {
      name: 'url',
      display: 'Website URL',
      rules: 'valid_url'
      },
      {
      name: 'cc-card',
      display: 'Credit Card',
      rules: 'valid_credit_card'
      }], function (errors, event) {
      if (errors.length > 0) {
        alert(errors.length);
```

```
        var msg = "";
        errors.forEach(function(elem,indx,arry) {
          msg+=elem.message + '<br />';
        });
        document.getElementById("results").innerHTML=msg;
      }
    });
    </script>
```

Or use a jQuery dependent solution, such as the jQuery Validation Engine plugin:

```
<form id="example" name="example" action="" method="post">
<fieldset>
    <legend>Example</legend>
    <div class="fld">
        <label for="name">Name (required):</label>
        <input type="text" id="name" name="name"
              class="validate[required]"
              data-errormessage-value-missing="Name is required"
           value="" />
    </div>
    <div class="fld">
        <label for="email">Email (required):</label>
        <input type="text" id="email" name="email"
              class="validate[required,custom[email]]"
              data-errormessage-value-missing="Email is required"
              data-errormessage-custom-error="Format: name@service.com"
           value="" />
    </div>
    <div class="fld">
        <label>Website:</label>
        <input type="text" id="url" name="url"
              class="validate[custom[url]]"
              data-errormessage-custom-error="Web URL"
            value="">
    </div>

    <div class="fld">
        <label>Credit Card:</label>
        <input type="text" id="cc-card" name="cc-card"
            class="validate[creditCard]"
            data-errormessage-pattern-mismatch="CC format is incorrect"
            value="">
    </div>
    <div class="fld">
        <label>Expires:</label>
        <input type="text" id="expires" name="expires" value="">
    </div>
    <div class="fld">
        <label>CVS:</label>
        <input type="text" id="cvs" name="cvs" value="">
    </div>
```

```
    <div class="fld">
        <input type="submit" value="Submit">
    </div>
  </fieldset>
</form>
```

Include the libraries and stylesheet:

```
<link rel="stylesheet" href="css/validationEngine.jquery.css" />
<script src="//code.jquery.com/jquery-2.1.1.js"></script>
<script src="js/languages/jquery.validationEngine-en.js"></script>
<script src="js/jquery.validationEngine.js"></script>
```

And instantiate the validation engine:

```
<script>
$(document).ready(function(){
    $("#example").validationEngine();
    });
</script>
```

Discussion

By now, we should not be writing our own forms validation routines. Not unless we're dealing with some really bizarre form behavior and/or data. And by bizarre, I mean so far outside the ordinary that trying to incorporate a JavaScript library would actually be harder than doing it ourselves—a "the form field value must be a string except on Thursdays, when it must be a number—but reverse that in even months" type of validation.

You have a lot of options for libraries, and I've only demonstrated a couple. The Validate.js library is a nice, simple, easy-to-use library that provides validation for most form types and in most circumstances. It doesn't require that you modify the form fields, either, which means it's easier to just drop it in, instead of reworking the form. Any and all styling and placement of error messages is developer dependent, too. In Figure 17-1, I used minimal CSS styling and just placed the error messages in a div element placed before the form.

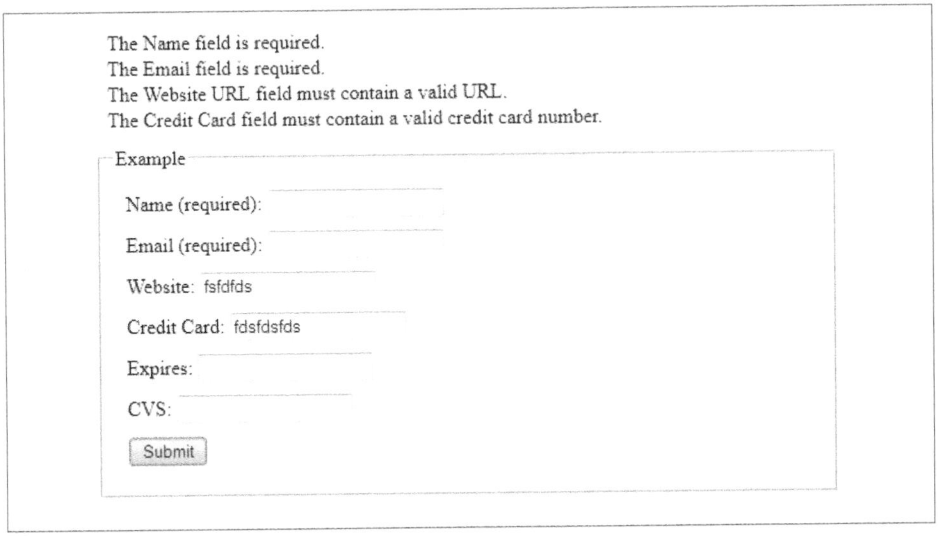

Figure 17-1. Form validated with the Validate.js library

In the solution, the code creates a new `FormValidator` object, passing in the name of the form, an array of field/rule combinations, and a callback function that accepts an errors object as parameter. The example uses basic validation: it checks for required fields (`name` and `email`) and whether the formatting is correct for some others (`email`, `url`, and `cc-card`). In the callback, the error messages for each of the error objects is extracted and used to create a string that's published to the `div` element. I didn't take advantage of some of the more sophisticated form validation, including the ability to code in depedencies for a field, so my bizarre data validation scenario wouldn't fail with Validate.js—so no excuse on not using a form validation library.

If you're incorporating jQuery, you can use the jQuery Validation Engine, which has an added benefit of localization as well as nicely integrated graphics, as shown in Figure 17-2.

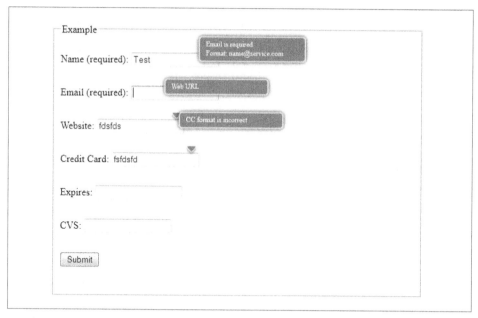

Figure 17-2. Form validated with jQuery Validation Engine plugin

The jQuery Validation Engine does make use of the `class` attribute to code in the validation rules and requirements, and the actual script is a simple instantiation of the process, as demonstrated in the solution. A new version that's still in development will replace the use of `class` with the more appropriate `data-` custom attributes. The `data-` attributes used in the solution contain the specialized error messages displayed for each field, and for each type of error. The jQuery Validation Engine supports several.

> Read about and download the jQuery Validation Engine plugin at *http://posabsolute.github.io/jQuery-Validation-Engine/*. Validate.js is available at *http://rickharrison.github.io/validate.js/*.
>
> You don't have use a plugin to work with jQuery and forms validation. Another popular validation library is Parsley (*http://parsleyjs.org/*), which requires jQuery, but isn't a plugin.

Sometimes you need a smaller library specifically for one type of data validation. Credit cards are tricky things, and though you can ensure a correct format, the values contained in them must meet specific rules in order to be considered valid credit card submissions.

In addition to the other validation libraries, you can also incorporate a credit card validation library, such as jQuery.payment (*https://github.com/stripe/jquery.payment*), which provides a very simple validation API. As an example, specify that a field is a credit card number after the form loads:

```
$('input.cc-card').payment('formatCardNumber');
```

And then when the form is submitted, validate the credit card number:

```
var valid = $.payment.validateCardNumber($('input.cc-card').val());

if (!valid) {
  message.innerHTML="You entered an invalid credit card number";
  return false;
}
```

The library doesn't just check format; it also ensures that the value meets a valid card number for all of the major card companies.

Lastly, you can pair client and server validation, using the same library, or different ones. One library, Validator.js, can be used in the client:

```
<script src="validator.min.js"></script>
```

or installed using npm:

```
npm install validator
```

Because it is a dual validation tool, it doesn't intercept the form submission. Instead, it provides a set of APIs that can be called to validate form fields:

```
validator.isEmail(formfield_value); // true if valid email
```

The advantage to the tool is you can validate fields in both the client and server using the exact same software. In addition, it gives you more finite control over when the validation happens, and what kind of message is displayed. Of course, this means more work for you, but nowhere near the amount you'd have to do if you had to manage every last aspect of the form validation.

Extra: What About HTML5 Forms Validation Techniques?

In "Extra: Why Not Just Use HTML5 and CSS3 for Managing Visual Effects?" on page 175 I gave some reasons why we can't rely totally on HTML5 and CSS3 to provide specialized visual effects. So, how about using the built-in HTML5 forms validation techniques?

I like the HTML5 forms validation techniques, and the fact that you don't have to code anything. However, as in "Extra: Why Not Just Use HTML5 and CSS3 for Managing Visual Effects?" on page 175, you have the same issues with form validation that you do with any of the other declarative capabilities: you don't have finite control over when events occur, and you don't have control over the appearance of the feedback.

However, work is underway on a new specification, the CSS Basic User Interface Module Level 3 (*http://dev.w3.org/csswg/css-ui/*), which does give us more visual control over some of the declarative functionality. But the control is still finite, the specification is still undergoing work, and the support is sketchy.

So the rules still apply: if you need finite control over the appearance and behavior of form validation, you're better off using a JavaScript library than depending on the HTML5 and CSS forms validation specifications. If you do, though, make sure to incorporate accessibility features into your forms. I recommend reading WebAIM's "Creating Accessible Forms" (*http://webaim.org/techniques/forms/*).

See Also

Validator is one of the Node modules most starred (favorited) in the npm registry. All of the Node modules in this chapter, and used elsewhere in the book, appear in this list. If you're working with Node, you should check out as many in the first page of the list (*https://www.npmjs.org/browse/star*) as possible. Like Validator, several in the list work equally well in the client, as in the server.

17.2. Persisting Information Using HTML5

Problem

You've looked at all the ways of handling the back button and controlling page state for an Ajax application, and you're saying to yourself, "There has to be a better way."

Solution

There is a better way—a much better way: using HTML5's `history.pushState` and `history.replaceState` methods to persist a state object, and the `window.onpope vent` to restore the page state:

```
window.history.pushState({ page : page}, "Page " + page, "?page=" + page);
    ...

window.onpopstate = function(event) {
    // check for event.state, if found, reload state
    if (!event.state) return;
    var page = event.state.page;
}
```

Discussion

To address the significant problems Ajax developers have had with trying to persist state through back button events or page reloads, HTML5 includes new `history` object methods, `pushState` and `replaceState`, to persist state information, and an associated `window.onpopevent` that can be used to restore the page state.

A popular approach to maintaining history in the past was to store the data in the page URL hash, which updates the page history and can be pulled via JavaScript:

```
http://somecompany.com/example.html#first
```

The problem with this approach is that if you hit the back button, the URL with the hash shows in the location bar, but no event is triggered so you can grab the data and restore the page. The workaround was to use a timer to check for the new hash and then restore the page if a new hash was found. Not an attractive solution, and one most of us decided just wasn't worth trying.

Now, you can easily store any object that can be passed to JSON.stringify. Since the data is stored locally, the early implementor, Firefox, limits the size of the JSON representation to 640k. However, unless you're recording the state of every pixel in the page, 640k should be more than sufficient.

In Example 17-1, the stored state object is extremely simple: a page property and its associated value. The history.pushState also takes a title parameter, which is used for the session history entry, and a URL. For the example, I appended a query string representing the page. The following is displayed in the location bar:

```
http://somecom.com/pushstate.html?page=three
```

The history.replaceState method takes the same parameters, but modifies the current history entry instead of creating a new one.

Example 17-1. Using history.pushState and history.replaceState to enable back button support

```
<!DOCTYPE html>
<head>
  <title>Remember me--new, and improved!</title>
  <meta http-equiv="Content-Type" content="text/html;charset=utf-8" />
</head>
<body>
  <button id="next" data-page="zero">Next Action</button>
  <div id="square" class="zero">
    <p>This is the object</p>
  </div>

  <script type="text/javascript">
    document.getElementById("next").onclick=nextPanel;

  window.onpopstate = function(event) {

  // check for event.state, if found, reload state
  if (!event.state) return;
    var page = event.state.page;
    switch (page) {
      case "one" :
         functionOne();
         break;
      case "two" :
         functionOne();
```

```
            functionTwo();
            break;
      case "three" :
            functionOne();
            functionTwo();
            functionThree();
   }
}

// display next panel, based on button's class
function nextPanel() {
   var page = document.getElementById("next").getAttribute("data-page");
   switch(page) {
      case "zero" :
            functionOne();
            break;
      case "one" :
            functionTwo();
            break;
      case "two" :
            functionThree();
   }
}

// set both the button class, and create the state link, add to page
function setPage(page) {
   document.getElementById("next").setAttribute("data-page",page);
      window.history.pushState({ page : page}, "Page " + page,
      "?page=" + page);
}

// function one, two, three - change div, set button and link
function functionOne() {
   var square = document.getElementById("square");
   square.style.position="relative";
   square.style.left="0";
   square.style.backgroundColor="#ff0000";
   square.style.width="200px";
   square.style.height="200px";
   square.style.padding="10px";
   square.style.margin="20px";
   setPage("one");
}

function functionTwo() {
   var square = document.getElementById("square");
   square.style.backgroundColor="#ffff00";
   square.style.position="absolute";
   square.style.left="200px";
   setPage("two");
}
```

```
  function functionThree() {
    var square = document.getElementById("square");
    square.style.width="400px";
    square.style.height="400px";
    square.style.backgroundColor="#00ff00";
    square.style.left="400px";
    setPage("three");
  }
</script>
</body>
```

When using the browser back button to traverse through the created history entries, or when hitting the page reload, a window.onpopstate event is fired. This is really the truly important component in this new functionality, and is the event we've needed for years. In order to restore the web page to the stored state, we create a window.onpopstate event handler function, accessing the state object from the event passed to the window handler function:

```
window.onpopstate = function(event) {
    // check for event.state, if found, reload state
    if (!event.state) return;
    var page = event.state.page;
    ...
}
```

In the example, when you click the button three times to get to the third *page*, reload the page, or hit the back button, the window.onpopstate event handler fires—perfect time to get the state data, and repair the page.

17.3. Using sessionStorage for Client-Side Storage

Problem

You want to easily store session information without running into the size and cross-page contamination problems associated with cookies, and prevent loss of information if the browser is refreshed.

Solution

Use the new DOM Storage sessionStorage functionality:

```
sessionStorage.setItem("name", "Shelley");
sessionStorage.city="St. Louis";
...
var name = sessionStorage,getItem("name");
var city = sessionStorage.city;
...
sessionStorage.removeItem("name");
sessionStorage.clear();
```

Discussion

One of the constraints with cookies is they are domain/subdomain-specific, not page-specific. Most of the time, this isn't a problem. However, there are times when such domain specificity isn't sufficient.

For instance, say a shopper has two browser tabs open to the same retail site and adds a few items to the shopping cart in one tab. In that tab, the shopper clicks a button to add an item because the page tells the shopper to add the item to the cart in order to see the price. The shopper does, but decides against buying the item and closes the tab page, thinking that action is enough to ensure the item isn't in the cart. The shopper then clicks the check-out option in the other opened tag, assuming that the only items currently in the cart are the ones that were added in that browser page.

If the user isn't paying attention, she may not notice that the cookie-based shopping cart has been updated from both pages, and she'll end up buying something she didn't want.

Although many web users are savvy enough to not make this mistake, there are many who aren't—they assume that persistence is browser page–specific, not necessarily domain-specific. With `sessionStorage` (to paraphrase the famous quote about Las Vegas), what happens in the page, stays in the page.

As an example of the differences between the cookies and the newer storage option, Example 17-2 stores information from a form in both a cookie and `sessionStorage`. Clicking the button to get the data gets whatever is stored for the key in both, and displays it in the page: the `sessionStorage` data in the first block, the cookie data in the second. The remove button erases whatever exists in both.

Example 17-2. Comparing sessionStorage and cookies

```
<!DOCTYPE html>
<html dir="ltr" lang="en-US">
<head>
  <title>Comparing Cookies and sessionStorage</title>
  <meta http-equiv="Content-Type" content="text/html;charset=utf-8" >
  <style>
    div
    {
      margin: 10px;
    }

    #sessionstr, #cookiestr
    {
      width: 100px;
      background-color: yellow;
      padding: 5px;
    }
  </style>
  <script src="cookie.js"></script>
```

```
  <script src="app.js"></script>
</head>
<body>
  <form>
    <div>
     <label for="key"> Enter key:</label>
       <input type="text" id="key" />
     </div>
     <div>
     <label for="value">Enter value:</label>
       <input type="text" id="value" />
     </div>
  </form>
  <button id="set">Set data</button>
  <button id="get">Get data</button>
  <button id="erase">Erase data</button>
  <p>Session:</p>
  <div id="sessionstr"></div>
  <p>Cookie:</p>
  <div id="cookiestr"></div>

  <script>

    document.getElementById("set").onclick=setData;
    document.getElementById("get").onclick=getData;
    document.getElementById("erase").onclick=removeData;

</script>

</body>
```

The *cookies.js* file contains the code necessary to set, retrieve, and erase a given cookie:

```
// set session cookie
function setCookie(cookie,value) {
  var cookieVal=cookie + "=" +
      encodeURIComponent(value) + ";path=/";
  document.cookie=cookieVal;
  console.log(cookieVal);
 }

// each cookie separated by semicolon;
function getCookie(key) {
  key = key.replace(/([.*+?^=!:${}()|[\]\/\\])/g, '\\$1');
  var cookie = document.cookie;
  var regex = new RegExp('(?:^|;)\\s?' + key + '=(.*?)(?:;|$)','i');
  var match = cookie.match(regex);

  return match && decodeURIComponent(match[1]);
}

// set cookie date to the past to erase
function eraseCookie (key) {
```

```
    var cookie = key +
                '=;path=/; expires=Thu, 01 Jan 1970 00:00:00 UTC';
    document.cookie = cookie;
    console.log(cookie);
}
```

And the *app.js* file contains the rest of the program functionality. No separate JavaScript
file is necessary for working with the sessionStorage object—another major difference
from cookies:

```
// set data for both session and cookie
function setData() {
  var key = document.getElementById("key").value;
  var value = document.getElementById("value").value;

  // set sessionStorage
  var current = sessionStorage.getItem(key);
  if (current) {
    current+=" " + value;
  } else {
    current=value;
  }

  sessionStorage.setItem(key,current);

  // set cookie
  current = getCookie(key);
  if (current) {
    current+=" " + value;
  } else {
    current=value;
  }
  setCookie(key,current);
}

function getData() {
  try {
    var key = document.getElementById("key").value;
    var session = document.getElementById("sessionstr");
    var cookie = document.getElementById("cookiestr");

    // reset display
    session.innerHTML = cookie.innerHTML = "";

    // sessionStorage
    var value = sessionStorage.getItem(key) || "";
    if (value)
      session.innerHTML="<p>" + value + "</p>";

      // cookie
      value = getCookie(key) || "";
      if (value)
```

```
        cookie.innerHTML="<p>" + value + "</p>";
    } catch(e) {
        console(e);
    }
}

function removeData() {
    var key = document.getElementById("key").value;

    // sessionStorage
    sessionStorage.removeItem(key);

    // cookie
    eraseCookie(key);
}
```

You can get and set the data from sessionStorage accessing it directly, as demonstrated in the solution, but a better approach is to use the getItem() and setItem() functions.

Load the example page, add one or more values for the same key, and then click the "Get data" button. The result is displayed in Figure 17-3. No surprises here. The data has been stored in cookies and sessionStorage. Now, open the same page in a new tab window, and click the "Get data" button. The activity results in a page like that shown in Figure 17-4.

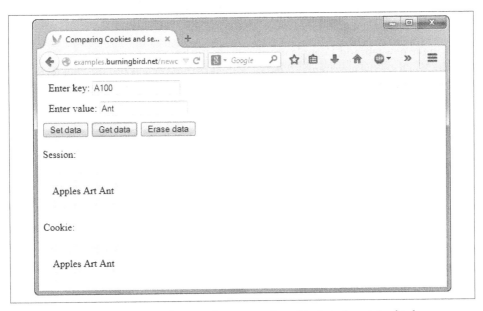

Figure 17-3. Displaying stored sessionStorage and cookie data in original tab

Figure 17-4. Displaying stored sessionStorage and cookie data in second tab

In the new tab window, the cookie value persists because the cookie is session-specific, which means it lasts until you close the browser. The cookie lives beyond the first tab, but the sessionStorage, which is specific to the tab window, does not.

Now, in the new tab, add a couple more items to the key value, and click the "Get data" button. You'll see the new items added to both sessionStorage and the cookie. Return to the original tab window and click the "Get data" button. As you can see in Figure 17-5, the items added in the second tab are showing with the cookie, but not the sessionStorage item.

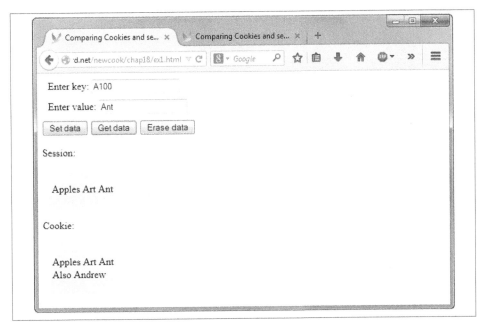

Figure 17-5. Returning to the original tab window and clicking "Get data" with A100 key

Lastly, in the original tab window, click the "Erase data" button. Figure 17-6 shows the results of clicking "Get data" on the original window, while Figure 17-7 shows the results when clicking "Get data" in the second tab window. Again, note the disparities between the cookie and sessionStorage. The first tab shows all of the data is gone for both cookie and sessionStorage, while the second tab still shows data in sessionStorage.

Figure 17-6. After clicking the "Erase data" button in the original tab window, and then clicking "Get data"

Figure 17-7. Clicking "Get data" in the second window, after erasing data in the first

The screenshots graphically demonstrate the differences between `sessionStorage` and cookies, aside from how they're set and accessed in JavaScript. Hopefully, the images and the example also demonstrate the potential hazards involved when using `session Storage`, especially in circumstances where cookies have normally been used.

If your website or application users are familiar with the cookie persistence across tabbed windows, `sessionStorage` can be an unpleasant surprise. Along with the different behavior, there's also the fact that browser menu options to delete cookies probably won't have an impact on `sessionStorage`, which could also be an unwelcome surprise for your users. On the other hand, `sessionStorage` is incredibly clean to use, and provides a welcome storage option when we want to link storage to a specific tab window only.

One last note on `sessionStorage` related to its implementation: both `sessionStor age` and `localStorage`, covered in the next recipe, are part of the W3C DOM Storage specification. Both are `window` object properties, which means they can be accessed globally. Both are implementations of the `Storage` object, and changes to the `proto type` for `Storage` result in changes to both the `sessionStorage` and `localStorage` objects:

```
Storage.prototype.someMethod = function (param) { ...};
...
localStorage.someMethod(param);
...
sessionStorage.someMethod(param);
```

Aside from the differences, covered in this recipe and the next, another major difference is that the `Storage` objects don't make a round trip to the server—they're purely client-side storage techniques.

See Also

For more information on the `Storage` object, `sessionStorage`, `localStorage`, or the Storage DOM, consult the specification (*http://dev.w3.org/html5/webstorage/*). See Recipe 17.4 for a different look at how `sessionStorage` and `localStorage` can be set and retrieved.

17.4. Creating a localStorage Client-Side Data Storage Item

Problem

You want to shadow form element entries (or any data) in such a way that users can continue where they left off if the browser crashes, the user accidentally closes the browser, or the Internet connection is lost.

Solution

You could use cookies if the data is small enough, but that strategy doesn't work in an offline situation. Another, better approach, especially when you're persisting larger amounts of data or if you have to support functionality when no Internet connection is present, is to use localStorage:

```
var value = document.getElementById("formelem").value;
If (value) {
   localStorage.formelem = value;
}
...
// recover
var value = localStorage.formelem;
document.getElementById("formelem").value = value;
```

Discussion

Recipe 17.3 covered sessionStorage, one of the DOM Storage techniques. The local Storage object interface is the same, with the same approaches to setting the data:

```
// use item methods
sessionStorage.setItem("key","value");
localStorage.setItem("key","value");

// use property names directly
sessionStorage.keyName = "value:
localStorage.keyName = "value";

// use the key method
sessionStorage.key(0) = "value";
localStorage.key(0) = "value:
```

and for getting the data:

```
// use item methods
value = sessionStorage.getItem("key");
value = localStorage.getItem("key");

// use property names directly
value = sessionStorage.keyName:
value = localStorage.keyName;

// use the key method
value = sessionStorage.key(0);
value = localStorage.key(0):
```

Again, as with sessionStorage, though you can access and set data on localStorage directly, you should use getItem() and setItem(), instead.

Both of the storage objects support the `length` property, which provides a count of stored item pairs, and the `clear` method (no parameters), which clears out all Storage. In addition, both are scoped to the HTML5 origin, which means that the data storage is shared across all pages in a domain, but not across protocols (e.g., `http` is not the same as `https`) or ports.

The difference between the two is how long data is stored. The `sessionStorage` object only stores data for the session, but the `localStorage` object stores data on the client forever, or until specifically removed.

The `sessionStorage` and `localStorage` objects also support one event: the `storage` event. This is an interesting event, in that it fires on all pages when changes are made to a `localStorage` item. It is also an area of low-compatibility among browsers: you can capture the event on the body or document elements for Firefox, on the body for IE, or on the document for Safari.

Example 17-3 demonstrates a more comprehensive implementation than the use case covered in the solution for this recipe. In the example, all elements of a small form have their onchange event handler method assigned to a function that captures the change element name and value, and stores the values in the local storage via `localStorage`. When the form is submitted, all of the stored form data is cleared.

When the page is loaded, the form elements onchange event handler is assigned to the function to store the values, and if the value is already stored, it is restored to the form element. To test the application, enter data into a couple of the form fields—but, before clicking the Submit button, refresh the page. Without `localStorage`, you'd lose the data. Now, when you reload the page, the form is restored to the state it was in before the page was reloaded.

Example 17-3. Using localStorage to back up form entries in case of page reload or browser crash

```
<!DOCTYPE html>
<html dir="ltr" lang="en-US">
<head>
<title>localstore</title>
<meta http-equiv="Content-Type" content="text/html;charset=utf-8" >
<style>
div
{
   margin: 10px;
}
</style>
<script>
   window.onload=function() {
      var elems = document.getElementsByTagName("input");

      // capture submit to clear storage
```

```
        document.getElementById("inputform").onsubmit=clearStored;

        for (var i = 0; i < elems.length; i++) {

            if (elems[i].type == "text") {

                // restore
                var value = localStorage.getItem(elems[i].id);
                if (value) elems[i].value = value;

                // change event
                elems[i].onchange=processField;
            }
        }
    }

    // store field values
    function processField() {
      localStorage.setItem(window.location.href,"true");
      localStorage.setItem(this.id, this.value);
    }

    // clear individual fields
    function clearStored() {
      var elems = document.getElementsByTagName("input");
      for (var i = 0; i < elems.length; i++) {

        if (elems[i].type == "text") {
            localStorage.removeItem(elems[i].id);
        }
      }
    }

</script>
</head>
<body>
    <form id="inputform">
        <div>
        <label for="field1">Enter field1:</label>
        <input type="text" id="field1" />
        </div>
        <div>
        <label for="field2">Enter field2:</label>
        <input type="text" id="field2" />
        </div>
        <div>
        <label for="field3">Enter field1:</label>
        <input type="text" id="field3" />
        </div>
        <div>
        <label for="field4">Enter field1:</label>
        <input type="text" id="field4" />
```

```
        </div>
        <input type="submit" value="Save" />
</body>
```

The size allotted for localStorage varies by browser, and some browsers, such as Firefox, allow users to extend the Storage object limits.

The localStorage object can be used for offline work. For the form example, you can store the data in the localStorage and provide a button to click when connected to the Internet, in order to sync the data from localStorage to server-side storage.

See Also

See Recipe 17.3 for more on the Storage object, and on sessionStorage and local Storage.

17.5. Using Squel.js to Query a MySQL Database

Problem

Your application uses a relational database, and you need to construct SQL to access it.

Solution

Use Squel.js to build your SQL statements. The following Node application uses Squel.js and the node-mysql module to access a MySQL database:

```
var mysql = require('mysql');
var squel = require('squel');

var connection = mysql.createConnection({
    host: 'localhost',
    user: 'username',
    password: 'password',
    database: 'dbname'
});

connection.connect();
var s = squel.select()
        .field('bTitle')
        .from('sc_tags')
        .from('sc_bookmarks')
        .where("sc_tags.tag = 'xhtml'")
        .where("sc_bookmarks.bId = sc_tags.bId");

console.log(s.toString());

connection.query(s.toString(), function(err, rows, fields) {
```

```
    if (err) throw err;

    rows.forEach(function(elem, indx, arr) {
      console.log(elem.bTitle);
    });

    connection.end();
  });
```

Discussion

Squel.js can be used in a client, but as the library developers note, you don't really want to send pre-formed SQL from the client to the server. It's too easy for SQL injection attacks to happen when you send SQL to the server.

Instead, we can use it in Node applications, and quite simply too. Although relational databases aren't as popular in Node applications as MongoDB or Redis, the node-mysql module does provide basic MySQL functionality, and Squel.js helps simplify the SQL formation.

In the solution, Squel.js performs a query on two tables, where rows with a tag name of *xhtml* in one table, sc_tags, is used to find identifiers, which are then used to query a second table, sc_bookmarks. The field we're interested in is bTitle.

The toString() function returns the formed SQL from Squel.js. In the example, the result is:

```
SELECT bTitle FROM sc_tags, sc_bookmarks WHERE (sc_tags.tag = 'xhtml')
AND (sc_bookmarks.bId = sc_tags.bId)
```

Squel.js supports a wide variety of SQL operations, including the basic CRUD (Create, Read, Update, and Delete), as well as many variations of queries: filters, subqueries, joins, and expressions. The queries can be manually created, but Squel.js provides cleaner, easier to read and maintain results.

As for node-mysql, it can also support basic CRUD, sophisticated queries, connection pooling, and basic transactions—all of the functionality you'll typically need with a relational database.

See Also

Access Squel.js at its main web page (*http://hiddentao.github.io/squel/*), and install it for Node using the following:

```
npm install squel
```

The node-mysql module can be installed with:

```
npm install mysql
```

Read more about it at *https://github.com/felixge/node-mysql*.

Another database option is MongoDB, demonstrated in Recipe 14.2.

Extra: Avoiding SQL Injection Attacks

The primary vulnerability to using a relational database is *SQL injection* attacks. They happen when a user is able to hand type in a query value, and he adds a little extra text to get more data than you want. For instance, if you ask for a username for the following query:

```
"select * from users where username = '" + username;
```

Instead of providing a username, he can provide the following:

```
shelleyp'; drop table users
```

Leading to the following SQL:

```
"select * from users where username = 'shelleyp'; drop table users"
```

To prevent SQL injections, values directly provided by the user are *escaped*, and node-mysql provides this capability. Depending on how you're connected, you can use either `pool.escape()` or `connection.escape()` to do this functionality:

```
var sql    = 'SELECT * FROM users WHERE id = ' + connection.escape(userId);
```

You can also defend against SQL injection using SQL *parameters*, in the form like the following:

```
connection.query('SELECT * FROM users WHERE id = ?',
  [userId], function(err, results) {
  // ...
});
```

Unfortunately, this structure does prevent using Squel.js, though the latter library does provide its own parameterized query:

```
console.log(JSON.stringify(
  squel.select()
    .from("users")
    .where("id = ?", 3)
    .toParam()
));
```

Resulting in the following output:

```
{"text":"SELECT * FROM users WHERE (id = ?)","values":[3]}
```

You'll have to map this object to what node-mysql requires, so it may not be as useful.

17.6. Persisting Larger Chunks of Data on the Client Using IndexedDB

Problem

You need more sophisticated data storage on the client than what's provided with other persistent storage methods, such as localStorage.

Solution

If your users are using newer browser versions, you can use IndexedDB.

The web page in Example 17-4 uses IndexedDB to create a database and a data object. Once created, it adds data and then retrieves the first object. A more detailed description of what's happening is in the discussion.

Example 17-4. Example of using IndexedDB to create a datastore, add data, and then retreive a data object

```
<!DOCTYPE html>
<html>
<head>
  <meta charset="utf-8">
  <title>IndexedDB</title>
</head>
<body>

<script>

  var data = [{name: "Joe Brown",age: 53, experience: 5},
              {name: "Cindy Johnson", age: 44, experience: 5},
              {name: "Some Reader", age: 30, experience: 1}];

  var delreq = indexedDB.deleteDatabase("Cookbook");

  delreq.onerror = function(event) {
       console.log("delete error", event);
       done = true;
  };

  var request = indexedDB.open("Cookbook", 1);

  request.onupgradeneeded = function(event) {

    window.db = event.target.result;
    var transaction = event.target.transaction;

    var objectStore = db.createObjectStore("reader",
              { keyPath: "id", autoIncrement: true });
```

```
objectStore.createIndex("experience", "experience", {unique: false});
objectStore.createIndex("name", "name", {unique: true});

transaction.oncomplete = function(event) {
  console.log('data finished');
};

var objectStore = transaction.objectStore("reader");
for (var i in data) {
  var req = objectStore.add(data[i]);
  req.onsuccess = function(event) {
    console.log('data added');
  };
}
};

request.onerror = function(event) {
  console.log(event.target.errorCode);
};

request.onsuccess = function(event) {
  console.log('datastore created');
};

document.onclick=function() {
  var request = db.transaction(["reader"])
                  .objectStore("reader").get(2);
  request.onsuccess = function(event){
                  console.log("Name : "+request.result.name);
  } ;
}
</script>

</body>
</html>
```

Discussion

IndexedDB is the specification the W3C and others agreed to when exploring solutions to large data management on the client. Though it is transaction-based, and supports the concept of a *cursor*, it isn't a relational database system. It works with JavaScript objects, each of which is indexed by a given *key*, whatever you decide the key to be.

IndexedDB can be both asynchronous and synchronous, but only the asynchronous API has been implemented at this time. It can be used for larger chunks of data in a traditional server or cloud application, but is also helpful for offline web application use.

Most implementations of IndexedDB don't restrict data storage size, but if you store more than 50 MB in Firefox, the user will need to provide permission. Chrome creates a pool of temporary storage, and each application can have up to 20% of it. Other agents have similar limitations. All of the main browsers support IndexedDB, except Opera Mini, though the overall support may not be identical.

As the solution demonstrates, the IndexedDB API methods trigger both success and error callback functions, which you can capture using traditional event handling, or as callback, or assign to a function. Mozilla describes the pattern of use with IndexedDB:

1. Open a database.
2. Create an object store in upgrading database.
3. Start a transaction and make a request to do some database operation, like adding or retrieving data.
4. Wait for the operation to complete by listening to the right kind of DOM event.
5. Do something with the results (which can be found on the request object).

Starting from the top in the solution, a data object is created with three values to add to the datastore. The database is deleted if it exists, so that the example can be run multiple times. Following, a call to open() opens the database, if it exists, or creates it, if not. Because the database is deleted before the example is run, it's re-created. The name and version are both necessary, because the database can be altered only if a new version of the database is opened.

A request object (IDBOpenDBRequest) is returned from the open() method, and whether the operation succeeds or not is triggered as events on this object. In the code, the onsuccess event handler for the object is captured to provide a message to the console about the success. You can also assign the database handle to a global variable in this event handler, but the code assigns this in the next event handled, the upgrade needed event.

The upgradeneeded event handler is only invoked when a database doesn't exist for a given database name and version. The event object also gives us a way to access the IDBDatabase reference, which is assigned to the global variable, db. The existing transaction can also be accessed via the event object passed as argument to the event handler, and it's accessed and assigned to a local variable.

The event handler for this event is the only time you'll be able to create the object store and its associated indexes. In the solution, a datastore named reader is created, with its key set to an autoincrementing id. Two other indexes are for the datastore's name and experience fields. The data is also added to the datastore in the event, though it could have been added at a separate time, say when a person submits an HTML form.

Following the upgradeneeded event handler, the success and error handlers are coded, just to provide feedback. Last but not least, the document.onclick event handler is used to trigger a database access. In the solution, a single data instance is accessed via the database handler, its transaction, the object store, and eventually, for a given key. In the solution, we went after the second object. When the query is successful, the name field is accessed and the value is printed out. Rather than accessing a single value, we can also use a cursor, but I'll leave that for your own experimentation.

The resulting printouts to the console are, in order:

```
data added
data finished
datastore created
Name : Cindy Johnson
```

I am ambivalent about IndexedDB. On the one hand, mobile application development based on web technologies needs a more sophisticated data storage mechanism than those discussed earlier in the chapter. On the other hand, it's a complex and not necessarily intuitive interface, leaving plenty of room to make typos that result in difficult-to-discover errors.

Still, IndexedDB is here to stay, so it's worth our time becoming familiar with how it works. Enjoy.

17.7. Accessing Data in the Cloud Using Dropbox Datastores

Problem

You have data in your application that you want to sync between all variations of your app: whether in a web page, an Android app, or a Node service.

Solution

Use a cloud-based datastore system, such as Google Drive, Amazon S3, or a Dropbox Datastore. For this recipe, I'm focusing on Dropbox.

To utilize Dropbox data storage in your application, you have to create a new app first. When you create the new app, Dropbox will ask if you're creating a Drop-in app or a Dropbox API app. Pick the latter.

Next, you'll be asked if you want to store "Files and datastores", or "datastores, only". Pick the "datastores only" option.

Last, the page asks for an app name. Once you provide it, you're all set. The tabbed page that opens provides the App key and App secret in the first tab page. You'll need the App key for the code in this recipe. For the example, you'll also need to provide a Redirect

URI for the OAuth 2.0 authentication purpose. This recipe is based on local development only, so use:

```
http://localhost:8080/
```

The server we're using is covered in the discussion.

Now, copy and paste or type the following code into an HTML file. Look for DROP BOX_APP_KEY and change the value to your newly created App key. This is the complete Dropbox datastore application allowing us to add key/value pairs to the datastore, review them, remove them individually or update them, or remove all of the key/value pairs in the default datastore:

```html
<!DOCTYPE html>
<html>
<head>
    <meta charset="utf-8">
    <title>Dropbox Data</title>
    <style>
      button {
         padding: 10px;
                 margin: 5px;
          }
         #control {
            margin-bottom: 20px;
            padding: 10px;
            background-color: palegreen;
            width: 300px;
         }
         #inputs {
            margin-bottom: 30px;
          }
         #addval {
            margin-top: 20px;
         }
    </style>
    <script
    src="https://www.dropbox.com/static/api/dropbox-datastores-1.2-latest.js">
    </script>
</head>
<body>
    <div id="control">
    <button id="dblogin" hidden>Login to Dropbox</button>
    <button id="dblogout">Logout and Cleanup</button><br />
    </div>
    <div id="inputs">
      <label for="newkey">Key:</label>
         <input type="text" id="dskey" name="dskey" />
      <label for="newval">Value:</label>
      <input type="text" id="dsval" name="dsval" /><br />
      <button id="addval">Add Record or Get Value</button>
         <button id="remrec">Remove Record</button>
```

```
        <button id="remrecs">Remove All Records</button>
</div>

<button id="showvalues">Show Values:</button>
<div id="result"></div>

<script>

      var DROPBOX_APP_KEY = 'yourappkey';
   var client = new Dropbox.Client({key: DROPBOX_APP_KEY});

      client.authenticate({ interactive: false });
      if (client.isAuthenticated()) {
             loggedIn();
      } else {
             document.getElementById("dblogin").removeAttribute("hidden");
      }

   document.getElementById('dblogin').onclick=function(e) {
       e.preventDefault();
        client.authenticate(function (err) {
       if (err) {
                console.log('Error: ' + err);
                   return;
             }
      loggedIn();
       });
      }

      function loggedIn() {
             document.getElementById('dblogin').setAttribute('hidden',true);
             var datastoreManager =
      new Dropbox.Datastore.DatastoreManager(client);

             datastoreManager.openDefaultDatastore(function (err, datastore) {
                if (err) {
                          console.log(err);
                             return;
                }

                var valueTable = datastore.getTable('values');

                document.getElementById('addval').onclick=function(e) {
                    var val = document.getElementById('dsval').value;
                        var key = document.getElementById('dskey').value;

                        var records = valueTable.query({'key':key});
                        if (records.length > 0) {
                            if(val && val.length > 0) {
                             records[0].set('value',val);
                             } else {
                             val = records[0].get('value');
```

```
                                      document.getElementById('dsval').value = val;
                                 }
                          } else {
                                 valueTable.insert({'key':key, 'value':val});
                          }

                  };

                  document.getElementById('remrec').onclick=function(e) {
                          var key = document.getElementById('dskey').value;
                          var records = valueTable.query({'key': key});
                          if (records.length > 0) {
                                 records[0].deleteRecord();
                          }
                  };

                  document.getElementById('remrecs').onclick=function(e) {
                          var records = valueTable.query();
                          records.forEach(function(record) {
                                 record.deleteRecord();
                          });
                  };

                  document.getElementById('showvalues').onclick=function(e) {
                  var records = valueTable.query();
                  var str = '';
                  records.forEach(function(record) {
                                 str+=record.get('value') + ' ';
                  });
                  document.getElementById('result').innerHTML = str;
                  };

              document.getElementById('dblogout').onclick=function(e) {
                  document.getElementById('dblogin').removeAttribute('hidden');
                  document.getElementById('result').innerHTML = '';
              client.signOut();
                  };
          });
       }
    </script>

  </body>
  </html>
```

Discussion

Most people think that Dropbox provides file-based cloud services, but like many other cloud systems, it also provides cloud-based data storage, too. Dropbox provides a set of Datastore SDKs for various environments:

- iOS
- OS X
- Android
- JavaScript
- Python
- HTTP

In this recipe, we're focused on the client-side JavaScript SDK, though the HTTP option would be good if you're interested in incorporating the data storage capability into a Node server app.

The Dropbox JavaScript SDK for data storage is available via CDN:

```
<script
src="https://www.dropbox.com/static/api/dropbox-datastores-1.2-latest.js">
</script>
```

Dropbox provides two example apps: Click the Box and Lists. I adapted Click the Box for the application covered in this recipe.

The app uses OAuth 2.0 authorization, which requires us to provide a Redirect URI in the Dropbox App page. You have to be precise, as you'll note from Figure 17-8, where I had to correct my Redirect URI after my first runtime error. You can also remove Redirect URIs.

Figure 17-8. OAuth requires precision—sloppy coding need not apply

You have two options for the type of Redirect URI you use. You can develop your application locally, and provide a localhost URI for the redirect; or you can serve the application via a web server that supports SSL (HTTPS). OAuth 2.0 doesn't *require* HTTPS, but because the data between the server and client is sent in plain text, most resources insist on HTTPS for all endpoint requests and authorization. Not all developers have access to SSL certificates, and some aren't equipped to provide support for HTTPS, so many resource providers also allow localhost URIs without HTTPS.

Thankfully, we as Node developers have other options, which I cover in detail in "Accessing Dropbox using OAuth 2.0 in a Web Page" on page 432.

The application in the solution, KeyValue, provides buttons to click to login to Dropbox and authorize, as well as log out and clean up, as shown in Figure 17-9. When the page is first opened, the Dropbox login button is displayed. However, the next time you access the page, you're already still logged in, so this button is hidden. It's only displayed again when we click the logout button.

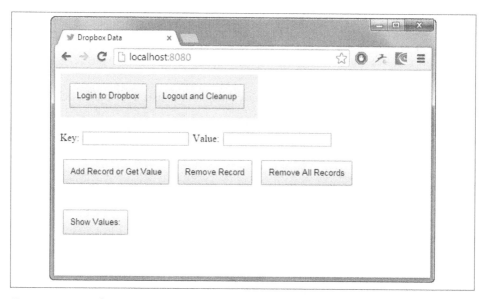

Figure 17-9. Application page when first loaded

Other buttons are used to add and edit key/value pairs, remove a single pair, display all existing values, and remove all key/value pairs from the datastore.

Returning to the JavaScript in the KeyValue HTML page, the very first action the code takes is creating a new Dropbox.client, passing the DROPBOX_APP_KEY —our app key assigned by Dropbox. Once the client is created, the authenticate is called, but with the option interactive set to false. The authenticate() method is what we use to trigger the authorization process, but we don't want to trigger this process if we're already authorized. Calling authenticate() with interactive set to false populates the Dropbox.client with information, including whether the application has been authorized data storage access or not.

In the next line of code, the code tests to see if the client object has been authenticated. If so, the code calls the function loggedIn(). If not, then the Dropbox login button is displayed, and the application waits for the user to click the button. The click event handler function calls authenticate() without the flag, which does trigger the authorization process. The user is taken to the Dropbox authorization page, shown in Figure 17-10, to authorize the app's access to the user's data storage.

Figure 17-10. Dropbox authorization page for authorizing the recipe app

After the user clicks the Allow button in the Dropbox authorization page, she's returned to the KeyValue app, where the Login button is now hidden. Now the application is ready to process requests to add data to the Dropbox data storage.

The highest level of object in the Dropbox data storage schema is the datastore, which is somewhat comparable to a relational database, at a very trivial level. It can be used by a single user, or it can be shared among Dropbox users in a work group situation (e.g., Dropbox for Business users). It can also be shared publicly. Be aware, though, that by default the datastore exists in isolation. If Person A uses KeyValue, the data is added to that person's own version of the default datastore—not a version shared by all users of the application (not unless the datastore is specifically shared with other individuals).

The details on data sharing are covered in the very good Datastore API (*https://www.dropbox.com/developers/datastore/docs/js*) for JavaScript documentation.

The datastore is managed via the `DatastoreManager` object instance, created as the first Dropbox operation in the `loggedIn()` function. We can create new datastores, but we can also make use of the default datastore (default, per user, of course). The key/value app created in the solution makes use of the default datastore, via the `datastoreManager.openDefaultDatastore()` function call, which has one parameter: a callback function. Most of the functionality for the app is defined in this callback.

Once the code has access to the default datastore, `datastore.getTable()` is called for a table labeled `values`. What follows is interesting, if you've primarily worked with relational databases. Tables aren't created, first, before use. Once the code to access the `values` table is processed, you won't find a copy of the table in the datastore. It won't exist until an actual record is added to the table. You can check this out yourself by browsing your app's datastores, once they're created, or data has been added. The entry point is accessible via the App Console, and the browser looks similar to that shown in Figure 17-11.

Datastores	Records	
▼ default	id	_183vd5fd1eg_js_QG7Vq
values	key	A1
▶ .4bSKEdppqvCcY5p3vcLLIoP...	value	Apples
▶ .8AEJfPFz_Q78yDOJqVdX-R8e...		
▶ .8JKqOVboCLXNSYpTeLCCyu...	id	_183vd5mmmvo_js_QQckF
▶ .8Wf-c_YAd2dn5Gm8umz4p...	key	A2
▶ .COlCC8jYEmcEtlekhjtSvfDSX...	value	Artichokes
▶ .D8YeRb4xbp4lEVd_KgaofGz...	id	_183vd5sc2mg_js_S_WT3
▶ .Evf8UpDpHpsTA_r0YHYb8Y...	key	B1
▶ .G0qnTF3JsasLszQ2XwP9f4Q...	value	Bananas
▶ .JxXjwWN6bxwgA4VzFFLr2dR...	id	183vd658o1o is DZuOu

Figure 17-11. Browsing among the Dropbox datastores for the KeyValue app

Dropbox doesn't create tables until a record is added, and doesn't maintain the shell of the table when the last record is deleted. It's more of a virtual grouping, than an actual physical implementation. When the code calls `getTable()`, what's happening is either a reference is returned to an existing table (previously created by the addition of a record), or a reference to a potential table is returned.

What you won't see in the code at this point is a call to setResolutionRule() on the table. The method is used to control how conflicts are managed when two sources are attempting to update the data at the same time. The method has the following format:

```
table.setResolutionRule('fieldname', 'rule');
```

Conflict resolution is at the field level, and resolution consists of one of the following values:

- remote: Remote change is selected to resolve conflicts
- local: Local change is selected to resolve conflicts
- max: Resolves in favor of the largest value, based on type ordering
- min: Resolves in favor of the smallest value, again based on type ordering
- sum: For numeric values, calculates all additions and subtractions to come to a final value; for nonnumeric, acts like remote

The remote rule is the default and that works for the KeyValue app.

The click event handler for the rest of the buttons are defined next in the solution.

The click event handler function for adding or editing a new key/value pair performs a datastore query using query() on the KeyValue table. The query() method searches for data matching the property/value pairs passed as an object to the method, returning matched records. By the very nature of the approach KeyValue is using, we don't have to worry about duplicate records for each key, because if the key matches, the new value just replaces the existing value.

The code checks if the key value exists. If it does, and the associated input field for the value isn't empty, then the record is *updated*, using the set() method. If the input field for the value is empty, then the process is treated as a retrieval, and the associated value field is displayed in the input field. Lastly, if the dskey value doesn't exist, a new record is created using insert().

Another approach to retrieve or insert the record is using an identifier and the record getOrInsert() method, providing all the fields as an object. Right now, the KeyValue pair is using default generated IDs for the record, as Figure 17-11 demonstrates.

The next click event handler is for the button to remove a record. The function queries for the record on the dskey, and if the returned array of records has at least one element, the first record is deleted with deleteRecord(). The code doesn't check for any others, because there should be only the one record. However, the code could be modified to delete all, just in case the delightful *unintended consequences* happen:

```
records.forEach(function(record) {
    record.deleteRecord();
});
```

The next `click` handler removes all records for a table by doing a `query()` with no parameter, returning all records, and then deleting each. This also, in effect, *deletes* the table, because a table is defined by its records.

The button to show all values triggers a full query, traverses all the returned records, and prints out the values, as demonstrated in Figure 17-12.

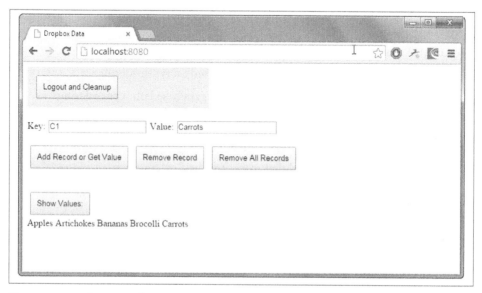

Figure 17-12. Showing all stored values currently in the datastore table

The last button is the one to log out of the application, and do general clean up. This means displaying the login button again, and setting the show values display result to an empty string. The `client.signOut()` method "invalidates and forgets the user's Dropbox OAuth 2 authorization tokens," as we'd all hope and expect that it would.

The server running the application is as simple as it can be—a Node server listening for specific routes, and serving up the appropriate response:

```
var http = require('http');
var router = require('router');
var route = router();
var fs = require('fs');

route.get('/', function(req, res) {
  fs.readFile(__dirname + '/index.html',
    function (err, data) {
```

```
    if (err) {
      res.writeHead(500);
      return res.end('Error loading index.html');
    }
    res.writeHead(200);
    res.end(data);
  });
});

http.createServer(route).listen(8080); // start the server on port 8080
```

Be forewarned, though, that the server will only work when run locally (using local host). A discussion why is covered in the section on the OAuth framework in "Extra: Setting Up HTTPS for Testing" on page 433.

The Dropbox datastore API is well documented, clean to implement, usable across a variety of enviroments, and makes a good application cache across devices.

## CHAPTER 18

JavaScript Hits the (Mobile) Road

JavaScript is more than client/server applications on traditional computers. Thanks to a plethora of Web APIs and new tools, JavaScript is now an integral part of mobile application development—whether as part of HTML5 applications in mobile browsers or standalone applications.

The types of mobile environments are increasing, too. Google's Android joins with Apple's iOS, Microsoft's Windows 8, and even less popular environments such as the Firefox OS and Chromebook's OS. Even online store king, Amazon, has introduced a variation of Android called Fire OS for its own devices.

In this chapter, I'm focusing primarily on variations of Android (including Fire OS) and HTML5 web apps, with a little exploration into Firefox OS and Chrome-flavored web apps.

 If you're interested in exercising your JavaScript skills creating iOS apps, I suggest Apple's own documentation (*http://bit.ly/1yI3vh7*), or *Programming iOS 7* (O'Reilly). And if you're interested in Windows 8 app development, Microsoft provides excellent documentation (*http://bit.ly/1E00Rn9*). Microsoft also provides a free e-book, *Programming Windows 8 Apps with HTML, CSS, and JavaScript* (*http://bit.ly/1E00R6o*).

18.1. Creating an Installable, Hosted Web App

Problem

You want to create a web app hosted on your server without having to target specific environments or devices. And you want the app to actually install, not sit there in a browser.

Solution

To create an installable web app, you only need to add some additional material to an already working web page application.

First, create a 128x128 pixel PNG file to add as your application's icon. In addition, if you expect your app to work offline, you need to provide an AppCache file. You'll also need to provide some meta elements to your primary web page's head element.

The following HTML page is set up for installation on an Android smartphone or tablet. The application gets your current location using the Geolocation API, and then gets a static map image from Google Maps with your location centered in the map:

```html
<!DOCTYPE html>
<html manifest="cache.appcache">
   <head>
      <meta charset="utf-8">
      <title>Where Am I?</title>
      <meta name="mobile-web-app-capable" content="yes">

      <link rel="manifest" href="manifest.json">

<!-- Fallback application metadata for legacy browsers -->
      <meta name="description" content="A Where am I map app">
      <meta name="application_name" content="Where Am I?">
      <meta name="viewport" content="width=device-width, initial-scale=1">
      <link rel="shortcut icon" sizes="128x128" href="img/icons/icon128x128.png">

<!-- Source files -->
      <link rel="stylesheet" href="/work/where/css/app.css">
      <script src="/work/where/js/map.js"></script>
      <script src="/work/where/js/app.js"></script>
   </head>
   <body>
      <section>
         <h1>Where Am I</h1>
         <p><button id="getmap">Get Map</button></p>
         <div id="out"></div>
      </section>
   </body>
</html>
```

Discussion

A web app is really any application that can be accessed in a browser on the Web, using HTML, CSS, graphics, JavaScript, and so on. An *installable* web app is the same, but with a few extra elements.

To demonstrate how to create an installable web app, we'll create a simple web application that uses the Geolocation API to find the individual's current location, and then uses this to get a copy of a static image from Google Maps, with the location centered in the map.

The application has two JavaScript files: an *app.js* file to set up the application, and a *map.js* file to get the location and the map.

The *app.js* file just has code to access the window.onload event handler, and then attaches an event handler function to the web page button's click event:

```
window.onload=function() {
    document.getElementById("getmap").onclick=geoFindMe;
}
```

The *map.js* file has code to call the Geolocation API's getCurrentPosition() method to get the current location's latitude and longitude. The geolocation object that implements the Geolocation API is accessible from the navigator object. When calling getCurrentPostion(), two functions are passed to the method: a success and a failure function. In the success function, the code then uses the position, passed as argument, to get the current longitude and latitude. These are used to form a REST request for a static map image from Google Maps. They're also printed out to the web page, as is an error message if the Geolocation method fails. The static map image is assigned to a new img element, which is appended to the page:

```
function geoFindMe() {
    var output = document.getElementById("out");

    if (!navigator.geolocation){
      output.innerHTML = "<p>Geolocation is not supported by your browser</p>";
      return;
    }

    function success(position) {
      var latitude  = position.coords.latitude;
      var longitude = position.coords.longitude;

      output.innerHTML = '<p>Latitude is ' + latitude + ' <br>Longitude is ' +
      longitude + '</p>';

      var img = new Image();
      img.src = "http://maps.googleapis.com/maps/api/staticmap?center=" +
      latitude + "," + longitude + "&zoom=13&size=300x300&sensor=false";

      output.appendChild(img);
    };
    function error() {
      output.innerHTML = "Unable to retrieve your location";
    };

    output.innerHTML = "<p>Locating…</p>";
```

```
    navigator.geolocation.getCurrentPosition(success, error);
  }
```

The CSS is very simple (defining a yellow background for the page just to jazz it up a bit):

```
html, body {
  margin: 0;
  padding: 0.5rem;
}

body {
  font-size: 1rem;
  background: yellow;
}

h1 {
  margin: 0 0 1rem 0;
}

p {
  font-size: inherit;
}
```

The *index.html* file should be more than familiar, except for the meta elements, and one link. The meta elements provide information about the page in a mobile setting, as well as providing metadata for all environments. The meta element for the viewport provides instructions for how the application is viewed in a mobile setting. The settings are standard for most mobile applications: the width=device-width sets the width of the application to the device's optimum width, and the initial-scale=1 sets the zoom scale, and the initial zoom value:

```
<meta name="description" content="A Where Am I app">
<meta name="application_name" content="Where Am I?">
<meta name="viewport" content="width=device-width, initial-scale=1">
```

The link for the icon specifies the icon that will represent the application when it's on the mobile device's *home screen*. Web apps should have, at minimum, one icon that's 128x128 pixels:

```
<link rel="shortcut icon" sizes="128x128" href="img/icons/icon128x128.png"
```

The manifest setting specifies the AppCache file for the application. Mobile devices can go offline, so it's important to ensure it works in all environments. Because the app we're creating really depends on Internet access, I didn't spend much time on offline fallback. The AppCache file I created, *cache.appcache*, is in the following code:

```
CACHE MANIFEST

# version
```

```
js/map.js
js/app.js
css/app.css
img/icons/icon128x128.png

NETWORK:
*
```

The resource files have to be listed, and the NETWORK setting allows any network resource access. The latter is essential, because we can't specify the RESTful request for the map image—it changes for every location.

 I derived my AppCache file based on advice in the absolutely essential and colorfully named A List Apart article "Application Cache is a DoucheBag" (*http://bit.ly/appcache-db*).

The last file, *manifest.json*, is based on work underway at the W3C to agree on a manifest file format for web apps. However, support for the file is limited in web apps, which is why I provide the fallback meta element definitions. Still, providing the file should help future-proof the app:

```
{
  "name": "Where Am I?",
  "short_name": "WhereAmI",
  "icons": [{
    "src": "img/icons/icon128x128.png",
    "sizes": "128x128",
  }],
  "start_url": "/work/where/index.html",
  "display": "standalone",
  "orientation": "portrait",
}
```

The entries should be self explanatory. Icons are listed in an array and described by attribute; in this case, src and sizes. The start_url ensures the right web page is loaded to start the app:

```
The specification for the manifest.json file is at
http://w3c.github.io/manifest/[http://w3c.github.io/manifest/].
```

It's linked into the *index.html* file:

```
<link rel="manifest" href="manifest.json">
```

The last unusual page entry is the following:

```
<meta name="mobile-web-app-capable" content="yes">
```

Chrome looks for this setting in the head element, to determine whether the application can run standalone in the mobile environment. It adds an "Add to homescreen" option to the browser menu when the app is loaded in the Chrome browser. Google insists on this attribute. A comparable item that Safari uses for the same principle in iOS is:

```
<meta name="apple-mobile-web-app-capable" content="yes">
```

Google originally supported this value, but has deprecated it, and warned about its use.

That's the last of the special settings. Because Chrome is now the default browser in Android devices (*not* Kindle Fire OS devices), your app should be installable in Android with the settings outlined. Once users upload the app and navigate to the app's directory, and the app is loaded, they'll be able to click the "Add to homescreen" option, to *install* it on the home screen, as shown in Figure 18-1.

Figure 18-1. Where Am I? web app installed on Nexus 7 tablet

I use italics with *install* because unlike native Android apps, the web app isn't technically installed in the device. A snapshot of the app is uploaded to the device, stripped of all browser chrome, and accessible by an icon. Underneath it all, though, it's still a web page in a browser. The browser is just not visible.

Browser-based or not, the app still has access to a considerable number of device-specific APIs, which I'll demonstrate later in the chapter.

See Also

For an excellent resource on the constraints of web apps, hosted or packaged, read "Installing web apps natively" (*http://bit.ly/1E04dGL*) by Dr. Axel Rauschmayer (my go-to guy for all things JavaScript).

The Where Am I? app gets moved to a native Android app, Firefox OS, Chrome, and Amazon Fire OS in the next several recipes. First, though, we're going to take web apps for a ride in the Amazon Appstore in Recipe 18.2.

18.2. Packaging Web Apps for the Amazon Appstore

Problem

You've created a web app that works as a hosted app, but you want to package it for distribution in Amazon's Appstore.

Solution

Change to the root directory for your web app, and zip the contents. In Linux, to package the Where Am I? web app for installing on Fire devices, run the following command:

```
zip -r where.zip *
```

You can then test the application using Amazon's Web App Tester app, which tests hosted and packaged apps.

Discussion

A web app for Amazon's Fire universe is probably the simplest of the web app environments. At the time this was written you don't need a *manifest.json* file, and Amazon provides a very detailed list of what specifications will and won't work. In addition, if you want to support in-app purchases, Amazon also provides a downloadable SDK, as well as APIs for various other functionality (maps, Amazon login, etc.).

Amazon expects the launch page for both hosted and packaged apps to be *index.html*. It has to be at the top level for the directory for the hosted app, and it must be at the top level of the zipped file. The Where Am I? app covered in Recipe 18.1 has the following directory structure:

```
cache.appcache
css/
    app.css
img/
```

```
icons/
    icon128x128.png
    icon16x16.png
    icon48x48.png
    icon60x60.png
    icon.svg
index.html
js/
    app.js
    map.js
manifest.json
```

Amazon doesn't require the *manifest.json* file, and the packaged app doesn't require *cache.appcache*, so both of these can be deleted. References to them should be removed from the *index.html* file, and the references to JavaScript and CSS files should be relative to the *index.html* file, not to the hosted environment:

```
<link rel="stylesheet" href="/work/where/css/app.css">
<script src="/work/where/js/map.js"></script>
<script src="/work/where/js/app.js"></script>
```

The Amazon documentation notes that the application is zipped outside of the project, but this fails, as the *index.html* file isn't at the top level. Instead, change to the project directory and run the zip command. In Linux:

```
zip -r where.zip *
```

Once the package is zipped, it's ready for testing. Amazon has a test tool, the Amazon Web App Tester, that you can install on a Fire device. It tests hosted and packaged apps, both verifying the app and then testing it. It can also install the app locally on the device. Figure 18-2 shows the results of running a test against two versions of Where Am I?— one where the *index.html* is top-level, and one not, which generates an error.

The Where Am I? app works without tweaks because, as Amazon's Device Component Support Matrix notes, the Geolocation API is supported in all Fire devices.

 The Amazon Web App portal page (*https://developer.amazon.com/ public*) is the place to start before porting your app into the Fire environment. The Amazon APIs (*https://developer.amazon.com/ public/apis*) lists all the various APIs you can utilize in your app, and the Device Component Support Matrix (*http://bit.ly/1yI3tFT*) provides very precise information about what JavaScript features work in which device.

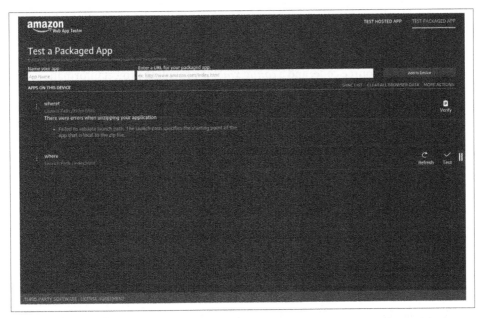

Figure 18-2. Testing two packaged apps in a Fire HDX tablet using Web App Tester

18.3. Building a Basic Android App Using Cordova (PhoneGap)

Problem

You want to create an Android standalone application, but you definitely aren't interested in getting deep into Java Development.

Solution

Use Cordova, the command-line tool that is the foundation for the more well-known PhoneGap.

Once Cordova is installed, create a directory for your work. In the directory, run a command similar to the following, but change the name *myapp* to your application name:

```
cordova create myapp com.example.myapp MyApp
```

Only the first argument for the `create` command, the name of the project directory, is required. Make sure you don't create the directory before running the command. The second argument is the reverse domain identifier for the project, and the third is the title for the application. The latter two arguments aren't required, but if you want to provide a project title, you do need to provide the reverse domain identifier—the arguments are place dependent. Cordova provides default values for both, so I strongly recommend using your own.

A directory is created and named *myapp*. In the directory are several directories containing generated source code, and a *config.xml* file providing project information. The directory of interest to you is *www*, which contains the source files you'll need to modify to create your application. The contents should be familiar to you—they're HTML, CSS, and JavaScript.

We're making an Android application, so we need to add support for the Android platform. In the top work directory, run the following command:

```
cordova platform add android
```

A new subdirectory named *platforms* is created and includes the Android support code. At this time, you can build the Android application and get the default Cordova Android application:

```
cordova build
```

You can run the application using the Android emulator:

```
cordova emulate android
```

Figure 18-3 shows the icon for the the generated application in the emulator, and Figure 18-4 shows the application after it is opened.

Figure 18-3. Displaying the icon for the default generated Android app

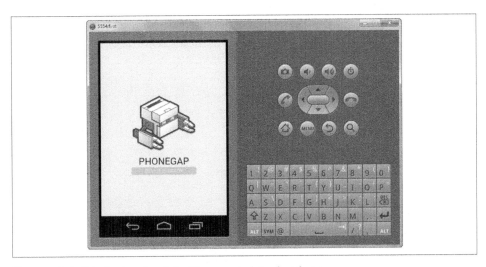

Figure 18-4. Displaying the default generated Android app

If you have an Android device, attach it via USB to the computer, and run the following to install and launch the application in the device:

```
cordova run android
```

More details on how all this works, and how to finish the full implementation of the application, are in the discussion.

Discussion

Cordova is the functionality behind the more well-known PhoneGap. When Adobe purchased the company behind PhoneGap, it split off the platform software and donated it to the Apache organization to maintain.

Cordova requires Node.js. Once Node is installed (in Windows, Mac, or Linux), you can install Cordova with the following:

```
sudo npm install -g cordova
```

> Access documentation for working with Cordova at *http://cordo va.apache.org/*.

Cordova is a command-line tool that has the advantage of being fast to learn and simple to use. Though this recipe is focused on Android, you can install additional platform support for other devices (which I'll cover later in the chapter). However, the platforms you can develop for depends on the operating system you're using for your development. If you're using a Mac, you can create applications for the following environments:

- iOS
- Amazon's Fire OS
- Android
- Blackberry 10
- Firefox OS

If you're using a Linux-based computer:

- Amazon's Fire OS
- Android
- Blackberry 10
- Firefox OS

And in Windows:

- Amazon's Fire OS
- Android
- Blackberry 10
- Windows Phone 7
- Windows Phone 8
- Windows 8
- Firefox OS

There are additional constraints for the environments, such as installing Visual Studio support for developing Windows apps, but for now, we'll focus on Android.

According to the Cordova Android Platform Guide (*http://bit.ly/1E070Q9*), you'll need to install the Android SDK (*http://developer.android.com/sdk/index.html*) before developing Android apps. You'll also need to install the Java JDK (version 6 at the time this was written), as well as Apache Ant.

Chances are you have a Java runtime on your computer, but you'll need the full Java Developer Kit (JDK) to work with Android. You can download the Java JDK at its download page (*http://bit.ly/TEA7iC*). Apache Ant can be downloaded from the Apache Ant site (*http://ant.apache.org/*). It can also be installed with npm:

```
npm install ant
```

Apache Ant is the Java version of Grunt, covered in Recipe 12.14. You don't have to be proficient with it to develop in Android. You just need to have the software installed.

You can install an Android installation package that also includes the Eclipse IDE (Integrated Development Environment), but for now, just install the standalone SDK. You'll also need to install support for at least one version of Android. Cordova supports Gingerbread (version 2.3), and 4.x versions. As a general rule, Cordova only supports versions with at least 5% popularity in the distribution dashboard that Google maintains, as shown in Figure 18-5.

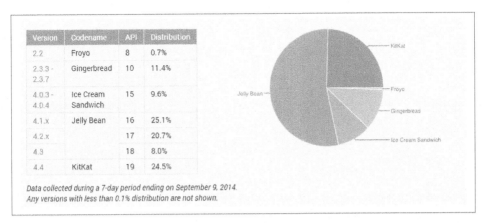

Figure 18-5. Android version distribution as of August 12, 2014

If you're developing in Windows, use the SDK Manager.exe tool to install the Android versions, as shown in Figure 18-6.

The Cordova documentation states that you can focus your mobile development two different ways: cross-platform, or platform specific. If you're only interested in developing Android applications, you might want to check out the IDEs, such as Eclipse, or Google's new Android Studio beta. However, if you're interested in developing apps for multiple device types, then you'll want to stick with Cordova, and the Cordova CLI, as your main development environment. This chapter focuses on the cross-platform approach.

Cordova comes with an emulator (and the Android SDK also provides access to an emulator), but if you want to try your app on the real thing, you'll need to connect your Android device(s) to your computer via USB cord. You'll also need to make sure your device is set up for Android debugging, and that you have the proper drivers installed.

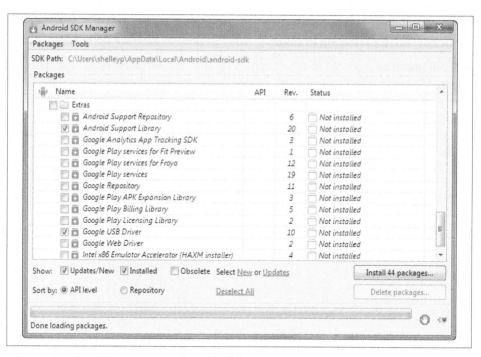

Figure 18-6. Installing versions of Android from the SDK

To set up USB debugging on your device, if your Android device is running a version of Android older than 4.0, the developer settings can be accessed via Settings→Applications→Development. If you're running a version between 4.0 and 4.2, access developer settings in Settings→Developer. If you're running a newer version of Android, this setting is actually hidden. To expose it, access Settings→About Phone, and then tap the Build number seven times. Yeah, I know—lame. But that's what you have to do.

In the Developer options window, check the option to enable USB Debugging, as shown in Figure 18-7.

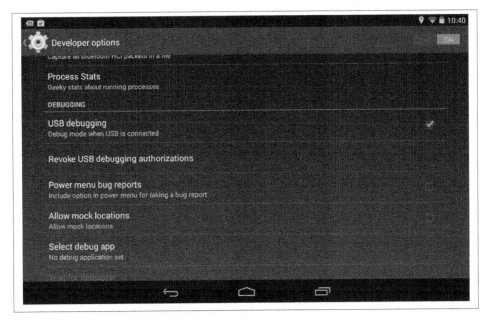

Figure 18-7. Checking the option for USB Debugging in Developer settings

You'll also need to set your PC to recognize your Android device. If you're using a Mac, you're all set, but if you're using Windows, you'll need to download a USB device driver from Google (*http://developer.android.com/sdk/win-usb.html*). If you're developing with Linux, the settings are defined in the Using Hardware Devices documentation (*http://developer.android.com/tools/device.html*).

Following the Windows route, I plugged in the Android phone, and then in the hardware manager, right-clicked on the device and chose the option to install the device driver downloaded from Google. Once the device driver was installed, and USB Debugging enabled, running the following command installed a debugging version of the Android app (an APK, with an .apk extension) on the device and launched it:

```
cordova run Android
```

Cordova finds the device and handles all of the build and installation for you.

Of course now is when the fun begins, as you design and build your own unique Android application; but for now, let's just assume the generated app is the one you want, and you want to finalize it as a standalone application. To create a standalone application, you'll need to digitally sign the APK with a certificate whose private keys are maintained by the developer. Then, you'll need to find a way to install the device on your Android devices.

If you don't have any other way of creating a *self-signed certificate*, you can use Keytool, which is part of the Java SDK. From a Windows command window, I ran the following command, which generates a key for an application named MyApp, stored in *release.keystore*, in a directory I added at the top level of my working environment:

```
keytool.exe -getkey -v keystore release.keystore
-alias MyApp -keyalg RSA -keysize 2048 -validity 10000
```

The tool will ask several questions, and prompt you for two passwords. Be sure you back up the generated key, because if you lose it, you won't be able to update your application in the Google Play store.

 For more information on signing the Android app, check out "How do I Create a Self-Signed Certificate for an Android App" (*http://bit.ly/1E08Bpd*), and the Android documentation on signing your app (*http://bit.ly/1E08wSf*).

Now that you have your key, you need to provide a way for the build process to know where to find it. This is where you'll need to modify the platform installation, even though Cordova warns against it. However, you're not modifying an existing source—you're just adding an Ant file with the path for the key.

In *platforms/android*, add a new file named *ant.properties*, and add the following lines of code to it:

```
key.store=/Users/whoareyou/work/keys/release.keystore
key.alias=MyApp
```

Change the code to match your own environment, and the alias you gave when you generated the key.

Now, to create a released version of the Android app, run the following:

```
cordova build --release
```

The build process will prompt you for the key passwords you provided earlier. A new released version of your app is created in *platforms/android/ant-build*, named something like *MyApp-release.apk*.

Now that you have your signed, released version of your Android application, how do you install it?

You can copy it over via the USB cord to a subdirectory on your Android device, but you may run into an odd parsing error if you do so. That's because of permission problems with the app, and the subdirectory where you loaded the app. You can use a file manager app to change these, but a simpler approach is to upload the APK file to Google Drive, Dropbox, or whatever cloud service you use with all your devices. Not only is this the simplest way to access your app, you can access the app with *all* your devices. Upload the Android app to your cloud drive, open up a reference to the drive in your Android device, and click on the app. The device will then begin the installation process.

You also have to enable *sideloading* for your Android device, which means loading apps from unknown sources. Check the option to enable sideloading in Settings→Security.

Congratulations, you just created your first standalone Android app.

18.4. Porting Where Am I? to Android

Problem

Web apps are all well and good, but you'd really like to package your web app functionality into a standalone Android app.

Solution

Now that we're set and ready to create all sorts of havoc in the Android world, let's take a shot at porting the Where Am I? geolocation app, developed as a web app in Recipe 18.1, into a native Android app.

Create a new directory in the work environment and call it *vanilla*, as in a plain vanilla Android app. In this directory, create a new Cordova project with the following command—changing the domain in the reverse domain to your own (or preferred) domain:

```
create whereami com.yourdomain.whereami WhereAmI
```

Next, change into the newly created *whereami* directory, and add support for Android:

```
cordova platform add android
```

The source files that the platform depends on are located in the top-level *www* directory. We're going to delete most of the generated code, because we want to create an interface as close as possible to the one we created for the web app.

The generated files and directories for the source files are:

```
www/
    css/
        index.css
    img/
        logo.png
    js/
        index.js
    index.html
```

We can use the generated *logo.png* file, or copy the *logo128x128.png* file from the web app over, and rename it *logo.png*. It's your call what you'd prefer to do.

I deleted most of the CSS in *index.css*, and added a few minor edits, resulting in the following:

```css
body {
    -webkit-touch-callout: none;
    -webkit-text-size-adjust: none;
    -webkit-user-select: none;
    background-color:yellow;
    font-family:'HelveticaNeue-Light',
      'HelveticaNeue', Helvetica, Arial, sans-serif;
    font-size:18px;
    height:100%;
    margin-left: 100px;
    padding:0px;
    text-transform:uppercase;
    width:100%;
}

button {
    padding: 10px;
}
```

I did the same with the *index.html* file. I removed portions, and added both the button and output div element, as well as a link to the new *map.js* file:

```html
<!DOCTYPE html>

<html>
    <head>
        <meta charset="utf-8" />
        <meta name="format-detection" content="telephone=no" />
        <meta name="viewport" content="user-scalable=no,
        initial-scale=1, maximum-scale=1, minimum-scale=1,
        width=device-width,
        height=device-height, target-densitydpi=device-dpi" />
        <link rel="stylesheet" type="text/css" href="css/index.css" />
        <meta name="msapplication-tap-highlight" content="no" />
        <title>Where Am I?</title>
    </head>
    <body>
        <h1>Where Am I?</h1>
        <button id="getmap">Get Map</button>
        <div id="out"></div>
      <script src="cordova.js"></script>
        <script type="text/javascript" src="js/map.js"></script>
        <script type="text/javascript" src="js/index.js"></script>
            <script type="text/javascript">
          app.initialize();
        </script>
    </body>
</html>
```

The *index.js* file was primarily a skeleton interface to several device—specific events. I left most of the skeleton, but trimmed out the comments and added the code to attach an event handler function to the button's click event into the onDeviceReady event handler:

```
var app = {
    // Application Constructor
    initialize: function() {
        this.bindEvents();
    },
    bindEvents: function() {
        document.addEventListener('deviceready', this.onDeviceReady, false);
    },
    onDeviceReady: function() {
        app.receivedEvent('deviceready');
        document.getElementById('getmap').onclick=geoFindMe;
                console.log('device is ready');
    },
    receivedEvent: function(id) {
        console.log('Received Event: ' + id);
    }
};
```

The deviceready event is called after Cordova is loaded, so the app can call Cordova JavaScript functions safely at this point. It's a good place to put our listener for the button's click event.

The *map.js* file is an exact copy of the *map.js* file created in Recipe 18.1:

```
function geoFindMe() {
  console.log('in geoFindMe');
  var output = document.getElementById("out");

  if (!navigator.geolocation){
    output.innerHTML = "<p>Geolocation is not supported by your browser</p>";
    return;
  }

  function success(position) {
    var latitude  = position.coords.latitude;
    var longitude = position.coords.longitude;

    output.innerHTML = '<p>Latitude is ' + latitude + '° <br>Longitude is '
    + longitude + '°</p>';

    var img = new Image();
    img.src = "http://maps.googleapis.com/maps/api/staticmap?center="
    + latitude + ","
    + longitude + "&zoom=13&size=300x300&sensor=false";

    output.appendChild(img);
  };
```

```
function error() {
  output.innerHTML = "Unable to retrieve your location";
};

output.innerHTML = "<p>Locating...</p>";

navigator.geolocation.getCurrentPosition(success, error);
}
```

We're done with the source files, but not the configuration. Because we're working with Geolocation, there is one other change we have to make. Back in the root directory for the application, add the Geolocation plugin:

```
cordova plugin add
  https://git-wip-us.apache.org/repos/asf/cordova-plugin-geolocation.git
```

Now, we're ready to build:

```
cordova build
```

To run the Android app in your device, make sure USB debugging is set up in the device, and connect it with a USB cable. Run the following command:

```
cordova run android
```

As an alternative, we can also run the app in an emulator:

```
cordova emulate android
```

The new app should load into the device/emulator. Once loaded, click the "Get Map" button and the map should display in the page, as shown in Figure 18-8.

Figure 18-8. The Where Am I? app displayed in a Nexus 7 tablet

Once you're satisfied, you can complete the rest of the steps to sign and package the app into a release APK, to send to friends and family.

Discussion

Existing web apps can be ported into a standalone Android app using Cordova. Once the project is created, modify the existing JavaScript, CSS, and *index.html* files to incorporate your web app functionality and look and feel. You can keep or delete as much of the generated content in the pages as you want. The important takeaway from the solution is that depending on what resources your web app accesses, you may need to take a couple of extra steps (adding a plugin and modifying the manifest and *config.xml* files to add permissions).

What underlies Cordova's web interface is Android's WebView component. This is a component that allows native Android developers (those working in Java) to embed a web app into their applications. WebView is based on Webkit, for older versions of Android, and Chromium, starting with KitKat (version 4.4).

Extra: Adding jQuery Mobile Support to a Cordova Android App

I'm not a web designer, as is probably apparent from my example screenshots in the book. If I want to publicly publish web pages or apps, I either use existing template/ themes, or use a library like jQuery Mobile to provide a more polished interface. Thanks to Cordova's WebView component platform, and the underlying Webkit/Chromium engine, what works in a browser like Chrome should work (with some constraints) in Cordova apps, and that includes incorporating support for jQuery Mobile.

To use jQuery Mobile, download the necessary JavaScript and CSS files, and add them as a separate subdirectory in your Cordova app's *www* directory. To demonstrate, we'll add jQuery Mobile support to Where Am I? and see if we can't jazz it up a little. At the time this was written, the additions of the jQuery Mobile files resulted in the following directory structure under *www/*:

```
css/
    index.css
img/
    logo.png
js/
    index.js
    map.js
lib
    jquery/
        css/
            /images
              ...
            jquery.mobile-1.2.0.min.css
        js/
            jquery.mobile-1.2.0.min.js
            jquery-1.8.2.min.js
```

The exact versions of the files will most likely be different when you try the example, but they're included in the examples as a snapshot. The *images* subdirectoy has all the possible images for the UI, so I haven't listed the files. You do need this subdirectory, or the application fails.

I'm not modifying the existing JavaScript files (*index.js* or *map.js*) at this time, but you can adapt them to use jQuery syntax. For now, I'm focused on adapting the HTML file. In the file, we'll add the jQuery JavaScript and CSS files. We'll also adjust the HTML to take advantage of jQuery Mobile's data- attribute names. The modified HTML file is displayed in Example 18-1. The minor modifications in the local CSS file is to add in the Where Am I? yellow background, and ensure the sections align nicely.

Example 18-1. The modified index.html incorporating jQuery Mobile structures

```html
<!DOCTYPE html>

<html>
  <head>
    <title>Where Am I?</title>
    <meta charset="utf-8" />
    <meta name="format-detection" content="telephone=no" />
    <meta name="viewport" content="width=device-width, initial-scale=1">
    <link rel="stylesheet" href="css/index.css">
        <link rel="stylesheet" href="lib/jquery/css/jquery.mobile-1.2.0.min.css" />
    <style>
          .ui-page, .ui-content { background-color: yellow; height: 100%}
        </style>
    <script src="lib/jquery/js/jquery-1.8.2.min.js"></script>
    <script src="lib/jquery/js/jquery.mobile-1.2.0.min.js"></script>
    </head>
    <body>
          <div data-role="page">
          <div data-role="header">
            <h1>Adventures in Geolocation</h1>
          </div><!-- /header -->
          <div data-role="content">
            <h1>Where Am I?</h1>

            <button id="getmap">Click Me!</button>
                      <div id="out"></div>
                      <img id="map" />
          </div><!-- /content -->
          <div data-role="footer" data-position="fixed">
            <h4>Wherever you go, there you are</h4>
          </div><!-- /footer -->
        </div><!-- /page -->

      <script type="text/javascript" src="cordova.js"></script>
      <script type="text/javascript" src="js/map.js"></script>
      <script type="text/javascript" src="js/index.js"></script>
              <script>
                app.initialize();
              </script>
    </body>
</html>
```

I built the example for both Android and Amazon Fire OS. Figure 18-9 shows the app loaded into my HTC smartphone.

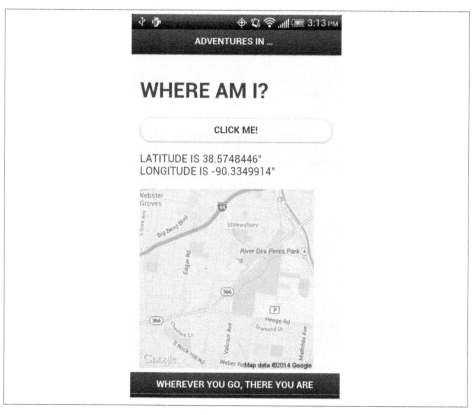

Figure 18-9. Screenshot of Where Am I? modified to use jQuery Mobile for interface improvements

See Also

The basic Android app of Where Am I? just created is also the basis for creating a version to run in a Kindle Fire device, covered in Recipe 18.7.

JavaScript Completely Out of the Box

There's another dimension to JavaScript development and that's the new open source hardware, DIY, and wearables. Yes, you can use JavaScript to build an air-quality control sensor. Or to control the pattern of LEDs sewn into a jacket, causing it to indicate how close you are to your target location. Or to operate a motion sensor and camera to create your own critter cam. Or...well, you get the point. The possibilities are endless.

But there are some topics that just can't be squished into single recipes, though I've tried a time or two in this book. The DIY, open source hardware development has preliminary

---

requirements and prerequisites beyond just being able to write the JavaScript. Not unless you want to fry your brand new microcontroller. Or the attached computer.

Most of the DIY microcomputers and microcontrollers do have built-in support for JavaScript (typically via Node.js), or there are libraries that bridge the gap between the native language and JavaScript. And with the new generation of wearables hitting the street, I expect we'll see a lot more of JavaScript out of the box.

18.5. Creating a Geolocation Firefox OS App

Problem

You want to try your hand at developing a Firefox OS app using the Geolocation API, but don't know where to start.

Solution

Creating a Firefox OS app is little different than creating a basic web application. The primary difference is a manifest file, and some design and API issues. Best of all, you can create and test your Firefox OS directly in your existing development environment.

Earlier in the chapter, we created a simple Geolocation app called "Where Am I?" as both web app, and standalone Android app. We'll now port it to the Firefox OS environment. The details for porting the Where Am I? web app, created in Recipe 18.1, to a Firefox OS app are covered in the discussion.

Discussion

To create an app, you create a web page with all the functionality, graphics, and style-sheets it needs. It requires some additional files, such as a *README.md* file and a *manifest.webapp* that defines the type of application, its name, and how to launch the app, but they're just plain text. All the files other than any graphics (with the exception of SVG files) can be created with your favorite editor, including the *README.md* file (the structure of which is discussed in "Extra: The README File and Markdown Syntax" on page 337).

You can use text, but starting with Firefox version 33, you can use the new WebIDE to not only test your Firefox OS apps, but create the individuals files as well. It can shorten the development time considerably, and is one of the better focused development tools I've used.

To start the WebIDE, look for the option for it in the Firefox Developer menu. Once opened, it asks what kind of project to build (a plain privileged template, or a wizard tool that will help you set up permissions), and the name of the project. For this recipe, we're creating a simple app that will get information about the user's geolocation. The Geolocation API requires a *hosted app* in the Firefox environment, where the files to support the application are installed on a web server. For this example, it's called Where AmI, and Figure 18-10 shows the WebIDE after the project has been created.

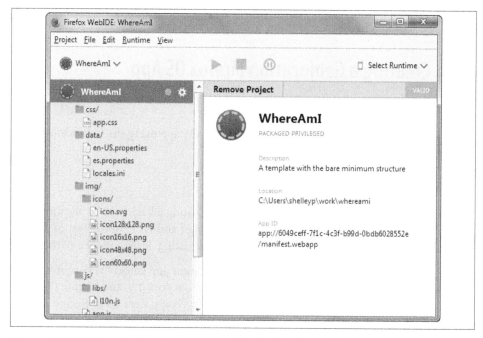

Figure 18-10. WhereAmI project generated in the Firefox WebIDE

Notice in the WebIDE that the tool automatically generates some basic files, including the icons. Mozilla requires one 128x128 pixel icon, and also recommends a second, larger 512x512 pixel icon with all Firefox OS apps. What the files are named isn't important, as they'll be linked as icons in the *manifest.webapp* file. At this point, we can use the generated icon, or we can use the icon we created for Recipe 18.1.

Following is the directory structure and files generated by the tool:

```
css/
    app.css
data/
    en-US.properties
    es.properties
    locales.ini
img/
    icons/
        icon.svg
        icon128x128.png
        icon16x16.png
```

```
            icon48x48.png
            icon60x60.png
    js/
        libs/
            l10.js
        app.js
    index.html
    LICENSE
    manifest.webapp
    README.md
```

The *index.html* file is where the application structure is created, and the *LICENSE* is licensing information. The *manifest.webapp* file is very similar to the *package.json* files used with Node applications and modules and the *manifest.json* file created in Recipe 18.1. In it, you'll list out the Firefox OS developer, how to launch the application, the icon names, permissions, and so on. I'll cover it later in this section.

The Geolocation code I'm using is an *exact* replication of the code I used in Recipe 18.1. This does demonstrate why it's essential to split your business logic out from your code to deal with the device mechanics—reuse!

```javascript
function geoFindMe() {
  var output = document.getElementById("out");

  if (!navigator.geolocation){
    output.innerHTML = "<p>Geolocation is not supported by your browser</p>";
    return;
  }

  function success(position) {
    var latitude  = position.coords.latitude;
    var longitude = position.coords.longitude;

    output.innerHTML = '<p>Latitude is ' + latitude + '<br>' +
                       'Longitude is ' + lngitude + '</p>';
    output.innerHTML = '<p>Latitude is ' + latitude + '<br>' +
                       'Longitude is ' + lngitude + '</p>';

    var img = new Image();
    img.src = "http://maps.googleapis.com/maps/api/staticmap?center=" +
              latitude + "," + longitude + "&zoom=13&size=300x300&sensor=false";

    output.appendChild(img);
  };

  function error() {
    output.innerHTML = "Unable to retrieve your location";
  };

  output.innerHTML = "<p>Locating¦</p>";
```

```
        navigator.geolocation.getCurrentPosition(success, error);
    }
```

The main entry point for the application is the *app.js* file. Most of it is commentary, which I stripped out. I also added the click event handler function to the app button:

```
window.addEventListener('DOMContentLoaded', function() {
  'use strict';

  var translate = navigator.mozL10n.get;
  navigator.mozL10n.once(start);

  function start() {

    var message = document.getElementById('message');
    document.getElementById("getmap").onclick=geoFindMe;

    message.textContent = translate('message');

  }

});
```

Another JavaScript file created for the app is is in *js/libs/l10n.js*, which provides *localization* capability for the app. It's part of the infrastructure for the frontend for the Firefox OS, known as *Gaia*. The message text in *app.js* is translated using the *l10n.js* library. The message itself is included in another file, *en-US.properties*, in the *data* directory for the app. It includes the title for the app, the description, and the `message` referenced in *app.js*. I modified the contents to the following:

```
app_title = Where am I?
app_description.innerHTML = It lives!
message = Being snoopy like a good app
```

The title that shows on the page for the app is defined in the `app_title` property, which might surprise you because you're assuming the title really comes in with the h1 header in the HTML page. The generated HTML with my own minor modification (the addition of a button) is shown here—this time I'm leaving in the generated comments, as they're quite useful:

```
<!DOCTYPE html>
<html>
    <head>
        <meta charset="utf-8">
        <title>Where Am I?</title>
        <meta name="description" content="A Where Am I app">

        <!--
            viewport allows you to control how mobile browsers will
            render your content.
            width=device-width tells mobile browsers to render your content
```

```
    across the full width of the screen, without being zoomed out
    (by default it
    would render it at a desktop width, then shrink it to fit.)
    Read more about it here:
    https://developer.mozilla.org/Mozilla/Mobile/Viewport_meta_tag
    -->

    <meta name="viewport" content="width=device-width">
    <link rel="stylesheet" href="css/app.css">

    <!--
    Inline JavaScript code is not allowed for privileged and certified apps,
    due to Content Security Policy restrictions.
    You can read more about it here: https://developer.mozilla.org/Apps/CSP
    Plus keeping your JavaScript separated from your HTML is always a
    good practice!

    We're also using the 'defer' attribute. This allows us to tell the
    browser that it should not wait for this file to load before continuing
    to load the rest of resources in the page. Then, once everything has
    been loaded, it will parse and execute the deferred files.
    Read about defer:
    https://developer.mozilla.org/Web/HTML/Element/script#attr-defer
    -->

    <script type="text/javascript" src="js/map.js" defer></script>
    <script type="text/javascript" src="js/app.js" defer></script>

    <!--
    The following two lines are for loading the localisations library
    and the localisation data-so people can use the app in their
    own language (as long as you provide translations).
    -->

    <link rel="prefetch" type="application/l10n" href="data/locales.ini" />
    <script type="text/javascript" src="js/libs/l10n.js" defer></script>
  </head>
  <body>
    <section>
        <h1 data-l10n-id="app_title">Where Am I</h1>
        <p><button id="getmap">Show my location</button></p>
        <div id="out"></div>
    </section>
  </body>
</html>
```

Note the reference to the *l10n.js* library, as well as the retrieval of another data file, *locales.ini*, listing the supported locales. In the generated application, U.S. English is the default language.

Read more about Mozilla's Firefox OS localization in "Localizing the Firefox OS Boilerplate App" (*http://mzl.la/1E0cGcT*) and about Gaia in the Mozilla Wiki (*https://wiki.mozilla.org/Gaia*).

The process that triggers the map to load involves clicking the button, and the associated code in *app.js*:

```
document.getElementById("getmap").onclick=geoFindMe;
```

The CSS is the same CSS for the web app:

```
html, body {
  margin: 0;
  padding: 0.5rem;
}

body {
  font-size: 1rem;
  background: yellow;
}

h1 {
  margin: 0 0 1rem 0;
}

p {
  font-size: inherit;
}
```

The directory structure for the app is the same as that listed earlier, except for the addition of the *map.js* file. That leaves us the last file to discuss, the *manifest.webapp* file, which pulls it all together.

For the `WhereAmI` application, I modified the *manifest.webapp* file to the following:

```
"version": "0.1.0",
"name": "WhereAmI",
"description": "A snoopy app that wants to know where you are",
"launch_path": "/work/whereami/index.html",
"icons": {
  "16": "/work/whereami/img/icons/icon16x16.png",
  "48": "/work/whereami/img/icons/icon48x48.png",
  "60": "/work/whereami/img/icons/icon60x60.png",
    "128": "/work/whereami/img/icons/icon128x128.png"
},
"developer": {
  "name": "Shelley Powers",
  "url": "http://burningbird.net"
},
"type": "web",
```

```
    "permissions": {
      "geolocation": {
        "description": "Needed to tell the user where they are"
        }
    },
    "installs_allowed_from": [
      "*"
    ],
    "default_locale": "en"
}
```

There are a couple of key takeaways from the file. First, because this application is web hosted, the `type` property for the app is set to `web`. In addition, all of the resources have to have an absolute URL location. Relative URLs can be used in the HTML file, but not the *manifest.webapp* file. Another edit I made to the generated *manifest.webapp* was to add a `permissions` property for the Geolocation. It's necessary for the application to work, and triggers the prompt for permission in order to ask the app user for his geolocation.

To try the app, we need to install simulator versions. We can do this by clicking on the "Select Runtime" option in the upper-right corner of the WebIDE. I installed all of the simulators, but you may want to only select the newest. Once the simulators are installed, we'll also access this option to run one of the simulators. Before we do, though, we'll need to install the files on a web host; Mozilla only allows Geolocation access from hosted apps.

The whole directory is copied to a web server, and now we're ready to try it out in the WebID using the newest simulator. From the "Project" menu opion, select the "Open Hosted App..." option. This opens up a window to type in the URL for the newly uploaded Firefox OS app directory. As long as there's no error in the setup, the app is loaded as valid. Run the app by clicking the Play arrow, which pops up the Firefox OS simulator. When you click the button the get the location, you'll first have to give permission to share your location with the app, as shown in Figure 18-11.

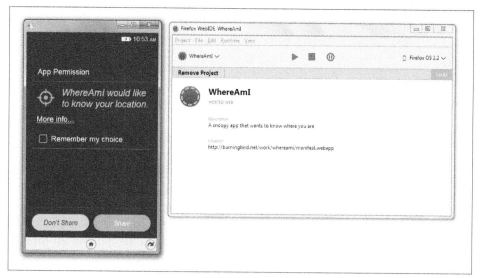

Figure 18-11. Getting permission from the user to access the person's current location

The app with a map loaded with my current location is shown in Figure 18-12.

Figure 18-12. The WhereAmI app in the Firefox OS simulator with a location loaded

It seems like a lot of work, but the WebIDE takes care of most of the work for you. And if you run into problems, it also provides the debugging tools you need. If you run the app in the simulator and it fails or doesn't act as you expected, pause the application by clicking the Pause button (a double quote in a circle) in the WebIDE. Pausing the app triggers the WebIDE to open an excellent debugger, as shown in Figure 18-13.

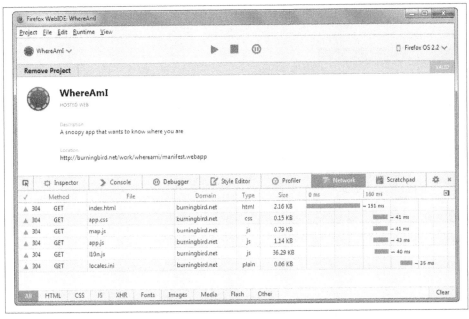

Figure 18-13. Opening a debugger in the WebIDE

Extra: Using Cordova to Generate a Firefox OS App

An alternative approach to using the WebIDE to create the Firefox OS app is to use Cordova.

Follow the instructions covered in Recipe 18.3 to create a new app, using the following:

```
cordova create findme net.burningbird.findme FindMe
```

Next, change to the newly created *findme* subdirectory, and add support for the Firefox OS platform:

```
cordova platform add firefox0s
```

Lastly, run the `prepare` command to finish the generation:

```
cordova prepare
```

The generated set of Web-based component files are located in */platforms/firefoxos/ www*. The files work in the older App Manager that Mozilla provided for working with Firefox OS apps, but at the time this was written, they didn't work directly with the WebIDE. If you load it as is, you'll get an error because the *manifest.webapp* file doesn't use an absolute URL for the `launch` property. It needs to be modified to:

```
"launch_path": "/index.html",
```

Now the app can be loaded into the WebIDE, though you'll get a warning about no icon files. Figure 18-14 shows the app loaded and ready for modifying.

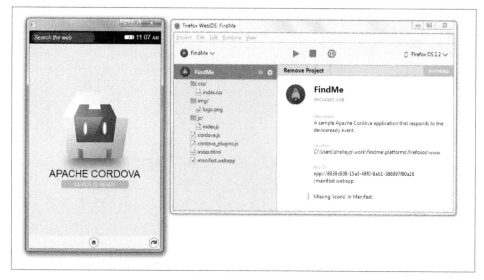

Figure 18-14. Running the Cordova-generated Firefox OS app in simulator

See Also

Mozilla provides a ton of helpful pages for creating Firefox OS apps, but I recommend beginning with the following:

- The Mozilla Developer Network App Center (*https://developer.mozilla.org/en-US/Apps*)
- The Firefox OS Quickstart guide (*http://mzl.la/1DGAncV*)
- Mozilla's WebIDE introduction (*http://mzl.la/1DGApla*)
- "Using geolocation" (*http://mzl.la/1DGAq8B*)
- "Firefox OS device APIs" (*http://mzl.la/1DGAuW2*)

For working with Cordova and Firefox OS:

- Apache Cordova's "Firefox OS Platform Guide" (*http://bit.ly/1DGAFQW*)
- "Cordova support for Firefox OS" (*http://mzl.la/1DGAKnM*)
- "Cordova Firefox OS plugin reference" (*http://mzl.la/1DGALrX*)

18.6. Porting the Geolocation App to a Google Chrome App

Problem

You're interested in porting the Where Am I? app to the Google Chrome environment, but don't know how.

Solution

Creating a Chrome OS app is simple. The steps, as defined in Google's starter documentation (*https://developer.chrome.com/apps/first_app*), are as follows:

1. Create a manifest file.
2. Create a background JavaScript file to build the app's interface.
3. Create icons.
4. Launch that puppy.

Discussion

Creating a Chrome app is simple, but it's made more so with a new Chrome Dev Editor (CDE), still in beta at the time this was written. It's installed as a Chrome App, and accessible via the equally new Chrome App Launcher.

> Download the CDE from *http://bit.ly/1z2EyL0*. You'll need to access the resource page with Chrome.

When you start the application the first time, it asks for the location of the top-level work directory. It then asked for a new project name, and project type. I entered "WhereAmI" as project name, and selected "JavaScript Chrome App", as project type. The tool generated the following directory structure and files:

```
assets/
    icon_16.png
    icon_128.png
background.js
index.html
main.js
manifest.json
styles.css
```

The icons are self-explanatory, as are the *styles.css* and *index.html* files. As with the earlier recipes, if you want to emulate the Where Am I? web app created in Recipe 18.1, copy the icon from that app to the Chrome directory and name it accordingly.

The *background.js* file is where the application launching code is included, and is required for all Chrome apps. For the Where Am I? app, the code is:

```
/**
 * Listens for the app launching, then creates the window.
 *
 * @see http://developer.chrome.com/apps/app.runtime.html
 * @see http://developer.chrome.com/apps/app.window.html
 */
chrome.app.runtime.onLaunched.addListener(function(launchData) {
  chrome.app.window.create(
    'index.html',
    {
      id: 'mainWindow',
      bounds: {width: 800, height: 600}
    }
  );
});
```

The code adds an event listener for a Launched event, and creates the actual app window. There's also a onRestarted event handler, which is called when the app is restarted— this is important if you're working with data and application state.

The second JavaScript file is *main.js*, and contains the following very simple code:

```
window.onload = function() {
  document.querySelector('#greeting').innerText =
    'Hello, World! It is ' + new Date();
};
```

Traditional "Hello, World" behavior, with a Date twist.

Because we're porting the Where Am I? app created in Recipe 18.1, I need to modify some of the files, and add a new one for the map functionality. The first thing to modify is the stylesheet. The one generated by the CDE is a placeholder only, so in addition to adding in the yellow background color, I need to copy all of the CSS generated for the Firefox OS app to the new Chrome app:

```
html, body {
  margin: 0;
  padding: 0.5rem;
}

body {
  font-size: 1rem;
  background: yellow;
}
```

```
h1 {
  margin: 0 0 1rem 0;
}

p {
  font-size: inherit;
}
```

Of course, a published app would have more CSS, but this works for now.

 There is no "save" feature in the CDE: saving happens when you switch to another file.

Next up, we'll modify the HTML file to add both an output div element and a button, as well as move the *main.js* file to the head element, and add *map.js*:

```
<!DOCTYPE html>
<html>
<head>
  <title>WhereAmI</title>
  <link rel="stylesheet" href="styles.css">
  <script src="main.js"></script>
  <script src="map.js"></script>
</head>

<body>
  <h1>Where Am I</h1>
  <p><button id="getmap">Show my location</button></p>
  <div id="out"></div>
</body>
</html>
```

You might notice that the *background.js* file isn't listed. That's because it creates the app window, and is processed before the window is opened. In *main.js*, delete the existing code, and add the button onclick event handler:

```
window.onload = function() {
   document.getElementById("getmap").onclick=geoFindMe;
};
```

Last, create the *map.js* file by right-clicking the file listing area in the CDE and selecting "New file…" from the options. The *map.js* code is exactly the same as that used in the web app, Firefox OS, and Android app, so I'll forgo duplicating it here.

Just like with the Firefox OS app, we need to get permission for accessing Geolocation in the app to the manifest file. Before we move on, we must make one more change.

Open the *manifest.json* file in the CDE and modify the name, short_name, and descrip tion properties, and add permissions:

```
{
  "manifest_version": 2,
  "name": "Where Am I?",
  "short_name": "WhereAmI",
  "description": "So, where are you?",

  "version": "0.0.1.0",

  "icons": {
    "16": "assets/icon_16.png",
    "128": "assets/icon_128.png"
  },

  "app": {
    "background": {
      "scripts": ["background.js"]
    }
  },
  "permissions": ["geolocation"]
}
```

You're now ready to try the application. Click the Play button, located next to the file listing horizontal tab bar towards the top of the page. At the time I wrote this, I received an error when I played the app, as shown in Figure 18-15. I believe this was because of the use of the new Chrome App Launcher, and the CDE was expecting the app to be installed directly in Chrome.

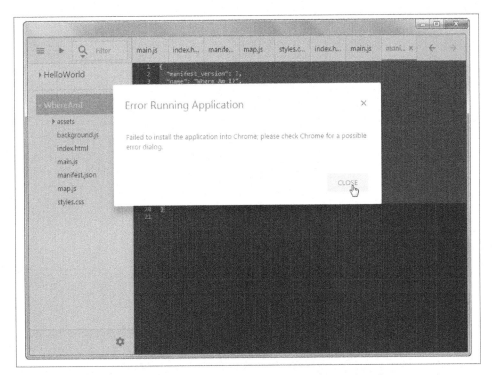

Figure 18-15. Chrome error that displays when first launching the Chrome app

If you look at the Chrome App Launcher window, though, you'll see the newly installed app, as shown in Figure 18-16.

Figure 18-16. New WhereAmI app installed in Chrome App Launcher window

Launching the app and clicking the button demonstrates that the Geolocation API call has worked. The longitude and latitude values are displayed in the page, but where's the map?

To debug the new app, right-click the background and choose the "Inspect Element" option from the menu. In the Developer Tools window that opens, select the Console, and then click the map button again. Here's the error that displays:

```
Refused to load the image
'http://maps.googleapis.com/maps/api/staticmap?center=38.574735499999996,
-90.3349295&zoom=13&size=300x300&sensor=false' because it violates the
following Content Security Policy directive: "img-src 'self' data:
chrome-extension-resource:".
```

Why the map doesn't display is where we get into a major difference between the Chrome App environment and the Firefox OS app environment. The Chrome App environment operates under a restricted Content Security Policy (CSP), which among other things, does not allow us to load external web content. This includes loading a new image.

To load external content, Chrome provides the webview tab, which acts like a sandboxed iframe. And to load an external image, you have to indulge in a bit of fudging to get the app to work.

 Read more about Chrome's CSP and view the workarounds in "Build a ToDo Chrome App" (*http://bit.ly/1DGC4ae*), and debugging in "Tutorial: Debugging" (*http://bit.ly/1DGC8Hb*).

We'll have to make an XHR (XMLHttpRequest) for the image, get the result as a blob, and then assign it to the image. We'll add the following function to the *map.js* file:

```
var loadImage = function(uri) {
  var xhr = new XMLHttpRequest();
  xhr.responseType = 'blob';
  xhr.onload = function() {
    document.getElementById("img1").src
      = window.URL.createObjectURL(xhr.response);
  }
  xhr.open('GET', uri, true);
  xhr.send();
}
```

And modify the success() function to incorporate a call to the function:

```
function success(position) {
    var latitude  = position.coords.latitude;
    var longitude = position.coords.longitude;

    output.innerHTML = '<p>Latitude is ' + latitude + '<br>Longitude is ' +
    longitude + '</p>';

    var img = new Image();
    img.id = "img1";
    var src = "http://maps.googleapis.com/maps/api/staticmap?center=" +
    latitude + "," + longitude + "&zoom=13&size=300x300&sensor=false";

    output.appendChild(img);
    loadImage(src);
};
```

We'll also have to modify the *manifest.json* file to add a new permissions entry:

```
"permissions": ["geolocation","<all_urls>"]
```

Running the app again and clicking the button not only loads the latitude/longitude pair, but also the map, as shown in Figure 18-17 (with the window manually downsized).

Figure 18-17. Chrome App with both geolocation and Google map image displayed

Extra: Chrome Apps and Cordova

As with the Firefox OS app, you can also use Cordova to generate the Chrome app. However, instead of using the Cordova installation created earlier in the chapter, we're using a variation Google created that works specifically with Chrome Apps.

Assuming Node.js is installed, install the Chrome/Cordova CLI using npm:

```
npm install -g cca
```

Because we already have an existing, working Chrome app, when we create the new project (which we'll call WhereAmI2), we'll use the option to copy files from an existing project. In my Chrome working directory, I typed:

```
cca create WhereAmI2 --copy-from WhereAmI/manifest.json
```

Providing the relative path to the original project's *manifest.json* file. The CLI copies all of the files from the original project. To create the Android implementation of the app, change to the newly created *WhereAmI2* directory, and run the prepare command:

```
cca prepare
```

To run the app in an emulator, type the following:

```
cca emulate Android
```

To run in an attached Android device:

```
cca run Android
```

The process is relatively quick and painless. There are some caveats about what's supported. Earlier, I mentioned the webview element, for external resources. Unfortunately, it's not supported in a Chrome app that's ported to Cordova.

 An excellent guide on porting a Chrome app to the mobile environment is Create Chrome Apps for Mobile Using Apache Cordova (*https://github.com/MobileChromeApps/mobile-chrome-apps*).

The Blurred Lines Between Chrome and Android

Thanks to the Cordova plugin, we can now port our Chrome apps to Android, but what about the reverse? Running all the many Android apps in Chrome?

Late in the summer of 2014, Google introduced the beta of the App Runtime for Chrome, which provides an Android runtime within Chrome. The company ported a set of popular Android apps, but not long after instructions popped up for sideloading any Android app to Chrome (*http://bit.ly/1DGCE86*). Of course, at the time this was written, the instructions were for experienced mobile developers, but by the time you read this, I expect the process will be simplified, officially sanctioned, and well documented.

But why stop at Android on Chrome? Why not Android everywhere?

Barely a week after the original sideloading hack was published, the original developer, who goes by vladikoff on GitHub, developed applications (*https://github.com/vladikoff/chromeos-apk*) that allow Android apps to be run in Windows, Linux, or the Mac.

The world of mobile apps has now become the world of apps.

18.7. Publishing Your Geolocation App in the Kindle Fire OS Environment

Problem

Your Geolocation app Where Am I? has now been ported to Firefox OS, Chrome, and Android, but what about running it in the Amazon Fire OS environment?

Solution

Developing a Fire OS Android app for Amazon Kindle is very similar to developing an Android app. What's needed is one of the files in the Amazon WebView SDK, *awv_interface.jar*. Once you download the SDK, extract the file, and add it to the Cordova installation. In Windows, *c:\Users\username\.cordova\lib\amazon-fireos\cordova \3.5.0\framework\libs* is the location for the file. If you're unsure of where to put the file, when you add the Fire OS platform support to an app without having copied the file, run the following:

```
cordova platform add amazon-fireos
```

You'll get an error pointing out the location where Cordova expects to find the file.

Once it's installed, and the platform is added, you're ready to develop. We'll cover porting Where Am I? to Amazon Fire OS in the discussion.

Discussion

Amazon's Fire OS is, first and foremost, Android. Therefore, the app is ported to plain vanilla Android, first (see Recipe 18.4). Once it's working in Android, we can just add support for the Fire OS and build the new version.

Assuming that you have a working Android app of Where Am I?, to set up Cordova for Amazon Fire OS, you first need to copy the file from the Amazon WebView SDK, as noted in the solution. Once you have copied the file, then add the platform:

```
cordova platform add amazon-fireos
```

The source code files for the Fire OS version of Where Am I? are the *exact* same source code files for the vanilla Android version created in Recipe 18.4. The files and app structure are:

```
www/
    css/
        index.css
    img/
        logo.png
    js/
        index.js
        map.js
    index.html
```

Now, we're ready to build.

```
cordova build
```

There is no Amazon Fire OS emulator in Cordova, so we'll need to test the app directly in a Kindle Fire device. We have to enable the Amazon Debug Bridget (ADB) in the device, first. How to do so depends on your device generation. I'm using a first-generation Kindle Fire HDX, and the option is available in Settings→Device. As for other devices, Amazon's documentation states:

```
On a 4th generation Fire tablet, tap Device Options, then Developer Options.
- or - On a 3rd generation Kindle Fire tablet, tap Device, then Developer
       Options.
- or - On a 2nd generation Kindle Fire tablet, tap Security.
```

Just switch USB debugging on. As the documentation notes, when not testing on the device, you should turn USB debugging off. This is true for all devices you're testing on.

The hardest part of setting up the Amazon Kindle device is setting up the device driver. You first have to install the device driver into the computer, from the executable file located in the Android SDK *extras* directory. Before you can do so, you have to run the SDK manager and add support for Amazon devices. This requires setting up an Android user add-on site, so that you'll be given the option of adding support for an Amazon Fire OS device.

Then, once you've done all of this, now you're ready to install the device driver for the device. If the computer has already installed a device driver, you'll need to delete it, and then add the ADB device driver. Lastly, you'll need to detect the tablet through the ADB.

Rather than detail all of this, which seems to change every few months or so, I'm going to point you to Amazon's detailed documentation. Check out the instructions in the pages accessible from the following links:

- "Setting Up the ADB Driver for Kindle Fire Devices" (*http://bit.ly/1DGD3ay*)
- "Connecting Your Fire Tablet for Testing" (*http://bit.ly/1DGD7ah*)

Once you've worked through the painful driver setup, loading the app in the Kindle is a piece of cake:

```
cordova run amazon-fireos
```

And your app is now running in Kindle Fire OS.

I was also able to run the vanilla Android app in the Kindle Fire OS. You can easily test whether your non-Fire OS Android app works in Fire OS by accessing Amazon's developer portal public web page (*https://developer.amazon.com/public*), and dragging your APK file to the box labeled "Drag and drop your APK here". The site first tests for compatibility, and then actually tests the app against both a Fire phone and various Fire tablets, as shown in Figure 18-18.

Figure 18-18. Testing standard Android standalone app in Amazon's developer portal

You can also sign up for a developer account with Amazon, and test your APK with the resources that Amazon provides to developers.

Again, most Android apps will work on Fire OS right out of the box, but I found the user interface was superior with the Fire OS flavored version, so you'll want to create a Fire OS specific version of the Android app if you want to support Amazon's devices. Once you have the debugger drive set up, it's incredibly simple to add the Fire OS plugin, and tweak the design to ensure a best look in a Fire device.

18.8. Debugging Your Android or Amazon Fire OS App

Problem

You uploaded your Android app to the device, and nothing happens. You know how to debug in a browser, but how do you debug in an Android device?

Solution

Standard Android apps and those created for the Fire OS environment both have debugging capabilities. See the discussion for more details.

Discussion

To debug a vanilla Android app, load the app into the Android device. Open a Chrome browser and type "chrome:\\inspect" into the location bar. Make sure the "Discover USB devices" option is checked in the page, and look for your device in the list. Most likely you'll see several different apps, but look at the bottom of the list, under the WebView listing associated with the reverse domain you've given the app. Click the "inspect" link underneath the app. A Developer Tools window opens with the files for the app you're debugging, as shown in Figure 18-19. You can now debug the app as you would debug any other JavaScript application.

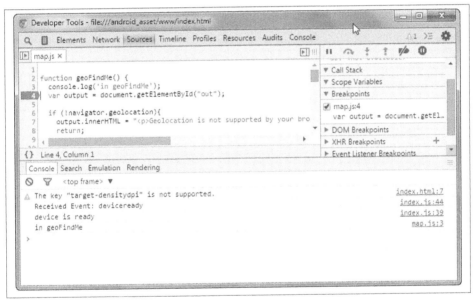

Figure 18-19. Debugging the Android app in Chrome

To debug an Amazon Fire OS app, you'll use the ADB command-line instructions, which is why it's so important to make sure the device is properly set up, first. You have several different command options, but the one I found to be the most helpful is the command that lists log data. To run it, in a Command window or terminal, type the following command:

```
adb logcat
```

Log data is printed to the screen, including errors in the Android app. Once the app is loaded, initiate action that is triggering the problem behavior, and any errors should show up immediately in the log data. I was able to discover that I hadn't correctly installed the Geolocation plugin when I first ran the Fire OS app on my Kindle Fire HDX by viewing the log file.

Thankfully, there's a simple fix. I just made sure I had the proper plugin the next go around, rebuilt the apps, and then launched the Fire OS app again. Relaunching an app closes the existing one, and replaces it with the new before popping it open.

If the log file isn't helpful, you can also use the Android Debug Monitor, located in the *tools* directory of the Android SDK. In Windows, it's a *.bat* file, and double-clicking the file loads the debugger.

The Debugger is really geared to native Android development, but you can view the log file more easily, though the verbosity of the tool can interfere with catching the data you need, as displayed in Figure 18-20.

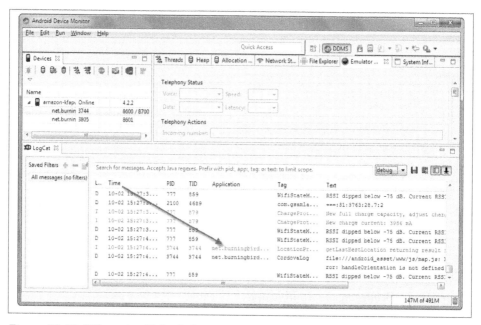

Figure 18-20. Where Am I? loaded in an Amazon Fire HDX tablet being debugged in Android Debug Monitor

Extra: Taking a Screenshot

You can use the Android Debug Monitor to take screenshots of the attached Android device (which is so much more handy than a complicated button combination that messes up the display).

When the app is loaded in the device, open the Android Debug Monitor, and click the little camera icon to take a screenshot. The screenshot capability works with standard Android devices, as well as the Amazon Fire OS devices.

 Read more about the Android ADB in the "Android Debug Bridge" documentation (*http://developer.android.com/tools/help/adb.html*).

18.9. Getting Information About the Device

Problem

You're ready to try your hand at mobile development, and are curious about what device functionality you can access from an Android app developed using Cordova.

Solution

Cordova provides a set of APIs for accessing information about the device. The documentation also clearly explains what is necessary in order to integrate the functionality into the app.

As an example, one of the plugins is the Device plugin that provides information about the device. To use it, you install the plugin in the following manner:

```
cordova plugin add org.apache.cordova.device
```

Then you can use the API in the Android app:

```
function onDeviceReady() {
    var element = document.getElementById('deviceProperties');
    element.innerHTML = 'Device Name: '    + device.name     + '<br />' +
                        'Device Cordova: ' + device.cordova   + '<br />' +
                        'Device Platform: ' + device.platform + '<br />' +
                        'Device UUID: '    + device.uuid      + '<br />' +
                        'Device Model: '   + device.model     + '<br />' +
                        'Device Version: ' + device.version   + '<br />';
    window.addEventListener("batterystatus", updateBatteryStatus, false);
}
```

But you're not restricted to just plugin functionality. Remember that the Cordova app is based on the Android WebView component, which is based on Chromium/Webkit (depending on the Android version). What works in Chrome should work in a Cordova app. For instance, if you're curious about the state of the battery, you can use the following, even though you haven't installed the Cordova battery plugin:

```
function updateBatteryStatus(battery) {
       var element = document.getElementById('battery');
               var batterystate;
               if (battery.isPlugged) {
                   batterystate = "Device is plugged in";
               } else {
                   batterystate = "Device is not plugged in";
               }

               element.innerHTML = 'Battery: ' + battery.level + '<br />' +
                                   batterystate;
       }
```

Discussion

Cordova provides a set of plugins that allow us to manipulate or get information about the device:

- Battery Status: Status about the battery
- Camera: Takes photos from the default device camera
- Contacts: Gets information about the device owner's contacts
- Device: Provides basic information about the device (used in solution)
- Device Motion: Accesses the device's accelerometer, and has the ability to get motion information in the x, y, and z direction
- Device Orientation: Accesses the device's compass and measures the direction in which the device is pointed in degrees from 0 to 359.99 (north is 0)
- Dialogs: Our old friends alert, confirm, and prompt, with the addition of beep
- FileSystem: Accesses the native filesystem in the device
- File Transfer: Uploads or downloads files
- Geolocation: Demonstrated in the Where Am I? apps
- Globalization: Localization of the device
- InAppBrowser: Opens a web browser view in the app (does not have access to the Cordova plugins)
- Media: Undergoing changes, but will eventually allow media files
- Media Capture: Allows access to audio and video capabilities
- Network Information: Accesses information about the network
- Splashscreen: Shows and hides the application splash screen

- Vibration: Vibrates the device
- StatusBar: Shows, hides, and configures the status bar

As you can see, you can have a lot of fun with your Cordova apps. Each plugin has different requirements, both to install and to use in Cordova.

 When accessing Cordova documentation, make sure you're looking at the correct version of the documentation. The documentation page features a dropdown at the top-right side of the page. Select the Cordova version you're using from the list.

You can find which version of Cordova you're using by typing:

```
cordova --version
```

Accessing the functionality is quite simple. Example 18-2 is the HTML page for a Cordova application accessing various information from the device.

Example 18-2. Android app querying the device for various information

```
<!DOCTYPE html>
<html>
  <head>
    <title>Device Properties Example</title>


  </head>
  <body>
    <p id="deviceProperties">Loading device properties...</p>
    <p id="battery">Getting information about battery...</p>
        <p id="compass">Getting compass heading...</p>
        <p id="accel">Getting Accelerometer information...</p>

        <script type="text/javascript" charset="utf-8" src="cordova.js"></script>
    <script type="text/javascript" charset="utf-8">

    // Wait for device API libraries to load
    //
        document.addEventListener("deviceready", onDeviceReady, false);


    // device APIs are available
    //
    function onDeviceReady() {
        var element = document.getElementById('deviceProperties');
        element.innerHTML = 'Device Name: '     + device.name     + '<br />' +
                            'Device Cordova: '  + device.cordova  + '<br />' +
                            'Device Platform: ' + device.platform + '<br />' +
                            'Device UUID: '     + device.uuid     + '<br />' +
                            'Device Model: '    + device.model    + '<br />' +
                            'Device Version: '  + device.version  + '<br />';
```

```
            window.addEventListener("batterystatus", updateBatteryStatus, false);
        }

            function updateBatteryStatus(battery) {
                var element = document.getElementById('battery');
                    var batterystate;
                    if (battery.isPlugged) {
                        batterystate = "Device is plugged in";
                    } else {
                        batterystate = "Device is not plugged in";
                    }

                    element.innerHTML = 'Battery: ' + battery.level + '<br />' +
                                         batterystate;
        }

            function onCompassSuccess(heading) {
            document.getElementById('compass').innerHTML = 'Heading: '
            + heading.magneticHeading;
        };

    function onCompassError(error) {
        document.getElementById('compass').innerHTML = 'CompassError: ' + error.code;
        };

            if (navigator.compass) {
            navigator.compass.getCurrentHeading(onCompassSuccess, onCompassError);
            } else {
                document.getElementById('compass').innerHTML = 'compass not supported';
            }

    function onSuccess(acceleration) {
    document.getElementById('accel').innerHTML ='Acceleration X: '
            + acceleration.x + '\n' +
            'Acceleration Y: ' + acceleration.y + '\n' +
            'Acceleration Z: ' + acceleration.z + '\n' +
            'Timestamp: '      + acceleration.timestamp + '\n';
        };

    function onError() {
        alert('onError!');
        };

            if (navigator.accelerometer) {
            navigator.accelerometer.getCurrentAcceleration(onSuccess, onError);
        } else {
            document.getElementById('accel').innerHTML = 'accelerometer not supported';
        }
        </script>
    </body>
</html>
```

Running the app in my Android tablet, I received the following response:

```
Device name: undefined
Device Cordova: 3.5.1
Device Platform: Android
Device UUID: (device's unique ID)
Device Model: Nexus 7
Device Version: 4.4.4

Battery: 75
Device is plugged in

compass not supported
accelerometer not supported
```

Not all functionality is going to work in all devices. I know for a fact that I have support for both the compass and acceleromter.

Cordova, like mobile devices, is a work in progress.

Extra: Discover Your Android's Capabilities

There are several apps you can download from Google Play that allow you to explore what sensors your Android device has. You'll never look at that little, flat thing the same when you realize exactly how many sensors most tablets and smartphone have.

Up and Running in jsBin and jsFiddle

Most of the examples are JavaScript code snippets, rather than HTML files with `script` elements. The snippets can be copied directly into jsBin or jsFiddle or, for the most part, run using Node. In this Appendix, I'll briefly cover the information you'll need to run the examples successfully.

The Console Is Your Friend

Formally, we should use unit testing for determing application state, but I've not found it to be as friendly or helpful as a good old print out of data. In the past, we used `alert()` to print out values, but now we have the console.

All the main browsers (i.e., Internet Explorer, Firefox, Chrome, Opera, and Safari) have access to a console, as does Node. Here's a quick cheatsheet:

- To access the console in Chrome, access the Chrome customize menu, then select Tools→JavaScript Console.
- To access the console in Opera, click Tools in the menu, then open up Opera Dragonfly and select the Console.
- In Safari, enable the Develop menu in Safari's Advanced preferences to access the Console.
- The Internet Explorer console can be accessed by pressing F12, or selecting "F12 Developer Tools" from the Settings menu.
- In Firefox, access the console by selecting Developer from the Firefox settings menu, and then choosing "Browser Console".
- In Node, output to the console prints to the standard output.

I used `console.log()` all throughout the book, but there are other methods you can use. Among my other favorites are the following:

- `console.assert(express, object)`: If the expression is false, the message is written to the console along with a stack trace (for some user agents)
- `console.count(label)`: Logs the number of times called
- `console.error(object)`: Outputs an error message (and a stack trace with some user agents)
- `console.time(label)`: Starts a timer with the label
- `console.timeEnd(label)`: Stops the timer associated with the label and prints out the elapsed time
- `console.trace()`: Prints out a stack trace
- `console.dir(object)`: Prints out an interactive listing of object properties

There are additional methods, but you can see the value of the console for more than printing out a message.

 Both Mozilla (*http://mzl.la/1DGFhGY*) and Chrome (*http://bit.ly/console_api*) provide documentation of the console methods, though the support isn't identical in both.

jsBin and jsFiddle: Online JavaScript Playgrounds

There are several HTML/CSS/JavaScript *playgrounds* (sites where you can test out code snippets), but I use two: jsBin and jsFiddle. Both sites are free to use, though jsBin now has a paid option providing additional functionality. Both sites provide the same basic types of functionality, though how they provide it does differ.

Most of my work is done in jsBin because I like the layout better. I like simple collapsible panels that can be closed, making room for the others. I also appreciate jsBin providing a Console panel, as shown in Figure A-1.

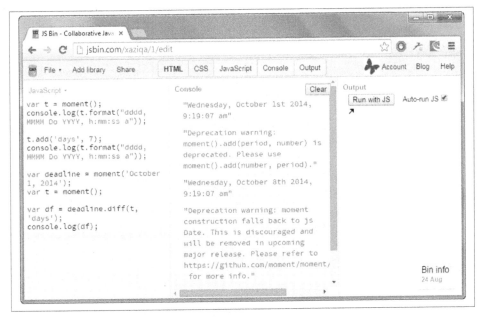

Figure A-1. Screenshot of jsBin showing a console panel with content

All jsBin "bins" are automatically saved. If you want to access previous bins, you need to set up an account in order to access the history. Otherwise, you can save the link that's automatically created for each. Once you have the contents of a a bin where you want it, you can use it as a template for future bins, clone it, or download it, and jsBin will create a clean HTML file that includes just the HTML, JavaScript, and CSS you provide. This latter capability is a particularly nice feature, and one I used with building example files.

jsFiddle also provides storage of "fiddles," as this playground calls them. Instead of using collapsible panels, jsFiddle separates HTML, CSS, JavaScript, and a result page, into four separate frames that can be resized, but not collapsed. If you need console access, you'll also need to use your browser's console, as jsFiddle doesn't provide one. An example of typical JavaScript testing with jsFiddle is shown in Figure A-2.

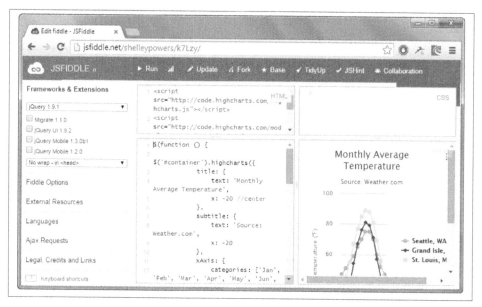

Figure A-2. Screenshot of jsFiddle showing an example of use for testing JavaScript

Both jsBin and jsFiddle provide access to various popular framework and utility Java-Script libraries you can include in your effort. Many popular libraries, such as jQuery and Underscore, are included.

One major difference between the two playgrounds is jsBin incorporates JSHint into the application automatically, while jsFiddle provides it as a selectable option. The issue with jsBin's incorporation is JSHint operates as you type, which means you're constantly getting immediate errors and warnings for code you're still adding. Frankly, it's excessively irritating. However, the jsBin creator, Remy Smart, notes that you can shut JSHint off using the browser console and typing in:

```
jsbin.settings.jshint = false;
```

jsBin provides a video detailing how to change editor settings (*https://www.youtube.com/embed/pzFqaRJwNQ8*). Note that Firefox's native JavaScript console doesn't seem to allow direct input, but Firebug's JavaScript console does.

The jsBin harness also seems to be more complex than jsFiddle, and did seem to interfere with some of the testing. However, because you can download a working example that's stripped clean, you can ensure clean testing source.

Both tools provide sufficient documentation for using their respective playgrounds.

To run the book code examples in either, just copy the complete HTML (if the example is packaged as an HTML file) into the panel labeled "HTML", or copy the JavaScript (if that's what's provided) into the JavaScript panels. Note that Node examples will not work in either tool, and any use of XMLHttpRequest is unlikely to work because of cross-domain restrictions. In addition, examples that require external script libraries that are not linked directly to a CDN and aren't included in either tool's set of libraries won't work, either. You'll need to run these examples directly from your browser, and from your example subdirectory.

Index

Symbols

!= operator, 12
!== operator, 12
$ (dollar sign), 172, 194, 197, 320
* (universal selector), 112, 123
* (wildcard), 449, 456
+ (plus sign), 17
:nth-child() pseudoclass, 123
; (semicolon), 195
== operator, 12
=== operator, 12, 144
_ (underscore character), 87, 181
_defineGetter method, 93
_defineSetter method, 93
{ } (curly brackets), 144

A

aboutAudio() event handler, 236
abstraction layers, 173
Access-Control-Allow-Methods header value,
    450, 456
Access-Control-Allow-Origin header value, 449
accessibility
    automatically updated regions, 163, 221
    highlighting errors, 156–162
    importance of, 143
accessor descriptors, 93
accidental closures, 74

accordion widget, 134
accounting libraries, 169
Accounting.js library, 169
add() function, 168
advanced math libraries, 170
Agile development paradigm, 148
Ajax
    automatic page updates with, 218–220
    making requests to other domains, 209–212
    processing JSON from requests, 212
    Promise object and, 270
    PUT requests in, 450–453
    sending binary data through, 453
    XML document handling, 199
alert boxes, 157
alert role, 142
algorithms
    recursive, 65–68
    specifying patterns in, 123
alternative testing, 153
Amazon Appstore, 541
Amazon Fire apps
    debugging, 580–583
    geolocation, 577–580
    packaging, 541
Amazon Web App
    portal page, 542
    tester app, 541

We'd like to hear your suggestions for improving our indexes. Send email to index@oreilly.com.

Immediately-Invoked Function Expression
    (IIFE)
        encapsulating objects in, 185
        global namespace clutter and, 313
        library sharing and, 330
        singletons and, 100
        using RequireJS with jQuery, 320
        wrapping variables/functions with, 82
imperative programming, 64
IndexedDB, 520–523
indexOf() method, 7, 43, 46
inflection rules, 420
inheritance, 88, 90, 107
init() function, 186
insertBefore() method, 124
instantiation, vs. declaration, 62
integration testing, 345
iOS apps, 149, 535
IP addresses, specifying, 276
iptables rule, 302
ISO 8601 format, 25–28
iterator protocol, 260

J

Jade, 393
Java Developer Kit (JKD), 546
JIT (Just-In-Time) compiler optimizations, 155
jQuery
        building on framework, 171–173
        converting libraries to plug-ins, 193
        using plugins, 174–176
        using with RequireJS, 319
        versions available, 172
jQuery Mobile, 556
jQuery Validation Engine, 497, 499
jQuery.hotkeys plugin, 177
jQuery.payment library, 500
JS Bin, 144
jsBin, 590
jsFiddle, 144, 590
JSHint, 143
JSLint, 45, 144
JSON
        accessing data RESTfully, 352–354
        converting objects to filtered/transformed
            strings, 208
        parsing/modifying, 206
        processing from Ajax requests, 212
JSON.stringify() method, 208

JsonClient, 357
JSONP (JSON with padding), 209–212
jsPerf, 153
just-in-time behavioral modification, 263

K

key/value pairs, creating unique, 255–258
keyboard shortcuts, 177–180
Keypress library, 177
keys() method, 54
Keytool, 549
Kindle Fire apps
        debugging, 580–583
        default browser and, 540
        geolocation, 577–580
        packaging, 541

L

l10n.js library, 562
lastIndex property, 22
lastIndexOf() method, 43
latitude/longitude pairs, 376
layers of abstraction, 173
leading spaces, removing, 9
length property, 4, 10
let keyword, 250–252, 283
libraries
        accounting, 169
        advanced math/statistics, 170
        basic utility, 180
        benefits of using, 165
        building on jQuery framework, 171–173
        chart making, 225, 476
        chart.js, 476
        combining several, 195–198
        converting to AMD format, 316
        converting to jQuery plug-ins, 193
        converting to Node modules, 328
        creating vs. using existing, 165, 182
        datetime functions, 170
        expanding Math object capability with, 168
        hosting, 189–192
        hotlinking to, 192
        keyboard shortcut support, 177–180
        loading with script loaders, 312–315
        locating, 165
        minifying, 187
        mylib.js, 317

O

OAuth 2.0, 379, 424, 527
OAuth framework, 422–435
object-oriented programming, 85
Object.create() method, 90
Object.defineProperties() method, 91
Object.defineProperty() method, 94
Object.freeze() method, 95
Object.isExtensible() method, 95
Object.preventExtensions() method, 94, 96
Object.seal() method, 96
objects
    accessing properties of, 4
    browser support for, 249
    chaining methods, 103–105
    controlling scope, 101–103
    converting to JSON-formatted strings, 208
    creating from JSON, 206
    creating using prototype, 87–90
    defining new properties, 92
    encapsulating data/functions, 97–100
    ES 6 standard, 249–272
    global, 285
    inheriting functionality, 90
    JavaScript's object-oriented capabilities, 85
    JIT behavioral modification to, 263–266
    keeping properties private, 86, 185
    literal, 98, 182
    preventing changes to, 95
    preventing extensibility of, 94
    Set object, 253
    vs. primitives and literals, 3–7
    weakly held, 255
Ocrad.js library, 489
octal sequence (3 digits), 15
odd argument, 123
ok test, 146
onblur event handler, 156
onchange event, 156
one-off object, 98, 186
one.js library, 317
onload event, 233
onsuccess event handler, 522
opacity settings, 132
Open Exchange Rates, 169
open source code, 189
open() function, 281
openFile() function, 295
Opera Mobile Classic Emulator, 149

Optical Character Recognition (OCR), 489
optimizations, 155, 187, 319
OPTIONS verb, 450
overlays, adding, 129–133
overrideMimeType() method, 200

P

package.json file, 335
page overlays, adding, 129–133
page state, 502
page updates, 163, 218, 221
Page Visibility API, 362
paragraph element, 126
paragraphs
    adding text to, 125
    inserting new, 124
parameterized queries, 519
parameters, default, 83
parentNode property, 108
parse() method, 28, 212
parseFloat() function, 34
parseInt() function, 34
partial application, 73, 77–79
Passport system, 423
path() method, 222
patterns
    dict pattern, 57
    finding/highlighting in strings, 18–22
    replacing with new strings, 16
    Unicode sequence, 16
performance testing, 152–156, 466
performance, improving with memoization, 80
permissions property, 565
PhantomJS, 483–488
PhoneGap, 543–551
play event, 236
playgrounds, 590
plug-ins
    converting libraries to, 193
    definition of term, 165
    proper word usage, 176
    using jQuery, 174–176
plus sign (+), 17
polling, 461
polyfills, 167, 249
pool.escape() function, 519
pop-up windows, 137–140
port 80, 275, 300
preflighting requests, 450

About the Author

Shelley Powers has been working with, and writing about, web technologies—from the first release of JavaScript to the latest graphics and design tools—for more than 12 years. Her recent O'Reilly books have covered the semantic web, Ajax, JavaScript, and web graphics. She's an avid amateur photographer and web development aficionado, who enjoys applying her latest experiments on her many websites.

Colophon

The animal on the cover of *JavaScript Cookbook, Second Edition* is a little egret (*Egretta garzetta*). A small white heron, it is the old world counterpart to the very similar new world snowy egret. It is the smallest and most common egret in Singapore, and its original breeding distribution included the large inland and coastal wetlands in warm temperate parts of Europe, Asia, Africa, Taiwan, and Australia. In warmer locations, most birds are permanent residents; northern populations, including many European birds, migrate to Africa and southern Asia. They may also wander north after the breeding season, which presumably has led to this egret's range expansion.

The adult little egret is 55–65 cm long with an 88–106 cm wingspan. It weighs 350–550 grams. Its plumage is all white. It has long black legs with yellow feet and a slim black bill. In the breeding season, the adult has two long nape plumes and gauzy plumes on the back and breast, and the bare skin between its bill and eyes becomes red or blue. Juvenile egrets are similar to nonbreeding adults but have duller legs and feet. Little egrets are the liveliest hunters among herons and egrets, with a wide variety of techniques: they may patiently stalk prey in shallow waters; stand on one leg and stir the mud with the other to scare up prey; or, better yet, stand on one leg and wave the other bright yellow foot over the water's surface to lure aquatic prey into range. The birds are mostly silent, but make various croaking and bubbling calls at their breeding colonies and produce a harsh alarm call when disturbed.

The little egret nests in colonies, often with other wading birds, usually on platforms of sticks in trees or shrubs, in reed beds, or in bamboo groves. In some locations, such as the Cape Verde Islands, the species nests on cliffs. In pairs they will defend a small breeding territory. Both parents will incubate their 3–5 eggs for 21–25 days until hatching. The eggs are oval in shape and have a pale, nonglossy, blue-green color. The young birds are covered in white down feathers, are cared for by both parents, and fledge after 40 to 45 days. During this stage, the young egret stalks its prey in shallow water, often running with raised wings or shuffling its feet. It may also stand still and wait to ambush prey. It eats fish, insects, amphibians, crustaceans, and reptiles.

Many of the animals on O'Reilly covers are endangered; all of them are important to the world. To learn more about how you can help, go to *animals.oreilly.com*.

The cover image is from Cassell's *Natural History*. The cover fonts are URW Typewriter and Guardian Sans. The text font is Adobe Minion Pro; the heading font is Adobe Myriad Condensed; and the code font is Dalton Maag's Ubuntu Mono.

Have it your way.

Get even more for your money.

Join the O'Reilly Community, and register the O'Reilly books you own. It's free, and you'll get:

- $4.99 ebook upgrade offer
- 40% upgrade offer on O'Reilly print books
- Membership discounts on books and events
- Free lifetime updates to ebooks and videos
- Multiple ebook formats, DRM FREE
- Participation in the O'Reilly community
- Newsletters
- Account management
- 100% Satisfaction Guarantee

Signing up is easy:

1. Go to: oreilly.com/go/register
2. Create an O'Reilly login.
3. Provide your address.
4. Register your books.

Note: English-language books only

To order books online:
oreilly.com/store

For questions about products or an order:
orders@oreilly.com

To sign up to get topic-specific email announcements and/or news about upcoming books, conferences, special offers, and new technologies:
elists@oreilly.com

For technical questions about book content:
booktech@oreilly.com

To submit new book proposals to our editors:
proposals@oreilly.com

O'Reilly books are available in multiple DRM-free ebook formats. For more information:
oreilly.com/ebooks

O'REILLY®

Lightning Source UK Ltd.
Milton Keynes UK
UKOW05f2339220816

281264UK00004B/7/P